PAKISTAN
THE ECONOMY OF
AN ELITIST STATE

PAKISTAN
THE ECONOMY OF
AN ELITIST STATE

Ishrat Husain

Karachi
Oxford University Press
Oxford   New York   Delhi

Oxford University Press, Great Clarendon Street, Oxford ox2 6dp

Oxford New York

*Athens Auckland Bangkok Bogotá Buenos Aires Calcutta
Cape Town Chennai Dar es Salaam Delhi Florence Hong Kong Istanbul
Karachi Kuala Lumpur Madrid Melbourne Mexico City Mumbai
Nairobi Paris São Paulo Singapore Taipei Tokyo Toronto Warsaw
and associated companies in Berlin Ibadan*

Oxford is a registered trade mark of Oxford University Press

Second Impression 1999.

ISBN 0 19 579014 6

*Printed in Pakistan at
Mas Printers, Karachi.
Published by
Ameena Saiyid, Oxford University Press
5-Bangalore Town, Sharae Faisal
PO Box 13033, Karachi-75350, Pakistan.*

CONTENTS

PREFACE

Economics is a dismal science and modern economics is considered boring, dull, and drab by ordinary readers due to an extensive use of high flowing jargon, and a preoccupation with mathematical precision. In Pakistan, unfortunately, the situation has become worse. Serious economic analysis and empirical inquiries have by and large been substituted by flawed economic logic, half-baked truths, selective or fabricated facts, speculative conjectures, and highly subjective assertions. Daily newspapers and their Economics and Business columns or the monthly magazines of general circulation have emerged as the popular medium of discourse. The influence that these columnists and reporters have unwittingly acquired in shaping popular public opinion in absence of any alternative means of discussion is simply astounding. Stories of doom and gloom, and negative reporting are slowly and gradually eroding people's confidence in the economy which is the main anchor for sustenance and nurturing in this era of globalization.

Paul Krugman of MIT has observed in his recent book *The Accidental Theorist* that 'plausible charlatans can often convince even the great and good that they are men of wisdom, that economic ideas of self-evident silliness often sound profound to the untrained ear'. This description is certainly apt for application to the Pakistani scene today.

There can be two responses to this dangerous trend of muddled and confused economic thinking getting hold of the popular imagination in the country. One is to keep silent and simply ignore and take no notice of what is being written. The second option is to make a modest contribution, in collaboration with others, in promoting some modicum of economic literacy hoping that the readers will themselves begin to question the 'conventional' wisdom being showered upon them. Like many trained economists, who have started to write sensible pieces in the popular press in Pakistan, I have also chosen the second option. There is always room for differences of opinion, healthy debate, and constructive dialogue because the truth emerges from such interactions. This book is a continuation of the effort to expand an informed understanding of the economic issues facing the country.

In addition, I also felt that there was a serious gap in our economic literature as the last comprehensive analytical history of Pakistan's economy was published more than a decade ago (*Management of Pakistani Economy* by Vaqar Ahmed and Rashid Amjad). Fortunately, a number of recent volumes (edited by Tariq Banuri et al. and by Shaharukh Rafi Khan), and books (by Parvez Hasan and Omar Noman) have partly filled this gap. The present book is also a humble attempt in the same vein, i.e. to facilitate an informed debate on the economic course this country should adopt based on the lessons drawn from an analysis of the first fifty years of its history.

I am fully aware that my past membership of the Civil Service of Pakistan and my current affiliation with the World Bank are likely to raise eyebrows amongst those who are always fond of finding motives rather than engaging in a substantive discussion of the issues. The book may also be ascribed as the defence or articulation of the World Bank viewpoint on Pakistan's economy.

I would like to make it abundantly clear that this book is motivated by one simple and pure consideration, i.e. to repay the immense debt and gratitude I owe to this country of mine which has provided me with numerous opportunities for personal and professional advancement. As far as the World Bank is concerned it has tremendous financial and intellectual resources at its disposal to defend itself, and present its viewpoint and does not require somebody like me to do so. The views and opinions expressed in this book are mine and do not in any way reflect those of the World Bank. I am, however, grateful to the South Asia region of the World Bank for allowing me to publish this work in its original form.

This book would not have been possible without the dedicated, untiring and competent research assistance provided by Ali Zafar. Ali was responsible for surveying the literature, preparing the basic data tables and the initial materials, making revisions and providing supplementary information during the entire course of this project. Ali Zafar carried out this work graciously, ungrudgingly and smilingly. I wish to express my deepest gratitude to him for his excellent assistance.

The National Bank of Pakistan and its past President, M.B. Abbasi and the present President, Mohammad Mian Soomro and its senior management deserve my appreciation for encouraging me to undertake this work and providing financial support for research assistance. Ahmed Jamal was particularly very active and helpful in the initial phases of this project.

Shahid Yusuf in his usual rigorous analytical frame of mind provided extremely useful and insightful comments on the earlier drafts. He was forthright in challenging and questioning some of my arguments and conclusions. I wish I could have stolen more of his valuable time for it would have helped to improve the quality of this book.

My assistants, Josie Carreon, Peter Scher and Chris de Serio worked beyond their normal duties to assist me in preparing and revising the manuscript at various stages. I wish to thank them profoundly for their support. I would also like to thank Ameena Saiyid, Yasmin Qureshi and Daleara Jamasji-Hirjikaka of the Oxford University Press for their patience, support, and professionalism throughout this period of our association. My dear friend of long standing Abdullah Memon who is an intellectual giant in his own right has been generous both with his time and ideas.

Finally, my wife, Shahnaz, and daughters, Farah and Uzma deserve the ultimate credit. They have been most understanding and supportive while I spent my weekends and evenings working on this book for the last two years.

Ishrat Husain
Washington DC, 1998

INTRODUCTION

The history of Pakistan has neatly coincided with the history of the economic development of more than a hundred low-income countries struggling to improve the living standards of their population. The record of the development experience has been mixed. A very small group of countries has been able to achieve success in graduating from the ranks of poor countries within a generation. Another group of countries, which includes the most populous country in the world, is moving rapidly in that direction provided there are no serious setbacks, while a very large number, particularly in Africa, have suffered reversals and are worse off today than they were at the time of their independence from colonial rule. Finally, there is a group of countries which are muddling through and moving forward with hiccups, but where the benefits of development are unevenly distributed and are highly concentrated in a small segment of the population.

Most of the discussion and debate in the literature of economic development explaining the above variances has centred around the dichotomous roles of the state vs the markets. In the 1950s and 1960s, the received wisdom was that the state through a strong interventionist and directive role, using the instruments of central planning and big-push, state-led industrialization, would break the low-level equilibrium trap of poverty in which developing countries were caught. The subsequent experience of the majority of the countries travelling this route exposed the weaknesses of this model, and the idealist concept of a benign and benevolent state acting in the larger interests of the population was replaced by that of a predatory state very much guided by the narrow and selfish interests of those in power.

The break-up of the Soviet Union was a wake-up call which completed the on-going intellectual revolution—decisively in favour of the superiority of markets. 'Government failure' was found to be a greater evil than 'Market failure'. 'Free enterprise' and 'deregulation' became the new buzzwords.

A more thoughtful and balanced analysis and interpretation of the past fifty years' experience leads to a more sobering view of the respective roles of the market and the state. An effective and capable state combined with properly regulated and well functioning markets in a competitive environment can bring a lot of good to the general welfare of the majority of the population in developing countries.

The East Asian economies, notwithstanding the current turmoil in their currency, financial, and stock markets, have demonstrated the power of this combination. The result, accepted by everyone irrespective of ideological predilections, has been a model of shared growth in which rapid economic growth has been accompanied by rapid reduction in poverty and a more equitable distribution of the benefits of development. New questions have emerged on the horizon in respect of the role of the government under the forces of globalization, liberalization, and integration of financial markets, but these will require a separate treatise of their own.

In contrast to this model of shared growth, there is an equally powerful model of elitist growth which characterizes a number of developing countries. Brazil, Mexico, Kenya, Nigeria, and Pakistan are the leading examples of this particular mode of development. Under this model, there is a complete reversal of the traditional roles of the market and the state. Markets are normally associated with efficiency and are found to be impervious to the considerations of equity and distribution. The state is usually thought of in terms of ensuring equity and access to opportunities. But under an elitist model, where both economic and political power are held by a small coterie of elites, the market is rigged and the state is hijacked in order to deliver most of the benefits of economic growth to this small group. The markets therefore produce inefficient outcomes that are detrimental to the long-term sustainability of growth, and the state, through its actions, exacerbates the inequities in the system.

This case study of the elitist growth model in practice focuses on Pakistan, which for the fifty years of its existence has followed this model with varying intensity. It traces the consequences of the various policies followed by seven successive non-military, nominated, appointed governments in the period up to 1958, the dictatorial regimes of Ayub Khan and Ziaul Haq, the socialist democratic era of Z.A. Bhutto, and the new, democratically-elected governments since 1988. What is most puzzling is that the forms of government—democratic, nominated, directly or indirectly elected, dictatorial—did not matter. Nor did the professed ideological inclinations of the government in power—liberal, conservative, Islamic, leftist, rightist—make any significant difference to the general thrust of this model. The PPP governments—supposedly leftist, liberal, and populist in orientation—performed as badly as the right-wing, conservative governments of the Muslim League. The Islamic dictatorship of Ziaul Haq was in no way distinguishable from the modernist, secular dictatorship of Ayub Khan. The same constellation of landlords, industrialists, traders, politicians, military and civil bureaucrats, and some co-opted members of the religious oligarchy and professional and intellectual groups dominated the scene under every single government. The faces did change from time to time, various relatives did appear or disappear over a specific period of time, but the stranglehold of this elite group, accounting for less than 1 per cent of the population, on the affairs of the state has remained unscathed. The capture of the institutions of the state and the market by the elite is complete.

The country has paid a heavy price in turn. The masses are labouring harder than before, but see only a general decay of institutions, lawlessness, lack of security of person and property, and widespread corruption and nepotism at every stage of any transaction, and there is deep anxiety for the future of their children. The irony is that the elites who are the main beneficiaries of this system are the most vocal in expressing their dissatisfaction and disenchantment, little realizing that they themselves are responsible for the current state of affairs.

Will the next fifty years witness a better period for the majority of the population? The answer is clear but difficult to implement. Unless this parasitic behaviour is replaced by a genuine desire to promote broad-based development that benefits most of the people irrespective of their ethnic, provincial, *biradri*, kinship, and similar other considerations, the game will go on. An agenda that lays down the main elements of a strategy which can bring about this change is presented in this study. What is required is strong political will and commitment, and patience, perseverance, and hard work by the whole society.

The present government, elected in 1997, has been given an extraordinary mandate by the people. The judiciary will support the suggested reforms as they will establish the supremacy of the rule of law. The public at large will welcome this relief as it will introduce fairness and equity in the system. Tough opposition will, of course, come from those who are operating the system and are its main beneficiaries. But it is incumbent upon the present government to rise to the occasion and to prove that the strong mandate given to it will be used only for one purpose, i.e., laying the foundations of a just and fair society. This is the only way to usher in the beginning of a new era for Pakistan.

Framework of Analysis and Organization of the Book

The organization of this book follows the basic framework adopted for analysis. This framework is illustrated in the chart below.

The current economic thinking about the process of development has evolved during the last five decades. Starting from the 1950s, when the simple relationship between investment in physical capital and growth in output reigned supreme, our understanding of determinants of growth and

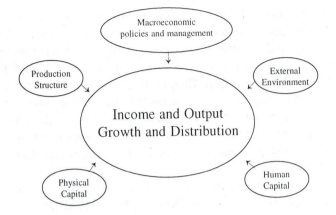

distribution in income and output has been enriched both by developments in theory and, more importantly by the evidentiary experience of the developing countries themselves.

The 1960s witnessed the emergence of Human Capital as a key variable along with Physical Capital. The oil price shocks of the 1970s and the subsequent debt crisis exposed the vulnerabilities of economies to distortions in macroeconomic policies and microeconomic incentives. Thus the whole set of macroeconomic stabilization and structural adjustment policies assumed a central place. The broader preoccupation with sustainable development in the 1990s introduced the concept of good governance, which embodied both economic management and the democratic exercise of power by the citizens on one hand, and equity and environmental protection on the other. Of course, the production structures inherited by a country and the external environment provide the backdrop and constraints within which an economy can function.

This book is organized along the same lines as the above framework. Chapter one provides an overview of the performance of the economy of Pakistan for the entire fifty-year period, followed by five sub-periods which correspond to different economic and political eras. Chapter two lays down the production structure—mainly those of the agricultural and industrial sectors—and outlines the changes which have occurred over the five decades. Chapter three summarizes the developments and outcomes in macroeconomic policies—Fiscal, Monetary and Exchange rate; other complementary policies—Trade, Debt, and Investment—are discussed in Chapter four, under the External Sector. Chapter five discusses Human Capital but extends into the issues of poverty and unemployment, an area of much concern to us. Chapter six presents the Physical Capital, which covers a broad range of components such as energy, power, transport, water and sanitation, and tele-communications.

Chapter seven attempts to present a cogent political economy explanation of the paradoxes exhibited by the Pakistani economy during the last fifty years. This draws upon the findings of the earlier six chapters—though not always explicitly and directly—to substantiate the main hypothesis advanced in this book.

The final chapter presents an agenda for economic and social reform that can help arrest the elitist growth model and move the country in the direction of the shared growth model.

CHAPTER 1

GROWTH AND STRUCTURAL CHANGE IN THE PAKISTAN ECONOMY

Pakistan's economic record for the past fifty years is both impressive and disappointing. It is impressive because economic growth rates and per capita incomes have more than doubled despite a quadruple increase in population, and have surpassed other countries in the region. The incidence of poverty has declined sharply, and a structural transformation has taken place from a predominantly agrarian economy to a more diversified production structure. Integration with the world economy has been fairly rapid, and liberalization and deregulation of the economy have begun to take root. Agriculture output has grown in excess of population growth rate.

But at the same time, there is a sense of disappointment. The potential for growth and development has not been fully realized and, relative to other countries at the same stage in the early 1960s, Pakistan has fallen behind. Human development indicators have lagged far behind other Asian developing countries. Adult literacy rates, infant mortality, and life expectancy are much below those justified by its per capita income level. Fiscal and monetary policies have been lax, and the gains achieved by establishing sound institutions in the earlier years are being gradually eroded. The physical infrastructure, particularly power and roads, has not kept pace with the speed and level of economic activity. Technological and scientific progress has been limited despite the acquisition of nuclear technology.

Estimates of the size of the economy vary widely depending on the particular index that is being used. In current rupee terms at market prices the overall GDP has grown to Rs 2500 billion from Rs 60 billion in 1972/3. If converted to US dollars at the official exchange rate, the size of GDP has multiplied ten times to US$65 billion, compared to US$26 billion in 1972/3. But the purchasing power parity calculations indicate that the size of the economy in 1995 was US$208 billion, or US$1,604 per capita. There are serious conceptual and measurement problems with each of these approaches but, as the purpose of the current exercise is to calculate the trends in growth and structural change over a long period of time, it is important to use time-series data of comparable quality. To do this, the changes in constant market prices in local currency are a more appropriate indicator. The difficulty in extending this series back to 1947/8 arises because prior to 1970/71 the national income accounts were calculated jointly for East and West Pakistan. Although some break-up of the accounts has been attempted, it is not free from serious measurement errors. Therefore it is prudent to present the trends that have occurred since 1972/3—the first year when independent separate national accounts were calculated for the present geographical territory of Pakistan.

The size of the economy in constant market prices has grown to over Rs 665 billion in 1996/7 from Rs 175 billion in 1972/3—the first year after the separation of East Pakistan. This represents an increase of slightly less than fourfold. The average annual rate of growth in this period has been 5.7 per cent. But the high population growth rate of 3 per cent a year could translate this impressive achievement into a modest per capita income growth rate of 2.6 per cent. In constant terms, an average Pakistani earned Rs 4,900 annually in 1996, compared to Rs 2,645 in 1972/3—almost twice as much. The above calculations of the size of the economy do not take into account the large underground or parallel economy that has grown rapidly, resulting from tax evasion, smuggling, corruption and illegal income accruals, drug trade, etc. An IMF estimate puts the parallel economy at around 30 per cent of the official economy. This translates into an adjusted per capita income of Rs 6,370 in constant prices.

But the recipients of this underground economy income (and here we are not talking about the unorganized informal sector) are largely concentrated in the top quintile income groups, which further exacerbates the already existing income disparities in the country. Income distribution had already worsened on the basis of officially recorded economy. The lowest 20 per cent of the population received 7.3 per cent of the total national income, while the highest 20 per cent increased its share to 44.5 per cent. Thus the ratio of highest to lowest income quintiles was up to 6.1 in 1990/1 from 7.9 per cent in 1971/2 and is perhaps higher for the later years of the 1990s. The Gini Coefficient also rose from 0.345 to 0.407 during the same period.

What happened to poverty incidence during this period? Based on 1991/2 rural prices the poverty line for Pakistan has been constructed at Rs 296 per capita per month. The number of poor people in Pakistan, i.e., those living below this poverty line, has actually declined from 43.5 million in 1984/5 to 38.6 million in 1990/1 despite the addition of 19 million people to the population during these six years. The incidence of poverty consequently declined from 46 per cent to 34 per cent, more sharply for the urban areas than the rural. The estimates of poverty incidence for the earlier years are not strictly comparable as they are based on slightly lower poverty lines. But other studies show that there has been a decline in the incidence of poverty since about 1970. A World Bank study estimated that the percentage of population living below the same comparable poverty line was almost identical in India and Pakistan in 1972 and 1962, respectively, i.e., 54 per cent. By 1983, India was able to bring this proportion down to 43 per cent while by 1984, Pakistan's population falling below this poverty line was only 23 per cent. The robustness of this conclusion is supported by available data on the real wages of agricultural workers. Both these series show that urban real wages increased annually by 1.1 to 2 per cent depending on location, while rural real wages by 2.1 to 3 per cent annually depending on whether the worker was in casual or permanent employment.

As per capita income growth has stagnated in the 1990s most analysts using indirect elasticity methods have concluded that this decline in poverty incidence has been arrested.

The poverty gap, based on survey data for 1984/5 and 1990/1, using the same reference poverty line, also fell, indicating a substantial decline in the depth of poverty. But it is not obvious if this will hold true for the 1991-8 period.

The average annual compound rate of decline in Pakistan's poverty head-count ratio was 4.9 per cent. A study of consumption poverty in six East Asian countries during 1970-90 estimates that the average annual decline was 6.1 per cent for the whole period, and a very high 8 per cent for 1980-90. Thus, Pakistan's record in reducing poverty was not as impressive as those of East Asian countries but better than other regions.

Pakistan also made some modest progress in human development from the early 1970s to the early 1990s, but the high population growth has marred this progress. Pakistan's population has grown at 3 per cent annually, and has expanded more than fourfold, from 30 million in 1947 to 136 million in 1997, while the proportion of people living in urban areas has increased by a factor of more than six. Almost one-third of the population lives in urban areas, compared to 18 per cent in 1950. The total fertility rate fell by 20 per cent to 5.1, life expectancy at birth increased from 34 to 75 years in the last fifty years and the infant mortality rate declined by one-third from 131 to 88. The adult literacy rate has increased to 38 from 15 in 1948. Gross enrolment in primary education has gone up to 74 from 12 in 1948, and enrolment in secondary education from 5 to 27 per cent. But despite this progress, Pakistan still lags far behind the averages for all low-income economies. Pakistan's total fertility rate is 65 per cent higher than the average for all low-income economies, its infant mortality is 30 per cent higher, its adult literacy rate is 25 percentage points lower, and its gross primary and secondary school enrolment ratios are not much more than half the average for all low-income economies. Moreover, the disparities in life expectancy at birth, the under-5 mortality rate, the adult literacy rate, and especially school enrolment ratios, are wider for females than for males. A recent World Bank study of the progress of 71 developing countries in reducing infant mortality rates during the 1960-90 period ranked Pakistan 50th. The same study placed Pakistan 35th out of 43 countries in terms of progress in increasing enrolment in primary education. Pakistan's performance in important human development indicators has all along been poor by international standards.

The main structural change that has occurred during the last five decades is that agriculture now accounts for twenty-five per cent of GDP compared to fifty per cent, and primary commodity exports are down from eighty to almost ten per cent. But half the country's population still derives its livelihood and employment from the agriculture sector.

Agriculture has generally performed well relative to other countries in the region. It has grown by more than 3 per cent a year over the past thirty years. Sources of growth, however, have changed over the years—from the seed, fertilizer, and irrigation package of the 1960s, to intensification of water and fertilizer use in the 1970s, to improvements in crop management and incentives in the 1980s. In the last decade, cotton has been a key source of growth, and livestock also did well. The aggregate agricultural performance stands up well with some other comparable countries, especially for the 1980s. The area devoted to cropland has risen to 28 per cent of total land area from 18 per cent in 1960, largely due to a doubling of the availability of irrigation water. This, complemented by high-yielding varieties of seeds and increased use of fertilizer, has enabled Pakistan to raise its foodgrain production faster than the population growth rate, thus increasing per capita food availability. Consequently, an average Pakistani today consumes 2,618 calories per day compared to 2,078 calories at the time of independence—an increase of 26 per cent, and higher than the average caloric intake of developing countries and the recommended dietary allowance.

Agriculture's contribution to manufacturing value-added is especially strong. Manufacturing value-added is highest in industries that have linkages to agriculture: food, beverages, tobacco, textiles and clothing. The indirect effect of agricultural growth is thus an important influence on Pakistan's overall growth performance.

But this increased forward and backward linkage between agriculture and the rest of the economy has also enhanced the country's vulnerability to natural exogenous shocks. Pest attacks, rains, floods, or other exceptional weather conditions depress the overall growth of the economy, exports, and foreign exchange reserves.

While the share of agriculture has declined to 25 per cent, that of industry has risen to 25 per cent, and services now claim 50 per cent of the GDP. The manufacturing sector has raised its share to 18 per cent. Both industry and services have been growing rapidly—about 7 per cent annually. The manufacturing base is, however, fairly narrow, consisting mainly of consumer goods such as cotton textiles, vegetable oil, and sugar, or intermediate goods such as cement. Capital goods production has not taken off, and many attempts, particularly in the 1970s, to rejuvenate this sector have not yielded any results.

In terms of natural resource endowments, Pakistan possesses one of the world's most extensive systems of irrigation canals, hydropower potential, and natural gas reserves. Irrigation water availability has transformed the semi-arid ecological zones into fertile areas of production, but environmental problems such as waterlogging and salinity have become a menace. Natural gas has helped in raising commercial energy use in the country, although it remains heavily dependent on imported oil for the bulk of its energy supply. Unless new sizable reserves are discovered, at the current rate of usage natural gas supplies will last no more than fifteen years.

Electricity generation capacity has grown much faster than the growth in both population and GDP. Large hydropower dams such as Mangla and Tarbela were instrumental in contributing to such rapid growth. Hydropower supplies 50 per cent of the total electricity generated in the country, but most new plants will be based on imported fuel oil.

Despite substantial expansion in the road network, air and sea transport, telecommunications, drinking water supply, and sanitation over the last fifty years, there are serious problems of underinvestment, poor maintenance, and unequal distribution. Public sector institutions that were formed to invest and maintain these services could not rise to the occasion as their capabilities were gradually eroded. Infrastructural deficiencies remain a constraint on rapid and sustainable growth.

Pakistan's integration with the world economy has been moderately rapid. The export-GDP ratio for Pakistan has doubled from 8 per cent to 16 per cent over the last twenty-five years. The average growth rate of merchandise exports was 8 per cent in 1980-90 in the period after a stagnation in the 1970s but only 4 per cent in the 1991-7 period. The terms of trade have remained favourable as there has been a relative shift in the composition of exports away from primary commodities to manufactured exports. Although the base remains narrow, the share of manufactures in total exports is 89 per cent compared to 59 per cent, in 1970. Textiles and clothing still account for the bulk of manufactured exports and the export concentration index has in fact risen. In terms of access to world markets, the only significant gain that Pakistan has achieved during the past five decades is its increased share in the world market for cotton. In 1950, Pakistan's share of world cotton production was 3 per cent. By 1995, it had more than tripled, to about 10 per cent. India, on the other hand, has maintained its share around 10 to 11 per cent during same period. Most of this increase can be attributed to a breakthrough in productivity growth.

The evolution of the Pakistani economy has been uneven throughout this fifty-year period. At least five different periods can be identified for analytical purposes. The first period, 1947-58, was devoted to managing the initial pains associated with the birth of a new nation and coping with the unprecedented scale of migration. The second period, 1958-71, witnessed greater attention to economic planning and development, but there were serious interruptions caused by the war with India in 1965 and the separation of East Pakistan in 1971. The following period, 1971-7, was a bold experiment in nationalization of large parts of the economy, accompanied by severe external oil price shock and vagaries of the weather. The military regime that followed during 1977-88 was favoured by large aid flows due to Pakistan's front-line role in the Afghanistan war, and by remittances from Pakistani workers abroad. The current period, starting with the restoration of democratically-elected regimes in 1988, has begun the process of liberalization and privatization of the economy, but governance issues and fiscal imbalance are creating serious difficulties. It is, therefore, important to analyse the aggregate trends in each of these periods separately.

Pakistan in 1996—fifty years after independence, and despite the structural changes described above—remains a low-income country, with a per capita income of approximately US$450. One-third of its population still lives below the poverty line (US$1 per day); the expanding parallel or unrecorded economy is sizable and has widened regional and inter-personal income inequities. (The observed Gini Coefficients do not adequately convey the extent of income disparities.)

The country enters the twenty-first century facing several formidable challenges. First, the domestic economic structure and the institutions supporting the economy are fragile. Second, the human resource and skill base is less developed compared to other countries in the region. Third, the forces of globalization and integration of the world economy impose severe penalties for poor internal economic management. Fourth, the competition from other developing countries for market share in international trade, and to attract foreign direct and portfolio investment and aid flows, has become fierce. Finally, the glaring income and social inequities, and the behaviour of many of the elite ruling Pakistan since independence, are becoming intolerable, diluting the mixture of social cohesion that binds different ethnic groups together.

TABLE 1.1
PAKISTAN'S GROWTH RECORD
(Annual Average Rates of Growth)

	Low Income Countries	Pakistan
	1965-96	1965-96
GNP	5.3	5.9
GNP per capita	3.1	2.7
Private Consumption	4.6	5.2
Exports	5.9	6.4
Investment	6.9	4.5

Source: World Development Indicators (World Bank, Washington DC 1998).

TABLE 1.2
STRUCTURAL CHANGES
IN THE PAKISTANI ECONOMY

	1950	1960	1980	1996
Agriculture production as % of total GDP	60	46	37	26
Manufactures as % of merchandise exports	0	22	48	84
Gross domestic investment as % of total GDP	5	12	18	19
Gross national savings as % of total GDP	5	7	14.3	12
Foreign savings as % of total GDP	—	7	3.7	7
External debt as % of total GDP	—	45.1[1]	42.4	56.6
Urban population as % of total population	18	20	28	32.5
Incidence of poverty	N.A.	40[2]	30	34
Percentage of share of income to lowest 20%	N.A.	6.4	7.4	8.4
Area under cropland as % of total land use	5	18	26	28

Source: World Development Report, 1978 and 1997.
[1] For 1970
[2] For 1963-64

THE EARLY YEARS

At the end of the Second World War, decolonization and the movement toward independence gathered critical momentum.

Empires were carved up, colonies liberated from colonial fetters, and new nations born. Pakistan, one of these new nations, was born on 14 August 1947. The partition of the Indian subcontinent created one country with two Wings, West Pakistan and East Pakistan, divided by more than a thousand miles of Indian territory.

Pakistani planners faced a plethora of difficulties from the outset. The complex task of nation-building required solid institutions, a functional administration, and a large cadre of technocrats and civil servants to formulate the country's economic policy. Unfortunately, the British withdrawal had been

Graph 1: Structure of Economy

1949-50   1995-96

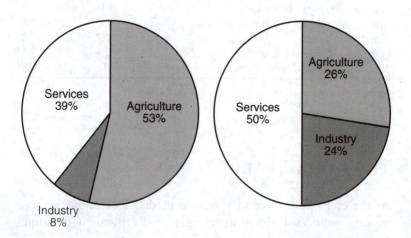

too speedy and chaotic for the policymakers to have put in place the appropriate institutions and regimes to manage the transition. Pakistan started its history with a net outflow of 'human capital', (Noman, 1994) as skilled Hindu businessmen and technical workers migrated to India, with virtually no indigenous industrial capacity at Partition, and without an entrepreneurial class that could fuel the industrial expansion. The prospects for Pakistan were not promising. The economic and social dislocations engendered by Partition created great difficulties for the planners, and many of the early years were spent in the rehabilitation of refugees. However, the inward migration of 6.5 million Muslims brought an influx of workers as well as a critical group of able civil servants who helped administer the country.

One of the few positive features in Pakistan in 1947 was the substantial irrigation network that had been developed during the heyday of British rule and continuously expanded in the subsequent years. This remarkable irrigation system, which represented one of the notable feats of public engineering, had evolved within the span of a century from a series of inundation canals which captured water for irrigation when river stages were high, to a network of 38,000 miles of canals and a series of river barrages and canal headworks which control the diversion of river flows into the canals (World Bank: Water and Power Resources of Pakistan, 1969). This system ensured that Pakistani agriculture would have a fertile milieu for the transfer of new technologies and institutions. Given the predominantly agrarian nature of the economy at Partition and the large dependence of Pakistani agriculture on cotton, rice, jute, and wheat production, a viable irrigation system was a necessary input into the production process. However, a critical deficiency of other infrastructure—roads, power, railroads—was a serious constraint on development. By all tokens, Pakistan was an agrarian society with marginal trappings of infrastructure.

The mixed initial endowment of resources and rudimentary institutions provided the critical background for Pakistan's attempts at nation-building. However, because the writing of a constitution and the development of viable political institutions were the main priorities in the early years, macroeconomic management and economic planning were placed on the back-burner.

The stylized facts and empirical evidence regarding the period are instructive. From 1947 to 1958, the Pakistani economy had an average annual GNP growth rate of 3.2 per cent, a sluggish rate that showed the structural weaknesses of the economy. However, manufacturing grew at an impressive 9.6 per cent and construction at a strong 6.8 per cent. By contrast, agriculture lagged considerably, growing at only 2.8 per cent. The reason why Pakistan had such a low overall growth rate is that the economy was mostly centred around agriculture, with agriculture contributing to more than 50 per cent of output. British colonialism had not bequeathed Pakistan a substantial industrial base, with East Pakistan being a predominantly jute-growing area and West Pakistan heavily based on cotton. The manufacturing rate was high because the country started from such a minute base in 1947. Much of the industrial growth was concentrated in the protected consumer goods sector, with the large-scale manufacturing sector accounting for 5 per cent of GDP.

An analysis of the economic policy from 1947 to 1958 shows a series of *ad hoc* reactions to crises (Ahmed and Amjad, 1984). After the refusal to devalue the rupee in 1949 had led to a severing of trade links with India, the Korean War proved a huge blessing for Pakistan by causing an upsurge in demand for Pakistani exports, mostly raw cotton and raw jute, and assisting in the creation of a nascent entrepreneurial class. A post-war recession led to a re-examination of policy, and a rigid system of import licensing was instituted to prevent Pakistan from having balance of payments difficulties and foreign exchange constraints (Islam, 1981). The idea was that the balance of payments position could only be maintained in equilibrium if imports were sharply curtailed through the licensing regime. Thus, what began as a series of exchange rate realignments was slowly evolving by the mid-1950s into a cumbersome web of administrative controls and intricate licensing systems that would form the backbone of Pakistan's import substitution industrialization (ISI) regime.

The ISI regime, which was to bring notoriety to Pakistan's trade and industrial structure in later years, was based on the idea that the development of a strong local industrial capacity was absolutely essential for development, and that dependence on agricultural commodities spelled disaster for an economy. An entire literature in development economics was arguing the merits of infant industry development and export pessimism, the idea that developing countries cannot be forever exporters of raw materials and depend on fluctuating demand in the industrialized countries (Maier, 1984). In order to develop the local industries, the government provided Pakistan's manufacturing sector with generous fiscal incentives, heavy protection, preferential access to foreign exchange allocation for imports of capital goods, and credit at low, controlled interest rates. A new class of industrialists developed who had accumulated large fortunes during the Korean War boom and who benefited from these concessions and collected sizable rents. Public policies, according priority to infrastructure in public expenditure and a business-friendly environment also helped them. These importers used their rents to invest in industry, reaping huge windfalls in the process (Noman, 1994).

Unfortunately, this policy regime set the foundation for rent-seeking by Pakistani businessmen. The flourishing of the black market in import licences, and the need for political connections to ensure access to cheap credit and fiscal incentives, paved the way for a private-public sector relationship where clientilism and patronage predominated. Rent-seeking behaviour was legitimized throughout the economy, and a class of industrialists was created who made huge markups for themselves and their families, but the spillovers to the rest of the economy were at best marginal. The state's capacity to tax these profits was virtually non-existent as the institutions had not been put into place. The simultaneous coexistence of large pockets of private wealth and low tax revenues had its unfortunate roots in the 1950s.

An important characteristic of this period, especially in contrast to later periods, was the very modest inflow of foreign capital, averaging about 1 per cent of GDP per year. Although Pakistan had joined CENTO in the mid-1950s to assist in the US doctrine of containment of the Soviet Union, inflows of foreign aid were still scarce. The international capital markets were still in inchoate form, and capital movements were quite meagre. Furthermore, the aggressive curtailment of imports meant that BOP problems were alleviated, and that dependence on foreign capital inflows could be avoided.

Two large transfers, however, compounded the anomalies in Pakistan's industrial policy of the period. The transfer of resources from East to West Pakistan, and from agriculture to protected and inefficient industry, were two of the worst legacies of the 1950s. Essentially, industrialization was encouraged in West Pakistan, while East Pakistan remained a raw jute exporter, with net transfer of resources estimated to have been equivalent to 2-3 per cent of West Pakistan's GDP during 1950-60 (Islam, 1981). In a similar way, the industrialization of West Pakistan was achieved at heavy cost to agriculture. The quantum of output was low in the 1950s due to poor public investment in agriculture, discriminatory pricing policies that kept the prices of manufactured goods high and those of raw materials and food low, and inadequate technology transfer. Food shortages were experienced during the period, and the fact that Pakistan became a net food importer in spite of such fertile agricultural land and a well-developed irrigation system speaks volumes of the anti-agriculture bias of Pakistan's ISI regime.

In sum, the 1950s were devoted to attempts aimed at the construction of a viable political and administrative system, with economic policy restricted to *ad hoc* reactions to short-term crises. The notable economic achievement of this decade was the development of an indigenous consumer goods sector, albeit protected from import competition.

THE AYUB DECADE

The period from 1958 to 1969 was dominated by the military rule of General Mohammed Ayub Khan, a leader whose regime was characterized by the paradoxical combination of the biggest growth rates in Pakistani history and large increases in income inequality, inter-regional differences, and the concentration of economic power. While the period had strong macroeconomic management, it paved the way for a series of problems that were exacerbated in subsequent regimes.

The economic indicators are extremely impressive. Agriculture grew at a respectable rate of 4.1 per cent over the period, while remarkable rates were achieved in manufacturing (9.1 per cent) and trade (7.3 per cent). GNP growth rates hovered near the 6 per cent mark throughout the decade. Economic growth was very strong on all fronts, especially in comparison to the 1950s and 1970s. In sectoral terms, agriculture shrank to 41.5 per cent of GDP, while manufacturing increased to nearly 15 per cent. The large-scale manufacturing sector doubled in importance as the economy coasted on the high growth rates.

However, the statistics on income distribution, wages, and human capital development tell a different story. Income inequalities increased substantially in the 1960s. The Gini Coefficients worsened, and the number of people below the poverty line, both absolutely and relatively, increased. Wage increases did not match productivity gains as living standards for a large majority of the population stagnated, with the index of real wages increasing by only 2 per cent in a ten-year period. Investment in the critical social sectors remained very poor, and population growth rates remained high inspite of a much-touted family planning campaign.

The centrepiece of Ayub's economic strategy was the commitment to rapid industrialization. Inheriting the prevailing wisdom that the benefits of economic growth would trickle down to the poorer segments of society, the Ayub administration showed a lack of interest in issues of equity and social justice.

Thus, distributional considerations took backstage to growth performance.

One of Ayub's main actions was to strengthen the administrative capacity. Political instability had characterized much of the 1950s, to the detriment of economic planning and management. With the benefits of authoritarian rule, Ayub proceeded to consolidate his power and put into place an administrative apparatus which would greatly facilitate the formulation and implementation of policies and programmes. Governance improved with a major expansion in the government's capacity for policy analysis, design, and implementation, as well as a far-reaching process of institution-building (Burki and LaPorte, 1984). A Planning Commission was created whose responsibility was to formulate a series of five-year plans that would define the economic objectives to be followed. There was a marked evolution of the Pakistani polity from being what political scientists called a 'soft state' to a developmental state that had acquired the semblance of political legitimacy (Noman, 1994).

The key priority of the Ayub administration was to achieve rapid rates of economic growth and develop Pakistan's industrial capacity. In explicit contrast to the Indian model of public sector-led industrialization, Ayub chose to centre his strategy on the private sector. In order to achieve this, the Second Five-Year Plan (1960-5) envisaged the removal of administrative controls and the maintenance of monetary discipline and price stability to provide a macroeconomic environment conducive to private investment.

Ayub's industrial policy was the hallmark of his rule. The key development was that the policymaking was tailored exclusively to promote industrial investment (Islam, 1981). This system provided a plan and procedure for investment licensing and credit dispersal. Furthermore, the Pakistan Industrial Development Corporation (PIDC) was formed to spearhead the industrialization drive by providing the critically-needed capital and then withdrawing in favour of the private sector, which lacked the skills or the finances to undertake very large projects.

However, the private sector's high industrial profits which had been common in the 1950s, continued unabated through the 1960s. Given the scarcity of finance for investment and the poor state of capital markets, profits accounted for a highly significant part of industrial investment during Ayub's rule (Islam, 1981). As the profits became more widespread, an entrepreneurial class emerged and provided the dynamism that had been absent in the 1950s. This class helped accelerate the rate of growth in the large-scale manufacturing sector to more than 15 per cent during the decade. Thus, Ayub's industrial policy stood vindicated.

In order to facilitate industrialization, Ayub instigated a series of reforms to alter the trade regime. The most significant reform was the introduction of the Export Bonus System (EBS), which gave a premium to exporters and introduced a system of multiple exchange rates favouring manufactured exports. Furthermore, preferential access to credit and a series of fiscal incentives were part of a policy package to give Pakistani exports international competitiveness. The export sector responded dramatically to these policies. The growth rate of exports jumped to 7 per cent a year. There was a large diversification of the composition of Pakistan's export portfolio, with cotton textiles and jute textiles slowly replacing primary commodity exports. The share of primary exports declined to 33 per cent by 1970. Ninety per cent of the export growth in the 1960s was due to the increase in manufactured exports which grew at an annual rate of 20 per cent. The strength of industry is revealed by the fact that, even before the export bonus scheme was introduced, several industries: cotton textiles, footwear, and leather, had become competitive enough to export at the overvalued exchange rate (Noman, 1994). Thus, these changes signalled the fact that Pakistan was moving up the ladder of industrial development. Complementing these changes, there was a significant dismantling of the import licensing regime and hence, greater ease in importing industrial raw materials and spare parts for industry.

However, in spite of the success in industrial diversification and export performance, the Ayub policies had several shortcomings. High rates of effective protection continued to make Pakistani industry inefficient, and a number of international studies documented Pakistan as one of the worst examples of ISI-industrialization (Balassa, 1971; Little, Scitovsky and Scott, 1970). Unlike the East Asian countries, where there was a judicious use of protection, the Pakistani use of tariffs and quotas was not carefully planned. The paradox of ISI industrialization was that, contrary to claims of reduced dependence on imports, the ISI regime resulted in a progressive worsening in the balance of payments, with the increase in machinery and raw material imports outweighing export performance. The ISI regime, by turning the terms of trade in favour of domestic industry, had an in-built long-term bias against manufactured exports, initial success in the 1960s notwithstanding.

The 1960s also mark Pakistan's increased reliance on foreign aid. The strategic plans of the Cold War and the project-related assistance of the international development institutions combined to provide vital resources to Pakistan. While the external economic assistance as a percentage of GDP was a modest 2.8 per cent in 1960, it became substantial within the next five years, reaching 6.6 per cent by 1965. The policymakers in Pakistan had expected that the foreign inflow would be temporary and that it would encourage filling in the gap between domestic savings and investment, which would then generate higher growth and higher domestic savings. These assumptions did not hold true and Pakistan's dependence on foreign aid and its external debt brought a lot of grief in subsequent periods particularly in the 1990s.

One of the more negative features of Ayub's industrial and trade policies was the deliberate repression of wages (Amjad and Ahmed, 1984). It was felt that low wages for industrial workers and the restriction of trade union activity would help industry acquire the critical mass needed for industrial take-off.

These features of authoritarian governance built up frustrations over time that would ultimately lead to Ayub's downfall.

The 1965 war with India disrupted the economic spurt Pakistan had embarked on. As foreign aid inflows were drastically reduced after the war as a result of sanctions imposed by the US and defence expenditures had to be raised, a reorientation of spending priorities had to take place. This, in turn, precipitated the re-imposition of import controls, the tightening of foreign exchange and imports, and a slowdown in economic growth. In the meantime, the growing concentration of wealth and the conspicuous consumption led many to question Ayub's industrial strategy. A statement by Mahbub ul Haq, Chief Economist of the Planning Commission, that twenty-two families controlled 66 per cent of the industrial wealth and 87 per cent of the banking and insurance in the country helped stir up public resentment against Ayub and his industrialization policies. Eventually, in 1969, a series of political protests by students and workers led to the downfall of Ayub and the change in leadership (Burki and LaPorte, 1984).

On a more positive level, one of the salient points of the Ayub decade was the reversal of the neglect in agriculture that had been conspicuous in the early 1960s. Although agriculture was still considered to be a supplier of foodstuffs and raw materials at cheap prices for industrial expansion, a series of reforms strengthened the Pakistani agriculture sector. Rural infrastructural investment was increased to improve the overall availability of irrigation water and the amount of cultivated land. The completion of the Indus Basin Works including the Mangla Dam was a major breakthrough. Furthermore, domestic terms of trade for agriculture were improved in the 1960s, thus reducing the bias that had crippled agriculture in the 1950s.

The two factors that contributed to the revival of Pakistani agriculture were the Green Revolution, characterized by the introduction of high-yielding varieties of rice and wheat, and the mechanization and diffusion of technology among agriculture producers. The Green Revolution of the mid-1960s provided a big boost to agricultural production. The introduction of high-yielding varieties of wheat and rice produced at international research centres gave an instantaneous boost to domestic food-grain supplies and dispelled the fears of an imminent food crisis. The disincentive effects of an agricultural pricing policy that deliberately kept agricultural prices below world levels, and a rationing system that provided subsidized foods to urban consumers, were mitigated by the enhanced productivity gains, reduced unit costs and thus higher incomes made possible by the diffusion and adoption of new varieties (Islam, 1981). In the latter half of the 1960s production of wheat and rice increased by more than twofold, especially in the irrigation-rich Punjab, as yield effects outweighed acreage effects. Cotton and sugarcane production also increased significantly in the 1960s, especially in contrast to their performance in the 1950s, but in their case, acreage effects dominated over yield effects. Furthermore, the Green Revolution proved to be scale-neutral, with the benefits dispersed to farmers regardless of income strata (Khan, M.H. 1975). The substantial increase in food-grain production in West Pakistan thus substituting for imported food contributed to an easing of foreign exchange constraints, liberalization of imports, and a revival of growth and stability in prices. The generous provision of subsidies for irrigation, fertilizers, and pesticides allowed farmers to obtain agricultural inputs and reduced their cost of production enabling them to maintain the upward movement in food-grain production.

Parallel to this shift was a rapid diffusion of agricultural technology: the installation of private tubewells, tractors, and chemical fertilizers proceeded at a rapid pace. While tubewells increased sixteenfold, fertilizer gained thirteenfold by the end of the decade. While contributing to growth, the tractorization and private tubewell expansion was to have adverse distri-butional implications subsequently as it was biased towards large farmers and capital-intensive practices. Income distribution in fact worsened in the rural sector, as mechanization had a displacement effect on the small tenant farmers and labourers. A study of income distribution for the period 1969 to 1979 showed that increased inequality of earnings in rural areas explained 33 per cent of total inequality increase (de Krujik and Van Leeuwen, 1985). To make the distribution of land more equitable, a land reform was instituted in 1959, but it proved only cosmetic because of the generous allowances given to landowners and weak implementation.

One of the major initiatives taken by Ayub was his quest to reduce the high population growth in Pakistan. A highly-publicized programme was launched in the mid-1960s. Based on a clinical approach to family planning that would involve rural midwives in the dissemination of contraceptive information, the programme received substantial international interest. However, within a couple of years the programme was abandoned because of serious implementation difficulties and resistance by religious leaders. The 1971 war led to the abandonment of this scheme and population control once again became a neglected issue.

In sum, the legacy of the Ayub years is mixed. While the consolidation of economic management and the high growth rates were important achievements, the growing income inequality and wage stagnation, the neglect of human capital, and the growing dependence on foreign capital inflows, (despite temporary reduction after the 1965 War) all promised a less than rosy inheritance for future regimes.

FLIRTATION WITH SOCIALISM

In 1971, Pakistan lay traumatized by the secession of East Pakistan and the defeat in the war with India. The end of the war marked the accession to power of Zulfikar Ali Bhutto, a charismatic leader who envisaged a broad restructuring of the country's industrial and agricultural sector. The period from 1971 to 1977 was to witness the most ambitious socialist oriented reforms in Pakistan's history and the strongest attempt to date to assert outside political authority over the country's bureaucracy and army.

In many respects, the performance of the economy during these years was the worst in Pakistan's economic history. Although the GNP growth rate was a respectable 5 per cent, agriculture and manufacturing had very sluggish growth rates, with agriculture growing at an average annual rate of 2.3 per cent from 1971 to 1977 and manufacturing not performing much better, hovering at the 3.2 per cent mark. In comparison with the very strong performance of the 1960s (8 per cent), these years represented a significant setback for Pakistan. An 8.9 per cent growth rate in the construction sector and a 4.4 per cent rate in the trade sector helped give Pakistan's GNP figures some respectability. Worst of all, the main plank on which the Bhutto government came to power—social justice—proved to be extremely weak. Between 1972 and 1980, all indicators suggest an increase in income inequality. The Gini values of overall income increased from 0.291 in 1972 to 0.355 in 1980 for farm households and from 0.231 to 0.263 for all households (Mohammed and Badar, 1985). The Gini Coefficient for urban areas rose from 0.363 in 1970 to 0.400 in 1979 (de Krujik and Van Leeuwen, 1985).

However, at a more disaggregated level, the economic performance was much stronger from 1971 to 1974 than from 1974 to 1977. In the first three years, the economy staged a recovery from the war and boosted its export performance and foreign reserves. The period from 1974 to 1977 was marked by the disastrous combination of macroeconomic and oil shocks, inclement weather and flooding, and the policy impact of nationalization.

This was also the period when Pakistan's domestic macroeconomic management was constrained by a series of exogenous shocks, causing significant macroeconomic instability. Firstly, the secession of East Pakistan after a brutal civil war led to a disruption of trade relations between the two countries and a loss for West Pakistan of half of its export market and one-fifth of its import source. This breakdown in inter-wing trade meant that Pakistan had to search for other markets for its manufactured exports. Secondly, the 1970s marked the beginning of a series of oil shocks induced by the newly-powerful OPEC cartel. The fourfold increase in petroleum prices led to great increases in Pakistan's import bill and a slowdown in exports due to the contraction in the world economy. The inflation rate rose during those years, averaging about 16 per cent during the period from 1971 to 1977 (the average inflation rate in the 1960s remained below 5 per cent). The acceleration in inflation was a reflection more of cost-push shocks than 'populist' demand-management and as such was less susceptible to macroeconomic control (Noman, 1994). Thirdly, the 1970s was a period of substantial fluctuation in the international prices of Pakistan's commodity exports—rice, cotton, and sugarcane-making export performance highly uncertain. Fourthly, a combination of bad weather, flooding, and pest attacks adversely affected the production of cotton, which considerably weakened the economy. All these factors combined to make macroeconomic management quite difficult.

In order to stimulate the economy, one of the key decisions of the Bhutto administration upon accession to power was the devaluation of the rupee in 1972. Prompted by concerns that the rupee had become overvalued during the Ayub years, this decision led to a phenomenal surge in exports as Pakistan found new markets to replace the loss of the East Pakistan trade (40 per cent growth in exports in the first two years after devaluation). Moreover, the administration began a serious attempt to liberalize trade by greatly simplifying the import system and removing the export bonus scheme in order to unify the exchange rates.

The most dramatic decision of the Bhutto regime was the nationalization of large private manufacturing and financial institutions. In 1972, all private banks and insurance companies, and a large number of manufacturing units, were taken over by the state with the avowed objective of reducing the concentration of wealth and diluting the power of the private industrialists. The Bhutto regime felt that nationalization would allow a more efficient resource allocation—the absence of competition in many industries was perceived to have led to a form of monopoly capitalism that was detrimental to the economy. The litany against the massive income inequalities and the large amount of wealth accumulated by private industrialists during the Ayub years found its voice in Bhutto's populist reforms. Bhutto's idea was to establish a powerful public sector that could govern the 'commanding heights' of the economy and spearhead the industrialization drive. The objective was to transform the industrial sector by moving the economic focus from an emphasis on consumer goods to one on building a capacity in basic industry. A critical Big Push by public investment was the central pillar of this strategy. Public investment rose sharply and was directed largely at the 'heavy industries' of steel, fertilizers, and chemicals.

The effect of the new industrial strategy on investment was striking and resulted in a dramatic reversal in investment mix (Naqvi and Sarmad, 1984). The composition of investment changed dramatically, with the private sector share in total investment decreasing from 51.3 per cent in the Ayub years to 33.8 per cent in the Bhutto period. Private investment fell from Rs 700 million in 1971 to Rs 183 million by 1975. By contrast, the public share increased to such an extent that by the end of the period it accounted for two-thirds of total investment. While in 1971 public sector investment had amounted to Rs 58 million, by 1977 it had risen to Rs 1,085 million. This fall in private investment was perhaps the most bitter legacy of the Bhutto years. The waves of nationalization had created an adversarial relationship between the private sector and the government sector that was to set the tone of the relationship for the next two decades.

However, in spite of the ambitious rhetoric, it is important to note the limited outcome of the nationalization campaign. The government takeover of capital and intermediate goods brought only 20 per cent of the total value-added of the large-scale manufacturing sector under government control, while leaving intact much of the privately-owned industry in the textile and consumer goods sector (Amjad and Ahmed, 1984). Pakistan's experience with socialism was far removed from the takeover of the entire industrial sector as was the case in Eastern Europe and the Soviet Union. But the impact on the private sector activity was highly negative and new entrepreneurial initiatives were stifled.

Nevertheless, the Bhutto reforms had far-reaching effects on the industrial structure of the economy, as well as on the nature of the relationship between the public sector and the private sector. The outcome of nationalization was not favourable. The large-scale manufacturing sector performed very sluggishly during this period, having a growth rate of only 3 per cent. Besides the contraction in the global economy in the wake of the oil shocks, the transfer of ownership that resulted from nationalization did much to weaken industrial performance. Inefficiencies proliferated as inexperienced managers operated public enterprises.

The nationalization of large-scale manufacturing industries had an unanticipated beneficial effect. It led to a rapid diversion of private investment to small-scale enterprises. As the performance of this sub-sector is less well-documented, the growth and expansion that took place during the 1970s is understated. But indirect evidence, particularly from the composition of manufactured exports and employment data, does provide strong indications that most of the increase in manufacturing stemmed from small-scale industry. The official statistics show that, while the share of large-scale manufacturing declined from 12.6 to 10.7 per cent of GDP between 1971 and 1977, the corresponding share of small-scale manufacturing rose from 3.8 to 4.5 per cent, and private investment in this sub-sector was also positive. The growth rate of small-scale manufacturing was 10 per cent per annum in this period compared to 4.2 per cent for the large-scale sub-sector (Afridi, 1985).

Having the outsider's distrust of entrenched bureaucracy, Bhutto resolved to conduct economic policy at the executive level. The hallmark of the Bhutto years was the replacement of centralized economic planning and its technical/institutional competence with a highly personalized and *ad hoc* approach to planning (Burki and LaPorte 1984). The Planning Commission was bypassed and the Ministry of Finance became more important. The levers of economic management shifted considerably, and economic decision-making became more politicized.

The inconsistent policy postures of the Bhutto government can best be illustrated by the example of the agriculture sector. A political party committed to the alleviation of poverty and improved living standards for the poorer segments of the population should have paid close attention to the agriculture sector. The majority of Pakistan's poor live in the rural areas and derive their livelihoods directly or indirectly from farm production, but, tragically, throughout the 1970s, the agricultural sector was plagued by stagnation, inter-crop disequilibrium, and a relative neglect of the non-crop sector (Naqvi and Sarmad, 1984). Agricultural growth slowed during much of the decade, due to a combination of exogenous and policy factors. Firstly, climatic shocks and viral diseases affected the crops, with marked damage to cotton production. Secondly, there was an overall shortage of the critical imported agriculture inputs that were needed to maintain the productivity gains of the high-yielding varieties. In spite of the tractorization and mechanization of the 1960s, inadequate supplies of water and fertilizer continued to constrain production (Naqvi and Sarmad, 1984). Finally, government pricing policy continued to discriminate against the agricultural sector by setting output prices well below those in international markets.

In response to the growing income inequality and unjust land tenurial arrangements, the Pakistan Peoples Party (PPP) promulgated an important land reform in 1972. However, as was the case in the late 1950s, the land reforms failed to take effect because of the low amount of land coverage (only 1.3 million acres), the small number of beneficiaries (76,000), weak implementation, and a series of transfers of land to non-existent relatives that helped many landlords avoid the reforms (Khan M. H. et al 1989). The only noteworthy feature was a provision to safeguard the rights of the tenant from landlord abuse.

However, in spite of this, land reforms did not make any significant dent in the inequities in agrarian structure.

One of the most unfavourable trends for the Pakistani economy in the Bhutto years was the exacerbation of balance of payments difficulties. While exports doubled from $591 million in 1971 to $1,141 million in 1977, imports increased fourfold from $638 million in 1971 to an astounding $2,325 million by 1977. While the export structure was less diversified at the end of the period than at the beginning, the import bill skyrocketed with the oil shocks. This dramatic difference between import and export growth paved the way for a sharply rising debt burden and dependence on external loans. The external debt problem grew rapidly in magnitude during the decade and was characterized by a sharp escalation in the net outstanding debt and a high dependence on external loan inflows including commercial loans. This growing dependence on foreign savings, with $ 3.9 billion in the form of loans and credits during this period, raised questions about the sustainability of Pakistan's balance of payments position (Khan, Mohsin, 1990) and prompted concern about the large gap between investment and savings, which reflected the inadequacy of the government's resource mobilization efforts. Savings remained at less than 10 per cent of GDP and accounted for only 60 per cent of investment through most of the period.

One of the most positive features of the 1970s was the large increase in worker remittances from Pakistani labourers, who flocked to the Persian Gulf in the aftermath of the oil shock. These remittances increased exponentially from $136 million in 1972 to $1,744 million by 1980, and were a huge blessing to the economy. The outmigration of labour had led to an infusion of capital, which greatly helped Pakistan alleviate its balance of payments difficulties. The remittance flow helped finance the trade gap between exports and imports and partially diminished the fears that the only means of financing the trade deficit was through capital inflows from foreign creditors. While exchange rate policies were useful, government policies to ease restrictions on outward migration and lobby the Middle East Governments to accept Pakistani labour proved far more important (Khan, Mohsin, 1990).

In sum, the 1970s was characterized by a combination of macroeconomic shocks, a mistaken nationalization campaign and neglect of agriculture. The most positive features of the Bhutto years was the rapid growth of the small-scale sector and the greater attention paid to protecting the rights of rural tenants and industrial workers.

BACK TO BASICS

The period from 1977 to 1988 coincided with the military rule of General Zia, who acceded to power with the goals of restoring political stability and the Islamization of society. The prime economic objectives of the Zia regime were a reversal of the nationalization policies of the Bhutto era and the attempt to liberalize the economy and encourage the return of private investment. The trade and industrial policy of the Zia era represented an attempt to heal the adversarial relationship that had developed between the public and the private sector as a result of nationalization.

At the institutional level, Zia restored the power of the Planning Commission to guide the economy. However, at the political level, he prohibited political party activity and limited participation in government to the local level in an attempt to create representative but decentralized institutions (Burki and LaPorte, 1984). This veneer of democracy masked the centralization of political power. Economic policy suffered to the extent that, contrary to the Ayub period, it was not the main objective of the government.

By observing the main economic indicators, it is fair to conclude that these were positive during the decade, but the foundations for macroeconomic instability were also laid in this period. The growth rate in GNP was over 6 per cent during the period, with agriculture having an average annual growth rate of 4 per cent and manufacturing 8.8 per cent.

In explicit contrast to the 1970s, the 1980s were a period of reversal from public sector-led growth strategy. Destabilizing exogenous shocks were absent in this period. The key macroeconomic problem was the widening gap in the balance of payments and the fiscal accounts throughout the 1980s. Despite average annual inflows of $3 billion of workers' remittances, the current account deficit averaged between 4 and 5 per cent of GDP. For several years in the 1980s, unsustainability in current account deficits, defined by conventional wisdom as a situation where deficits cannot be covered by normal capital inflows or drawdown of international reserves and where policies are urgently needed to correct this imbalance, was prevalent (Khan, Mohsin, 1990).

The international macroeconomic environment was much more favourable to Pakistan in the 1980s than it had been in the 1971-7 period. The collapse of the oil boom and the upswing in world trade in the late 1970s led to an appreciable increase in Pakistani exports, with exports of cotton and rice growing at a rapid rate and non-traditional exports, such as carpets and leather products, surging. One of the key reforms of the Zia years was the decision to put the Pakistani rupee on the managed float system, thus making the active use of the exchange rate a major policy instrument. As the overvalued rupee depreciated, export performance received a critical boost, averaging a 10 per cent growth rate for most of the decade.

The Russian invasion of Afghanistan in 1979 propelled Pakistan to the forefront of international political attention. Not only did it give political legitimacy to a regime which was facing credibility problems of its own, it also set the way for substantial infusions of foreign aid and war-related assistance that would, together with the remittances, provide a safety valve for the Pakistani economy. Aid inflows, which reached $2 billion annually by the mid-1980s, supplemented meagre domestic savings and helped establish some creditworthiness for Pakistan. These flows changed substantially over time—there was a shift in the composition of official capital inflows from grant-type assistance to loans and credits.

One of the negative effects of the Afghan war was the mushrooming of the parallel and illegal economy. The diversion of aid money, the growth of smuggling, the rise in sale of weapons, and the large drug business together created a subterranean economy that was estimated to be about 20-30 per cent of GDP. Estimates put the value of illegal imports at around $1.5 billion in the mid-1980s. A large untaxed component of the economy was growing at the same time as the fiscal burden was reaching 8 per cent of GDP.

The 1980s were the golden years of Pakistani remittance inflows. Averaging about $3 billion per year for most of the decade, these remittances accounted for 10 per cent of GDP and 45 per cent of current account receipts, eclipsing revenues from merchandise exports. The remittances generated a ripple effect on the rest of the economy. The flow of remittances supplemented household incomes and financed the private sector with a pool of funds that could be used productively for investment. They allowed private investors to find alternatives to the domestic financial system, which had already been pressurized to provide capital for the government's fiscal deficit. They allowed a closing of the 6 per cent gap between savings and investment, and financed much of the trade deficit. Given the financial repression prevalent in Pakistan, channels for the productive use of remittances were not easily found. There is some evidence to suggest that these inflows have retarded the domestic savings rate (Kemal and Durdag, 1990). The savings/GDP ratio in 1980 was only 14 per cent, a figure contrasted with the 30 per cent for East Asia and the mid-20 per cent in many of Pakistan's competitors, such as India.

One factor which surfaced in the 1980s to partially weaken the impact of the remittance inflow on the balance of payments was the flight of capital from Pakistan. It was estimated that deposits of Pakistani residents in foreign banks increased from $700 million in 1981 to $1.7 billion by 1987. Although the $1 billion increase was small compared to the annual remittance inflows of $3 billion dollars, it was nevertheless significant in that it allowed this capital to escape the tax net. Furthermore, it did nothing to assist the process of financial deepening that was so important for Pakistan's economic growth.

The 1980s saw the widening of fiscal deficits, which averaged 8 per cent as a proportion of GDP in the second half of the 1980s. Despite this development expenditure declined as a proportion of GDP from 8.6 per cent in 1980 to 5.9 per cent by the end of the decade. Non-development expenditures, including defence, public administration, and the subsidies on wheat, edible oils, and other goods, continued to increase (Kemal and Durdag, 1990). These growing fiscal deficits did not translate immediately into instability or weakened growth rates, but the accumulated domestic borrowing to finance these deficits had serious repercussions for public finances and macroeconomic stability in the 1990s. Inflation, according to the official statistics, averaged 7.6 per cent compared to the high 13.9 per cent average for the 1970s. Monetary policy remained conservative as the rate of money creation was slow by international standards; in part the budget deficit was financed by attracting private savings at higher than market interest rates.

The financing of the deficit through non-bank borrowing avoided the twin evils of monetization of the deficit leading to inflation, and large external financing leading to external debt crises. Thus, Pakistan avoided the macroeconomic destabiliz- ation that afflicted much of Latin America in the 1980s. But the government's diversion of non-bank savings into its own exchequer created several strains on the financial system, most notably the upward pressure on interest rates (Kemal and Durdag, 1990). This also led to crowding out, with high interest rates deterring investment. Furthermore, to the extent that higher interest rates attract foreign exchange funds, this could have caused an upward pressure on the exchange rate and hence, may account for the failure to increase and diversify exports (Kemal and Durdag, 1990). At constant prices, exports declined from $ 409 million in 1980-81 to $ 355 million in 1989-90.

On the industrial front, the Zia regime began to deregulate and liberalize the economy to encourage private-sector investment. The denationalization of certain public-sector projects, the provision of a package of fiscal incentives to the private sector, and the liberalization of regulatory controls characterized the government's industrial policy in the 1980s. Tax holidays, the granting of rebates, the streamlining of investment licensing procedures, and the removal of price distortions were instituted to improve private-sector investment. While the initial reactions of the private sector to the reform packages was slow, by the mid-1980s there was a movement toward greater investment. The share of the private sector in total investment increased from 33 per cent in 1980 to 46 per cent in 1989. However, the perennial problem of low employment expansion in the large-scale manufacturing sector continued to perplex the policymakers. The 1980s has been characterized as a period of relatively easy, soft-option industrial growth that did not rely much on improvements in international competitiveness and technological competence (Noman, 1994).

The two big success stories of Pakistani industry in the 1980s were the continued spectacular growth of the small-scale sector and the development of the intermediate and capital goods sector. Ignored in the early years due to the capital-intensive bias of Pakistan's trade and industrial regimes, denied access to cheap finance and credit by the government's stringent credit policies, and penalized by a clientilistic industrial policy, the small-scale sector transformed the critical boost that it had received from the nationalization campaigns of the 1970s into full industrial success in the 1980s. Entering industries as diverse as leather manufacture, sporting goods, and surgical goods, the small-scale entrepreneurs helped in the diversification of Pakistan's industrial profile.

Similarly, the intermediate and capital goods sector finally made some modest progress by the mid-1980s. The culmination of the ISI regime, which Pakistan had begun in the 1950s, was finally reached in the mid-1980s, as Pakistan developed industrial capacity in the steel, automobile, and light engineering sectors, and the chemical industry. Although a plethora of problems pervade this sector of the industry, including the absence of technological sophistication and linkages between sectors, the formation of these industries showed that industrial diversification was possible in Pakistan. Whether the financial performance of these industries was affected by their ownership pattern and the management structure or they were not competitive to begin with is difficult to disentangle. But the favourable spillover effects of these industries downstream have not yet been realized.

The 1980s was a time of significant structural change for Pakistani agriculture (Khan, M.H., 1991). While the share of agricultural products in total exports had almost halved and the share in GDP significantly reduced, agriculture still formed the backbone of the economy, industrialization notwithstanding. The military government, upon accession to power, commenced a process of deregulation of markets and production. Policies to revamp the agricultural sector after years of government regulation included the deregulation of the sugar, pesticide, and fertilizer industries, the removal of the monopoly power of the Rice and Cotton Export Corporations, and the removal of bans on the private sector's import of edible oils. The pricing support system, which had been established in the 1970s to stabilize agricultural price levels, was reformed as the subsidies on pesticides and fertilizers were removed, and consequently, the price system became more market-oriented. In addition, there was a large increase in agricultural credit as the formal lending institutions, led by the Agricultural Development Bank, finally addressed the credit shortages in the rural sector. The agriculture growth rate thus averaged 4 per cent—the highest rate for any decade.

However, in spite of these changes, the industrialization bias continued to hurt the agricultural sector. While industry enjoyed effective protection rates of over 25 per cent, agriculture continued to have negative protection. Historically, compared with a broad range of countries, the effect of protection of other sectors on agriculture was relatively high. Furthermore, a whole series of indirect taxes, especially export taxes on agricultural products, further penalized the agricultural sector. Recent estimates of the average annual range of intersectoral flow of resources range from 1.3 to 13 per cent (Nasim, Hamid and Nabi, 1990). Furthermore, as Pakistan reduced its development expenditures to tackle the problems of the growing fiscal deficit, agriculture's share in public development expenditure declined from 20 per cent at the beginning of the decade to 13 per cent. Agriculture was one of the first victims of budgetary cuts as investment in both rural infrastructure—irrigation systems, roads, extension services—and in the social infrastructure—education, training, sanitation—were conspicuously absent in the 1980s.

The great success story of Pakistani agriculture remained the spectacular performance of cotton as new varieties led to a rapid increase in yields. Cotton production doubled during the decade as higher-quality seed, increased pesticide use, attractive incentives, and the depreciation of the rupee spurred cotton growth (Faruqee, 1995). Given the intrinsic link between cotton production and economic growth in Pakistan, this was an important achievement.

In contrast to the success story of cotton was the disastrous wheat policy, as Pakistan became more and more dependent on expensive wheat imports. The goals of self-sufficiency in food production faded away as Pakistan's imports of wheat (although Pakistan enjoys comparative advantage in wheat) increased from 4 per cent at the beginning of the decade to 10 per cent at the end. Grain output per capita, which had increased significantly in the 1960s, declined from 185 kg in the early 1980s to 172 kg in the late 1990s. This dependence on imports came at a time when development expenditures were being slowly squeezed curtailing investment in rural infrastructure.

Unfortunately, most of the increases in agricultural growth were due to the increased utilization of land, and yield increases, with the notable exception of cotton, were few. Thus, the tapering of agricultural output in the wake of the Green Revolution continued its course in the 1980s. The Zia years closed with a series of deliberations on the viability and consequences of the implementation of agricultural income tax, but no consensus could be reached in face of the vehement opposition of the large landowners.

In the 1980s the high population growth rate of 3.1 per cent became a matter of immediate policy attention. Started with much fanfare in the 1960s, halted in the 1970s in the aftermath of the Indo-Pakistan War, crippled by financial constraints, administrative *ad hoc*ism, and religious opposition, the family planning programme was reintegrated into the health ministry in the 1980s and contraceptive information disseminated through a multitude of channels. That the programme failed to even make a dent in Pakistan's population growth rate speaks volumes for the obstinate resistance of cultural factors, of organizational uncertainties, of gender biases, of religious antagonisms. By the end of the decade, population growth continued unabated, causing increasing demands and pressures on infrastructure, on agricultural output, and on increasingly scarce resources.

In sum, the 1980s were a period of substantial macroeconomic stability and revival of private investment, as well as significant structural change in agriculture and industry, but the burgeoning trade and budget deficits did not bode well for the economy in the subsequent period.

MUDDLING THROUGH

The period from 1988 onwards witnessed the revival of democracy in Pakistan and the difficult transition to civilian rule after years of military dictatorship. In spite of the strong political opposition between Benazir Bhutto, the leader of the Pakistan People's Party, and Nawaz Sharif, the leader of the Muslim League, there was a fundamental consensus on basic economic policies, but a lack of continuity of programmes and policies. Administrative *ad hoc*ism and policy reversals and adventurous economic initiatives failed to cash in the advantages of this economic policy consensus. Instead, each group used these mechanisms to establish political power and supremacy.

Although, in retrospect, this turned out to be a myopic approach, the damage to the economy has been irreversible.

Overall, there has been a deceleration in the rate of GDP growth—down to 4 per cent, with agriculture growing at a rate of 3.3 per cent and manufacturing at a rate of 5.9 per cent. Export growth at constant prices has been negative, current account and fiscal deficits have widened and external debt servicing has risen significantly to almost 40 per cent of export earnings—an unbearable burden on the economy. Incidence of poverty is estimated to have worsened.

In early 1989 the newly-elected government embarked on a programme of financial reform that was meant to remove the distortions that had been created as a result of years of overregulation and mild financial repression. In the late 1980s Pakistan's financial system was characterized by a combination of captive commercial banks required to hold government debt, administered interest rates that frequently had no relation to the cost of capital, and credit ceilings that forced banks to lend according to sanctioned criteria. The government's process of depending on non-bank borrowing to finance the deficit had created differential interest rate structures in the economy and had drained deposits away from the banking system (Kemal and Durdag, 1990). The effect on macroeconomic management had been deleterious, with financial disintermediation becoming more and more systemic. The deepening of a country's financial institutions, the growth of the capital markets, and the freeing of its banking system from government dictates are linked to economic growth. With this in mind, a series of financial reforms were instituted to correct the various distortions and strengthen the operational autonomy of the banking system. The government implemented reforms to allow a freer flow of private capital and allow unlimited quantities of foreign currency to enter the domestic banking system. This elimination of exchange controls was meant to reverse the capital flight and to link domestic interest rates with international ones. Preliminary estimates showed a strong response to these changes, with capital flowing in at significant rates. Foreign currency accounts had risen to almost $11 billion by 1998. But the overall level of national savings and investment has remained stagnant. Investment/ GDP ratios are significantly higher in comparable Asian countries.

At the same time, Pakistan compares very unfavourably with other fast growing economies in basic transport, power and telecommunications, poverty, and other social indicators. Private capital stock in industry is antiquated and badly maintained and needs to be upgraded and expanded in order for Pakistan to remain competitive in world markets. Thus the demand for financing infrastructure remains strong but the capital market development which can supply this capital has been hindered by the Government's growing claims on private savings—both domestic and foreign.

While the government resorted to non-bank borrowing in the 1980s to finance the budget deficit, which served to mitigate the inflationary consequences, this policy choice left a legacy of debt and debt servicing in the 1990s, with total interest payments amounting to one-third of expenditures (Husain, 1992). The persistently high deficit/GDP ratio, which averaged 6.8 per cent during the 1990s, was beginning to take its toll on the economy. While the deficits were large compared to other developing countries, the inflexibility in expenditure reduction imposed by domestic debt servicing obligations and defence outlays did not permit much room for manoeuvre to reduce current expenditures. Studies have shown that a fiscal deficit in excess of 4 per cent throughout the 1990s will have adverse macroeconomic consequences, with the possibility of a high inflationary bout (Haque and Montiel, 1991). A reduced fiscal deficit will also provide space for private-sector access to credit and investment.

Another area where significant reforms were initiated is in the trade sector. In the 1990s, a series of policies were introduced that reduced the items on the Negative List, abolished industrial licensing, and simplified procedures for foreign investors. Furthermore, a generous package of incentives was given to exporters. These reforms represented the strongest measures to date to dismantle the ISI edifice that had been part of the

Pakistani economy since the 1950s. The initial reaction of exports to these changes was dramatic, with exports growing at a rate of 10 per cent per annum, with a surge in nontraditional exports, but this temporary upsurge was negated by other disincentives including an overvalued exchange rate.

The Uruguay Round of international trade, the most comprehensive set of trade negotiations ever, negotiated in the early 1990s, presents Pakistan with substantial possibilities as well as major challenges. While Pakistan can gain from liberalization by increasing the volume of its manufactured exports, it risks being marginalized as international capital flows to fewer and fewer developing countries, as the regionalization of the world economy into separate trading blocs becomes more complete, and as the long-run income elasticities for textiles and garments remain low. As the economy is increasingly integrated, vulnerability to external shocks becomes more likely. Protectionism continues to be prominent in a large number of industries, and Pakistan's caution in reducing its tariff rates, as well as non-tariff barriers, makes it vulnerable to the risk of losing its market share as lower-cost exporters compete and more liberalized economies derive greater benefits from open trade regimes (Riordan and Srinivasan, 1996). The phasing out of the Multi-Fibre Agreement (MFA) means that Pakistan's leading export, i.e., cotton textiles, will face increased competition.

Two further trends that will reduce the foreign exchange availability in the 1990s are the decrease in remittances and the dwindling flows of foreign aid. Historically, from the mid-1970s to the early 1990s, Pakistan relied on both sources of finance to supplement its meagre domestic savings, which in the 1990s amounted to 15 per cent of GDP, in contrast to the East Asian Tigers' 30 per cent. The remittance inflows, which averaged $2 billion per year in the 1990s, show signs of reduction as the economies of oil exporting countries are no longer expanding at the same pace as in the earlier decades. Consequently, the Gulf demand for foreign labour has diminished. Similarly, the reduction in aid that followed the end of the Cold War spells increasing financial difficulties for Pakistan at a time when its fiscal deficit is becoming clearly unsustainable. While bilateral aid halved from the 1980s to the 1990s, among official creditors there has been a shift from grants to loans and from concessional to non-concessional lending. As Pakistan's strategic importance diminished with the break-up of the Soviet Union, aid started to flow to other areas of the globe that were politically and strategically more important, such as Eastern Europe.

One of the areas where the 1990s saw a radical departure from previous regimes was in industrial policy. Weakened by high protection rates that resulted from years of ISI-industrialization, damaged by the nationalizations of the 1970s, and threatened by marginalization from world export markets after the Uruguay Round of world trade, Pakistan's industrial sector struggled to maintain its viability in the 1990s after a respectable performance in the 1980s. In response to the perception that the public enterprises, which accounted for 40 per cent of total fixed investment, were riddled with waste, operational efficiencies, and poor mandates, a package of policies were introduced in 1990 to encourage the deregulation, liberalization, and privatization of industry. A combination of fiscal incentives—tax holidays, delicensing of investment regimes, reduction of tariffs on capital goods—were meant to encourage the flow of private investment, which had been reduced to a trickle since nationalization.

In accordance with this change, privatization programmes became a staple part of economic policy to reduce the budgetary deficit, broad-base equity-capital, reduce waste and inefficiency, and revamp the industrial structure. Prescribed as the panacea for the dilemmas of Pakistani industry, privatization policies had become popular the world over as it became apparent that the bureaucrats were not ideally suited to running businesses. By 1995, 90 units had been privatized, although the pace has been slower than planned. Larger units, including telecommunications, gas, and power companies, are currently up for sale, with the government planning to raise $3 billion from privatization proceeds. If these proceeds are applied to paying back the domestic debt, the debt servicing burden will be reduced by $400 million annually.

However, the reaction of the private sector to privatization has not been strong. It still maintains a cautious attitude toward the public sector after the nationalization policies and is fearful of policy reversals. Moreover, there has been a perception that the privatization procedures are not transparent, and allegations of favouritism weaken the response. Private fears of being saddled with excess labour after privatization, and the feeling that government might relinquish shares but maintain ownership, compound the problems (Kemal, 1990). Finally, the financial repression which resulted from the government's deficit financing strategy has diverted valuable capital from the private sector and created a credit crunch, thus making it financially impossible for private firms to buy manufacturing units.

As time has progressed, criticism of public inefficiencies has been matched by criticisms of inappropriate privatization. Privatization will only change the locus of ownership; it will achieve few economic gains if the trade regime continues to display abundant levels of effective protectionism and other competitive measures are not put in place. Poor performances in the steel, automobile, and chemical sectors, an inability to build a strong capital goods sector, technology-intensive export products and, a heavy dependence on cotton-textile production are the more obvious structural weaknesses of Pakistani industry in the 1990s. As countries in East Asia move rapidly up the hierarchy of industrial specialization, Pakistan remains mired in the production of cotton-textiles and other light industrial products.

On a more positive note, during the 1990s Pakistan succeeded in attracting significant foreign direct investment (FDI) for the first time in its history. The streamlining of administrative regulations and the removal of the investment licensing regime led to the inflow of $500 million by 1998. Given the growing importance of private capital, Pakistan's success in attracting FDI, which currently represents about 7 per cent of private fixed investment spending in Pakistan, contrasts favourably with competitors such as India and other lower income countries (Riordan and Srinivasan, 1996).

Agriculture performance during the 1990s was mixed. Heavy flooding and pest attacks during 1991 and 1993 reduced cotton output and exposed the vulnerability of the Pakistani economy to its dependence on the vagaries of the weather and a single crop. Agricultural growth in the 1990s equalled the trend rates of growth, although the potential for higher achievement remains unrealized. The inefficient and wrong utilization of scarce irrigation water remains the single most important impediment to accelerated, efficient, and equitable growth in the agriculture sector. As the cultivable area reaches its limits, measures are needed to boost a total factor productivity growth, and better utilization of irrigation water can contribute to this. Output prices of agricultural commodities are being brought closer to export/import parity levels thus reducing the implicit tax on the agriculture sector. This will also help the supply response and productivity improvements.

As Pakistan's fiscal system came under growing pressure, the interim government of Moeen Qureshi, for the first time in the nation's history, instituted an agricultural income tax, which was vehemently opposed by the large feudal and land-owning interests. Based on a system that would assess income according to the productive capability of land (PIU), this new tax could bring in some semblance of inter-sectoral equity in tax burden.

One area where the 1990s marked out a significant role for the private sector was in the provision of infrastructure. Energy policy centred on the opening of the power sector to private capital. Assisted by international donors like the World Bank and The Consortium, a major oil-fired power project was built in Hub near Karachi to improve the supply and distribution of power. The implications of this project for industrial output were assessed to be very favourable.

In sum, the 1990s have presented the Pakistani economy with a series of challenges as well as opportunities. The economic policy formulation has been in the right direction but actual implementation has been erratic, inconsistent and poor. The external sector and particularly the management of debt has put the economy under severe pressure. The cumulative imbalances of fiscal and current accounts combined with the decay of key institutions and rapacious governance have neutralized the liberal economic policy regime.

CHAPTER 2

PRODUCTION BASE:
AGRICULTURE AND INDUSTRY

HISTORICAL PERFORMANCE

The agricultural sector in Pakistan has performed respectably over the last fifty years, averaging a 3 per cent growth rate. In spite of low growth rates in the 1950s and the 1970s, strong performances in the 1960s and 1980s have enabled the country to double agricultural output in spans of twenty-five years. Although its share of GDP has halved to almost a quarter from one-half at the time of independence, it continues to be an important mainstay of the economy. It provides employment to half the labour force, the bulk of the country's exports are based on cotton, and agriculture has been a conduit for extracting surplus for investment in the manufacturing sector. Most of the gains have occurred since 1967; the index of agricultural productivity has almost tripled since then and has kept pace with the population increase. Improved technology, the Green Revolution seed and fertilizers, new variety of cotton seeds, expansion in irrigation water, exchange rate policy, liberalization of price and marketing policy, and improved farming practices have all contributed to this increase. But the recent stagnation of agricultural productivity is a source of concern.

Food production increased more than fourfold in the last five decades (from 5.5 million tons in 1947-8 to 23.0 million tons in 1995-6) at a rate slightly faster than population growth (from 30 million to 130 million over the same time period). Unfortunately, the country has not been able to achieve self-sufficiency in

Graph 2: Agricultural Production

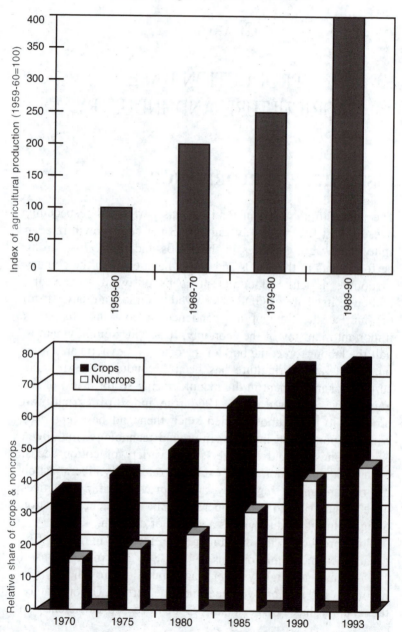

Graph 3: Industrial Production Index

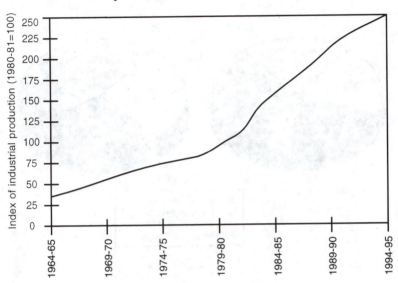

Graph 4: Industrial Production (Per cent Increase)

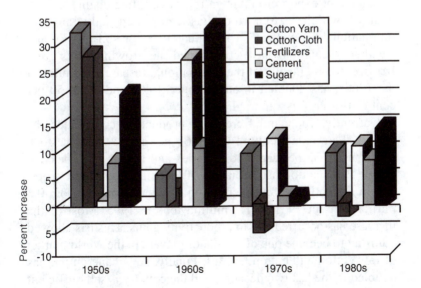

Graph 5: Structure of Manufacturing

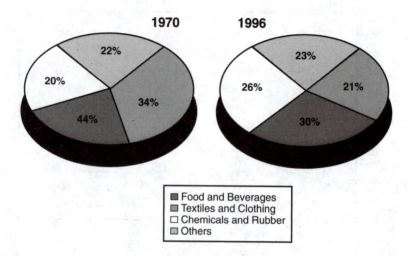

producing the main staple, wheat, and has to import, on average, 10 to 12 per cent of the country's total consumption. Basmati rice, a major export crop known for its very fine quality, 25 per cent of which is exported, has catapulted Pakistan into international prominence. Unfortunately, poor soil quality and weather fluctuations have constrained the growth of this crop. Irri rice, the brainchild of the international research institutes of the 1960s, has doubled in output since 1970, and about 50 per cent of this crop is exported.

Currently, food and fibre crop production contributes the largest share of agriculture GDP (63 per cent), with livestock contributing 32 per cent and fisheries and forestry 15 per cent. (Table 2.1). Cotton has been one of Pakistan's strongest crops, with a dramatic fivefold increase in lint cotton output from 0.3 million tons in 1961 to 1.7 million tons in 1995. Most of the increase has occurred due to productivity gains. This has allowed Pakistan to become one of the major players in the world market of raw cotton and cotton textiles. Finally, sugarcane output has doubled in the last two decades, and the country is self-sufficient where sugar is concerned. But there is a serious question about the economic viability of sugarcane production in Pakistan. The average recovery rate of sugar and low yields of cane production do not seem to justify the costs of water and other inputs applied to this crop if valued at international prices of output and inputs. Table 2.2 documents the area and yield increases of principal crops and shows the improvement since 1947 in the production of cotton, wheat, sugarcane, and rice. Table 2.3 that there has been an increase of 22 per cent in per capita food availability from 2078 calories to 2542.

Although the share of food grains and cash crops has increased, that of pulses and fodder has reduced. Moreover, non-tradable crops have not been accorded as much attention as food and cash crops, and hence their supplies have dwindled. One final success of Pakistani agriculture is the livestock, fisheries, and forestry sector. Livestock now contributes about one-third to agricultural GDP. Currently, about 5.5 million households own livestock, generally in small mixed farming systems.

Pakistani agriculture has made impressive strides in utilization of land (Table 2.4). Since 1960, the cultivated area in Pakistan has increased by over 5 million hectares, cropped area by about 8 million hectares, and cropping intensity by 15 per cent. This extensive, as opposed to intensive, agriculture, however, has its costs, particularly for the environment (Faruqee,. 1994). Output increase can come either from more inputs or from a more efficient output per input ratio. Pakistan has chosen the former instead of the latter, with adverse implications for efficiency and long-term growth. Waterlogging and salinity—the twin menaces facing Pakistan's agriculture—have stemmed largely from lack of attention to the drainage system. Although gradually tubewells have helped in lowering water tables in the sweet aquifer areas, the saline water areas have elsewhere been devasted.

The two leading successes of Pakistani agriculture were the Green Revolution in the late 1960s, where the introduction of high-yield varieties of wheat and rice led to spectacular increases in their production, and the tripling in cotton production over the last decade due to the use of quality seed and proper incentives to the sector. The other success factor was the expansion of irrigation water which has almost doubled in the last five decades.

The 'sources of growth' analysis of four major crops—wheat, rice, sugarcane, and cotton—for the period 1960-75 shows that the largest contribution to output of these crops has been made by changes in yield per acre (Khan, M.H., 1981) (Table 2.5). But the contribution was far more limited for cotton and sugarcane than for wheat and rice. However, the situation changed dramatically in the 1980s, as the high-yielding varieties of cotton made substantial inroads in boosting overall production while wheat and rice production remained stagnant.

In sum, Pakistani agriculture has performed respectably, especially in comparison to pre-Partition days. Crop output has been substantial, land use has been extensive, water and other input use has accelerated and technological change has been used for expanded wheat and rice production in the 1960s and cotton production in the 1980s. The daily calories supply per capita exceeds the recommended daily allowance and has risen by 10 per cent. Per capita consumption of cereal has also increased by 15 per cent in the last fifty years.

In spite of its manifest successes, the Pakistani agricultural sector is plagued with a series of major problems, whose solutions look increasingly difficult.

Firstly, despite the policymakers' stress on crop diversification, the economy is dependent on cotton for more than half of its export earnings. This strong dependence is dangerous given the climatic and viral-induced setbacks that cotton production has historically experienced throughout Pakistan's history. As the relationship between cotton growth and overall growth seems very strong, the recent tapering off in productivity levels of cotton without a matching increase in productivity levels of other crops has enhanced the vulnerability of the national economy to the fluctuations in cotton output. The poor performance of the economy in the early 1990s is attributed to the failure of the cotton crop in three successive seasons.

Secondly, the avowed objective of food security, which should have been possible given the favourable resource endowment of the country—one of the largest irrigation systems in the world—has not been achieved so far. Although wheat is the most important food grain, and is estimated to contribute more than half of per capita caloric intake and 85 per cent of total protein intake, adequate attention has not been paid in recent years to proper and efficient utilization of land and water resources, or to the supporting policies and infrastructure, which could easily make Pakistan self-sufficient in wheat production.

Thirdly, the rapid increase in population, with the growth rate estimated at 3 per cent has substantially reduced the per capita agricultural production rate. Unless significant effort is made to reduce the population problem, Pakistan's natural environment will be put under severe stress if the agriculture, output is accelerated beyond a certain level.

Fourthly, growth in the most recent decade has come from more extensive, and not intensive, agriculture (Table 2.5). Before and after the Green Revolution, the production expansion of wheat and rice can be attributed to increases in the cropping area, while during the Green Revolution, yield effects predominate; since then, yield increases have been achieved only for cotton (Faruqee, 1994). This reliance on area expansion will inevitably meet with land and water resource constraints.

Fifthly, productivity growth in agriculture has been small according to a number of indicators—output per hectare, output per unit of a single factor, yield gaps between average and best farmer yields, and total factor productivity (Byerlee, 1994). Total factor productivity, perhaps the best measure of agricultural growth due to its comprehensive comparison of an index of all outputs with an index of all inputs, stagnated or declined in post-Green Revolution Pakistan. The reasons cited for the stagnation are many. Poor input and output price signals, weak irrigation networks, low levels of human capital, inefficient seed supply and distribution systems, resource degradation, and poor research and extension systems have played their part in reducing agricultural productivity.

Sixthly, the government price system has been criticized for inducing a number of distortions and incorrectly trying to remedy the situation through a series of input subsidies (Hamid, Nabi and Nasim, 1990). The poor alignment between support prices and world prices has created serious disincentives for farmers to produce export products. Unless these distortions are corrected, and agricultural prices made to reflect actual costs, the disincentives will continue.

Finally, erratic and inconsistent policies and poor planning and management, for example of the irrigation system, deficiency in providing fertilizer, lack of quality control on pesticides, inadequate investment in rural infrastructure, and improper research and extension services, have all played havoc with Pakistan's agriculture.

The performance of the agriculture sector has varied over time and the average outcomes mask the enormous differences across policy regimes. It would be useful here to examine the evolution of the agriculture sector across the five decades.

EVOLUTION OF THE AGRICULTURAL SECTOR

THE FLAT FIFTIES

The question preoccupying the early economic planners of Pakistan was how to transform the agrarian economy, inherited as a result of the Partition of the Indian subcontinent, into an industrial one. This was in consonance with the key insights of development economics literature of the late 1940s and early 1950s. The early models, most notably the Lewis model, argued that the predominance of surplus labour in the rural sector, with a marginal productivity of zero, translated into a large army of reserve labour that could fuel the industrialization process. All the dualistic development models of the period stressed the parallel coexistence of a backward, stagnant agricultural sector with a dynamic, modern industrial sector (Maier, 1984). The goal of development was to ensure that the structural transformation of the economy was accelerated. Consequently, agricultural development was ignored in the early models and its role in development consigned to being a hinterland that provided the burgeoning industrial sector with food and raw materials.

The quantum of output was quite low in the early years as public policy discriminated against agriculture, and PL-480 food aid was the principal source of feeding the population. The combination of cheap food imports and disincentive prices turned the terms of trade against agriculture throughout the 1950s (Islam, 1981).

Consequently, the performance of the agricultural sector in the years from 1947 to 1958 was dismal. A growth rate of 2.8 per cent, compared to a growth rate of 9.6 per cent for manufacturing, speaks volumes for the priorities of the policymakers. The index of agricultural productivity showed very little increase during the period. A series of stringent import controls kept the prices of manufactured goods high, while the prices of food and raw material were kept below world market prices, thus redistributing income from agriculture to industry through terms of trade adverse to agriculture. According to one study, the ratio of agriculture's domestic terms of trade to those of industry at world prices during the first half of the 1950s was less than two-fifths (Islam, 1981). Lewis has argued that the early industrialization of Pakistan was financed by the agriculture sector (Lewis, 1970). Other studies have supported this finding by stressing that the first decade of Pakistan was one of declining per capita agricultural production, and that food shortages were experienced in all but two years during the period (Amjad and Ahmed, 1984). Unfortunately, Pakistan's growing dependence on food imports was a legacy of this period. Food imports, like aid flows, became very important for the economy. Thus, due to a combination of factors—declining terms of trade against agriculture, poor public investment in agriculture, the absence of a policy framework to tackle the problems, and weaknesses of agricultural research—the early years were disastrous for Pakistani agriculture.

THE GOLDEN SIXTIES

The era from 1958 to 1969 can best be characterized as the golden years of Pakistani agriculture, thanks to a variety of favourable developments. The high agricultural growth rate of 4.1 per cent, the highest in the entire history of Pakistan and comparable to the most successful developing countries, was a result of Ayub's policies emphasizing and encouraging the transfer and diffusion of new agricultural technology.

The basic premise of the agricultural policy under the new government was that greater attention to agriculture would help accelerate economic growth and reduce poverty. Agriculture can help economic expansion by supplying foodstuffs to the growing population and raw materials to expanding sectors of the economy, providing an 'investible surplus' of savings and taxes to support investment in the dynamic industrial sector, selling a marketable surplus for cash that will increase the demand of the rural population for manufactured consumer goods, and relaxing the foreign exchange constraint. The idea was that agriculture was to be viewed more as a partner of the industrial sector than as a backwater of primitive means of production.

Besides the policy reversal, large public investments were made in irrigation and drainage works following the Indus Water Treaty with India in 1960. The installation of private tubewells at a very fast pace during the period 1960-5 enabled the farmers to intensify irrigation and make changes in cropping patterns. The overall availability of irrigation water increased from 82 to 117 MAF (Million Acre Feet) i.e., a 43 per cent quantum jump during the decade, helped to boost agricultural productivity.

The major problem confronting decision-makers was how to increase the yields of food and cash crops. There were two points of view on this debate (Hussain, 1970). One group argued that a rapid increase in all inputs, seed varieties, pesticides, fertilizer, and tractors, as well as the provision of increased water supplies through large-scale government projects, was the solution. Rapid increase in inputs should lead to rapid increase in output. Others held the view that one has to prioritize, and that increased use of fertilizer and water should accomplish the task. Exogenous shocks, both positive and negative, led to the almost automatic resolution of this debate.

The conflict with India in 1965, resulting in a suspension of US aid, and a very severe drought in 1965-6, however, made it difficult for the government to obtain food aid supplies and ensure the availability of food grains at the old subsidized prices.

This period of scarcity fortunately coincided with the advent of the Green Revolution, characterized by the introduction and subsequent diffusion of high-yielding varieties of wheat and rice, which had been respectively developed in the research institutes of Mexico and the Philippines. These new varieties were being experimented with in the Punjab by 1965. The idea behind the Green Revolution was that a technical, scientific breakthrough could dramatically boost agricultural productivity without resorting to land area expansion. The speed at which new wheat and rice varieties were adopted was very rapid, especially in the irrigated areas, where they proved technically and economically superior to the local varieties. The impact of these technical changes on the production of wheat and rice was astounding. Wheat production jumped by 91 per cent in one decade, and the rice output expanded by 147 per cent. Independent of the Green Revolution, sugarcane production also increased by 147 per cent (Table 2.6).

In the most significant study on the effects of the Green Revolution on Pakistani agriculture, several important conclusions emerge (Khan, M.H. 1975). Firstly, the new wheat and rice varieties were more profitable than the local ones. Secondly, the benefits initially went to larger rather than smaller farms, and more to provinces well-endowed with irrigation facilities than to others. Subsequently, the demonstration effect of higher yields and rising profitability persuaded the small farmers to adopt new technology. Thirdly, the new technology was scale-neutral, in other words, both small and large farms could achieve identical efficiency. Lastly, in the areas in which the new varieties were introduced, they did not generate more output per unit of land than their local counterparts unless accompanied by better water supply and fertilizer. The use and profitability of these new seeds was constrained by the topography of the area as well as by social and economic factors. It is no accident that the Punjab, with its large areas of irrigated land, was the prime beneficiary of the Green Revolution.

The use of mechanical inputs such as tractors was also encouraged by a liberal policy of imports, subsidized credit by the government-owned Agriculture Development Bank, and artificially cheap capital costs due to overvaluation of the exchange rate, lower interest rates, and reduced import duties and taxes. The number of tractors expanded from a negligible quantity to more than 100,000 in this period. The combination of new seed availability, fertilizer use, increased irrigation water, and tractorization had a positive impact on cropping intensity, yield level, land preparation, and post-harvest operations. On the other hand, it has been contended that tractorization and other mechanical improvements, such as wheat harvesters, resulted in the displacement of labour, tenant evictions, and expansion of the already large landholdings. The empirical studies on this issue remain inconclusive.

The use of chemical fertilizers was unknown in Pakistan's agriculture in the 1950s, but it exhibited a growth rate of more than 80 per cent per annum between 1959-60 and 1964-5. This continuing upward trend in fertilizer use brought total fertilizer consumption to more than 300 thousand nutrient tons by 1969-70. The availability of high-yielding varieties of wheat and rice in the 1960s contributed to the rapid growth of fertilizer consumption in Pakistan.

The experience of the 1960s amply demonstrated the bankruptcy of two popular myths about small farmers' behaviour. First, the small farmers were just as responsive to price signals as the large and medium scale farmers. Second, the adoption and diffusion of new technology was equally widespread among small and large farmers. This insight is very helpful in designing realistic policies and technical packages for the agriculture sector in such a way as to benefit the farmer irrespective of the size of his holdings.

THE SOCIALIST SEVENTIES

The years from 1971 to 1977 were characterized by a slowdown in agricultural production. The sector was plagued with stagnation, inter-crop disequilibrium, and relative neglect of the non-crop sector (Naqvi and Sarmad, 1984).

Agricultural output slowed throughout the sector, with the crop subsector having the lowest growth rate. The sectoral growth rate stumbled to 1.8 per cent from the 4.1 per cent achieved in the 1960s due to a stagnation in major crop production (Table 2.7).

With the accession of Z. A. Bhutto in 1971, the Pakistan People's Party embarked on a series of legislation to increase state intervention in the agricultural sector. In 1972 the open market sale of sugar was banned and rationing begun, fertilizer distribution was taken over by the state, and firms involved in the tractor industry were nationalized. By 1973 rice and cotton exports were transferred to monopolies, and the Rice Export Corporation and Cotton Export Corporation were established. In 1974 all private vegetable ghee mills were nationalized. By 1975, two parastatals were established at the federal level for the procurement, storage, and marketing of agricultural commodities. By 1976 all flour mills, rice mills, and cotton ginning factories were nationalized. Thus, the state attempted to regulate the agricultural sector with a heavy hand.

The poor performance of the agriculture sector cannot be attributed to the public policy stance alone. Several additional factors also contributed. Firstly, severe climatic shocks and a cotton virus that depressed production for most of the decade were to blame. Secondly, the diminished returns that had set in after the initial spurt of the Green Revolution had peaked. The performance of all crops except wheat and rice remained unchanged and thus the sectoral growth, after the initial gains from the Green Revolution were internalized, slowed down. In Pakistan, the positive effects were mostly in the Punjab; and to some extent in the irrigated areas of Sindh, consequently, regional inequality increased. A further problem with the Green Revolution was that the high-yielding varieties of wheat and rice were more sensitive to pests, disease, weather, and fluctuations in the supply of chemical inputs (Khan, M.H., 1975). In fact, the third reason for the poor outcome in the agriculture sector in this period was that there was an inadequate supply of vital agricultural inputs (Naqvi and Sarmad, 1984). Average farm productivity could have doubled or even tripled if adequate supply of inputs was provided. According to several estimates, the supply of fertilizer was sufficient to meet only 30 per cent of requirements and that of irrigation water only 40 per cent of actual requirements. The low efficiency of the water system and its distributional networks, as well as inefficient use of fertilizer, were the main contributory factors to lower-than-expected productivity. Fourthly, agricultural credit was heavily biased in favour of large farmers and utilized mostly for tractor purchases, hence ignoring the importance of other inputs (Faruqee, 1994). Fifthly, agricultural research was completely neglected. Agricultural development efforts seemed to be concentrated on major crops such as rice, wheat, and cotton, ignoring minor crops, fisheries, and livestock.

The setback to the agricultural sector in the 1970s was not intentional but the consequence of misguided policies, adverse exogenous shocks, and disruption in the supply of critical inputs.

REVIVAL IN THE EIGHTIES AND NINETIES

The period from 1977 to 1996 witnessed the revival of agriculture, with growth rates averaging 4 per cent. A combination of sound government policy with a series of very fortunate circumstances gave rise to this outcome.

Although agriculture was still an important sector of the economy, its role and structure had changed considerably. Agriculture's share in GDP declined from about 31 per cent in the early 1980s to a little over 26 per cent by 1996. The share of agriculture products in exports had declined from about a third in the late 1970s and early 1980s to less than one-fifth by the mid-1990s. The fluctuations in agricultural output during the period are reflected in the dramatic increase in the index of total output to 6 per cent in the 1980s, falling to 2.7 per cent in the 1990s. Production of fibre crops, as a result of the cotton boom, rose more significantly than that of food crops. While the grain output per capita declined from 185 kg in the early 1980s to 172 kg by the early 1990s, the wheat output stayed around 130 kg, with considerable fluctuations. Pakistan continued to import wheat, with the amount of wheat imported tripling from the early 1980s to the mid-1990s.

The 'sources of growth' analysis for the period from 1981 to 1993 shows that 62 per cent of the increased crop output was due to productivity gains arising out of technological progress, and the rest due to additional quantities of land, labour, and capital (Khan, M.H., 1991). The technological breakthrough in boosting the yield of cotton in the 1980s, liberalizing the market in pesticides and fertilizers, and bringing domestic purchase prices up to international market prices were some of the factors for this productivity increase. The enhanced availability of major farm inputs to farmers, with additions in fertilizers, irrigation water, credit, and tubewells, played an equally important part as a source of growth in the 1980s and 1990s.

The military government initiated a process of gradual deregulation of markets and production, which was continued by successive elected governments (Khan, M.H., 1991). The pace of agricultural reform in the initial period was quite rapid as it had to reverse the decisions of the 1970s. By 1985, the Zia government had denationalized the flour and rice mills and the cotton ginning factories, deregulated the sugar and pesticide industry, and allowed the voluntary procurement of wheat. In the next five years, fertilizer, rice, and cotton trading were substantially deregulated. The removal of the monopoly of the Rice Export Corporation of Pakistan (RECP) and the Cotton Export Corporation (CEC) in export trade facilitated the entry of the private sector into these markets.

The agricultural sector performed reasonably well in the early 1980s and agricultural productivity went up. Wheat output increased by a third, and cotton output doubled during the decade (Table 2.8). Overall, fibre crops did extremely well, doubling production during this period. Several factors contributed to the improved performance in this sector. First, a whole series of government policy measures gave private farmers more incentives and removed constraints to produce. There was an impressive growth in the use of improved seed and fertilizer per hectare of land, and the supply of irrigation water and farm credit also increased. Second, the major breakthrough during this period was the development of a new, high-yielding variety of cotton by the National Agriculture Institute. This variety was diffused and adopted fairly rapidly among the farmers in southern Punjab, the cotton belt of Pakistan. The adoption of this new variety, and greater use of pesticides, led to a tripling of production in a span of six years. Third, weather conditions remained favourable and, no major natural disasters or catastrophes occurred during this period.

In the later half of the 1980s and the earlier years of the 1990s, the pace of reforms slowed down and, although there was a basic consensus over the kinds of policy to be achieved, the sense of direction seemed to have been lost and administrative *ad hoc*ism governed the period. Growth rates in this period were lower than in the early 1980s, about 3.3 per cent per annum between 1988 and 1996.

The variability in output was more pronounced in this period and could not be ascribed only to vagaries of the weather. A combination of flood-related damage to crops and infrastructure, as well as a strong virus that damaged the cotton crop, had caused agricultural output to be lower than expected. But there were other factors at work too.

Public investment in agriculture was curtailed significantly, decreasing from about 20 per cent in the Fifth Five-Year Plan (1978-83) to 13 per cent in the Seventh Five-Year Plan (1988-93). Investment in rural infrastructure which slowed down in the early 1980s also suffered serious cutbacks as efforts were intensified to reduce the fiscal deficit. Although the shift in some of the responsibilities to the private sector and the reduction in subsidies for inputs such as fertilizers also explain this decline in the public expenditure share of agriculture, it is clear that these shifts and cutbacks did have an impact on the profitability levels that farmers had previously enjoyed.

The more worrying aspect of agriculture was the enormous gap between the average and the best farmer yields (Faruqee, 1994), and the failure of agriculture extension services to bridge this gap. In some instances, for example, rice, the average farmer was producing only half of the potential yields. Total factor productivity in this sector, therefore, suffered. Outdated land tenure arrangements, erratic macroeconomic policies, a slow-down in development of new technical packages, and a weak institutional support system did not help, and may have contributed to this stagnation.

FUTURE OUTLOOK

The future outlook for agriculture growth in Pakistan depends on the changes in its land tenure system, public policies and initiatives affecting this sector, and the weather condition.

LAND TENURE SYSTEM

Pakistan's agrarian structure had been shaped by both the Mughal period and the British colonial era. At the time of Partition Pakistan had two land tenure systems existing side by side (Khan, Naqvi, and Chaudhry 1989). The first type, which was quite widespread, was of the *zamindari* (landlord-tenant) system. Basically, the *zamindars* (landlords) and *jagirdars* (non-revenue paying landlords) possessed large tracts of land which were divided into small areas and cultivated by sharecroppers, while the majority of landlords were absentee owners and lived from the tenants' rent. This system, which became known as the *batai* system, had two main elements. Firstly, there was the distribution of cropshare between the landlord and tenant on a 50:50 or 40:60 basis. Secondly, the landlord charged the tenant a fee, which varied from five to twenty per cent of the tenant's share of the produce. This system had all the trappings of an exploitative feudal culture. Any forum for the settlements of disputes was heavily biased in favour of the *zamindars*, and consequently, the peasants were without legal protection. The second major type of land-tenure system was peasant proprietorship, under which peasants cultivated small amounts of land owned by them. In this system, which played a role in the Punjab and irrigated areas of the North-west Frontier, the peasants were obviously more powerful, but this was only a small fraction of the rural population. Although these two systems were relics of the Mughal and British agricultural systems, there were different objectives underlying them. While the *zamindari* system in Mughal times had been based on the state's raising of tax revenues to finance the costs of administration by squeezing the profit from the tenants, the British added a novel twist by defining more clearly the property rights structure. As a result of all these forces, Pakistan inherited a feudal structure in 1947 that was internally inconsistent. The agrarian system of Pakistan differed substantially from that in many developing countries, for example, Latin America, where large landowners possessed most of the land and a large group of small peasants occupied a small part of it, or Malaysia, where large rubber plantations produced primary commodities for export, or those countries where socialist forms of land tenure existed and where egalitarian distribution of land gave more autonomy to the peasantry. The combination of tenant farming and rural landlessness seems particularly prominent in South Asia.

One highly contentious issue that has been widely debated and discussed in Pakistan for the last five decades is the question of land reforms (Khan, Naqvi, and Chaudhry, 1989). Several attempts have been made over the years to come to grips with this issue, but the outcomes have been unsatisfactory in terms of implementing the objectives or altering the historical power relationship.

In the early 1950s there were two pieces of strong legislation enacted in Punjab, Sindh, and the Frontier to improve the landlord-tenant relationship (Khan, Naqvi, and Chaudhry, 1989). A series of provincial tenancy acts sought to convert the occupancy owners into full owners, provide greater security of tenure to tenants-at-will, and increase the tenant's share in total produce by enhancing his share in the crop-sharing agreement. In Sindh, after the publication of the *Hari* Inquiry Committee Report, which tried to redress the peasant's grievances, the Sindh Tenancy Act was passed in 1950. This Act granted permanent tenancy rights to the *haris* who cultivated a given average of land, and made their eviction more difficult. A second piece of legislation was the abolition of the *jagir*. *Jagirdars* did not cultivate the land themselves but engaged tenants-at-will called *haris* who had few legal rights. A *jagirdar* paid no land revenue to the government. Unfortunately, these acts proved to be of only cosmetic significance and did not do much to alter the unjust and asymmetrical relationship between landlord and tenant. The landlord class represented a powerful political lobby, and the tenants were disorganized and diffused.

The inability to bring about serious land reforms is particularly vexing as empirical studies undertaken in Pakistan show an inverse relationship between farm size and productivity (Khan, 1981). Large farms tend to incur higher costs than small farms because of the high capital intensity of their operations. Small farms also make more judicious use of agricultural land as they cultivate it more intensively. According to the 1980 Census of Agriculture, the average land use intensities for small and large farms were 100 and 60 per cent respectively. Similarly, small farms had a cropping intensity of more than 150 per cent, which compared favourably with the 88 per cent cropping intensity of the large farms. If these trends have persisted over time, then the efficiency argument for land redistribution reinforces that of equity and income distribution.

This inherited structure of land tenure has played a powerful role in shaping the country's political system, institutions, and societal norms. The influence of the feudal system—a purely agriculture sector phenomenon—has spilled over into the industrial and bureaucratic spheres of life and reinforced the elitist growth model, with serious consequences for the country's transition to a modern state. The subsequent periods of Pakistan's economic history should thus be examined in this context.

By the late 1950s, the issue of land reform had become a salient feature of the political agenda. The Ayub administration embarked on the first serious land reforms in Pakistani history. Under Martial Law Regulation no. 64, about 2.5 million acres were resumed and 2.3 million acres distributed among about 185,000 tenants (Khan, Naqvi and Chaudhry, 1989). Unfortunately, the area involved was only about 5 per cent of the total landholding in Pakistan. The rationale for this limited area was that the Land Reform Commission gave very generous allowances for exemption from land acquisition. Furthermore, the *zamindars* colluded with the local revenue officials to alter the records. Thus, although an important milestone was reached, the policy did not go deep enough to redress the grievances of existing tenants.

The Bhutto government seemed to be more successful with its attempt to create a more egalitarian distribution of land. In 1972, a Regulation was promulgated which for the first time in Pakistan's history, made significant changes in the tenancy laws in order to safeguard the rights of tenants. These laws gave the tenant greater power to avoid eviction, and ensured that he had no responsibility for land revenue, the water rate, or the cost of the seed. Under this rule, about one million acres were distributed to the peasantry. Unfortunately, even this strong measure seems to have done little to reduce the concentration of land ownership that had become a staple part of Pakistan's feudal culture. In 1977, additional measures were implemented that reduced the ceiling on the individual holding to 100 acres irrigated or 200 acres unirrigated. The land revenue was abolished and replaced by a tax on the income of large landowners. However, after the overthrow of Bhutto the legislation on land reforms and agricultural taxation introduced in the 1977 Finance Act was suspended by General Zia.

By the late 1980s there had been three major changes in the ownership of land relative to the late 1960s. Firstly, the ownership and area under small holdings had increased due to the subdivision of holdings under the laws of inheritance and because of population growth. Secondly, there was a significant decline in the numbers and area of very large landholdings due to intra-family land transfers as a result of the land reform acts and the threat of future land reforms. Thirdly, the middle-size holdings, especially in Sindh, had gained both in numbers and in terms of area. Although these changes were important, they have not altered the fundamental feudal structure of Pakistan.

In sum, three land reform acts have been implemented, but little is known of their impact on productivity, employment, and income distribution due to the absence of systemic micro-level studies. Only 1.4 million hectares have been distributed to 288,000 beneficiaries, and the total area resumed has been 1.8 million hectares, which represents less than 10 per cent of the total cultivated area.

Land reforms seem to have been unsuccessful because the resumption and distribution of land was greatly diluted by numerous exemptions in the Acts, by evasion during the implementation process, and by the influence of the large owners in the land reform administration. Furthermore, a follow-up support system providing protection to new landowners was conspicuously absent. Finally, major shortcomings in the sharecropping system were not addressed.

The concentration of land continues to be the dominant feature of Pakistani agriculture, having changed little since Partition—a high concentration of land in the hands of a few coexisting with the feudal tenancy system in which landless peasants sharecrop the land. Table 2.9 shows how little land concentration has changed over the years. The coefficients measuring land distribution have remained relatively constant over time. There has been a decline in feudal tenancy in the irrigated districts, as farming based on hired labour and mechanization has become more prominent, and also because of an increase in the number of small owner-operators, but the declining land base of the workers has turned them into landless wage-labourers. Land fragmentation in small holdings due to a variety of reasons, ranging from the law of inheritance to productivity differences in different classes of soil, has been the trend among the smaller landholdings, thus increasing the gap between large landlord and small farmer/tenant (Khan, 1991). It is fair to say that land reforms have not made any major contribution in redirecting the process of differentiation in Pakistan's agrarian structure. Nor is it obvious that there is likely to be strong political will and determination for land reforms in future.

PUBLIC POLICIES AFFECTING THE AGRICULTURE SECTOR

PRICING POLICY

In Pakistan, all major crops are covered by a guaranteed minimum price or support price programme, determined by a consultative process that takes into account many factors, including domestic and world demand and supply, production costs, prices of competing crops, and intersectoral considerations (Faruqee, 1994). According to this system, the respective government agencies must purchase all quantities offered to them at the guaranteed minimum price if the market price falls below a certain level.

The rationale for these policies is based on several premises. Firstly, the programme is designed to combat drops in price immediately following harvest, which would force farmers with limited storage to sell at depressed prices. Secondly, balance of payments considerations and government policies attempting to either maximize foreign exchange earnings in the case of export crops (cotton and rice) or minimize imports in the case of deficit crops (wheat and sugar) have weighed heavily. Thirdly, these programmes are meant to provide urban consumers with subsidized food prices at lower than parity prices. The historical evolution of the pricing strategy is very interesting.

In the early years of Pakistan's history, governmental intervention in the agricultural market was pervasive. It affected the agriculture sector indirectly through the exchange rate policy. An overvalued exchange rate penalized the agricultural sector by making domestic agricultural output very expensive relative to import substitutes (Islam, 1981). More directly, the prices of agricultural products were kept below the world level through the compulsory procurement of major crops at pre-determined prices, and by imposing major taxes and export duties on agricultural commodities. Thus, the terms of trade were turned against agriculture. The underlying assumption, which proved incorrect, was that the farmers were not responsive to price changes and therefore peasant production would not be affected by a reduction in prices resulting from high export taxes and compulsory government procurements. By the early 1960s, it had become obvious that this policy was flawed, and that domestic food production was not adequate to meet the needs of the growing population. The chronic food deficits that had afflicted the Pakistani economy in the early years led to a reconsideration of the discriminating policy against agriculture.

The wheat market was the first that the government intervened in directly (Nabi, Nasim and Hamid, 1990). Historically, wheat had been subjected to a very comprehensive price control, in which the government procured a stock of wheat from the cultivators according to a target. In this system, the procurement price of wheat remained stagnant as Pakistan became more and more dependent on imports of US wheat under PL-480. This was creating pressure on the balance of payments, as relatively more expensive wheat imports (compared to domestic wheat) were financed by taxing and monopolizing the export trade in cotton and rice. By the late 1960s, the government, in an attempt to redress the problem, intervened by raising the producer price of wheat. The government felt that the private traders were taking advantage of the seasonal glut in the market to push down the price at harvest time; consequently, it was decided to purchase wheat directly from the farmer at harvest time at remunerative prices in competition with the private traders. Interestingly, by 1982 the government was procuring 73 per cent of the marketable surplus in the Punjab. What was initially conceived as a back-up system to ensure a minimum price to the farmer had grown over time so that by the 1980s it was handling most of the marketed wheat, and the role of the private traders had been reduced to that of mere commission agents (Nabi, Nasim and Hamid, 1990). In order for the government to meet its twin and contradictory objectives of providing urban consumers with wheat flour at low prices and protecting the farmers from seasonal price fluctuations, a subsidy was provided to consumers to obtain wheat at cheaper prices.

Another important area where the government intervened heavily was in cotton pricing. Cotton had historically been the most important crop in pre-Partition India and, given its importance as an international cash crop, a vast and sophisticated pricing mechanism and a system of intermediaries had developed between the grower and the final consumer of the raw material. After letting the market system operate in the early years, the government began intervening in the cotton market. With its ISI strategy and the consequent multiple exchange rates, a three-tier structure emerged in which the exporter of raw cotton faced an unfavourable exchange rate, the exporter of yarn faced a better rate, and the exporter of cloth manufactures faced the best rate. This manufacturing-biased policy was a strong disincentive to cotton producers. By the mid-1970s the government had moved from partial control and indirect price setting to a complete takeover of the cotton trade. A Cotton Export Corporation (CEC) was created that procured cotton from farmers, operated a price support system for raw cotton, and exported cotton abroad. Sales could not take place below a Minimum Export Price (MEP). Thus, as time progressed, the government's price intervention resulted in increasing conflicts between the growers, the manufacturers, and the users. This policy was pursued for over fifteen years, and not until 1988, when liberalization set in, was the private sector allowed into cotton export.

The story for rice is very similar to that for cotton, with the Rice Export Corporation of Pakistan (RECP) performing a similar role to the CEC. The REC held a monopoly on the procurement and export of rice, maintaining procurement prices substantially lower than world prices in order to protect urban consumers from high food costs.

A parallel set of input subsidies on irrigation water, fertilizer, electricity, and pesticides, to counter the effects of declining agricultural output prices, were adopted in the 1970s. These subsidies, which have been progressively dismantled in recent years, were the government's attempt to compensate for its low output prices.

The result of all these policy measures was that government intervention in pricing and trading of major agricultural commodities (wheat, rice, cotton, sugar, and edible oils) and input subsidies (fertilizer, irrigation water, and electricity) was so pervasive that the private sector was reduced to a passive spectator. Considerable resource transfer out of agriculture occurred as a result of these policies (Table 2.10), estimated at about 3.4 per cent of GDP (Nabi, Nasim and Hamid, 1990). The subsidization of inputs and the procurement of major farm products at prices far less than the world market price was so strong that, by the end of the 1980s, the domestic procurement price of rice was about 50 per cent of the export parity price, while the price of wheat was around 75 per cent of the international market price. Similarly, Pakistani cotton prices were kept substantially below international prices, with the average price of cotton being 55 per cent below world prices. According to some studies, the gap between producer prices and border prices increased for all crops except sugarcane (Faruqee, 1994). These policies continued the trend, started in the 1950s, of a large net resource transfer from the agricultural sector to the growing industrial sector. Studies show that these transfers amounted to as much as 11 per cent in the earlier period, but subsequent corrective policies had reduced these transfers to more modest levels by the late 1980s.

In the mid-80s, the government created the Agricultural Prices Commission (APCOM), which was established to advise the government on changes in support prices for major crops. While this institution was primarily an advisory body, it could provide much-needed information on elasticities and appropriate pricing mechanisms.

The reforms in Pakistan's pricing polices arrived in consonance with changes in the development economics literature, which was slowly recognizing the importance of getting prices right (Griffin, 1989). Empirical studies from a large number of countries demonstrated that peasant farmers were responsive to price signals and increased their supply if the prices were favourable. There was a growing recognition of the relationship between proper pricing policy and growth rates. The pace of agricultural growth, although based on a solid resource endowment, was found to be largely determined by the rate of technological change, which in turn was determined by the level of profitability (Mellor, 1991). Moreover, the correlation between the growth of the non-agriculture sector and rising rural incomes suggested that price policy, by affecting the relative profitability of specific commodities, could influence this relationship. Thus, pricing was found to be vital to any agricultural strategy.

Did government intervention in price-setting for key agricultural commodities help either the efficiency or the poverty reduction objectives? The evidence from Pakistan suggests that the actual consequences of pricing policies were totally different from the intended objectives. The inter-sectoral transfer of resources out of agriculture led to what an influential study termed the 'plundering of agriculture', with an adverse impact on the rural poor and a repressed environment for enhanced agricultural production. It was only when the relative prices were aligned with the border prices and marketing was liberalized that agriculture growth was once again revived in the 1980s.

TAXATION POLICY

Throughout Pakistan's history, the agriculture sector has not been directly taxed. The main argument against direct taxation has been that a whole series of indirect taxes, and policies favouring the manufacturing sector, had already created a substantial burden, and, as pointed out above, intersectoral transfer of resources was taking place from agriculture to industry. For the opponents of the tax, agriculture was already an overtaxed and neglected sector. In the light of Pakistan's growing fiscal deficit and an increasing difficulty in mobilizing resources, strong pressures against fiscal evasion by the agricultural sector have resurfaced.

In 1993, the interim government of Moeen Qureshi introduced reforms to the agriculture income tax and the wealth tax. This was the first time in the nation's history that an agriculture income tax was actually legislated. The income tax was to be based on the productive capability of land, which was assessed in terms of the Produce Index Units (PIU). Basically, the tax rate was Rs 2 per PIU between 4,000 and 6,000 PIUs, and Rs 3 per PIU between 6,000 and 8,000 PIUs.

The use of PIUs was one of the major areas of contention. A relic of post-Partition days, PIUs were designed in the 1940s and 1950s when attempts were made to settle the land claims of Muslim refugees after independence. PIUs were meant to establish equivalence between land parcels having different soil and water conditions, but they seem to bear little relationship to the current productive capacity of the land. It is, therefore, vital that a revamping of the PIU-based system take place in order to make a realistic assessment of agriculture tax. The implementation of the tax on agriculture has yet to take place.

The major taxes on agriculture historically have been the provincial land tax and *ushr*, which is leviable on all Muslim landowners at the rate of 5 per cent of the share of the output (Nasim and Akhlaque, 1992). Due to poor administration, abuse of the principle of 'low average yields', whereby tax burdens were to be proportional to incomes, and a whole series of loopholes, less than 5 per cent of *ushr* has been collected. In 1989-90 the potential for *ushr* collection was Rs 2,855 million against the actual collection of Rs 134 million.

How much direct tax can be raised from agriculture? As the sectoral contribution of agriculture to GDP is 25 per cent, the maximum potential from this source is 3 to 4 per cent of GDP (total tax revenue is 14-15 per cent). Estimates about the actual revenue that can be obtained from such a tax vary (Azhar, 1991). One study finds the potential for agricultural income tax plus land revenue and *ushr* to be around Rs 1 billion in 1986-7 (Nasim and Akhlaque, 1992). Other work suggests a much higher magnitude, in the order of Rs 3 billion. The underlying assumptions indicate generous threshold levels and high costs of administration and collection. Although the studies disagree on a variety of points, the consensus is that the landlords in the upper income groups are currently being undertaxed.

This tendency to exempt large landowners from the taxation net weakens the incentives for overall tax collection and heightens the probability of fraud as people with non-agricultural income masquerade their income as agricultural.

As output prices are being aligned closer to border prices, and inter-sectoral transfers get smaller, the case for horizontal equity in tax collection is becoming more persuasive. While the net proceeds from agriculture tax would remain modest, the round-tripping on non-agricultural incomes that is pervasive under the current system would improve the overall collection.

Besides the direct taxes, a whole series of indirect taxes affect the agriculture sector. One of the major ones has been the export tax on agricultural products, providing a major source of revenue for the government. The government has used its monopoly position in the export trade of rice and cotton to reap huge windfalls. The revenue from the export tax on cotton has fluctuated widely, but reached about Rs 2 billion in 1988-9. The Rice and Cotton Export Corporations have also made profits by buying the produce at lower domestic prices and selling them at higher prices.

Another important policy affecting the agriculture sector is the subsidization of inputs (Faruqee, 1994). Subsidies for fertilizer and tubewells and a host of other products, as well as a whole battery of concealed subsidies on water, electricity, and credit, confer some benefit to agriculture. The estimates suggest considerable gains for the sector as a whole. While the subsidy on fertilizer declined from its peak of Rs 3.6 billion in 1979-80 to Rs 1 billion in 1989-90, the subsidies on irrigation, water, and electricity increased from Rs 1 billion in 1980 to Rs 3 billion in 1990. But these subsidies have had a differential impact, favouring the large influential farmers and bypassing the small farmers who are below the technological production frontier. The subsidies have thus created inefficiencies and are inequitable.

The studies of taxation and agriculture subsidies are emphatic in asserting that the net burden of this complex set of measures falls disproportionately on the poor and small farmers. The poor do not benefit from the subsidies but pay indirect taxes and implicit taxes through lower output prices. The large farmers who receive most of the subsidies—credit, irrigation water, tractors, electricity for tubewells—do not pay direct taxes and their indirect tax burden is almost identical, in proportional terms, to that of the small farmers. This inter-personal inequity in economic power has been reinforced by the influence and connections of the large land-owning classes which have held the reins of political power since independence.

CREDIT POLICY

The problem of capital scarcity for the underdeveloped agrarian sector is well-known in development economics. Pakistan has historically lagged behind other developing economies in terms of a solid credit policy to aid the agriculture sector, thereby hindering its growth and productivity.

Access to credit has many positive consequences for the agricultural sector. Research has found that higher credit use is correlated with higher input use and higher output, as well as being important in the alleviation of poverty and in financing small-scale projects in the rural non-farm sector (Faruqee, 1994). Moreover, it is particularly important in the emerging sectors, such as export horticulture, which require both short-run and long-run investment.

The provision of credit in Pakistan is shared by both official and non-institutional sources of credit disbursement. At the official level, institutional sources comprising the ADBP, commercial banks, provincial governments, and co-operative institutions have emerged as major credit suppliers in the agricultural sector. These institutions together supplied Rs 15 billion to the agricultural sector in 1990-1, about 7 per cent of sectoral value-added. While this may not be large compared to the (very rough) estimates of the amount of money flowing in the unorganized markets, it is significant when compared to the Rs 3 billion in 1979-80 (4.5 per cent of sectoral value-added). Nevertheless, the credit gap remained significant as credit lagged significantly behind sectoral value-added and has widened in the mid 1990s. (Table 2.11).

Credit disbursement which was nonexistent in the 1960s and 1970s, accelerated uptil the mid 1980s, and tapered off gradually by the early 1990s. Lending by all agencies increased until 1987, but lately the stagnation in lending and the recent bail-out of the agricultural co-operatives are signs of major problems in the rural financial systems. The formal sector is characterized by its failure to mobilize deposits and the inability to respond dynamically to changed circumstance. The 1972 banking reform forced commercial banks to meet a target level of lending to the agricultural sector, but the lending is conducted at non-economic rates, for non-viable projects, and directed to the large landowners. Furthermore, the credit system is poorly enforced and there are many non-performing loans, with attempts at recovery taking years. The clear class bias is demonstrated by the requirement for large collateral, which means that many tenant farmers are unable to benefit from credit disbursements.

Given the low level of financial intermediation and the ineffectiveness of banking institutions at transfering funds to the rural sector, it is no surprise that non-institutional sources of credit such as moneylenders, relatives, commission agents, and rural landlords are the major source of private capital for the rural farmers. This informal finance, which is estimated to account for 80 per cent of agricultural credit, is geared towards meeting short-term credit and consumption loans. In situations where the tenant has little recourse to the financial system, the rural moneylenders intervene, granting short-term loans largely against personal security. These moneylenders have an intimate knowledge of the borrower, as well as of local conditions, and demand repayment within a period of months. This system has been characterized as exploitative and undesirable due to a variety of factors (Faruqee, 1994). Firstly, the lender is indifferent to the uses of the money, and thus, it may be used for unproductive purposes. Unfortunately, most of the loans from non-institutional sources are used for consumption purposes. Secondly, a higher rate of interest is offered than in the organized financial sector. These higher rates reflect the informal lenders' high screening costs, since they must undertake high-risk lending without collateral. One estimate shows that rejection rates can reach as high as 50 per cent for rural loans from this informal credit market. Thirdly, the government is unable to tap into the resources of the unorganized sector, and its conduct of monetary and fiscal policy must operate outside this very important money market.

Although the difficulties of financial intermediation in predominantly agricultural rural markets is well-known—

dispersal of clients, poor infrastructure, fluctuations in farmer incomes—there is room in Pakistan for the creation of integrated rural financial markets, where less profitable farmers can have access to credit. There is a role for a Grameen bank-type institution in conjunction with the commercial banks.

INSTITUTIONS SUPPORTING AGRICULTURE DEVELOPMENT

One of the key characteristics of the agricultural sector is the proliferation of public institutions that are involved in a whole range of activities, from input supply to infrastructure provision to output price intervention. These institutions have become generally inefficient and inflexible over time.

The marketing of agriculture produce is an area where Pakistan has lagged behind many developing countries. While much input has gone into increasing crop productivity and bringing technical changes into agriculture, little attention has been devoted to the marketing side. By the four crucial standards used to evaluate the strengths of a marketing system—the level and quality of competitive conditions, the relative predictability and stability of prices, product standardization, and the effectiveness of market regulation—Pakistan has a very poor record.

The transportation network in Pakistan is one of the worst in the world. Fewer than a third of of the country's 45,000 villages have access to wholesale trading centres, and the roads, the main thoroughfares for commerce are poorly maintained. Thus, a weak investment in roads has been a strong barrier to the successful marketing of agricultural products. It has been estimated that inadequate road standards increase transport costs by 30-40 per cent. Furthermore, the non-availability of storage accommodation compels a farmer to sell his produce immediately after harvest, and thus reduces his staying power.

The supply of inputs is another area where Pakistani agriculture has performed weakly (Faruqee, 1994). Large distortions in the fertilizer, pesticide, and seed markets have created numerous problems for farmers. The fertilizer policy imposes large hidden costs on farmers, including search costs for scarce supplies, panic buying due to uncertainty about availability, and depressed yields through lack of availability at the required time—fertilizer is rarely delivered on time, and it has been a chronic complaint of farmers since the seventies that agricultural output would be tremendously boosted if a strong fertilizer distribution system was in place. It is interesting to note that, although the recommended ratio between nitrogen and phosphate is 1:1 for most crops, the ratio in Pakistan is 3:1 due to the poor level of phosphate imports.

The supply of pesticides has been very strong since the subsidy was ended in the 1980s, and it has become common knowledge that one of the key factors responsible for the dramatic growth in cotton yields in the 1980s was the widespread availability and use of pesticides. The case of pesticides is an empirical verification of the idea that agricultural liberalization can be very successful.

A final input whose provision has been inadequate has been seed. The success of the Green Revolution has not been repeated in recent years as Pakistan has struggled with seed distribution and pricing policy. Problems of availability, accessibility, and quality of seed are rampant.

While the overall effectiveness of agricultural research and extension services has been widely debated, there is general consensus that Pakistan's system needs a major overhaul. In response to the growing needs of farmers to improve their productivity, the World Bank and bilateral donors began assisting the government in the early 1980s to strengthen research and extension services.

Agricultural research in Pakistan, spearheaded by the PARC and the NARC, has not kept pace with the times. Due to paucity of funds, bureaucratic infighting, bad equipment, and vague organizational structures and mandates, these institutions have not fostered a strong research environment.

Basically, agricultural research in Pakistan covers two areas—plant breeding research and crop and resource management research. While plant breeding research has been satisfactory, it takes very long to get results to the farmer. Similarly, crop and resource management research lack a systems perspective and ignore interactions between different crops and agronomic issues.

Similarly, the extension system in Pakistan is plagued with multiple problems—severe organizational problems, low funding, and poor staff training and education. Given the importance of input efficiency in the future growth of agriculture, a better system will have to be developed. A number of innovative approaches to farmer training and dissemination of knowledge of best agricultural practices have been successfully applied in a number of developing countries. But organizational inertia, lack of imaginative leadership, and outmoded technical skills have not permitted Pakistan's farmers to benefit from these innovations.

SUMMING UP

Pakistan's overall record of agriculture growth has varied widely. The future of agriculture in Pakistan is uncertain and is highly dependent on a number of institutional reforms and appropriate policies to improve agricultural productivity. The growth rate of agriculture can be accelerated through improved technology and a shift towards the production of high value products. The direct and indirect effects on the rest of the economy through demand stimulus, expansion in employment, and stable prices can be highly favourable. To achieve this, the government must formulate an appropriate programme to tap the hidden potential of Pakistan's agriculture. The past success of the agriculture sector was built on a programme of effective public price support for major crops, subsidies to popularize new inputs, and enhanced credit facilities to enable the farmers to adopt modern inputs and technologies. Some elements of these policies will have to be retained while others, such as subsidies for fertilizers, will need to be discarded. New elements such as rationalizing and phasing out some of the public-sector marketing and supply organizations, and ensuring efficient use and cost recovery of irrigation water charges, have to be implemented. Much attention should be paid to developing new seed varieties of wheat, rice, and maize suitable for Pakistan's soils and ecological habitat. Import substitution in edible oils has been made possible in India by a package of price incentives, technological and institutional support, and government policy. This high-value crop can also be expanded in Pakistan, provided the right mix of pricing, technology, and institutions is adopted along with high-value fruits, vegetables, and livestock products. This goal is by no means incompatible with the goal of self-sufficiency.

Given Pakistan's strong comparative advantage in wheat, basmati rice, and cotton, due to a Domestic Resource Cost (DRC—the ratio of domestic nontraded inputs to the value of foreign exchange per unit of the crop) of less than one, measures must be undertaken to increase their productivity. Wheat self-sufficiency is a must, as Pakistan cannot keep on depending on expensive wheat imports.

Secondly, increasing pressure on land will require a shift toward higher-value, higher-yielding crops, and toward higher cropping intensities. The amount of cultivable land is shrinking, and attempts must be made to increase yields, thus making agriculture more efficient.

Thirdly, the success of agriculture depends on the pace of government liberalization and its commitment to proper pricing. The web of interventions, which are a legacy of the early years, must be progressively dismantled. While government interventions in output prices to reduce farmer uncertainty have been moderately successful, the average foreign exchange foregone as a result has been estimated to be 150 per cent. This is a huge cost.

Fourthly, some method must be found to ensure fertilizer and water availability. One of the lessons of the 1970s is that poor input supply is devastating. Pakistan will have to avoid repeating that experience.

Unless these reforms are undertaken, the future of Pakistani agriculture is bleak. As the world approaches the millennium, Pakistan cannot rest on the laurels of its Green Revolution success and cotton boom of the 1980s. New policies must be formulated to move it forward.

STRUCTURE AND EVOLUTION OF INDUSTRY

The central pillar of Pakistan's development strategy over the last fifty years has been industrialization. From the very beginning, Pakistan made the development of a strong industrial sector a vital priority. Through import substitution industrialization, it has sought to develop its infant industries and give its manufacturing sector the ability to compete in export markets, and to build an indigenous consumer and capital goods sector, thus reducing the economy's dependence on imports.

Furthermore, as the forces of globalization and economic integration are getting stronger, it has become imperative for developing countries to benefit from this larger economic pie by developing a comparative advantage in particular branches of industry. The process of structural transformation itself involves the transition from a purely agrarian to an industrial economy. No country has succeeded on the sole basis of agriculture. Thus, an assessment needs to be made of the structure and evolution of Pakistani industry over the last fifty years, the strengths and weaknesses analysed, and the implications for the future examined.

An analysis of the stylized facts gives some useful insights. Manufacturing's share in value-added increased from 7.8 per cent in 1950 to close to 18 per cent by 1995 (Table 2.15). The index of industrial production, perhaps the single best indicator for industrial output, increased from 22.6 in 1950-1 to 1,347 by 1994 (but growth has slowed down since then). This represents an almost sixtyfold increase in a span of fifty years. But since the initial base was so small, this statistic is not very meaningful. Even if the early years are ignored, production quintupled from 1965 to 1990. This record is impressive, but the employment generated by the manufacturing sector was less than 11 per cent of the employed labour force. This low employment elasticity has its historical roots in the preferential treatment meted out to both private and public industrial firms in the form of cheap capital. Within the industrial sector, the proportion of workers employed in the capital and intermediate goods industry has remained stagnant for the last two decades, and the proportion in the intermediate industry has increased only threefold since 1970 (Table 2.16). Currently, investment in the manufacturing sector averages about one-fourth of the total fixed capital formation.

Pakistan's manufacturing sector has had strong growth rates in the last fifty years, averaging about 7 per cent annually. There have been variations in the rates of growth in the different periods, ranging from 11 per cent in the early 1960s, to 4 per cent in the first half of the 1970s, but the persistent trend in most of the period has been 7 to 8 per cent. The only aberration in Pakistani industrial success, which occurred in the 1970s, was caused by a combination of powerful exogenous shocks and ill-guided nationalization policies.

The structure of the industry has changed considerably since Partition (Table 2.17). In the early years, most of the manu-facturing capacity was concentrated in textiles, garments, leather goods, and other simple consumer goods, but by the 1970s, spearheaded by the public sector, there were large investments in industries such as steel, chemicals, fertilizer, and cement. By the 1980s the private sector was investing in sophisticated intermediate goods and capital goods industries (Noman, 1992). However, technological backwardness and low productivity still characterize many of these industries. While Pakistan was succcessful in the first-stage ISI and built a substantial consumer goods sector, it has had only partial success in developing a capital goods sector or intermediate goods industrial base. The backward linkages of agro-processing industries are fairly strong but the forward linkages are underdeveloped.

Table 2.18 shows the annual average growth of selected industrial items and shows that non-textile—fertilizer, cement, and sugar—have had strong growth, averaging more than 10 per cent annually over the span of several decades. They show the partial success of industrial diversification in Pakistan.

The leading sector of Pakistani industrialization has been the cotton textile sector, where output increased from 114 million kg of yarn in 1955 to 1,300 million kg in 1995. Pakistani industry had achieved great success in translating its comparative advantage in the production of raw cotton into manufacturing success. Pakistan's share in world export of cotton yarn is 30 per cent, and its share of cotton cloth is 7 per cent. Table 2.19 shows the growth rates of cotton yarn and cotton textiles for various time periods.

However, the sector has been plagued with inefficiencies (Riordan and Srinivasan, 1996). In spite of enjoying high protection and benefiting from a government policy of deliberately keeping cotton prices low, the textile industry suffers from several deficiencies. Its very meagre contribution to world textile exports (less than 2 per cent) suggests that output performance has been much below potential. The textile industry hardly maintains any quality control system and confines the spinners to the production of lowest value-added coarse counts, the weaving mills to coarse fabrics, the knitting units to low-priced basic T-shirts in bulk, and the garment units to items lacking innovative design. Furthermore, perennial conflict between cotton growers, spinners, weavers, and garment manufacturers has hindered the development of a long-term strategy. Despite the fact that cotton and cotton-based products account for over 60 per cent of Pakistan's export earnings, an integrated approach to strengthening the textile industry has yet to emerge.

The small-scale sector, which was a negligible part of the economy in the 1950s and 1960s, received a boost from the nationalization of large-scale manufacturing in the early 1970s.

Currently about 30 per cent of total industrial output is supplied by the small-scale sector. Although penalized in earlier years by exchange rate, financial, and fiscal policies, the liberalization policies have gradually done away with the problems of differential access and reduced the cost diasadvantages of small entrepreneurs. Despite the issues of formal credit, marketing, and quality that still loom large, the small-scale sector has made an invaluable contribution to the growth of manufactured exports.

Small-scale manufacturing has also been relatively more successful in generating employment opportunities. Studies have shown that the annual average rate of growth in value-added has been identical to the growth in employment in this sub-sector. It is reasonable to assume that the employment elasticity is close to one for small-scale manufacturing.

It is also argued that the statistical foundations for estimating the trends in investment, value-added, and employment in small-scale manufacturing are weak, and that the actual contribution of this sub-sector is much larger than is indicated by the national income accounts. There are very good reasons for these small-scale entrepreneurs to underestimate and underreport their incomes and output. As most of the investment is self-financed, there are strong incentives to maximize cash flow and after-tax profits. The largely undocumented nature of business transactions does in fact facilitate and reinforce these incentives.

However, any balanced assessment of Pakistan's industrializ-ation experience must take into account the critical shortcomings. The most glaring weakness of Pakistani industrialization has been its inability to diversify its structure of manufactures. Although the share of manufacturing sector in GDP has risen to 18 per cent, the base is too narrow—50 per cent of value-added originates largely in textiles and food processing industries. Domestic steel production is insignificant and uncompetitive, thus downstream industries that use steel have not been successful. Furthermore, Pakistan's cotton textiles have low value-added and have undergone only a few stages of processing. Cotton yarn is the main manufacturing product along with the lower end of cotton cloth.

Secondly, Pakistan's industrialization has come at a high cost. Pakistan has historically been in the higher rungs of the ladder of developing countries with large effective protection rates (Kernal and Naqvi, 1991; Winters and Ingco, 1995) (Table 2.20). Many industries continue to provide low or negative value-added at world prices. Although gradual liberalization efforts have been made at various points in time, the continued high rates of tariff protection and other discretionary rules and regualtións, some of them mutually inconsistent, have not allowed Pakistan to move into efficient industrialization that can compete in the world markets. Its inability to take full advantage of the Uruguay Round is just one glaring example. Only 25 per cent of manufactured goods were covered by tariff bindings that are reasonably acceptable (Winters and Ingco, 1995; Low, 1995).

Thirdly, the large scale private sector in Pakistan seems to want a cozy relationship with the government, and this kind of relationship is not particularly healthy. The nationalization of the 1970s created a climate of distrust, which seems to have lasted, on and off, for an extended period. Private entrepreneurs are always keen to maximize economic rents for their industries by blocking competition and channelling selective funds from the government. Other successful countries have demonstrated that an effective government-private sector partnership under a competitive market structure is an important means of promoting socially efficient investment.

Fourthly, the small-scale sector, a dynamic and flourishing sector, has not been given equal attention by the government. Industrial policy has always favoured large-scale organizations, with their capital-intensive policies and their organizational power. The myriad advantages to small size, such as innovation, flexibility, and dynamism, that are an asset in today's world, have been ignored in policy formulation.

Fifthly, ISI industrialization has resulted in a heavy tax on agriculture, which is the mainstay of the Pakistani economy (Islam, 1981). Intersectoral transfers have been quite high, until recently, when attempts have been made to redress the grievances of the agricultural sector. This discrimination against the agriculture sector, which still employs half of the country's labour force, has not allowed demand for simple labour-intensive goods to be maximized. The chain of industrialization starts organically with a strong consumer demand arising from the higher incomes generated in the agriculture sector.

Sixthly, a heavy burden on Pakistani industrialization has been its export performance, especially in the last two decades. Anti-export bias has not been corrected despite the recognition that export promotion is the preferred option for the country. The weakness of Pakistan's export performance can be gauged by the fact that not only has it fallen massively behind South-east Asian countries with respect to total manufactured goods, but it has been particularly unsuccessful in four of the labour-intensive industries that have been important in the early phases of industrial development in most labour-abundant countries— garments, footwear, electronics, and furniture (Noman, 1992). The Philippines, which until 1985 had a lower level of manufactured exports than Pakistan, has been able to increase manufactured exports ten times during the decade, while Pakistan had achieved a fourfold expansion in the same period.

Thus, in sum, the Pakistani industrialization record, like its agriculture and trade record, presents a mixed picture, being neither a glaring disaster nor an unmitigated success.

CONSTRUCTING AN INDUSTRIAL BASE

In 1947 there was hardly any industry of significance in the provinces now forming Pakistan. For a variety of reasons—the peculiar nature of British colonial rule, the resource endowments of the area, the control of trading by Hindus and Parsis, who were located in other parts of India the dependence on agriculture and the inertia this caused, and finally, a complete absence of interest in industry on the part of those living in the area which formed Pakistan—the country inherited a weak industrial base at the time of Partition. Moreover, the mass migrations after Partition wreaked havoc on whatever minimal indigenous small-scale manufacturing capability there existed.

At Partition, the country had no large-scale manufacturing capacity except for a few rudimentary textile mills, an oil refinery, and some capacity in sugar refining, tea processing, and cement (Noman, 1992). Furthermore, in the textile business, Pakistan was still a substantial net importer, with imports accounting for all domestic absorption of modern manufactures. The main trading partner was India, with whom Pakistan exchanged agricultural goods for manufactured products. One good index of the strength of the manufacturing sector, the ratio of large-scale manufacturing to GDP, reveals an interesting comparison. While the ratio in Pakistan was 1.4 per cent, the Indian figure was 6 per cent.

To compound these problems, Pakistan did not have a strong entrepreneurial class, which could have catapulted private industry into prominence. The indigenous commercial class could neither provide the drive nor the capital that is so vital to industrial success. To remedy this situation, the founder of Pakistan, Mohammad Ali Jinnah, invited leading Muslim industrialists of India, including the prominent Habibs and Ispahanis, to come to Pakistan and build industry. They filled the vacuum left by the departing Hindu merchants.

Industrialization was the rage in development economics in the late 1940s and 1950s. Proceeding from the observation that rich countries tend to be industrialized, economists argued that growth can only be achieved through industrialization. A voluminous body of research found large generalizations in the pattern of development across several countries, and concluded that economic growth is synonymous with a declining share of output and employment in agriculture and an increasing share of output and employment in industry (Maier, 1984). The argument was that industry grows at a faster pace than agriculture because of economies of scale, a higher capital intensive nature, complementarities between projects, and externalities not found in the agriculture sector. Industry enjoys higher productivity, which is crucial for development. Thus, the mantra of the early years was that industrialization was the recipe for success.

These findings from development economic literature had strong implications for development policy. The idea was that government policy—through the acceleration of investment, through the provision of the critical 'Big Push', through the construction of a trade regime that protects local infant industries, through the supply of critical inputs like capital, managerial talent, and resources at subsidized prices, and through central allocation of key raw materials, imports, and foreign exchange—could spearhead the drive to industrialization and thus, accelerate the growth rate. Pakistan attempted to implement these ideas in concrete policy actions.

The first key decision that affected industry in Pakistan was the government's decision not to devalue its currency when both the pound sterling and the Indian rupee were devalued (Ahmed and Amjad, 1984). One of the important considerations behind this decision was the desire to obtain imported capital goods needed to establish industries at cheaper prices. However, the Korean War boom, resulting in a dramatic increase in the prices of jute and raw cotton, created a commodity boom whereby many traders rushed into the import/export business to make quick profits. The combination of an overvalued exchange rate, a high tariff structure, a vacuum caused by the trade disruption with India, and the fertile commodity market, created Pakistan's first class of nascent entrepreneurs. These merchant capitalists bought raw materials from the agricultural sector at cheap prices and sold them in the foreign markets at very high mark-ups (Islam, 1981; Noman, 1992). However, the end of the Korean War left these merchants with reduced profit opportunities in the import trade.

The government, which had followed a liberal import policy during the war, reacted to the fall in commodity exports and the consequent foreign exchange crisis by re-imposing adminis-trative controls. These controls, mainly on the import of consumer goods, increased the prices of these goods and set the terms of trade heavily in favour of industry and against agriculture (Islam, 1981). This resulted in a large profitability for the industrial sector, even in comparison to the trading sector. Interestingly, the rate of return on industrial investment was so high that industrialists were able to recover their initial investments in one or two years (Papanck, 1967). This was remarkable considering that the conventional gestation period for industry is much longer. Thus, traders who had earlier made high profits and amassed surpluses during the Korean War boom converted merchant capital into industrial capital by importing industrial machinery and producing consumer goods, especially cotton textiles.

The first stage of Pakistan's ISI trade strategy was under way, in which the imports of non-durable consumer goods, such as household goods and clothing, were replaced with domestic equivalents. Furthermore, manufactures slowly began to displace primary commodities as Pakistan began its industrial process. Given that Pakistan's resource endowment heavily favoured the export of jute and cotton, the first industries to develop in the area were naturally cotton and jute-based manufactures. The second-stage ISI, in which imports of intermediate goods and producer and consumer durables were replaced by domestic products, started in the mid-1960s.

In the 1950s and 1960s the Pakistan government came to the aid of industry in a variety of ways. First and foremost, it set up the Pakistan Industrial Development Corporation (PIDC), whose objectives were to initiate pioneering ventures in many new areas of industry and to supplement private enterprise where the existing number of private units was not sufficient in relation to demand (Islam, 1981). The main areas where PIDC was to intervene were in heavy engineering (including iron and steel), shipbuilding, and jute paper. The units that were successful were then to be handed over to the private sector after completion. In a large number of projects, the private sector worked closely with PIDC in the form of joint ventures, partly because this ensured easy access to foreign capital and partly because PIDC could secure government sanctions speedily. In the early years, much of PIDC's work was in the underdeveloped parts of Pakistan, where roads, infrastructure, and power projects had to be built. Thus, PIDC spearheaded the industrialization drive in Pakistan. It provided that critical 'Big Push' and initial capital investment without which the private sector could not operate because of its skill limitations, capital constraints, and long gestation periods.

Secondly, a systematic policy of industrial licensing was formulated and implemented in the late 1950s and 1960s (Islam, 1981). During the Second Five-Year Plan (1955-60) and the Third Five-Year Plan (1960-5), a consistent industrial development programme was formulated, and an industrial investment schedule was designed to provide guidelines for investors. It is important to note that the import licensing regime was mainly concerned with the allocation of imports among large-scale commercial importers or large-scale industrial establishments because the larger enterprises were easier to deal with administratively. This resulted in a notable neglect of the flourishing small-scale sector, which accounted for a significant amount of employment and income in Pakistan. The small-scale industries, defined as establishments that use motive power and do not employ more than 50 workmen, were industries characterized by a lower capital intensity than their large-scale counterparts. Due to restricted access to credit and bank financing, difficulty in obtaining imported capital equipment, economies of scale and the consequent disadvantages of size, and discriminatory treatment in fiscal and exchange rate policies, the small-scale sector, a vital source of employment and broad-based industrialization in countries as diverse as Italy and Taiwan, remained suppressed as a result of Pakistan's lopsided industrial policy.

Thirdly, the Government provided heavy protection in the form of tariffs in order to strengthen the infant industries. The import controls instituted in the 1950s, which were originally aimed at solving the balance of payments difficulties, did not disappear with time. The infant-industry argument does justify some protection for a limited period, allowing industry to gain experience from learning-by-doing, but, like many developing countries, this form of protection became open-ended, with no time limit.

In an important study, the Tariff Commission compared the ex-factory prices (a good indicator of domestic costs of production) with the prices of imported goods in industries between 1951 and 1966 and found that factory prices were 50-100 per cent higher in one-third of the industries and 100-200 per cent in about one-fifth (Islam, 1981). This was a huge burden on consumers. Furthermore, empirical studies of the magnitude of protection of Pakistani industries in the 1950s and 1960s reach disturbing conclusions, showing very high rates of protection for a whole array of industries, ranging from cotton textiles to sugar and edible oils (Little, Scitvosky and Scott, 1970).

As a result of all these policies, Pakistan had a phenomenal growth rate of manufacturing between the 1950s and the 1960s—an average annual growth rate of more than 9 per cent. This is especially large in comparison to the meagre 2.6 per cent for agriculture and the 3 per cent for trading. The high rate was no doubt facilitated by the non-existent industrial base at Partition, but it is nevertheless a strong achievement.

An assessment of Pakistan's industrialization experience in the 1960s has revealed two starkly different interpretations. Some have found Pakistan's industrialization experience to be highly problematic, resulting in an inefficient and misguided attempt to develop local industry (Little, Scitovsky and Scott, 1970; Balassa, 1971), while others have found it remarkably successful in creating an industrial infrastructure for the economy (Noman, 1992).

On the negative side, it has been argued that the home market for manufactured goods was so strongly protected by tariffs, controls, and multiple exchange rates that Pakistan had astronomical levels of effective protection, with average levels of protection exceeding 100 per cent. The effective protection rates, the percentage by which import restrictions enable the value-added in production to exceed what it would have been in their absence, has been so high that Pakistan had negative or negligible value-added at world prices. In major industries, such as cotton textiles and jute textiles, more than two-thirds of value-added was due to protection. In other words, the cost of the imports was not less than the value of the final output.

Secondly, the industrialization policies of the 1950s and the 1960s spawned huge inequalities between the agricultural and industrial sectors in Pakistan. By promoting industry, they indirectly taxed agriculture and thus put agricultural exports at a disadvantage. The effective exchange rates for the agricultural sector were between Rs 3.00 and Rs 4.25 per dollar during the 1950s, whereas for imported manufactured goods, they were between Rs 9 and Rs 10 per dollar; by 1960 the agricultural sector received Rs 5 per dollar for its purchases and paid Rs 10 for its purchases (Islam, 1981). Thus, there was a large intersectoral transfer of resources due to the declining terms of trade for agriculture and the government policies to assist industry. Estimates of the intersectoral resource transfer for West Pakistan was about Rs 8 billion, most of which was concentrated in East Pakistan.

Several arguments have been made in defence of the early industrialization strategy in Pakistan. Firstly, high protection in the early years did not affect the pattern of industrialization, but merely influenced the rate. In a situation of generally high and assured profitability and tight rationing of foreign exchange, the size of the domestic market, access to raw materials, and cost advantages had a decisive effect. Thus, the high protection rates were not the only factor responsible for resource allocation. Secondly, in spite of the inefficiencies, there was susbstantial improvement in labour productivity in the 1960s. The manufacturing sector demonstrated a high capacity for technological adaptation and innovation, and this led to advances in labour productivity. In another influential study, it was found that most of Pakistan's manufacturing industries can survive without protection (Kemal, 1991). Although government policies made the acquisition of imported inputs for second-shift operations relatively expensive and new capital cheaper, resulting in low rates of capacity utilization, this did not hurt the competitiveness of Pakistani industry. Thus, according to this view, the negative effects of protectionism on industrial performance were overstated.

Nevertheless, the 1960s was the most dynamic period in Pakistan's industrialization policy, and, notwithstanding its strong demerits, and there are many, it managed to provide a base for industrial capacity in Pakistan.

STATE OWNERSHIP OF INDUSTRIES

In 1971, with the secession of East Pakistan, the Pakistan's People's Party came to power under the leadership of the charismatic Zulfikar Ali Bhutto. The concentration of industrial power in the hands of a few families had provided ample ammunition for Bhutto and the PPP to win popular support in the 1970 elections. He was, therefore, obligated to uproot the existing structure and replace it with a new one. The PPP had opted for socialism as the main plank of its economic policy. The nationalization of large-scale industry after the PPP government assumed power was widely expected.

In January 1972, in the most dramatic reforms in Pakistani history, the banking and insurance comapanies were nationalized, and the government took over the management of thirty-one major manufacturing enterprises covering ten sub-sectors, including engineering, oil refining, and the ghee industry. A Board of Industrial Management (BIM) was set up to supervise the entire structure. By 1974, ten public-sector corporations had been established to run various industries, including fertilizer, automobiles, steel, and cement. Spurts of nationalization continued intermittently throughout the Bhutto years.

The reasons advanced to justify nationalization were many. Firstly, there was the attempt for the state to take over the 'commanding heights' of the economy and assume responsibility for investment and growth. Secondly, the nationalization campaign was a response to the perceived failure of the 'trickle-down' growth that had been prominent in the first two decades of Pakistan's existence. The idea was that only through large public investment and redistribution could income distribution be improved and workers earn higher wage incomes. Nationalization had as its logic the idea that only through governmental control of industry could correct allocative decisions be made. Throughout the world, the state had taken over sectors of the economy for a variety of reasons—regulation of market failures, command of strategic sectors, provision of physical infrastructure, the assurance of equitable prices, and distribution of goods to the population. Nationalization represented an attempt to expand the locus of the state still further. Thirdly, the reforms were meant to reduce the concentration of economic power among the leading industrialists, the famed 'Twenty-Two Families'. The growing concentration of wealth in Pakistan had provoked major concern, and the PPP had voiced popular demands for some action.

Unfortunately, the 1970s was also a period characterized by strong exogenous shocks to the Pakistani economy. It was a time of macroeconomic instability, the Indo-Pakistan war of 1971, the OPEC oil price shocks of 1973, and a series of adverse weather conditions and disease-related attacks on crops throughout the period, did not help Pakistani manufacturing. The government also decided in 1972 to devalue the currency massively and to remove distortions in the exchange rate regime.

Pakistani manufacturing performed quite badly during the period. The growth rate of manufacturing was a little over 3 per cent annually. Interestingly, the large-scale manufacturing sector, which accounted for more than two-thirds of the total value-added in manufacturing, had a stagnant production during the period, but the rapid and unanticipated expansion of the small-scale manufacturing sector was the most positive outcome of this period. The growth of this sector demonstrates the unintended consequences of public policy. Nationalization proved a bane to large-scale industry but a boon to small-scale enterprise.

Small-scale industry had been neglected during the 1960s due to the preference for large-scale enterprises, but the devaluation of 1972 provided a tremendous boost to profitability in this sector. As large-scale industry lost its cost advantage, acquired through access to subsidized foreign exchange and imported raw materials and capital goods, small-scale industry began to expand rapidly in all sectors, especially the consumer goods sector, machinery and fabricated goods in the engineering sector, and the export-oriented sector, including carpets, garments, textiles, and sporting goods. Furthermore, the government's import liberalization measures allowed the small industrialist greater access to capital and imported machinery. As small-scale industry was declared exempt from nationalization, much of the private capital was diverted to investment in smaller units of industry. As relative profitability had improved in the aftermath of devaluation and import liberalization, and there was no fear of takeover by the government, it made perfect sense to put money in this sector. In sum, Pakistan was finally beginning to diversify from its earlier emphasis on cotton and jute textiles, using a more efficient mode of industrialization.

An examination of the investment statistics clearly shows the expanded role of the public sector in this period (Naqvi and Sarmad, 1984) (Table 2.21). The public sector investment grew by over 25 per cent annually raising the share of public investment in total investment from 12.6 per cent in 1972-3 and to 79.9 per cent by 1977-8. The dominant fact of the 1970s was the radical upsurge in the role of the public sector in large-scale manufacturing.

Besides the adverse business climate that had been created as a result of nationalization, the antagonistic public/private relationship, and the series of external shocks, Pakistani industry was affected by another problem. Basically, the combination of overvalued exchange rates, high tariffs, cheap imports of capital goods, and easy access to credit that had protected and sheltered Pakistani industry from foreign competition during the 1960s was being progressively dismantled. The devaluation of 1972 and the import liberalization policies in the early 1970s left many of the industries facing less protected and more competitive markets. The heyday for Pakistani industrialists was clearly over.

The short-term transitional costs of this change in industrial policy should have been managed in an orderly manner and ought to have had beneficial effects over time. But the lack of trust on the part of private investors in the government's policies and the inherent fear of takeover deterred new investment flows in the large-scale industries that had become more profitable in the aftermath of devaluation and import liberalization. Thus, the normal expected effect of devaluation, i.e., expenditure switching through reallocation of factors of production, did not take place in this period to the extent necessary, and the beginning of an efficient structure in large scale industry was thwarted. As stated earlier, however, the small-scale industries, did thrive and contributed to the diversification of manufactured exports.

LIBERALIZATION, DEREGULATION, AND PRIVATIZATION

In 1978, the military government under General Zia attempted to restore the private sector to its cardinal role in economic activity. In 1977, the cotton, rice, and flour mills were denationalized, and in 1978 the government issued the 'Transfer of Managed Establishments Order' allowing for the denationalization of units, mainly manufacturing ones. In the Fifth Five-Year Plan, public sector investment was confined to the completion of ongoing projects, and emphasis was placed on the self-financing of industry. Furthermore, an Expert Advisory Cell was added to the Ministry of Production to monitor public sector performance. Unfortunately, the pace of divestiture and liberalization was extremely slow, and the public sector continued to grow. Notwithstanding divestiture, the public enterprise sector grew both in absolute terms and in terms of its share of GDP between 1975 and 1985, although new investment had come to a halt.

However, the divestiture strategy under the Zia regime was not particularly successful for a variety of reasons (Kemal and Naqvi, 1991), mainly because the government had fixed the prices of units way above their replacement value, and that it wanted to relinquish shares but retain ownership. Investors in Pakistan have a short-term time horizon and are not interested in buying loss-making units at such high prices and recouping them through profits generated as a result of improvements in productivity. The uncertainty in Pakistan's political and economic environment contributed to this attitude. Finally, investors were scared of the excess labour which would be difficult to get rid of after the transfer of ownership.

The post-Zia period, despite many changes in the political regimes, has proved to be more consistent in its policy stance towards liberalization and, particularly, privatization of public enterprises. The modalities and the process of sale and divestiture could have been more transparent, but the policy objective has not been tampered with.

In 1989, the new Pakistan People's Party government led by Benazir Bhutto established a Board of Investment which had the responsibility of laying down policy guidelines affecting industry. An Industrial Policy Statement was issued which increased the sanctioning limit for new investment to Rs 1 billion and simplified and streamlined the licensing process. Moreover, a list of 'key industries' was introduced, including the engineering, fertilizer, and electronic industries, and these units were given tax holidays and exemptions from custom duties. Furthermore, Ms Bhutto continued the divestiture and liberalization policies of her predecessor and vowed to strengthen private industry.

In 1990, the new Nawaz Sharif government, in the most ambitious economic reforms since the nationalization of the Bhutto years, announced a series of policy reforms to stimulate investment in manufacturing, including the removal of the complicated investment licensing regime, the liberalization of exchange controls, the facilitation of easy access to credit, and the granting of further tax incentives to industrialists (Noman, 1994). By 1991, the privatization of public sector industries had begun in earnest, with the offer of sale of over 100 companies. By 1996, with the second Benazir Bhutto government in power, over eighty units had been privatized. Thus, from 1978 to 1996, the Pakistani polity engaged in a series of measures to denationalize industry and provide strong incentives for the private sector to invest.

The ideological origins of the privatization measures stemmed from the growing experience of failed public sector enterprises in a large number of developing countries in the late 1970s and early 1980s. In the 1980s, privatization had been the buzzword in development circles. Privatization programmes, first developed and implemented in the UK, were adopted in a number of countries, particularly in Latin America and East Asia. Privatization, i.e., any transfer of assets from the public sector to the private sector with the explicit aim of enhancing private sector development, was motivated in Pakistan by a reaction to the dismal record of the nationalized industries. It was also felt that by extending its sphere of activities to production, distribution, and trading—the areas which private owners can operate more efficiently—the government was neglecting its fundamental responsibilities of law and order, infrastructure development, provision of basic social services, and human capital formation. The bureaucrats, who are normally risk-averse and have no aptitude or training for managing entrepreneurial activity, were not suited to operating public enterprises.

By 1990, the public sector units, also known as government-sponsored enterprises, held assets of Rs 700 billion, which was equal to Pakistan's GNP (Kemal and Naqvi, 1991). Furthermore, they had a share of 40 per cent of the total fixed investment in the economy and contributed 6.7 per cent to the economy's value-added.

The litany of complaints against them had escalated over the years. Firstly, they were accused of being inefficient and using their social objectives to mask poor performance. Secondly, the post-tax return on equity had been only 10 per cent, with sharp fluctuations in different units. According to some estimates, the corresponding private sector returns averaged 15-20 per cent. Also, continuing the trend of many private industries in the 1960s, many of them were inefficient as they added negative value-added at border prices. Thirdly, the growing fiscal burden of the economy was increasing rapidly. The overall fiscal deficit, the excess of total public expenditures over total revenue receipts, had increased in the 1980s because government saving declined sharply, from 2.8 per cent in 1980 to -1.4 per cent by 1989. The fiscal deficit had reached 8 per cent by 1988. This represented a tremendous burden on the economy because the deficit was eating up valuable resources that could have been used for productive investment. Under these circumstances, the public-sector corporations were viewed as prime villains, and their privatization was seen as an important way to alleviate the fiscal deficit. Among policymakers there was a fear that the high interest rates were crowding out private investment, although the evidence suggests that credit rationing has been much more important than rising interest rates in suppressing private investment. While there is some evidence of partial crowding out in the large-scale manufacturing sector, this is not as important as the government licensing regimes and credit programmes.

One important hindrance to the privatization schemes has been the high protection rates enjoyed by industry in Pakistan, which averaged 66 per cent in 1980-1. It has been argued that as long as tariff levels remain high, a change in the locus of ownership will not affect enterprise performance. In an important study (Kemal and Naqvi, 1991), which assessed the impact of the structure of protection on the pattern of domestic resource allocation in the early 1980s, but which is of considerable relevance to the present, it was found that the implicit effective protection rate (IEPR), the percentage excess of value-added at domestic prices over the value-added at world prices, was 66 per cent, while the domestic resource cost, the value at shadow prices of domestic resources employed over the value added, was 3.43. The study was based on a sample survey of 750 firms drawn randomly from ninety industries, and the authors drew a series of very interesting conclusions (Kemal and Naqvi, 1991). Firstly, the average level of protectionism is moderate although the range of variation around the average is very large, with nine industries characterized by negative value-added. Secondly, the distortions induced by protectionism have resulted in considerable allocative inefficiency, estimated at a staggering 10 per cent of GDP. Thirdly, there has been a secular shift from quota restrictions and tariffs to export subsidies, with export industries having the highest incidence of protection and inefficiency. Fourthly, it was found that protectionism does not increase with the stage of processing.

The implications of these findings of Pakistani industrial policy are important. It follows that there must be a readjustment in the system of industrial protection involving the replacement of quantitative restrictions by import duties to increase government revenue (Kemal and Naqvi, 1991). Domestic taxes and subsidies must take the place of trade restrictions, and export subsidies must be reduced because of the low contribution of export industries to economic growth. Interestingly, effective protection rates are generally lower in industries where public industrial enterprises dominate, and the domestic resource cost is the same for both the private and the public sector, indicating that the locus of ownership is not so important. An important academic finding suggests that the worst kind of allocative efficiency is in the private sector (Kemal and Naqvi, 1991). While 91.4 per cent of private sector industries may be characterized as inefficient, the proportion of inefficient industries in the public sector is only about 75 per cent.

In the period from 1978 to 1996, the performance of Pakistani industry was respectable. The high growth rates that the Pakistani economy achieved during the period can be attributed to the strong performance of the industrial sector. The manufacturing sector averaged a growth rate of about 7 per cent annually, which was a great improvement over the previous period's 3 per cent.

One of the leading success stories was the dramatic growth of the small-scale sector, which averaged growth rates of 8 per cent during the 1980s. The small-scale sector, which was a beneficiary of the nationalization of large-scale industries, devaluation, and liberalization policies of the 1970s, firmed its roots in the 1980s. Interestingly, the rapid growth of the heavily subsidized large-scale manufacturing sector suggests relatively higher levels of efficiency in the small-scale industries, but few small enterprises have graduated to become medium or large-scale enterprises. This anomalous fact suggests that there are several constraints to enterprise size. Various reasons have been cited for this (Kemal, 1994). Lower capital intensity in the small-scale sector (with capital-labour ratios only 20 per cent of the large-scale sector) and a crippling lack of finance due to the government's stringent credit policies (with formal credit only 10 per cent of investment) seem to account for the difference. The smaller industries had larger productivity of capital (two and a half times the level of the large-scale enterprise, perhaps due to the higher number of working hours in the small-scale sector).

One of the partial successes of industry in the 1980s was its shift towards building a sophisticated and intermediate capital goods industry, although this sector was plagued with problems. In one of the studies that focused on textile products and the chemical and engineering sectors, which accounted for a little less than half the value-added in manufacturing and more than 60 per cent of employment, it was found that technological backwardness, low productivity, and under-utilization of capital, with rates ranging from 30 per cent to 70 per cent, characterized these sectors. The steel, automobile, and engineering sectors were among the weakest performers of the 1980s, with cement and fertilizer being amongst the strongest.

Unfortunately, industrial diversification in Pakistan has not proceeded according to the development of linkages between sectors. While the textile industry has concentrated on spinning low-quality yarn rather than developing more forward linkages with the weaving sector, the engineering sector is dominated by either assembly operations based on imported parts, or the production of basic components. Industrial depth has, therefore, eluded Pakistan despite the import substitution strategy of the 1960s, nationalization, the jump in public industrial investment of the 1970s, and continued support of the industrial sector throughout the period.

INDUSTRIAL POLICY—AN INTERNATIONAL COMPARISON

The chaotic and haphazard nature of Pakistan's industrial policy can best be seen when comparing it with a broad spectrum of developing countries, especially the East Asian economies. Industrial policy, defined as government efforts to alter industrial structure, has also been an important aspect of Pakistani economic policy, but the results have been entirely different from the East Asian economies. In the latter set of countries, industrial policy was aimed at promoting productivity-based growth through a combination of learning, technological innovation, and catching up to international best practices. In Pakistan, industrial policy has given rise to highly protective and inefficient industries generating large private benefits and insignificant social gains.

Table 2.22 presents an international comparison between Pakistan and a broad array of developing countries in order to assess industrial growth patterns. The evidence overwhelmingly indicates that industrial diversification in Pakistan has been quite difficult to achieve. From 1970 to 1986 the share of value-added as a share of manufacturing value-added in food, beverages, and tobacco has increased from 24 per cent to 30 per cent, and that of chemicals and dyes increased from 20 per cent to 26 per cent. In the critical areas of electronics, machinery, and metal products, Pakistan has had hardly any shift, while the share of apparel and textile industry has declined from 34 per cent to 21 per cent. The high-growing Asian economies have had spectacular increases in the relative size and growth rates of these two important subsectors—metal products and machinery, and textiles and garments.

The well-documented examples of Japan, Taiwan, and Korea bear ample evidence to the fact that a sound government strategy can have a beneficial impact on industrial performance. Although there is considerable controversy among academics arguing the relative importance of industrial policy in East Asia's economic miracle, it is beyond contention that a correct set of incentives, a co-operative public sector-private sector relationship, contestable markets, and an open trade regime are vital ingredients of industrial success.

The experience of Pakistan with respect to industrial policy should be contrasted with that of Japan, Korea and Taiwan. All the essential ingredients of industrial policy—subsidized credit, preferential treatment in allocation of foreign exchange and imports, tax holidays, exemptions, industrial sanctions, publicly provided infrastructure—were also present in the case of Pakistan but the outcome was totally different from the Far Eastern one. The policy has, in many ways, retarded the growth of industry and distorted the pattern of development. The inefficiency of its industry has made Pakistan unable to compete internationally. The negligible exports of the large-scale manufacturing sector have forced Pakistani industry to focus on internal demand, and consequently, it has been unable to grow faster than domestic demand and has not become an engine of growth for the rest of the economy as earlier envisaged. The value-added in large and small scale manufacturing sectors as a proportion of total gross output is the lowest among all the sectors of the economy (Table 2.23).

One of the most pernicious aspects of the industrial policy was the reduction in the cost of capital relative to labour and the consequent adverse effect on the employment generation capacity of the large-scale manufacturing sector. This high capital-intensive approach to development has limited labour absorption in the large-scale manufacturing sector. The small-scale sector has had higher elasticities of labour absorption but the poverty levels in this sector have been quite high. It has been estimated that the reduction in capital cost due to concessionary interest rates and an eight-year tax holiday comes to about 25 per cent (Hamid and Kemal, 1991). A whole range of incentives, from tax holidays to exemptions of custom duty on machinery and equipment to subsidized credit, have not only led to diminished government revenues, but have had a series of negative spillover effects on the whole economy. Firstly, the level of private investment has not been influenced by these policies because supply, rather than demand, has been the critical constraint on investment (Hamid, 1992). In other words, the financial repression prevailing in Pakistan has been the major factor in determining the low level of investment. Secondly, the political considerations in the sanctioning of loans have not rewarded the most financially and economically viable industrial projects, and the bias in the allocation of credit towards new units has not made proper use of the economies of scale of existing units (Hamid, 1992). Thirdly, while fiscal incentives have failed to divert industry to backward areas due to the absence of infrastructure in these areas, the investment has been diverted from developed areas of the country to industrial estates in their vicinity (Hamid, 1992). The conspicuous feature of these estates has been the lack of linkages with the rest of the economy. Fourthly, the allocation of industrial licences and credit was guided by considerations of patronage. Financial viability has frequently been ignored as a criterion in the sanctioning of a loan or credit. The nexus between corrupt industrialists and nepotistic bureaucrats has consolidated the elitist strains in the Pakistani economy. Finally, the economic and industrial structure of Pakistan has remained decidedly oligopolistic, market reforms notwithstanding. The barriers to entry into a large majority of industries have remained quite high. Room for new entrepreneurs has been scarce. The economy-wide policies of liberalization, on the other hand, have been conducive to the expansion of small-scale industry in the last two and a half decades.

In sum, industrial policy in Pakistan, in alliance with trade policy, has had a retarding effect on industrial development. The manufacturing sector as a whole has not properly played its role of income generation, and has thus consolidated the elitist structure of the economy. Industrialization has reinforced the elitist nature of the Pakistani economy and concentrated the fruits of economic success at the upper rungs of society.

PREPARING FOR COMPETITION IN THE TWENTY-FIRST CENTURY

As the next century approaches, Pakistan's industrial sector faces a series of critical challenges. The growing integration of the international economy, the Uruguay Round and its aftermath, and the increased flow of capital, all carry serious implications for Pakistan's manufacturing sector. The expected stronger growth in world economy, an opening of the markets in textiles and related goods covered by the MFA, and significant potential in the 'long-distance' services trade provide an opportunity for Pakistan to increase its share in the world market (Riordan and Srinivason, 1996). But this will require resolution of a number of issues facing the industrial sector.

The toughest problem facing Pakistan is the future demand for its cotton textiles. Unfortunately, the long-run growth in basic manufactures is expected to be fairly modest, given the fundamentals of comparatively low income elasticities of demand. The cotton textile industry is characterized by low barriers to entry. Other low-cost producers are already entering the market and threatening the Pakistani exports. As income levels grow over time, the wage costs will also rise. Pakistan will have to reduce its dependence on low value-added cotton-based manufactures and diversify into other sectors, especially high value-added apparel and garments, as well as non-traditional exports such as sporting goods, surgical items, leather products, and carpets. The combined share of textiles and clothing exports, which is currently about 60 per cent, has also enhanced the risks and increased the volatility of export earnings. The failures of successive cotton crops in the mid-1990s demonstrated the vulnerability of Pakistan's economy to this excessive dependence on cotton-based exports. Although income from textiles and clothing products is predicted to increase with the elimination of the Multi-Fibre Agreement, there can be no long-run security founded on cotton-based exports alone.

As the world becomes increasingly competitive, new sources of comparative advantage must be created to face the challenges. In the traditional criteria used to understand the comparative strengths and weaknesses of nations, factor conditions (the nation's natural and human resource endowments), demand conditions (the nature of demand for an industry's products), related and supporting industries (the presence of linkages with other related sectors of the economy), and firm strategy (the conditions in the nation governing the creation and organization of companies) (Porter, 1990), Pakistan lags far behind many nations. Its human factor endowments are not abundant, and its comparative advantage in cotton and in textiles is in the lower order of the hierarchy of comparative advantages. Comparative advantages based on high skills, product differentiation, and new technologies last much longer. The development of a comparative advantage based on lower labour costs is unlikely to be sustainable in today's world, where a new competitor can produce with even lower labour costs.

The principal danger facing Pakistan in the aftermath of the Uruguay Round is that the policymakers, entrepreneurs, and industrialists will not rise to the challenge (Winters and Ingco, 1995). Pakistan is still left with a complicated, overly protective, and inefficient trade regime. Given the tailor-made, special-interest nature of the tariff system, the rates of effective protection vary enormously and foster inefficient production but maximum private gains to those who benefit from the system. The proliferation of import taxes—customs duties, import surcharge, *Iqra* surcharge, import licence, and sales tax on imports only—complicates the administration of the system and, when combined with duty exemptions and tax concessions, makes it highly discretionary and open to abuse. In 1993-4, the simple average tariff was 60 per cent, with the rates on imports of industrial raw materials and intermediate goods ranging between 20 per cent and 50 per cent, while imports of capital goods were charged tariffs between 40 per cent and 80 per cent. Meanwhile, the tariff structure based on statutory tariff rates shows some degree of escalation, with the imports of primary products facing average tariffs of about 45 per cent and semi-processed items facing 52 per cent (Winters and Ingco, 1996). This escalated tariff structure means that it makes economic sense to have higher value-added products. For Pakistani industrialists, the Uruguay Round's dismantling of tariff and non-tariff barriers means that their industries will have to become more efficient to compete internationally.

Unless Pakistan diversifies its industrial output, the prospects for retaining even the current share of the world market (0.20 per cent) do not look promising. The threat from countries endowed with high human capital but low labour cost, such as China, Vietnam, and India, has to be contained by further liberalization of the tariff regime and support for industries that have the potential for developing dynamic comparative advantage.

TABLE 2.1
AGRICULTURAL PERFORMANCE 1970-93
(Billions of Rupees)

Sector	1970	1975	1980	1985	1990	1996
Crops	35.9	41.7	49.8	62.9	74.5	88.8
Wheat	12.5	13.8	16.1	20.2	21.7	25.5
Rice	7.2	7.7	8.5	8.6	9.8	12.7
Cotton	5.4	7.3	10.2	18.3	24.8	28.0
Sugar	7.2	7.5	8.7	7.9	10.3	15.1
Noncrops	15.6	18.5	23.6	30.6	40.0	51.1
Livestock	15.3	16.9	20.1	25.9	34.1	46.2
Fisheries	0.2	1.4	2.7	3.6	4.4	4.9
Forestry	0.1	0.2	0.8	1.1	1.5	1.0
Total	51.4	60.2	76.4	93.5	114.5	140.9
Share of GDP						
Agriculture	40.4	32.9	29.2	25.0	25.1	24.6
Crops	28.2	22.8	19.8	16.8	16.3	15.6
Noncrops	12.2	10.1	9.4	8.2	8.8	9.0

Source: *Economic Survey* (various issues), Ministry of Finance, Government
of Pakistan, Islamabad

TABLE 2.2
AREA, PRODUCTION, AND YIELDS

	Area (Mill. Ha.)	Production (Mill. tons)	Yield (Kg./Ha.)
Cotton			
1948-9	2.65	NA	NA
1971-2	2.0	0.7	364
1996-7	3.1	1.5	503
Wheat			
1948-9	4.24	4.0	10.2
1971-2	5.8	6.9	11.9
1996-7	8.11	16.6	20.5
Rice			
1948-9	2.0	0.73	9.6
1971-2	1.45	2.16	12.0
1996-7	2.25	4.32	19.2
Sugarcane			
1948-9	0.46	5.44	330
1971-2	0.53	25.9	461
1996-7	1.05	53.0	504

Source: Computed from *Pakistan Economic Survey* (various issues)

TABLE 2.3
PER CAPITA FOOD AVAILABILITY

	1949-50	1979-80	1996-7
Calories/day	2078	2301	2542
Cereals (kg)	139.3	147.1	156.4
Pulses (kg)	13.9	6.3	8.1
Sugar (kg)	17.1	28.7	28.4
Milk (kg)	107.0	94.8	10.6
Edible oils (kg)	2.3	6.3	
Protein/day	62.8	61.5	68.6

Source: Computed from *Pakistan Economic Survey* (Various issues), *FAO Year Book* (various issues)

TABLE 2.4
LAND UTILIZATION
(Million Hectares)

Year	Cultivated Area	Cropped Area	Cropping Intensity
1960	16.5	14.7	0.89
1970	19.2	16.8	0.88
1980	20.2	19.2	0.95
1990	21.0	21.5	1.02
1996	21.6	22.9	1.06

Source: *Economic Survey* (various issues), Ministry of Finance, Government
of Pakistan, Islamabad

TABLE 2.5
DECOMPOSITION ANALYSIS OF PRINCIPAL CROPS
(Percentage)

Period	Area	Yield	Multiple
Wheat			
1961-7	111.4	-9.9	-1.5
1967-76	13.7	75.7	10.6
1976-89	40.0	47.3	12.7
Rice			
1961-7	44.5	46.2	9.3
1967-76	18.6	73.6	7.8
1976-89	78.5	16.5	5.0
Cotton			
1961-7	45.8	39.9	14.3
1967-76	1.7	91.2	7.1
1976-89	19.1	58.4	22.5

Source: Faruqee, Rashid, *Structural and Policy Reforms for Agricultural
Growth: The Case of Pakistan*, World Bank, Washington, DC, 1994.

TABLE 2.6
AGRICULTURAL GROWTH DURING THE 1960s
(000 tons)

Year	Wheat	Rice	Sugarcane
1960	3814	995	10662
1965	4591	1350	18668
1970	7294	2401	26370
Change 1960-70	+91 per cent	+141 per cent	+147 per cent

Source: *Economic Survey* (various issues), Ministry of Finance, Government
of Pakistan Islamabad

TABLE 2.7
GROWTH RATES OF VALUE-ADDED
IN AGRICULTURE
(1970s and 1980s)

Sub-Sector	1969-79	1980-95
Major Crop	1.2	3.0
Minor Crop	4.9	4.8
Livestock	2.1	5.7
Fishing	-9.9	4.0
Forestry	–	1.0
Total Agriculture	1.8	4.2

Source: Naqvi and Sarmad, *Pakistan's Economy Through the Seventies*,
Pakistan Institute of Development Economics, Islamabad, 1984

TABLE 2.8
GROWTH OF MAJOR CROPS DURING THE 1980s
(000 Tons)

Year	Wheat	Rice	Cotton	Sugarcane
1980	10,587	3126	728	27,498
1985	11,703	3315	1008	32,140
1990	14,316	3220	1456	35,494
Change 1980-90	+35 per cent	+3 per cent	+100 per cent	+29 per cent

Source: *Economic Survey* (various issues), Ministry of Finance, Government of Pakistan, Islamabad

TABLE 2.9
CHANGES IN LAND CONCENTRATION IN PAKISTAN
1950-81—GINI COEFFICIENTS

	Land Ownership				Operational Holdings			
Year	Pakistan	Punjab	Sindh	NWFP	Pakistan	Punjab	Sindh	NWFP
1950	0.64	0.62	0.66	0.49	NA	NA	NA	NA
1961	NA	NA	NA	NA	0.62	0.59	0.51	0.73
1972	0.57	0.53	0.59	0.41	0.52	0.49	0.43	0.64
1976	0.55	0.52	0.58	0.41	NA	NA	NA	NA
1981	0.53	0.49	0.55	0.38	0.53	0.51	0.47	0.57

Note: These figures are the Gini Coefficients for landownership and land use. Data was obtained from provincial Land Revenue Departments and various Agricultural Censuses.

Source: Khan, Mahmood Hassan, 'The Structural Adjustment Process and Agricultural Change in Pakistan in the 1980s and 1990s,' *Pakistan Development Review*, 1994

TABLE 2.10
TRANSFERS FROM AGRICULTURE DUE TO OUTPUT
AND INPUT PRICE INTERVENTIONS
(Billions of Rupees, 1985-6 Prices)

	Direct Transfers	Total Transfers
Output Prices	9.8	21.0
Input Prices	-2.6	-5.2
Net Transfers	7.2	15.8
Share of Agricultural GDP	6.4	13.6
Share of GDP (per cent)	1.6	3.4

Source: Hamid, Nabi, and Nasim, *Trade, Exchange Rate, and Agricultural Pricing Policies in Pakistan*, World Bank, Washington DC, 1990

TABLE 2.11
CREDIT GAP
(Rs. Million)

Years	Value-added in Agriculture	Credit Need	Credit Available	Credit Gap
1959-60	7,711	1,927	87	1,840
1969-70	15,964	3,991	155	3,835
1979-80	62,164	15,541	2,859	12,681
1989-90	181,138	45,284	13,834	31,450
1990-1	214,070	53,517	14,858	38,658
1996-7	38,658	123,299	19,187	123,299

Source: Sohail Malik et al., *Pakistan's Economic Performance, 1947-1993* (Sure Publishers, Lahore). *Pakistan Economic Survey*, Government of Pakistan, Islamabad; (various issues)

TABLE 2.12
LAND RESOURCES FOR AGRICULTURE

	Million Hectares	Per cent
Irrigated Areas	35	70
Perennial	20.2	40.4
Non-perennial	14.3	28.6
Commanded	5.0	10.0
Other	5.5	11.0
Other Areas	15	30
Barani	9.1	18.2
Riverain	3.1	6.2
Torrent	2.8	5.6

Source: *Economic Survey*, Ministry of Finance, various issues

TABLE 2.13
DISTRIBUTION OF CANAL COMMAND AREA

	Perennial	Non-Perennial
NWFP	0.732	0
Punjab	12.485	7.827
Sindh and Balochistan	7.626	5.929

Source: *Economic Survey*, Ministry of Finance, Islamabad, (various issues)

TABLE 2.14
STRUCTURE OF WATER SUPPLY
(MAF)

Year	Canal Head Withdrawal (Farmgate availability)	Public Tubewells	Private Tubewells	Total
1947-8	50.25	Nil	Nil	50.25
1959-60	45.61	0.47	3.27	49.35
1969-70	59.91	3.54	12.05	75.50
1979-80	63.14	7.03	23.97	94.14
1989-90	NA	NA	NA	114.66
1994-5	105.98	NA	23.67	129.65

Source: *Agricultural Statistics of Pakistan*, Food and Agriculture Division, Islamabad, (Various Issues).

TABLE 2.15
CHANGES IN THE INDUSTRIAL STRUCTURE
(Share in Value-Added at Constant Prices)

	1949-50	1959-60	1969-70	1979-80	1989-90	1995-6
Industry	9.6	15.5	22.7	25.6	25.5	26.5
Manufacture	7.8	12.0	26.0	17.0	17.6	18.0
Large-Scale	2.2	6.9	12.5	12.4	12.7	12.1
Mining	0.2	0.4	0.5	0.5	0.5	0.5
Construction	1.4	2.5	4.2	5.1	4.1	3.9
Electric & Gas	0.2	0.5	2.0	3.0	3.3	4.1

Source: *Economic Survey* (various issues), Finance Division, Government of Pakistan, Islamabad

TABLE 2.16
CHANGES IN TOTAL INDUSTRIAL EMPLOYMENT

Industry	1954	1960	1965	1970	1977	1980	1985	1987	1995
Consumer Goods	79.7	73.8	73.9	71.8	68.3	67.5	61.1	62.6	64.4
Intermediate Goods	2.3	2.8	2.0	4.3	10.3	12.0	13.8	12.4	11.7
Investment Goods	12.0	13.3	12.2	12.3	9.2	9.1	13.2	13.2	13.7
Capital Goods	6.0	10.1	11.9	11.6	12.1	11.4	11.8	11.7	10.2
TOTAL	100	100	100	100	100	100	100	100	100

Source: Malik, Sohail, *Pakistan's Economic Performance 1947-1993: A Descriptive Analysis*, Sure Publishers, Lahore

TABLE 2.17
CHANGES IN TOTAL INDUSTRIAL VALUE-ADDED

Industry	1954	1960	1965	1970	1977	1980	1985	1987	1995
Consumer goods	84.4	73.3	76.5	71.7	67.0	57.0	57.0	55.5	59.3
Intermediate goods	3.5	3.2	2.4	12.9	16.6	18.7	16.9	21.6	17.4
Investment goods	8.8	14.5	10.8	9.0	8.2	13.8	17.8	16.0	14.0
Capital goods	3.2	9.0	10.3	6.3	8.1	10	8.3	6.9	9.2
Total	100.0	100.0	100.0	100.0	100.0	100.0	100.0	100.0	100.0

Source: Malik, Sohail, *Pakistan's Economic Performance 1947-1993: A Descriptive Analysis*, Sure Publishers, Lahore

TABLE 2.18
ANNUAL GROWTH OF
SELECTED INDUSTRIAL ITEMS (%)

Decade	Cotton yarn	Cotton cloth	Fertilizer	Cement	Sugar	Veg. ghee
1950s	32.8	27.9	NA	10.3	20.9	19.0
1960s	5.6	3.1	27.4	10.7	34.2	12.5
1970s	3.3	5.2	13.2	2.5	2.2	13.3
1980s	9.9	1.1	10.7	8.6	14.4	3.3
1990s	5.4	-0.1	2.0	1.0	4.5	-1.3

Source: *Economic Survey*, Statistical Supplement, Finance Division, Government of Pakistan, Islamabad

TABLE 2.19
COTTON TEXTILE STATISTICS:
TREND AVERAGE ANNUAL GROWTH RATES

Time Period	Cotton Yarn	Cotton Cloth
1947-8 to 1990-1	8.2	2.3
1947-8 to 1959-60	29.7	25.8
1959-60 to 1969-70	4.9	2.1
1969-70 to 1976-7	1.3	-6.7
1976-7 to 1979-80	8.5	-6.7
1979-80 to 1984-5	3.8	-3.5
1984-5 to 1990-1	14.9	2.3
1990-1 to 1996-7	12.1	1.9

Source: Malik, Sohail, *Pakistan's Economic Performance 1947-1993: A Descriptive Analysis*, Sure Publishers, Lahore

TABLE 2.20
EXPLICIT AND IMPLICIT NOMINAL PROTECTION
RATES IN 1985-6

Major Industry Group	Explicit Nominal Protection	Implicit Nominal Protection
Air Conditioner	146	46
Television Sets	124	29
VCRs	90	40
Synthetic Fabrics	146	24
Plastic Crockery	146	25
Meat Mincers	124	24
Electric Irons	124	23

Source: Noman, Akbar, 'Pakistan—A South Asian Miracle' (draft), World Bank, Washington, DC

TABLE 2.21
TREND GROWTH RATE OF INVESTMENT IN
LARGE-SCALE MANUFACTURING
(AT CONSTANT PRICES OF 1969-70)
(Annual Averages)

Time Period	Private Sector	Public Sector	Total
1963-4 to 1990-1	3.8	9.2	5.0
1963-4 to 1969-70	-2.9	11.3	-1.9
1969-70 to 1974-5	-21.9	27.0	-10.1
1974-5 to 1979-80	7.5	24.7	18.8
1979-80 to 1984-5	12.5	-13.9	-1.6
1984-5 to 1990-1	14.3	-17.7	8.4
1989-90 to 1996-7	-2.5	0.9	-0.21

Source: Malik, Sohail, *Pakistan's Economic Performance 1947-1993: A Descriptive Analysis*, Sure Publishers, Lahore

TABLE 2.22
CURRENT PRICE VALUE ADDED AS A SHARE OF
MANUFACTURING VALUE-ADDED:
INTERNATIONAL COMPARISON

Economy	Year	Food	Textl.	Chem.	Mach.	Others
Hong Kong	1973	0.05	0.48	0.12	0.23	0.09
	1988	0.06	0.38	0.10	0.33	0.11
Indonesia	1973	0.59	0.14	0.16	0.05	0.05
	1988	0.26	0.15	0.15	0.14	0.28
Japan	1973	0.09	0.16	0.16	0.24	0.31
	1988	0.09	0.05	0.16	0.46	0.22
Korea	1986	0.23	0.19	0.21	0.13	0.21
	1988	0.11	0.15	0.18	0.36	0.18
Malaysia	1969	0.16	0.05	0.27	0.06	0.25
	1988	0.18	0.07	0.27	0.27	0.20
Singapore	1969	0.14	0.05	0.30	0.29	0.19
	1989	0.05	0.04	0.20	0.61	0.08
Thailand	1968	0.26	0.17	0.09	0.12	0.35
	1986	0.42	0.22	0.09	0.11	0.16
India	1970	0.12	0.21	0.18	0.25	0:22
	1986	0.12	0.15	0.24	0.29	0.20
Pakistan	1970	0.24	0.34	0.20	0.05	0.09
	1986	0.30	0.21	0.26	0.04	0.09
Brazil	1970	0.17	0.13	0.19	0.20	0.29
	1985	0.14	0.12	0.24	0.27	0.20

Source: Page, John, et al., *The East Asian Miracle*, World Bank,
    Washington DC

TABLE 2.23
BACKWARD LINKAGES OF PAKISTANI ECONOMY
(As % of Total Gross Output)

	Inter-Industry Transactions			Value-added
	Total	Domestic	Imported	
Major Crops	42.7	40.7	2.0	57.3
Minor Crops	40.6	39.6	1.0	59.4
Livestock	43.2	43.2	NA	56.8
Fishing	13.9	13.9	NA	86.1
Forestry	21.0	21.0	NA	79.0
Mining	36.2	30.4	5.8	63.8
LS Manuf.	81.5	62.8	18.7	18.5
SS Manuf.	83.4	77.6	5.8	16.6
Construction	56.7	42.9	13.8	43.3
Elec.& Gas	21.5	21.5	NA	78.5
Transp.& Comm.	62.5	29.6	32.9	37.8
Trade	5.5	5.5	NA	94.5
Banking	27.1	25.3	1.8	72.9
Dwellings	10.0	10.0	NA	90.0
Public Adm.&Defence	46.4	45.4	1.0	53.6
Other Serv.	4.2	4.0	0.2	95.8

Source: National Accounts of Pakistan

APPENDIX:
RESOURCE ENDOWMENTS FOR
AGRICULTURE

LAND RESOURCES

Pakistan covers an area of 310,403 square miles, 183,840 of which in the north and west is mountainous terrain and tableland, and the remaining 126,563 make up a flat gradational surface, including a large amount of desert land. The Himalayan and Hindu Kush mountains define the north-west contours of the country, while a desert defines much of its common eastern boundary with India. In the southern and western parts, a series of plateaus and plains provides a topographical contrast to the structure of the northern part.

The major agricultural areas lie within the basin formed by the Indus river and its tributaries, which run in a general north-west/south-west direction from the points where the rivers enter Pakistan to the mouth of the Indus at the Arabian Sea east of Karachi; the basin extends into the north-west to include parts of the North-west Frontier Province as well. One of the four cradles of civilization in ancient times, the Indus has defined the agricultural structure of Pakistan. The most productive agricultural area in Pakistan lies in the Punjab, watered by the Indus and its tributaries, the Jhelum, Chenab, Ravi, and Sutlej. This Indus Basin agroclimatic zone provides a very fertile alluvial plain for agricultural production (World Bank, 1969).

Of the total land area of Pakistan, half is composed of mountains and deserts, a quarter is accounted for by towns, roads, water areas, and wasteland, leaving just over a quarter for agricultural cultivation. Of the total agricultural area of Pakistan which is about 804,000 square kilometers or 79.6 million hectares, 20.8 million hectares (roughly 26 per cent) is cultivated, of which 11.5 million hectares lies in the Punjab and 5.4 million hectares in Sindh. The irrigated area is 35 million hectares, while the non-irrigated area, including *barani* (rainfed), is about 15 million hectares (Table 2.12).

The fertility of the Indus Basin soil has historically been the foundation of Pakistani agriculture (Faruqee, 1994). According to the Soil Survey of Pakistan, carried out in 1993 as part of the National Conservation Strategy, in which soil data was combined with climatic, hydrological, plant, and other relevant information, Class I land, defined as the most arable land, occupied 5.2 million hectares, with predominance in the Punjab. Twenty-six per cent of the total arable land in Pakistan was of excellent quality, with all this area being under irrigation. Of Class II land, arable due to soil with a high clay content, but permeable to surface ponding, sandiness, and salinity, 7 million hectares were of good quality, although subject to erosion and poor climate. Of Class III land, moderately arable but affected by salinity for irrigated land and floods for dry land, 2.1 million hectares are of moderate quality rainfed land. The last category of arable land, Class IV land, categorized as poor and marginal lands with little potential for agriculture crops, occupies 3 million hectares. Thus, a significant portion of Pakistani arable land is very fertile.

In spite of the presence of 15 million acres of good arable land, there are two severe constraints on Pakistani agriculture. The first is the narrow scope for utilization of additional land. The present land base has been abundantly used for agricultural production, and there remains hardly any other land to use for cropping. The second is that soil erosion, by water on hillsides and along river banks, and by wind, more prevalent in areas lacking vegetation and in arid zones, together have affected more than 16 million hectares of Pakistani soil. Meanwhile, flood damage as a result of soil erosion is becoming more prevalent, especially in areas where the natural vegetation has been removed.

From the point of view of topography and agricultural structure, crops are the most important agricultural sub-sector, with production concentrated in three agroecological zones— irrigated lowlands, rainfed lowlands, and mountain areas (World Bank, 1969). Currently, crop production is well diversified, with more than half the area devoted to cereals, one-fifth to cash crops, and the rest to vegetables and fruits. Livestock production is an important agricultural sub-sector that has historically accounted for an average of 15 per cent of GDP.

Between 1960-1 and 1996-7, the cultivated area increased by about 5 million hectares, while the double-cropped area went up from 1.59 million hectares to 4.36 million, a 174 per cent increase. Consequently, the total cropped area increased from 14.7 million hectares to 22.9 million—an increase of 55 per cent in thirty-five years (Table 2.4).

WATER RESOURCES

Pakistan has an abundant system of water resources to supply its agricultural sector. The total water supplies available to agriculture within the Indus Basin system derive from three sources: rainfall which occurs directly on the cropped land, surface water from the River Indus and its tributaries, and usable groundwater from the aquifers underlying the Indus plain. Since rainfall has historically been inadequate to supply Pakistan's agricultural sector with water, the sector has become dependent on one of the world's largest irrigation networks, that was developed in the Indus Basin alluvial plains over the last one hundred years. Geometrically, the system can be described as a funnel, with numerous sources of water at the top converging into a single stream which flows into the Arabian Sea east of Karachi (World Bank, 1969).

The rainfed area in Pakistan is mostly arid, with the pattern of rainfall highly variable depending on seasonality. The range of mean average annual rainfall extends from less than four inches in Sindh to more than thirty inches in the foothills of the northern mountains; the latter amount occurrs during the monsoon period but, due to rapid runoff, much of it is unavailable for agriculture. Currently constituting about 5 million hectares, the rainfed areas mostly produce wheat, pulses, and livestock. However, yields are low due to poor fertility conditions, fertilizer deficiency, and fragile topsoil, flood proneness. Rainfall is in general, so meagre or unreliable that it is a distinct constraint on Pakistan's agriculture, and rainfed areas constitute only a minor part of the total area under cultivation.

Pakistan's irrigation system is the largest contiguous system in the world and the fourth largest in the world in terms of land area, with its 17 million hectares of irrigated land ranking behind China, India, and the United States, countries with far greater landmasses and natural resource endowments. Currently supplying more than three-fourths of total agricultural land, the irrigation system has been growing at the average rate of 1.5

per cent a year for the last two decades. Furthermore, since the early 1960s, while the total cultivated area has been relatively constant, the expansion in irrigated land has come at the expense of the rainfed area. In recent years, there has been little expansion of irrigated land, suggesting that there are constraints on the water resources. However, the sector is the backbone of Pakistan's agriculture—the production of three of Pakistan's leading crops, cotton, rice, and sugarcane, is virtually confined to the 19 million hectares of canal irrigated area, and wheat is dependent for more than three-fourths of its productivity on the canal irrigation system.

In the span of a century the irrigation system has been transformed from a series of inundation canals, which captured water for irrigation when river stages were high, to a network of 38,000 miles of canals and a series of river barrages and canal headworks which control the diversion of river flows into the canals (World Bank, 1969). This remarkable feat of public engineering was begun in the nineteenth century, when weirs and barrages were constructed, and developed into a series of high-powered projects in the postwar years. The irrigation system was continuously expanded, and now includes four barrages on the Indus main stem which increase the irrigated area by 9 million hectares, a series of relatively small hydroelectric projects on the canals, and an upsurge in the exploitation of groundwater. The main purpose of the canal systems has historically been to command as much land as possible, with large cropping intensities not a major consideration. By design, the canal system takes variable flows from the rivers up to the limit of the canal capacity, but delivers to the farmer a fairly constant capacity.

Since Partition, the irrigation system has been greatly expanded, particularly along the main stem of the Indus. Some nine million acres have been added to the Canal Command Area (CCA), and new link canals have been built to transfer water from the Jhelum and Chenab to the Ravi and Sutlej. Average annual irrigation diversions have increased from about 67 MAF in 1950 to 106 MAF in 1995. Average *kharif* (spring) diversions have increased by 40 per cent, while average *rabi* (autumn) withdrawals have increased by 85 per cent, primarily due to the Tarbela and Mangla dams. As a result of the Indus Basin Plan investments, the capacity of the irrigation system to use river inflows has increased from 52 per cent in the 1950s to 77 per cent in 1979. The distribution of canal command areas in the four provinces is given in Table 2.13.

Water availability has grown at an annual rate of 2.4 per cent since 1965-6, with the Indus Basin Works and the expansion in tubewell installation which started at about the same time. An overall increase of 62 per cent in water availability has taken place since 1947. This development has increased the extent of irrigated lands, but the increased water input and the lack of proper drainage have contributed to an increase in waterlogging.

Due to the absence of major storage reservoirs, the system is based entirely on natural river flows. Unfortunately, given the seasonal variation in rainfall, with the majority falling in the summer, there is an inadequate supply of water for most of the year (i.e., the non-summer months). Thus, canal capacities are clearly inadequate and unreliable for optimum crop production. A further complication is that there is a lot of irrigable land in the eastern part of the Punjab, while the bulk of the water supplies are in the western part.

One key problem for the canal irrigation system is low delivery efficiency (Faruqee, 1994). As a result of age, overuse, and poor maintenance, average delivery efficiency is now only 35-40 per cent from the canal head to the root zone, with a large portion of the losses occurring in the watercourses. As with other sectors of Pakistan's infrastructure, poor maintenance has led to a rapid deterioration of the irrigation and drainage system, with waterlogging and salinity becoming pressing problems. At present about half a million hectares of non-saline, cultivated land in the CCA is severely to moderately waterlogged. The total extent of saline lands is far higher, at 5.81 million hectares, 3.2 million of which is in the canal command areas.

The two main contributory factors to the deteroiration of the irrigation system in Pakistan are the erosion of management capability and a poor financial structure, with low water charges that have not kept pace with maintenance needs or inflation, and which account for only 5 per cent of farm income or the cost of production. The government's inability to formulate an appropriate pricing regime in accordance with the opportunity cost of resources has led to improper maintenance. This represents a major shortcoming in Pakistan's capacity to make efficient use of a scarce source of critical importance.

In order for Pakistan to increase the efficiency of its irrigation network, policies to improve service delivery are essential. A combination of public investment in irrigation, provision of market-determined incentives, and decentralization of water provision are central components of any policy reform package. Given the constraints on cultivated area, these measures need to be implemented in order to overhaul the current system.

A second development in Pakistan's water resources management has been the installation of private tubewells. Due to one of the key weaknesses of the Indus system, a lack of drainage, under the Salinity Control and Reclamation Projects (SCARP), a network of private tubewells were installed in order to increase agricultural production by the provision of additional irrigation supplies and by control of the water table. Groundwater pumpage increased from 3.77 MAF in 1959-60 to 23.67 MAF in 1994-5. The tubewells have been quite successful, and now account for 22 per cent of total irrigation water supply in the country. Table 2.14 shows the respective roles of canals and tubewells in the structure of water supply.

One project that has been remarkably successful outside the canal system has been the Tarbela Dam project, completed in the mid-1960s, to harness unregulated and wasteful water flows. As a result of the signing of the historic Indus Waters Treaty in 1960 with India, which allowed Pakistan the right to full use of the Indus itself and the western tributaries, the Jhelum and Chenab, but allowed India to divert the eastern tributaries for its use, Pakistan needed an additional dam to exploit unused capacity in the western Punjab. The dam was immensely successful, providing a large augmentation of irrigation supplies and a major step in surface water development. The farm-gate availability of water, accounting for losses and runoffs, has doubled from 50 MAF in 1960-1 to over 100 MAF by the next quarter century. Irrigated area increased by 70 per cent, from 10 million hectares to 17 million. The amount of water per unit of irrigated area has increased from 2.04 to 2.57 acre feet. Part of the enhanced water availability has been used to cultivate more land and part has been utilized to raise the cropping intensity of existing lands and to increase crop yields.

The British bequeathed Pakistan the rudiments of one of the largest canal networks in the world, and after the war, Pakistan greatly increased the capacity and structure of its irrigation system. The canal and tubewell systems have been a mainstay of the Pakistani agricultural sector. Although the Indus Basin is an extremely fertile land, low rainfall and extreme seasonality due to a subtropical and semi-arid climate, with hot summers and cold winters, do not militate in favour of Pakistan's agriculture. Thus, although Pakistan's factor endowments are not too good and its mineral and other resources not too abundant, the presence of a large irrigated network has given Pakistan a strong comparative advantage in agricultural production. Unfortunately, unless maintenance is dramatically improved in the future, Pakistan risks losing this competitive edge.

HUMAN RESOURCES

Pakistan has one of the largest populations in the world, currently estimated at 130 million. Of them, 88 million are located in the agricultural sector, which provides the livelihood for the majority of the population. This large rural population is dependent on the land for its direct subsistence and employment. A high proportion of the population has settled in the irrigated areas, where climate and conditions are more favourable to agricultural production, and consequently, the Indus Basin has the most densely populated conglomeration of people in Pakistan.

Estimates of the size of the labour force available to agriculture vary, with labour force participation rates fluctuating between 25 per cent and 30 per cent in recent years. In 1998 the labour force was about 37 million, with about 26 million in the rural sector and 11 million in the urban sector; about 10 million were actually wage earners in the agricultural sector. Since only about a quarter of the labour force is working, the rest of the agricultural sector represents a high dependency burden. In spite of this strong endowment of human resources, seasonal unemployment and localized shortages have presented a few problems for the sector. Nevertheless, the factor of labour does not appear to pose a serious development constraint.

Like other developing countries, urbanization in Pakistan has been proceeding at a rapid pace, with the urban population doubling over the last two decades. Annual average growth rates of 4.5 per cent for the last two decades have changed the urban/rural relationship. Thus, while the absolute numbers of rural people is increasing, their share in Pakistan's total population is decreasing substantially. The implications of rapid rates of urbanization on agriculture are uncertain, but at present urbanization has not had a negative effect on agricultural production.

One factor which has been crucial for agriculture is education. Pakistan's overall education levels compare unfavourably with other countries, and are characterized by low educational spending and primary school enrolment. Current literacy rates of 38 per cent (25 per cent for women, 50 per cent for men) inhibit agricultural productivity—the agricultural workforce does not have the necessary technical skills to increase production. In a study of total factor productivity (TFP) in Pakistan during the 1955-85 period, it was found that a 10 per cent increase in rural male literacy increased total factor productivity by 2.7, while gains in the area under irrigation and gains in the share of high-yielding varieties caused smaller increases in TFP (Faruqee, 1994). Education is linked to such factors as fertilizer use, knowledge of seeding varieties and patterns, ability to utilize new technologies, and ability to benefit from extension services. Moreover, quality of education and level of education are also correlated with productivity. Thus, it is abundantly clear that human capital deficiencies lower the return to labour.

In sum, while the quantity of workers in the agricultural sector is a vital asset, the serious limitations in quality due to poor education represent a critical shortcoming. Unless measures are undertaken to improve the qualitative side of human capital, Pakistan's agriculture remains condemned to poor future performance.

CHAPTER 3

MACROECONOMIC FOUNDATIONS: FISCAL, MONETARY, AND EXCHANGE RATE POLICY

Cross-country experience over the last decade or so has amply demonstrated the unambiguous efficacy of a stable macroeconomic environment in the process of economic growth and development, including poverty alleviation. There is a common understanding that inflation not only creates uncertainty in the field of new investment but is also inimical to the goal of poverty alleviation. In fact, inflation has proved to be the worst enemy of the poor segments of the population, as the poor do not have any means of sheltering themselves from the attack of general price increases, while the rich have recourse to asset substitution and capital flight, etc. to insulate themselves.

The traditional instruments of macroeconomic policies are fiscal, monetary and credit, exchange rate and trade policies. This chapter focuses on the first three instruments; trade policies in the context of the external sector are discussed in Chapter 6. Fiscal deficit has become a major issue in the macroeconomic management of Pakistan, and the tax and expenditure patterns and policies have a direct bearing on aggregate demand, external balances, and domestic credit expansion and inflation. The monetary and credit policies can either be accommodating or put a brake on expansionary fiscal policies. The recent turmoil in Asian markets has brought to the surface the importance of a healthy and vibrant financial sector. Exchange rate and trade policies affect not only the current account balances and external debt profile of the country, but also have powerful incentive effects on production for domestic markets versus the foreign markets.

The interrelationship between these various instruments calls for a consistent framework in which the growth objective can be reconciled with macroeconomic stability. This chapter is divided in three parts—the first section deals with the fiscal policy, the second with the monetary and credit policies, and the final section focuses on exchange rate issues.

FISCAL POLICY

The large fiscal deficit that has persisted for the last two decades has emerged as Pakistan's key macroeconomic problem in the 1990s. The increasing gap between expenditure and revenue has had a series of negative ramifications on the rest of the economy and brought the Pakistani economy to international attention. Growing pressure from international organizations, especially the International Monetary Fund and the World Bank, has spurred Pakistan to put its macroeconomic house in order. The fiscal deficit/GDP ratio, which had reached an alarming 8 per cent in the 1980s, has persistently clung to the 6-7 per cent mark in the 1990s. The high deficit has diverted valuable resources away from the private sector, it has also had negative effects on the interest rate structure in the economy, it has contributed to low investment rates, and has partially damaged Pakistan's export performance.

The roots of the fiscal deficit date back to the 1970s. As has been shown in two different studies, the origin of fiscal deficits in Pakistan can be traced to an upsurge of externally-financed development spending during the mid-1970s, mainly in the form of investment by public enterprises. This spending proved to be permanent, and the public sector was unable to generate the revenues, either from taxation or from direct return on investments undertaken, to close the fiscal gap (Kemal and Durdag, 1990). Thus, what began as temporary spending to boost economic activity through a strong public sector became an intractable problem two decades later as deficits moved out of control.

In 1971 the Bhutto government, assisted by cheap concessional flow of funds through generous aid from the OPEC countries in the 1970s, motivated by socialistic plans to control the commanding heights of the economy through a surge in public spending, and influenced by plans to use fiscal policy for redistributive purposes, began a programme of fiscal expansion that was unprecedented in Pakistani history. During the period from 1971 to 1977, development expenditures—consisting of investment by the federal and provincial governments in infrastructure, in industry, and in production subsidies—doubled their share in the total expenditure. The four major factors that were responsible for this increase in public expenditure were (a) the very sharp increase in defence expenditure in the aftermath of the 1971 War—defence expenditures as a percentage of GDP increased from 3.7 per cent in 1970 to 6.3 per cent by 1975; (b) the subsidies on wheat, edible oils, and other goods consumed by the poorer section of the population which increased from being virtually non-existent in 1970 to amounting to 2 per cent of GDP by the mid-1970s; (c) the government's public investment in the economy, which increased from 7 per cent of GDP in 1970 to 9.8 per cent of GDP by 1975 and finally, (d) the sharp increase in internal debt that resulted from the higher interest rates precipitated in the aftermath of the oil shocks (Kemal and Durdag, 1990). Together these factors led the fiscal deficit to more than triple during the 1970s. However, there was no equivalent increase in revenues as the tax/GNP ratio remained stable at around 14 per cent, thus causing the fiscal deficit /GDP ratio to widen from 1.3 per cent in 1970 to 5.3 per cent in 1980. The significant failure of the Bhutto years was the incapacity of the administration to realize that expenditures needed to be funded from a stronger tax system. The expansionary fiscal policy resulted in large current account imbalances—10 per cent of GNP—which were financed mainly from external capital from the friendly oil-exporting countries in the Middle East.

In 1977, the accession to power of the military regime resulted in a reversal of the economic regime and fiscal retrenchment through both expenditure cuts and revenue increases. Under the sponsorship of the IMF, Pakistan initiated a short-term stabilization programme that was to reduce the fiscal deficit by de-emphasizing the role of the public sector. It has been estimated that the revenue resulting from the discretionary revenue measures during the period amounted for less than a sixth of the total increase in tax revenue, with trade taxes contributing to the majority of the gain (Haque and Montiel, 1993). The implications of this for tax reform suggest that trade booms may be more revenue-producing than reforms in tax collection and administration. Nevertheless, as a result, the fiscal deficit fell from 8 per cent in 1977 to 5 per cent by 1982. However, the situation changed dramatically as the 1980s progressed.

The fiscal deficit, which continued to worsen as expenditure growth outpaced revenue growth, reached 8 per cent of GDP by the end of the decade. Although the government did succeed in containing public expenditure, the non-development expenditures, including defence, public administration, and subsidies, continued to grow at a rather sharp rate. The most rapidly increasing category of spending during the 1980s was interest on public debt as government resorted to non-bank borrowing to finance the deficit. Avoiding the twin evils of monetization of the deficit leading to higher inflation and external financing of the deficit, the government resorted to tapping the non-bank system through a series of measures. The distinctive features of the government's non-bank borrowing include a heavy and growing reliance on short-term securities, and a tapping of the resources of financial institutions at low interest rates of between 5 and 6 per cent (Kemal and Durdag, 1990).

The government's success in mobilizing large amounts of funds by offering attractive interest rates has had a ripple effect on the country's financial markets: there was an upward pressure on the interest rates in both formal and informal credit markets, with rates rising from 10-14 per cent in the late 1970s to 16-20 per cent by the late 1980s in the formal markets, and above 30 per cent in the kerb market. The negative consequences of this high interest on private investment and on the international competitiveness of tradeables through upward pressures on the exchange rate thus became more obvious as time went on (Kemal and Durdag, 1990). Furthermore, it has been argued that the rising interest rates failed to induce the public to economize on its holding of money balances, as the velocity of money has been declining since the early 1980s (Kemal and Durdag, 1990).

An econometic study which investigated the relationship between the budget deficit and the economic growth found that private savings were used largely to finance the budgetary deficit. This diversion of savings crowded out private investment. The overall savings rate remained unaffected (Kemal and Durdag, 1990). The authors conclude by arguing that the growing burden of servicing the domestic and foreign debt requires over half of government revenues with very serious implications, for liquidity, for money supply, and for private investment.

One question that perplexed several analysts during the 1980s was the absence of high inflation in Pakistan in spite of high fiscal deficits. One study shows that the availability of cheap financing resulted in a statistical illusion, whereby both domestic and foreign debt were below international interest rates for most of the 1970s and 1980s, which, coupled with high growth performance expanding the revenue base, allowed sustainable high deficits without the ignition of an inflationary episode (Haque and Montiel, 1993).

The pattern of financing the deficit continued well into the 1990s as expenditures continued to increase significantly. However, tax reform did make some contribution towards reducing the deficit to 6 per cent by the mid-1990s, in contrast to the high 8 per cent in the late 1980s. Under a plan worked out with the International Monetary Fund, Pakistan committed itself to reducing the fiscal deficit to 4 per cent of GDP by 1996-7. Under this new structural adjustment programme, the IMF held back its third tranche of $600 million in order to test the government's commitment to alleviating the deficit. Currently, defence expenditures and debt servicing continue to account for 60 per cent of government expenditure, and together they account for more than the total tax revenues. Fiscal retrenchment in Pakistan has meant that spending on the social sector, especially education and health, remains at less than 15 per cent of total expenditure.

In sum, the fiscal policy's role in raising domestic resources for economic growth has not been impressive either in relation to the country's investment needs or in comparison to other countries at a similar stage of development. The inability to widen the tax net, and the overdependence on debt payments, have placed serious constraints on the effectiveness of fiscal policy.

PUBLIC EXPENDITURE

More than three-fourths of the total public expenditure (consolidated Federal and Provincial) is carried out by the Federal government (Table 3.1). The division between the two main components of public expenditures, current and development, shows an alarming secular trend of decline in the development component. From almost one-third of the total expenditures allocated for development in 1980-81, the share has come down to one-sixth in 1995-6, creating an alarming situation for the future economic growth of the country. The Provincial governments, which are responsible for most of the social services and other amenities that affect the daily lives of the common man, have suffered the most. Development expenditures of the Provincial governments have been cut by almost one-half (as a share of GDP) in the last decade. The congestion in urban areas, pollution and environmental degradation, and almost total breakdown of essential services are reflections of this neglect.

Although Table 3.1 shows that the level of public expenditures has remained unchanged over the last three decades, the fiscal situation remains precarious and difficult. Pakistan's fiscal difficulties that have surfaced in the mid-1990s owe their origin to the profligate public expenditures incurred during the 1980s. The average level of fiscal deficit in the 1980s has hovered around 8 per cent. This was financed mainly by forced savings from the banking system, including the Central Bank at interest rates much lower than the market rates. When the government decided to liberalize the interest rates and resorted to rolling over its accumulated domestic debt and borrowing its incremental requirements at the market rate of interest from banking as well as non-banking sources, the true burden on the budget became apparent. Interest payments as a percentage of GDP have almost tripled between 1980 and 1995. This elimination of implicit transfer from savers to the public sector and the actual reflection of the true cost of borrowing in the budget has exacerbated the fiscal problems. Although the level of public expenditure in fact declined by almost 3 percentage points between 1985 and 1995, the fiscal deficit remained stuck between 5 and 6 per cent in the first half of the 1990s. Interest payments, which now account for almost 6 per cent of GDP, are equivalent to the fiscal deficit. These have added an additional burden of about 3 per centage points to the total expenditure, and in turn have crowded out development expenditures. The decline in development expenditures is the mirror image of the rise in interest payments.

Contrary to popular belief, defence expenditure has, in fact, been curtailed by 1.6 percentage point of GDP over the last ten-year period. Expenditure on subsidies has also declined significantly, to almost one per cent of GDP. Excluding defence and interest payments, current Federal spending on general administration has risen significantly over time and is almost twice that of the social services.

This rise in general administration is surprising because the Federal government employment figures seem to have declined since 1988-9. The estimated government employment in 1988-9 was 1.8 million, of which about a third worked for the Federal government and the balance for the Provincial governments (40 per cent of the total government employees were on the payroll of the Punjab government). The current budgetary estimates show that there has been an overall decline in the number of Federal government employees. The data on this subject is contradictory and of a highly dubious nature, and it is hard to come to any definitive conclusion. But the budgetary data on the wage bill of the Provincial governments certainly shows a significant increase more rapid than that of the Federal government. The total wage bill of government employees in Pakistan is 4.2 per cent of GDP, which is higher than Indonesia but lower than other Asian countries. The average annual wage implied by the data (US $2,127) was almost 4.8 times per capita income, which is low by international standards. Compared to 1989-90—when the implied average wage was 1.8 times per capita income—this suggests a worsening of the gap between civil service wages and average incomes of the population at large.

One prominent feature of the expenditure system in Pakistan is the overdependence on Federal government revenues to finance expenditure at the provincial and local levels (Tables 3.2 and 3.3). While the Federal government collects 90.7 per cent of the total revenue, its share of the expenditure is 67.1 per cent, suggesting a large vertical imbalance. Furthermore, the sub-national tax-GDP ratios (local and provincial) have not shown any appreciable increase in the last two decades (Table 3.4) The weak provincial and local revenue generation is of major concern and should become an area of examination and policy reform.

An examination of the relative growth rates of the various components of Federal government expenditure (Table 3.5) confirms that debt servicing is causing the major imbalance. While the growth of defence expenditure was contained in the

1970s and 1980s, it has been further curtailed in the 1990s and is about the same as the average rate of inflation. In other words, in real terms the expenditure on defence has remained unchanged in the 1990s. Development expenditures have not only been drastically cut back in real terms, but the nominal growth rate is abysmally low. Contrary to the popular rhetoric, social sector expenditures under the consolidated Federal and Provincial governments have grown in the last decade at 19 per cent annually.

TAXATION SYSTEM

In recent years, the role of taxation in development has been reaffirmed. After a neglect of domestic public finance in the earlier days of development planning, when external assistance seemed to be at its prime, the macroeconomic instability of the 1970s and 1980s and the decline in the volume of concessional aid brought to the forefront the importance of an effective tax system in dealing with fiscal imbalances. Structural adjustment and stabilization required a tax and public expenditure system that was rational and effective. In Pakistan, the imbalance between rising expenditures on debt, defence, and social spending, and the non-expanding revenue base, has prompted concerns that the tax system is inefficient, outdated, and dysfunctional and needs serious reform. The system has neither addressed the equity issues satisfactorily nor been an aid in promoting efficiency.

The distortions in the tax system are partially responsible for a host of economic problems—fiscal deficits, balance of payments difficulties, capital flight, concentration of industrial wealth and, inadequate infrastructural investment. Pakistan's inadequate tax system has had a negative ripple effect on the rest of the economy, with the high fiscal deficits representing the reigning macroeconomic problem of the 1990s. Thus, fiscal adjustment is now one of the most important items in Pakistan's policy agenda, and Pakistan's success across a whole gamut of activities will depend critically on its ability to widen the tax net and find more efficient and equitable ways of mobilizing resources.

CHARACTERISTICS OF PAKISTAN'S TAX SYSTEM

The 1973 Constitution delineates the responsibilities of the Federal government (Federal Legislative List)—international trade, macroeconomic management, industrial development— and the areas of responsibilities (Concurrent Legislative List) which the Federal government is to share with the Provinces— population planning, social welfare, and educational policy (Sadiq, 1994). However, in practice, the Federal government has encroached on the lower levels of government in Pakistan, usurping many of the responsibilities of provincial and local governments. This wide interepretation of its constitutional mandate has resulted in a crowding out of the private sector in industry, in educational and health services, and in banking; undermined efficiency and equity in public-sector provisions by creating an overcentralized system largely unresponsive to local needs; impaired the accountability of the public sector by the separation of tax and spending decisions; and weakened the local governmental sector (Sadiq, 1994). The centralization of decision-making, of financial support, and of administration by the government has hindered the Provincial governments in catering to the needs of their citizens with regard to health facilities, schooling, water supply, etc.

Furthermore, while the Federal government generates almost all of the tax revenue, accounting for almost 90 per cent of the tax revenue in the 1990s, the provincial and local contribution is very meagre. The distinguishing feature of the constitutional assignment of taxing powers to the Federal government and to Provinces in Pakistan has been the tendency to assign major tax bases exclusively to one area of government or another, without any revenue-sharing system (Sadiq, 1994). Historically, the

Pakistan tax system retains the essential characteristics and problems arising from the Government of India Act of 1935, although it has evolved as a series of *ad hoc* measures dictated by short-term pressures. Fundamentally, in terms of general structure, the tax system has remained remarkably constant since Partition.

An examination of a series of stylized facts shows the interesting evolution of the tax system. The tax/GDP ratio, the best indicator that relates revenue generated to total economic production, was 5 per cent in the first decade, reached 9 per cent by 1960, and has not moved beyond the 12-13 per cent mark for the last two decades (Table 3.7). The greatest change has been in the composition of taxation. While in the first two decades of Pakistan's existence, income tax and sales taxes were increasing relative to customs tax, which formed almost half of Pakistan's total tax revenue at Partition, over the last two decades, income tax and domestic taxation have declined in significance while customs duties became more and more important, increasing from 35 per cent of total revenue in 1969-70 to 44 per cent in 1989-90. (Table 3.8) While the income tax reached about 17 per cent of tax collection at the beginning of the 1980s, by the end of the decade it had declined to 13 per cent. However, since the early 1990s, this trend has been partially reversed as tax policy reform has resulted in a reduction in the reliance on taxes on trade and a greater emphasis on both sales and income taxes, which together accounted for over 40 per cent of tax revenue in 1995. The recent reduction in import tariff rates will minimize the dominant position of custom duties in the total tax revenue collection.

There is a consensus in both academic and policy circles that Pakistan's tax system is beset by a number of structural problems, including an overdependence on indirect tax (and on international trade tax) for over three-fourth of revenues (Table 3.9) and the negative implications for both efficiency and equity are manifested in the form of a narrow tax base coupled with high levels of taxation, and, the escape of large pools of income from the tax net (Husain, 1984). Regressive in nature, outmoded in procedures, corrupt in performance, Pakistan's tax system has failed to meet the demands of the economy and needs serious restructuring.

The heavy reliance on customs duties as the main tax lever has brought quite serious distortionary influences to bear in the structure of production and consumption, promoting widespread smuggling which penalizes domestic industry and has led to collusion between importers and custom officials, thus depriving the exchequer of large sums of duties. There have been a series of negative consequences for domestic industrial development. The short-term advantages in terms of revenue collection have to be weighed against the longer-term negative effects on the domestic production structure and incentives. Since the majority of Pakistan's imports in the 1990s were raw materials or capital goods, reflecting second-stage ISI where firms set out to develop a viable manufacturing and capital goods base, the high duty penalizes both local industries and exporting companies dependent on these foreign sources. The reliance on these indirect taxes on trade has played no small part in Pakistan's weak industrial capacity and its poor performance in exporting manufactured goods.

Coupled with this reliance on taxation of trade has been the poor effort in collecting direct taxes on income, wealth, and property. The income tax system in Pakistan is characterized by a large number of exemptions and credits for such items as agricultural income, capital gains on financial assets, major public corporations, and tax holidays (Dept. of Income Tax, 1995), so that revenues foregone, are over 2 per cent of GDP, thus explaining Pakistan's low direct tax/GDP ratio of 3 per cent in comparison to the 7 per cent of developing countries at a comparable stage of development. It has been estimated that, if all the allowances are availed of by an individual, the tax exemption limit will be over twelve times the per capita income. These allowances along with high marginal tax rates for both personal and corporate income tax of more than 50 per cent, fuel tax evasion. Of the total income tax collected in 1995, corporations paid over 80 per cent of the total income tax, with the number of private individuals escaping the tax net reaching staggering proportions. Estimates based on government taxation sources suggest that only one million people out of a population of 130 million pay income tax, thus showing rampant patterns of evasion. Studies calculating the taxable capacity of Pakistan show that less than 50 per cent of taxable capacity is being utilized, thus showing abundant areas for the mobilization of new revenue.

Furthermore, the low income elasticity of the tax system has been the crucial factor in determining its ineffectiveness in providing revenues for the government. Historically, tax revenues have not responded to income changes.

INTERNATIONAL COMPARISONS

A comparison with the tax systems of other developing countries does not show Pakistan in a favourable light (Ahmed, 1992). Countries as diverse and poor as Kenya, Gambia, Nicaragua, Egypt, India, and Sri Lanka have achieved much higher tax-GDP ratios than Pakistan. There is little reason to think that, by improving tax administration and realigning the tax structure, the yield could not be raised from the present low levels.

Tax-GDP ratios in Pakistan bear more similarity to sub-Saharan Africa than they do to India and Latin America, where direct taxes and corporate taxes constitute a larger source of revenue. A comparison with India is instructive. The Indian tax-GDP ratio of 17 per cent by the mid-1980s contrasted dramatically with Pakistan's 11.2 per cent. While India, in tune with its quasi-autarkic ISI policy, saw a large drop in the relative importance of customs as a source of tax revenue, Pakistan has relied deeply on the taxation of trade for revenues, with trade taxes constituting over half of indirect taxes (Ahmed, 1992). While India has managed to achieve some success in taxing personal and corporate income tax, Pakistan has had much more modest success. Pakistan has meanwhile avoided India's heavy dependence on a cumbersome system of excises and the cascade of indirect taxes that is a consequence of such a system.

Another interesting comparison is with Bangladesh. With a tax-GDP ratio of only 7 per cent in 1985, Bangladesh, like Pakistan, depended heavily on the taxation of international trade for a large amount of its revenue. But the introduction of value-added tax in the early 1990s reversed this course, and there has been an overall improvement in total tax collection, reduced reliance on taxes on international trade, and a strengthening of fiscal account.

The evidence shows that as a country becomes more modernized, the direct-tax-to-GDP ratio increases and the proportion of trade tax is susbstantially reduced. The expansion and monetization of domestic spheres of activity means that the recourse to trade taxes can be avoided by using stronger income taxes, sales taxes, or value-added taxes. The international comparison shows that Pakistan lags behind other low-income countries in sales tax / VAT and income/ corporation tax.

Estimates of elasticities of four major taxes with respect to their bases (Table 3.10) show there is considerable scope for improvement. With the exception of sales tax on domestic goods, all other elasticities have been declining over time. If measures are taken to strengthen tax coverage, assessment, and collection, and the elasticities attain their values of the 1960s, the tax-GDP ratio would rise and become more comparable to other countries at the same level of income and development.

POLICY REFORM

In the early 1990s, in the wake of both domestic and international criticism of Pakistan's tax structure, a series of reforms were enacted to make the tax system more efficient, more progressive, and more buoyant. This was accomplished by withholding taxes at the source, removing exemptions and concessions and, extending the coverage of the General Sales Tax (GST). A series of tariff reform also strengthened the tax base.

Perhaps the most successful of the government reforms was the introduction of the withholding tax. The percentage of income tax relative to total tax revenue surged from 14.5 per cent in 1990-91 to 24.2 per cent in 1995-6 (Table 3.11). These withholding taxes, used to extend the coverage of income tax to various forms of capital or unearned income, were not restricted only to deductions at source, but were also levied at points where one could get a proxy for the income of a taxpayer (Pasha, 1995). While the empirical estimates of the extent of income and corporate tax evaded in Pakistan varied, there was a strong consensus that withholding taxes could tap this large pool of resources and bridge the gap between incomes liable for tax payment and the inability of the tax administration to collect the tax. The extension thus made can not only contribute to a growth in revenue, but also increase equity. As income tax is progressive in its incidence and the previously evaded incomes are taxed, the capital income earned by the upper middle class and the elite is taxed, the benefits are manifold. This is likely to contribute to a greater elasticity of income tax revenue by being linked to fast-growing income streams such as interest income from bank deposits, income from government securities, and other related activities (Pasha, 1995). These reforms were in consonance with the rich insights of the political economy literature on tax reform suggesting that the deduction of tax at source is a formidable tool against the corruption of income tax officers and that the minimization of contact between tax officers and citizenry in developing countries should be encouraged.

The withholding tax represents the best attempt in the short and medium run to alleviate the budgetary pressures of the government. Possibilities for rapid improvement in Pakistan's tax administration, notwithstanding ambitious plans, are scarce. The preponderance of indirect taxation in most developing countries is a clear indication of the severe constraint imposed on the nature of tax reform in developing countries by administrative limitation; in almost every developing country in which taxes have increased significantly, the increased revenues have not come from direct taxes on income and expenditures, but from a variety of indirect taxes on consumption (Khalilzadeh and Shah, 1991). Pakistan is no exception in this regard. The international literature on taxation in developing countries is rife with reports of poor administration and collection, and rampant tax evasion. In this regard, Pakistan is no exception. The problems of tax regimes are essentially problems of governance and reflect more on weak states and the underdevelopment of political institutions than on the incapacity of economic planning. Taxes in Pakistan must be designed both to be politically acceptable and to work with a poor administration (Khalilzadeh and Shah, 1991). Given the political clout of both the urban industrialists and the feudal landlords, there is little possibility of targeting and taxing their income directly. Experience in developing countries suggests that the key to success with income taxes is a good withholding system supplemented by some sort of legally-based presumptive assessment on hard-to-tax groups, with both these systems having the virtue of reducing the opportunity for face-to-face negotiations between taxpayers and tax officials. Beyond that, the sales tax and a series of other indirect taxes are critically important.

The second key reform was the conversion of a general sales tax to a value-added tax (VAT) in 1990-1 and the extension of this tax to over 300 additional goods by 1995. However, this tax has not had a strong effect since many of these industries are small in terms of value, and attempts to extend GST to the wholesale and retail trade sector, giving it the character of a consumption tax, have been met with vehement political opposition from the business and trading interests.

Pakistan's attempt to institute a value-added tax is a reflection of international trends that mark the introduction of VAT as the most significant event in the evolution of tax structure in the last half of this century (Khalilzadeh and Shah, 1991). Basically involving a transaction tax on all goods and services at all stages of production and distribution, VAT has the advantage relative to the income tax of raising more revenue with less administrative and economic costs than other broad-based taxes.

Harder to evade than income tax, administratively less cumbersome, reflecting the principles of tax neutrality, VAT has been instituted in over fifty-five countries worldwide, most notably in Latin America, with considerable success.

The Pakistani conversion of GST to VAT has been half-hearted and incoherent. The lack of commitment to a pure form of VAT is revealed by the eagerness with which improvisations in the form of presumptive, fixed, or non-invoicable GST have been adopted. The reform process in Pakistan has been *ad hoc* and piecemeal, with little understanding of the intricacies of VAT. However, given the inflationary and regressive nature of most sales taxes and the administrative and political impossibility of substantial increases in income tax, the imposition of a broad-based VAT represents the best means to provide revenues in the medium run.

A series of international studies has conclusively shown that the value-added tax is the instrument of choice for most developing countries contemplating reform of their sales tax. VAT has been empirically shown to increase revenue and economic efficiency, improve vertical equity by reducing rents accruing to wealthy recipients of foreign exchange or import licences, and assist in the collection of other taxes (Khalilzadeh and Shah, 1991). In spite of certain limitations of VAT, such as its inability to target and tax the urban informal sector and the frequent exclusion from its range of basic necessities and foods in order to protect the poor, it represents the best hope for Pakistan of improving its difficult fiscal position.

Improvements in tax administration, strengthening of withholding tax on presumptive income, further horizontal expansion of VAT, and extending the coverage and base of tax payers offer the best hope for increased revenue performance. The budgetary deficit can be reduced to 4 per cent of GDP by the year 2000 if strenuous efforts are made on the tax side of the equation. Any further cuts in development expenditure to contain the fiscal deficit would prove counterproductive in the medium term—they would hurt the production capacity of the economy as well as retard efforts to invest in human development.

MONETARY AND CREDIT POLICIES

Monetary management refers to policies, practices, and institutional arrangements that seek to attain certain objectives for the macroeconomy by operating on a country's money and credit supply (Mohammed, 1992). The main goal of monetary management is to maintain the stability of the currency and ensure that there is a smooth flow of money throughout the economic system.

Monetary policy affects the entire economy through a multitude of channels. Besides the obvious effect on the rate of inflation, monetary policy affects the economy in more subtle ways. The growth pattern of the real sector, the investment rate, the credit availability to industry, the interest rate structure of the economy, the savings-investment profile, the effects of foreign trade are all highly sensitive to monetary policy. Although taxation and budgetary issues are much more likely to generate public interest than money supply matters, escpecially in a developing economy like Pakistan, the importance of monetary policy and the financial system cannot be exaggerated. When used effectively by a government in conjunction with other macro policy instruments, it can not only regenerate stagnant economies, but it can also cushion the myriad exogenous shocks that affect developing economies in the post-Uruguay Round international economic system. While historically, in most developing countries, monetary policy has been a relatively passive instrument, the imperatives of macroeconomic adjustment and stabilization policies have brought it to the forefront. An efficient and effective financial sector facilitates the operation of a monetary policy consistent with stabilization and growth.

While positions differ on the optimal policy reforms and the proper sequencing of changes, there is a strong consensus on the nature of the maladies afflicting the sectors. A combination of deterioration of the loan portfolio, a slowdown in the rate of domestic deposit growth, a segmentation of financial markets and a corresponding differential interest rate structure, and an eroding capital base, all have brought the issue of banking reform to the forefront. Similarly, the financial sector is crippled by significant financial repression and distortionary interest rate policies. In the light of these problems, financial liberalization, with banking reform at its forefront, will determine Pakistan's success in solidifying its financial institutions and thus improving prospects for economic growth. A sound monetary policy, in accordance with these changes, will be instrumental in maintaining the strength of the financial sector.

The financial system plays a critical role in economic development. Money and finance facilitate the exchange of real goods and services in the market and reduce transaction costs. Likewise, credit and capital market instruments facilitate exchange and expansion of the market for real goods and services. Recent empirical work demonstrates the relationship between financial systems and growth, and concludes that the level of the financial system is highly correlated with long-run economic growth (King and Levine, 1992). The size of the financial sector in relation to GDP, the importance of banks in relation to the Central Bank, the proportion of credit allocated to the private sector, and the ratio of credit allocated to private firms to GDP, are all consistently correlated with efficient capital accumulation (Bencivenga and Smith, 1991). The contribution of the financial systems to growth is related to its ability to increase efficiency. A large body of econometric work shows strong positive relationships between financial variables and rates of economic growth.

The goal of financial-sector reform is to establish a flexible system of financial intermediation in which a variety of instruments are made available to savers and borrowers through stable financial institutions.

A rich theoretical literature on endogenous growth has focused on the importance of financial systems in helping to improve not only the quantity but also the quality of productive investment (Romer, 1986, 1990). In this framework, financial institutions can help individuals to reallocate their portfolios in order to economize on savings. Such policies improve the productivity of capital and hence, foster economic growth.

While much of the early development literature had postulated the Harrod-Domar model and the importance of strong investment ratios in generating growth, it was the changed economic circumstances of the late 1970s which finally propelled a change of policy. The dependence on commodity exports and foreign borrowing to pay for imported inputs became more and more difficult as interest rates rose in the late 1970s and commercial banks in developed countries reduced their lending portfolios (World Bank, 1989). The economic contraction in the aftermath of the OPEC oil shocks and the debt crisis led to a contraction in foreign capital flows, thus heightening developing countries' concerns to accelerate their own savings rate through financial sector reform. The recent East Asian crisis had highlighted the importance of an efficient and well regulated financial sector.

EVOLUTION OF MONETARY POLICY

Monetary policy in Pakistan has evolved along with the changing paradigm of development management. From highly-regulated and tightly-controlled allocation of credit with administratively determined interest rates, the policy stance currently is relatively more market-determined in terms of both quantity and price.

The State Bank was established in 1948 with a mandate to control the money supply in the economy. Monetary policy was framed in accordance with the larger economic objective of encouraging industrial development and commercial expansion in the economy in the absence of an industrial base. In the 1950s the monetary policy was heavily influenced by changes in the balance of payments position (Malik, 1994). The first serious change in monetary policy was in the aftermath of the

1949 decision not to devalue in the wake of India's devaluation. This led to a trade deficit and a consequent monetary expansion. The value of the money supply rose from Rupees 3,226 million in 1949- 50 to Rupees 3,738 million in 1950-1. A decrease during the Korean War-led boom due to the strong export expansion, the depletion of foreign exchange reserves, the importation of large quantities of food, and general economic contraction led the government to engage in serious deficit financing, resulting in a contraction of the money supply (Malik, 1994).

The situation changed in the 1960s when Ayub's industrialization policies necessitated a need for money to finance the economic growth. In the first half of the 1960s a combination of private-sector demand for capital, liberalization of commercial policy after the ISI-induced restrictions of the 1950s, and credit market expansion led to over 10 per cent growth rates of money supply (Malik, 1994).

After a monetary contraction in the late 1960s due to the balance of payments difficulties, the 1970s witnessed major changes in monetary policy (Naqvi and Sarmad, 1984). Deficit financing became a major element of monetary policy. The annual growth rate of 16.5 per cent in the money supply was in excess of the annual growth rate of 2.8 per cent of the commodity-producing sectors and of 4.6 per cent of GDP in real terms, while the GDP deflator was in single digits. A combination of stagnant productivity in the commodity-producing sectors and an increase in the general price level in the aftermath of the early 1970s OPEC oil shocks led to an expansionary monetary policy in order to accommodate these increases. By the mid-1970s the nationalization of the commercial banks had taken place, and the government imposed strict controls to regulate the banking sector, with negative effects on the rate of monetary growth.

This policy continued into the 1980s as the rupee was delinked from the dollar and monetary expansion was only used to ease balance of payments crises. The overall rate of inflation for the 1980s averaged 6.6 per cent. However, in the 1990s a combination of increases in government borrowing, financial liberalization and the abolition of credit ceilings, and the increase in liquidity ratio to 45 per cent, led to an increase in the money supply and a rise in inflationary pressures.

In sum, the primary function of monetary policy in Pakistan remains the easing of balance of payments disequilibrium.

The determination of an optimal monetary policy has been difficult in Pakistan because of very inconclusive estimates of income velocity and money demand. A large number of studies on the relationship between income velocity and per capita income have very divergent results, heavily dependent on the time period studied. The hypothesis that the velocity of money declines as income rises is true for certain time periods but not true for the entire period since 1947. Similar ambiguities dominate the literature on money demand. Although there have been many studies on money demand, there is no consensus on the stability of the money demand function. One of the studies has found that the narrow money demand function is more stable than the broad money demand. This means that a narrow aggregate can be used for monetary targeting in Pakistan and that the monetary authorities should direct their focus to ensuring price stability (Hossain, 1994). Thus, monetary policy cannot be predicated on a stable demand function, hence undermining its effectiveness.

INFLATION

Pakistan, like other South Asian countries, has been a low inflation country. Since the 1970s, inflation has assumd increased importance in the context of macroeconomic stabilization. The OPEC-induced oil shocks contributed to increasing inflation in the developing world. The remarkable acceleretion of inflation worldwide, however, did not touch East Asia and South Asia as much.

Low rates of inflation have been identified as vital prerequisites for sound macroeconomic management in developing countries. Inflation can have a series of adverse consequences for the economy. Firstly, inflation erodes the purchasing power of the population and hence, leads to a contraction in economic growth. Related to this is the increase in macroeconomic instability as an inflationary environment creates many uncertainties. Secondly, inflation has regressive consequences on the poverty profile of a country. The increase in .overall prices hurts the poor more since their consumption basket becomes significantly reduced in every inflationary bout. Thirdly, inflation can damage a country's competitiveness by leading to an appreciation of the local currency and a consequent overvalued exchange rate. This will have a negative effect on exports. In recent work, price stability, in combination with fiscal discipline and policy credibility, has been identified as one of the key factors explaining Asian success and Latin American failure in policy reform over the last three decades (Caprio et al, 1990).

The basic trend in inflation in Pakistan, as in other developing countries has been a long-term low rate compared to other developing regions such as Latin America or parts of Africa (Table 3.10). The inflation rate remained below ten per cent, which is especially low in comparison to the over 50 per cent rates of many of the Latin American countries in the wake of the OPEC oil shocks (Table 3.11). By a broad range of monetary indicators, Pakistan has done well by international standards. Pakistan's annual average inflation rate (using the GDP inflator) from 1980 to 1993 was 7.4 per cent, significantly below not only the hyperinflationary Latin American economies— Argentina, Mexico, and Brazil—but also lower than its South Asia neighbours (Table 3.12). In fact, the low inflation puts Pakistan in the same league as the successful East Asian economies, such as Indonesia and Korea. However, the recent acceleration in inflation in the mid-1990s will reverse this trend.

The same trend can be observed in the growth of money stock. Pakistan has had a very conservative rate of increase in money stock when compared internationally. The State Bank has allowed the money supply to increase by only about 15 per cent per year between 1970 and 1993. This is low in comparison to rates above thirty per cent for a range of developing countries including Turkey, Brazil, Indonesia, and Korea. The conservative monetary policy of the State Bank can be gauged by the fact that it is very hard to find developing countries with substantially lower rates of monetary creation than Pakistan. This shows that monetary expansion by providing critical liquidity has not been used to stimulate economic growth.

Until recently, a combination of manageable levels of deficit financing and heavy resort to external aid and borrowing, and the avoidance of monetization as well as conservative monetary policy, have permitted a more reasonable control on inflation.

The volatility of inflation has not been particularly inimical, although peaks were recorded in 1957-8, 1966-7, 1973-7, and 1980-2. The mid-1970s was the most inflationary time in Pakistan's history, with inflation rates averaging more than 15 per cent annually. The oil price increase and major nationalization of the economy combined to create inflationary pressures of an unprecedented nature for the Pakistan economy. Accommodating monetary expansion played a much greater role in fuelling inflation in the 1970s. Currency devaluation and devastating floods affecting Pakistan's agriculture exacerbated these pressures. By the early 1980s, a combination of improved performance of the commodity-producing sectors and lower rates of public investment led to a restoration of trend rates (Malik, 1994).

The 1990s have witnessed an end to the period of low inflation and the trend is moving towards accelerating inflation. Given Pakistan's general price stability during the last three decades of its history, the upsurge in the 1990s has threatened to reduce the rates of return on financial assets and create a general climate of uncertainty. The wholesale price index (WPI) almost reached twenty per cent by the middle of the decade, with the consumer price index (CPI) not lagging far behind. Compared to the historical level of single digits, the inflation of the 1990s has created a serious disturbance. Although the factors explaining this phenomenon are not clear, the role of public policy has not been insignificant. The conclusions on the causes of inflation in Pakistan remain inconclusive, with both monetary and structural factors held responsible (Bilquees, 1988; Hossain, 1990). Heavily dependent on specification, the varying econometric results have yet to resolve the debate. One of the empirical studies found that, contrary to popular perceptions about the contribution of monetary expansion and supply shocks to inflation, it was the rise in procurement prices (especially of wheat) and administered prices (mainly of energy inputs), as well as the increase in indirect taxes in the 1994-5 budget, that explain the spiralling inflation (Hasan, Khan, Pasha and Rasheed, 1995). The implications of this study are that government demand management policy, in the form of reducing the rate of monetary growth and controlling the budget deficit, was not too successful in combating inflation in the absence of controls on procurement prices of wheat and administered prices of fuel, gas, and electricity.

Another study supports the contention that changes in the real money balance in Pakistan have contributed to the acceleration of inflation, while other estimates suggest that the financing of the budget deficit has done so. It has also been argued that the money supply in Pakistan has not been exogenous, but rather it depends on the position of international reserves and the fiscal deficit (Chaudhry and Ahmad, 1995).

CHARACTERISTICS OF THE FINANCIAL SECTOR

BANKING SECTOR

The financial structure of Pakistan is an agglomeration of myriad banking and financial entities, dominated by the commercial banks. Currently, the financial system of Pakistan consists of the State Bank of Pakistan, 3 nationalized commercial banks, 2 partially privatized banks, 21 foreign commercial banks, 9 private domestic banks, 2 provincial commercial banks,

9 development finance institutions, 45 *modarabas* (mutual funds), 3 stock exchanges, and 60 insurance companies.

The State Bank, the country's central bank, is the principal hub of the banking system. Aside from fulfilling the functions of a central bank, it regulates credit and is an important source of financing for the government and certain state-owned development finance institutions. However, due to the limited autonomy it had until recently, in disciplining the nationalized banks as well as the development financial institutions, it could not successfully or effectively oversee the banking system. The State Bank was granted autonomy through legislation introduced in 1996.

In the banking sector, the three nationalized commercial banks (Habib Bank, National Bank, and United Bank) and the two partially-privatized banks (Muslim Commercial Bank and Allied Bank Limited) account for the lion's share of deposits, holding 70 per cent of total deposits, while foreign banks account for 17 per cent, and private domestic banks for 13 per cent.

A comparison of the performance of these banks, divided into NCBs, partially privatized banks, foreign banks, and private domestic banks, provides some interesting insights. The most striking feature of the Pakistani banking system is the noncompetitiveness of the nationalized commercial banks. The return on equity is a bare 3 per cent, in contrast to the 53 per cent of the foreign banks and the 11 per cent of the partially-privatized banks. Similarly, the return on assets is only 0.1 per cent, in contrast to 2.8 per cent of foreign banks. The poor performance of the NCBs can be gauged by the fact that if credit losses had been adequately provided for, they would have shown negative returns and net worth; furthermore, if sufficient provisions were made, all NCBs would have been insolvent with a negative capital base of between 8 and 10 per cent of total assets.

The poor performance of the banking sector has been attributed to a variety of reasons—the nationalization wave of the 1970s and the bureaucratic managerial culture that it engendered, the heavy burden of non-performing loans, the political pressures to grant loans to political cronies and affiliates, overstaffing and promotions based on seniority and not performance, large overhead costs, and sensitivity to political changes. The erosion of the capital base of NCBs has been so large that the total advances of NCBs characterized as bad and doubtful have increased from Rs 25 billion in 1989 to Rs 135 billion by 1998, which amounts to over 20 per cent of the NCBs' lending portfolio (Haque and Kardar, 1993). In order to improve the operational efficiency of the banking system, measures are needed to isolate the infected portfolio, build up the capital base according to adequacy standards, and strengthen professionalism among the nationalized banks. Estimates from the Bank of International Settlements show that the cost of recapitalizing these banks could reach a staggering $6 billion.

However, the predominance of non-performing assets is not unique to Pakistan. Recent World Bank research lists thirty-three countries experiencing serious problems of non-performing assets in their banking systems (World Bank, 1989). Government intervention, in the form of pressures to achieve mandatory credit disbursement targets, has been one of the main reasons for the large number of nonperforming assets in the Indian banking system (Morris, 1985). The major causes of high arrears in India—the failure to tie lending to productive investment, defective loan policies, ineffective supervision, and lack of responsibility and supervision by the bankers—hold considerable validity for Pakistan. Another prominent international example is the Republic of Korea. The Korean government, in its drive to industrialize heavy and chemical industries in the 1970s, coerced the banks into making risky long-term loans. By 1987, nonperforming assets had risen to 20 per cent of total bank loans (Park and Kim, 1990). The recent financial crisis in this eleventh largest economy of the world was triggered by the poor health of the financial institutions.

The partially-privatized banks are in relatively sounder financial health than their public counterparts. The privatization policies of the early 1990s seem to have paid good dividends as these banks, although plagued by a low yield on the old stock of loans and an inherited cost base, have improved loan recovery and reduced costs since privatization.Although their return on assets is still a meagre 0.2 per cent and their efficiency ratio only 84 per cent, their return on equity has reached over 10 per cent. However, a combination of high personnel costs due to the recruitment of more qualified staff without a retrenchment of unqualified personnel, growing position risks, interest rate risks, and a poor loan stock show that the required capital of 3 per cent of liabilites is grossly inadequate. Of all the banking institutions, the foreign banks are the best performers. Even though the twenty-one foreign banks make up only 21 per cent of the sector, they have been consistently earning about two-thirds of the industry's profits, with earnings primarily coming from trade finance and foreign currency deposit collection surrendered to the State Bank with good margins. Characterized by highly technical management skills, better access to international financial markets, low administrative costs, and political noninterference, the gross revenues of foreign banks have been spectacular since the deregulation of the banking sector in the late 1980s. The share of foreign banks in total after-tax profits of all scheduled banks increased from less than 20 per cent in the mid-1980s to over 60 per cent by the mid-90s (Haque and Kardar, 1993). By a wide variety of empirical indicators, the foreign banks have been the most dynamic sector of the Pakistani economy in the last decade. However, one important caveat to consider in comparisons between foreign banks and local banks is that these two types of banks are not competing in the same markets, and the foreign banks are not subjected to the same political pressures to hire staff and advance/reschedule loans. Thus, the NCBs and the foreign banks have fundamentally different cost profiles (Haque and Kardar, 1993). Nevertheless, the infusion of the foreign banks has provided the necessary measure of competition that was conspicuously absent from the oligopolistic structure of banking that had dominated Pakistan for decades.

The fourth of the banking groups, the private domestic banks, are doing quite well, with return on equity averaging 25 per cent. A combination of rapid growth, a solid efficiency ratio, and containment of administrative costs has propelled this sector to prominence, in spite of its small size and vulnerability to banking crises.

NON-BANKING FINANCIAL SECTOR

The financial sector in Pakistan is characterized by seven industrial and development finance institutions (DFIs), each with a special mandate to address the long-term financing needs of specific sectoral clients, with the Industrial Development Bank (IDBP) established to provide term finance to small industries and the Pakistan Industrial Credit and Investment Corporation (PICIC) providing term finance to the medium and large industries. As with their counterparts in the banking sector, the wave of nationalization had negative effects. In recent years, in spite of success in mobilizing short-term deposits, a combination of drying up of international credit line sources and weak collection performance has made the DFIs as a group illiquid.

ASSESSMENT OF THE FINANCIAL SECTOR

The intellectual framework for analysing financial-sector and policy advice lies in the models of Ronald McKinnon and Edward Shaw, who made the central argument that financial repression in the form of indiscriminate distortions of financial prices including interest rates and foreign exchange rates reduces the rate of growth of the economy and retards the development process (McKinnon and Shaw, 1973). For a variety of reasons, such as the development of an industrial sector and the financing of government deficits, developing countries engage in a host of policies that basically impose a discriminatory tax on financial intermediation. These policies distort the structure of incentives to savers and worsen income distribution. Their argument is that financial liberalization through the overhaul of this large web of controls is absolutely central to economic growth. The McKinnon-Shaw model has spawned a vast body of empirical research verifying the predominance of financial repression in developing countries and its hindrance to successful growth.

Pakistan's experience fits very neatly into this analytical framework.The key characteristic of Pakistan's financial markets for most of its history has been its financial repression. A combination of direct controls on deposit and loan rates, credit controls involving bank-by-bank credit ceilings and mandatory credit programmes, and concessionary finance to various sectors has resulted in a distorted and regulated interest rate structure (Haque and Kardar, 1993). The large fiscal deficits that have been prominent in recent years have resulted in the government's large taxing of the financial and banking system in order to finance the deficit. The ripple effect this has generated on the whole interest rate structure has had very serious implications for the level and composition of investment (Kemal and Durdag, 1991).

The predominant trend in the Pakistani banking system has been the conspicuous absence of financial deepening.[1]

The level of financial depth has barely kept pace with the rest of the economy.[2]

In sum, financial deepening has proved an elusive goal for Pakistan.

In the last decade, the Pakistani economy has experienced serious financial disintermediation due to the means used by successive governments to finance the fiscal deficit. Firstly, the remarkable stability of the interest rates on deposits over the

---

[1]The ratio of M1/GDP, which measures the amount of currency in circulation, and demand deposits has declined in the last thirty years, while the M2/GDP, which is a broader definition of money supply including time deposits, has registered a decline from close to 50 per cent in 1961-70 to 44.6 currently (Table 3.13).

[2]The income velocity of M1 and M2, which is another indicator expressing the depth of the financial sector, has remained relatively constant over the past two decades.

last decade has resulted in negative real interest rate, with very adverse consequences for domestic savings. Secondly, a combination of high rates on national savings instruments (averaging 14 per cent in 1996) combined with low deposit rates (averaging 8 per cent in 1996), high reserve requirements for the banking system, and low rates on subsidized credit has resulted in a heavy cost on the financial system by diverting money from deposits in commercial banks to National Savings Schemes. The spread between these two yields on government securities (the sovereign risk) and private sector debt (the commercial risk) is too large for any healthy financial sector to maintain. Such a divergence in interest rates can have deleterious effects on capital formation in the banking sector.

Another trend with negative effects on the domestic banking system has been the rise in foreign currency deposits (FCDs) introduced in the early 1980s as a key component of the government's financial liberalization efforts. The opening of the FCDs has proceeded at such a rapid pace that by June 1998, they accounted for US$ 11 billion (40 per cent of total bank deposits). A combination of movement of local depositors from rupees to dollars with the active encouragement of the State Bank which provides a heavily subsidized foreign exchange cover to foreign bank branches, giving banks attractive margins, has been instrumental in determining this shift. This growing trend toward asset substitution into dollars had created serious problems for monetary policy and exchange rate management.

CREDIT POLICY

Domestic credit policy in Pakistan has historically relied on a system of global ceilings with direct and selective controls being the primary instrument for the regulation of the growth and distribution of domestic credit by the banking system. Under this system, there are three fundamental sources for generating high-powered money: changes in foreign exchange reserves, State Bank of Pakistan credit to the government, and State Bank credit to scheduled banks and nonbank financial institutions. Thus, State Bank credit is the principal axis on which the system in Pakistan has historically revolved.

Every year the National Credit Consultative Council meets and sets the ceiling for credit to be disbursed to the various sectors and determines the interest rate to be charged. After an overall credit expansion target has been reached, the SBP determines the relative allocation to the private and the public sector. While the allocation of credit to the public sector takes into account the estimates of targeted budgetary support, the credit needs of the private sector are determined on the basis of overall as well as sector-wise targets for investment and production. Through this vast framework of detailed quantitative control of overall credit expansion, the State Bank regulates the money entering the credit expansion, which has been used to finance the economic industrialization of Pakistan and ensure that critical resources for development are easily available to the private sector.

The evolution of the credit system has been interesting, with an increasing percentage going to agriculture and services (Table 3.14). Originally founded in the late 1950s, the credit system was mainly used to aid private industrialists in setting up viable projects and foreign traders interested in finance for import/export activities. Thus, manufacturing and commerce took the lion's share of early investment, receiving up to 80 per cent of credit disbursed by the early 1970s.

In the mid 1970s the pattern changed with the nationalization of the commercial banks. Agriculture, which had been a neglected sector with an allocation of below 10 per cent in the first two decades, had an increase in its allocation to about 15 per cent by the mid-1970s. Although the amount of credit in terms of sectoral value-added was still slight, the reversal of neglect was an important development.

By 1990 agriculture held close to 30 per cent, manufacturing about 40 per cent, and commerce about 20 per cent of credit allocations. By the early 1990s the government, in an attempt to liberalize the financial system, abolished the system of monetary credit targets and instituted a system whereby commercial banks are required to extend 32 per cent of the value of their deposits as credit. However, to counterbalance any undue expansion in the money supply that may result, the State Bank raised the liquidity ratio.

The system of directed credit, while helping in the industrialization of Pakistan, unfortunately had a series of pernicious effects on the economy. The policies induced a series of distortions in the economy: lower deposit rates, lower savings, and inefficient resource allocation. Perhaps the greatest weakness of the credit regime, paradoxically, was the reduction in supply of credit to economically poor sectors. By keeping both the deposit and the loan rates below their market equilibrium values, the policies reduced the aggregate supply of investible funds. Abundant international evidence suggests that the two premises that form the foundation for selective credit policies—planners' knowledge of investments to be undertaken, and the optimal role of credit allocation to ensure that these investments are undertaken—are both flawed. Credit policies seem to be the ideal recipe for reducing the quantity and quality of productive investment by decreasing the efficiency of resource allocation by financial intermediaries.

Jagdish Bhagwati and T.N. Srinivasan have made the important argument that development plans in India, as well as in most developing countries, seem to have favoured, through import licenses and selective credit policies, investments with low social returns and high domestic resource costs (Bhagwati and Srinivasan, 1993). The conventional argument that selective credit policies have encouraged investments with high social returns does not match with the available evidence.

FINANCIAL SECTOR REFORM

As the accumulation of savings in the form of financial assets rises with the increase in per capita income, the financial institutions, infrastructure, and financial policies have to evolve to make this possible. In the early stages of Pakistan's development, informal finance involving direct lending by the saver to the investors was the predominant means of financial intermediation. The network of family, friends, and money-lenders was the major source of lending. But over time, formal financial institutions have taken root. The government played a very proactive role in laying down the rudimentary infrastructure. Banks and development financial institutions were the ones to be established first. With the passage of time, mixes of formal financial institutions and informal kerb markets, private and public finance companies such as *modarabas*, leasing companies, etc. have proliferated. Market segmentation, however, remains pervasive despite this proliferation and expansion. Small and medium firms are still rationed out of formal credit markets, and institutional agriculture credit, despite mandatory requirements, remains paltry in relation to the requirements of the sector.

In the 1990s, Pakistan began the process of financial liberalization. This was partly in response to growing evidence that government policies and interventions holding nominal interest rates down to low levels under inflationary conditions had produced low or negative real rates of return and discouraged financial savings. Loanable funds remained in short supply and the financial sector remained shallow, with low-risk lending to government and to larger scale establishments dominating the activities of the bank. Controls on interest rates were accompanied by directed allocation of credit determined by the preferences and priorities of the government. The public sector absorbed 48 per cent of domestic credit. On the other hand, countries with a higher share of credit to the private sector have tended to attain higher rates of economic growth in Asia.

Thus, in 1989, the Pakistani government embarked on a series of policies to smoothe the functioning of the financial system and dismantle the regime of financial controls that had accumulated over several decades. The main thrust of the government's reforms focused on: privatization policies to improve the competitive environment in which banks operated, and a greater reliance on market forces, liberalization of exchange controls, the deregulation of the structure of interest rates and a gradual dismantling of the system of directed credit, permission for foreign ownership of equity, and improved bank supervision (Haque and Kardar, 1993). The main objectives of these programmes was to alleviate the growing strains on the banking circle that were a result of decades of misguided policies that had repressed the financial sector. The reforms were meant to enhance economic efficiency and contribute to financial intermediation. The thrust of the reform programme is the improvement of the environment for bank owners, bank regulators, markets and courts to enhance governance and financial discipline.

The key reform of the early 1990s was the privatization of the banking system. Hurt by the nationalization of the 1970s, weakened by years of government patronage and coercion, financially crippled by a huge nonperforming loan liability, and mismanaged by a cadre of political appointees, Pakistan's banking system struggled to maintain viability in the 1990s. The main goal of privatization was to achieve good governance by selling the NCBs and DFIs to private investors who possessed the integrity, capital, banking expertise, management and technology to run these institutions efficiently and to promote greater market competition. To this end, the full privatization of Habib Bank, United Bank, National Bank, and the National Development Finance Corporation has been envisioned. By the middle of 1997, Allied Bank and Muslim Commercial Bank have been fully privatized and plans are under way to remove two of the remaining three banks from the locus of state ownership. However, plans to downsize have met with considerable resistance and the pace of reform has slowed down.

Concomitant with these changes, in 1991 the government introduced an auction system for government securities, with commercial banks as the primary dealers. The introduction of two debt instruments—6-month Treasury Bills and 3 to 10 year Federal Investment Bonds—has injected some freshness into the financial system.

A second key area of reform, as mentioned above, was the relaxation and liberalization of exchange controls. Originally installed to maintain the stability of the local currency, the exhange controls had long outlived their purpose and were detrimental to economic growth. Moreover, given the large informal trade in foreign currency that had circumvented the organized financial system for decades, this measure represented a legalization of what had become common practice.

A third area of reform was in the equities market. The low capitalization of the stock market in Pakistan had prevented the capital deepening that Pakistan has historically lacked. A thin market, characterized by rampant insider trading, with prices not reflecting their actual share value, the stock market had failed to keep pace with changing international economic realities. Of the private companies that declared cash dividends in the 1990s, only one-fourth of them gave a dividend value of 10 to 15 per cent on the par value of the share, while the remaining gave either very thin dividends or none at all. Another factor influencing the thinness of the equity market has been the liberal credit policies of the government. The easy availability of credit from public-sector banks and development financial institutions to blue-chip companies has made debt the preferred instrument over equity for raising capital and hence, slowed the development of the capital markets. This low level of equity market development has not only had adverse effects on domestic finance but also discouraged foreign investment. However, recent regulations by the State Bank to decrease the debt/equity ratio to 60:40 seem to have had some effect.

A fourth line of reform has been to develop a regulatory and supervisory system that would assess the condition of banks and financial institutions. The system would define and regulate capital requirements, loan concentration limits, accounting standards, and provisioning norms in order to strengthen the financial system. This would also harmonize Pakistan with international standards. The inspection and auditing of a nationalized bank's portfolio is a vital pillar for the proper implementation of monetary policy.

Two critical factors for Pakistan are the presence of macro-economic stability, without which even the most well-intentioned reform is destined to failure, and the importance of institutional reform and regulatory mechanisms, which provide an adequate framework for change. The market by itself does not suffice in the case of the financial sector.

The key factor that has repeatedly threatened to thwart Pakistan's financial reforms is the absence of fiscal discipline, which has clearly emerged as a vital prerequisite to successful monetary policy. The key lesson that has emerged from developing-country reform in the last two decades is the fundamental importance of fiscal prudence. Without the underpinnings of fiscal discipline, even the most radical institutional reforms of the banking and financial sectors will prove ineffective.

Financial liberalization is likely to succeed when it is accompanied by reforms that eliminate distortions in goods, labour, and foreign exchange markets. This will ensure that the savings accumulated through the financial intermediaries are being put to the most efficient use in sectors and activities in which Paksitan has competitive advantage. If access to these savings remains restricted and new businesses and entrepreneurs are unable to obtain credit, the effects on the real sectors of the economy are unlikely to be positive.The continued crowding out of private sector due to privileged or preferential borrowing by the government and public enterprises will also impede the development of the financial system.

Low-cost arrangements to mobilize savings in the rural areas and to target credit at the less well-to-do households and firms have proven effective in a number of developing countries. Bangladesh, Bolivia, Indonesia, and a number of other countries at similar levels of low per capita income have succeeded in mobilizing savings and channelling credit to the rural areas.

EXCHANGE RATE POLICY

A country's exchange rate, which measures the price of its currency against a foreign currency, helps to determine an economy's competitiveness and the strength of its currency. Intersecting with monetary policy and fiscal policy, the exchange rate policy determines the economy's vulnerability to external shocks, its terms of trade and, its current account balance. While frequently a reflection of economic fundamentals—productivity, savings, unit labour costs—the exchange rate helps in influencing these fundamentals.

A misguided exchange rate policy can have pernicious spillover effects on the rest of the economy. The maintenance of overvalued exchange rates has been one of the key mistakes of developing-country governments in the last four decades. Exchange rates that do not reflect the proper prices in the economy create a web of distortions that considerably hurt an economy.

Empirical proof of this phenomenon can be analysed through a comparison of the macroeconomic experiences in East Asia and Latin America, suggesting that the management of the exchange rate has played a major role in the contrasting experiences of these countries (Khan, 1986, Balassa, 1986). In the analytical framework of the McKinnon-Shaw model, a flexible exchange rate has been viewed as a crucial element in financial stabilization and liberalization programmes. Other research in economics relates economic success to soundness of the exchange rate regime.

Pakistan, like other developing countries, has had a variety of exchange rate regimes and an evolution of exchange rate policy in response to changing domestic priorities and international considerations. While the exchange rate policy in the first three decades left much to be desired, since 1982 it has been relatively sound, with the exchange rate used as an active instrument of policy.

The current world exchange rate system, after the collapse of the Bretton Woods system, is characterized by a system known as 'dirty float', in which governments intervene in the markets in the short-run to smooth out the fluctuations in the exchange rate, but allow the market to determine the long-run equilibrium rate. Under a freely floating exchange rate system, where the government does not have to take explicit account of the balance of payments when formulating policy, it has more autonomy in determining its objectives. However, given the greater integration of the financial system, shocks are easily transferable between countries. The success of an exchange rate regime depends on its abiltiy to weather these shocks and create minimum disruption to the orderly functioning of the currency market.

EVOLUTION OF EXCHANGE RATE POLICY

Pakistan's exchange rate regime has gone through three different phases. In the first phase, from 1947 to 1972, the exchange rate was not used as a policy instrument, but was used to respond occasionally to balance of payments crises. In the second phase, from 1972 to 1982, the rupee was unified and the system of multiple exchange rates which had developed in the 1960s was abolished. In the third period, from 1982 to the present, the rupee was put on a managed float system, and a deliberate policy was followed to achieve a targeted path for the nominal effective exchange rate. Important objectives of the new policy were to boost Pakistan's monetary stability and to increase its competitiveness.

The first stage of Pakistan's exchange rate policy was characterized by a fixed exchange rate regime. Characterized by the nonuse of the rupee as a policy instrument, this regime had occasional devaluations in response to payments crises. In accordance with the stipulation of the International Monetary Fund that a currency could only be devalued if there was a fundamental imbalance in the balance of payments position, Pakistan only devalued in response to these crises. After a decision not to devalue in 1949 in spite of the neighbouring

Indian devaluation, Pakistan devalued the rupee in 1955 by 33.5 per cent in response to a balance of payments crisis. However, the response of exports to the change was not dramatic. In the 1960s the exchange rate was a passive instrument, with concentration on export incentive schemes rather than devaluation to boost export performance and improve the current account.

The second stage of the exchange rate regime was the period from 1972 to 1981, when the exchange rate was closely tied to the dollar. On 12 May 1972 the Bhutto administration, in the most major exchange rate reform in Pakistani history, devalued the real effective exchange rate by 62 per cent, unified all existing multiple exchange rates, and established a new par value of Rs 10 per US dollar (Mohsin Khan, 1990). Thereafter, it was kept fixed to the dollar for almost ten years. Although the nominal rate was relatively constant over the next decade, the real rate fluctuated in response to changes in the dollar's international position and international inflation. During this period, as in the previous one, the exchange rate was still not used as an active instrument. In spite of the uncertain international macroeconomic environment and the necessity of maintaing the stability of the exchange rate system, Pakistani policymakers were averse to broadening the exchange rate policy. Two major reasons were advanced for not using the exchange rate to achieve balance of payments objectives (Khan, 1990). Firstly, it was postulated that foreign trade flows, especially workers' remittances, were not responsive to changes in relative prices. The implication that followed from this line of thinking was that an exchange rate policy would be powerless and ineffective. Secondly, it was apprehended that further devaluation of the rupee would create inflationary pressures, which the government wanted to avoid in the inflation-prone international economy of the 1970s.

A series of econometric studies have shown the erroneous nature of the government's contention that exchange rate policy was ineffective. One study confirmed the hypothesis that an appreciation of the real exchange rate would affect both exports and imports and reduce the inflow of worker's remittances (Khan, 1990). In another study estimating equations for various categories of imports from 1969-70 to 1983-4, it was found that the relative price elasticities were statistically significant for many categories of imports (Sarmad and Mahmood, 1987). The main finding was that trade and services are sensitive to exchange rate changes.

The third stage of the exchange rate regime started in 1982, when the government adopted the managed float. Faced with a balance of payments crisis and an appreciating currency, the government de-linked from the dollar and adopted a flexible exchange rate policy. While the US dollar remained the intervention currency, the official dollar/rupee exchange rate was changed continuously to achieve a targeted path for the nominal effective exchange rate (Haque and Montiel, 1991). The main rationale for the change was to sustain a desired level of external competitiveness through the management of a nominal exchange rate system to achieve a desired outcome for the real effective exchange rate.

An analysis of the exchange rate movement since 1982 yields very interesting conclusions (Haque and Montiel, 1991). Firstly, the real effective exchange rate has not remained constant for any significant stretch of time since the managed float system was adopted. In fact, there has been a steady depreciation since that time. Secondly, the US dollar exchange rate has been relatively smooth, contrary to what one would have expected from an economy hit by a series of macroeconomic shocks— high external interest rates, oil price hikes, and reduced remittance inflows (Haque and Montiel, 1991). Thirdly and most significantly, the nominal effective exchange rates (NEER) and the real effective exchange rate (REER) have had a remarkably close association. Since the NEER is a nominal, policy-determined variable while the REER is an endogenous variable, this correlation need not be true (Haque and Montiel, 1991).

In an important paper, two divergent reasons were cited for this association (Haque and Montiel, 1991). On the one hand, the stickiness of the domestic price level has been perceived as allowing the authorities to achieve a secular appreciation of the REER, making the real rate a policy variable rather than an endogenous variable. On the other hand, the close association between the two exchange rates was achieved through a nominal depreciation rather than through an adjustment in relative price levels between Pakistan and its trading partners. The authors find that the depreciation in the REER since the adoption of the managed float significantly reflects a decrease in external receipts of workers' remittances and official transfers during this period. This finding goes against some international evidence that suggests that nominal exchange rates have been driven by pressures arising more from the capital account than the current account (Goldstein et al, 1992).

Regardless of the causes of this depreciation, one of the striking facts about the Pakistani economy during the post-1982 period was the low export elasticity to exchange rates. In spite of notable depreciations in currency, the current account was not significantly affected. Lack of econometric work notwithstanding, a casual analysis of the data shows a significant discrepancy between the magnitude of exchange rate depreciation and export expansion. The pattern of the early years is repeated as devaluation fails to lead to an export surge. Various explanations seem to be plausible. Sophisticated 'elasticity' pessimists argue that devaluation in the South Asian context cannot work simply because the government's control regime can weaken the supply response (Joshi and Little, 1994). Other arguments range from weaknesses in incentives to exporters to adverse terms of trade to the fixed quota for textile exports—the largest component of Pakistan's total exports. Conventional economic theory suggests that, due to downward rigidity in wage and prices, nominal devaluation in an economy will improve the current account only if it is accompanied by a reduction in expenditure. All explanations agree that lack of change in the fiscal and trade outcomes will mitigate any positive effects of devaluation.

FUTURE OF THE EXCHANGE RATE REGIME

As Pakistan enters the twenty-first century, it can be seen that there are considerable benefits as well as dangers in economic integration with the wider world economy. There is significant debate in both academic and policy circles regarding the advantages and disadvantages of the managed float system. While proponents of the 'dirty float' suggest that the system gives governments flexibility in adjusting to macroeconomic and structural changes and protects the economy from exogenous monetary shocks, critics argue that the new system creates considerable uncertainty, actually heightens vulnerability to shocks, and results in an exchange rate structure that is not reflective of real economic 'fundamentals'.

Nadeem ul Haque and Peter Montiel have argued that part of Pakistan's relatively satisfactory performance during the 1980s and 1990s can be attributed to a fairly skilful management of this regime, allowing Pakistan to avoid the severe external crises associated with fixed nominal pegs and the inflationary repercussions of certain external shocks under a fixed real peg (Haque and Montiel, 1991). They stress the way the authorities have tracked the depreciation. They conclude that, while short-run exchange policy must be guided by the current state of the real effective exchange rate relative to its perceived equilibrium level, in the long run, exchange rate policy depends critically on the economy's long-run inflation target, which itself depends on fiscal policy and on the methods Pakistan chooses to finance its growing fiscal deficit.

Arguments suggesting that it is the exchange rate depreciation itself which is responsible for the fiscal problem do not seem plausible in Pakistan's case. Evidence from India suggests that devaluation does not have a contractionary effect on government finance.

Vijay Joshi and I.M.D. Little, in their seminal book on the Indian economy, which has considerable applicability to Pakistan, have argued that the exchange rate cannot be a prime factor in explaining the fiscal deficit. Responding to the structuralist contention that the direct effect of devaluation is to worsen public finances, they argue that the combination of positive net transfers from abroad, high tariff rates that ensure an increase in government revenue in case of an appreciation of the currency, and the cost-plus basis of public sector enterprise financing have ensured that currency depreciation would not have adverse fiscal consequences.

One important point to examine is the linkages between fiscal, monetary, and exchange rate policies—their points of congruence as well as their points of departure. It is this growing conflict with fiscal and monetary policy that may weaken exchange rate policy. In Pakistan, one of the foremost objectives of monetary policy has been price stability. In order to accommodate this, interest rate policy has been aggressive, conflicting with the objective of achieving exchange rate stability. A policy of maintaining the growth of money supply at stable levels in order to minimize inflationary dangers has' created a very distorted interest rate structure in Pakistan, and thus can have negative effects on the exchange rate, which is linked to the interest rate. Thus, the presence of dual and conflicting objectives creates a policy dilemma for the government. In a similar vein, fiscal policy objectives— broadening tax base, financing deficit through monetization— may not coincide with the aim of exchange rate stability. This disharmony between policies, especially at a time when fiscal deficits in Pakistan have clearly become unsustainable, can undermine exchange rate stability.

The implications of exchange rate variability on the Pakistani economy are still not fully understood. There is some empirical evidence that the move to floating exchange rates has increased uncertainty, and that this has reduced both the level of international trade and its rate of growth (Peree and Steinherr, 1989). Whether exchange rate variability increases in coming years as financial systems get more integrated and shocks can be passed on relatively easily remains to be seen.

In conclusion, the success of Pakistan's economic policy will depend on its ability to maintain fiscal discipline. The growing fiscal deficit is an omen hanging over exchange rate policy. The resolution of Pakistan's fiscal crisis will determine the future of its exchange rate regimes.

INTERNATIONAL FACTORS

Pakistan's concerns about exchange rate fluctuation come at a time when there is considerable criticism about the demerits of the post-Bretton Woods system. Critics of the managed float system have viewed the excessive swings in real exchange rates as potentially damaging to developing economies. The reasons cited for the high variability of the present exchange rate system boil down to a combination of two factors—volatility and misalignment (Goldstein et al, 1992). Volatility, referring to short-term fluctuations, and misalignments, persistent departures of real exchange rates from their equilibrium values, have prompted a re-examination of the premises of the floating exchange rate system.

Real exchange rates have fluctuated much more since the breakdown of the Bretton Woods system in the early 1970s. While the positive view of this fluctuation suggests that they facilitate adjustment to changes in real economic conditions, the negative view argues that real exchange rates move for reasons that have nothing to do with real productivity. The empirical fact that movements in the nominal exchange rate over the last two decades have far exceeded changes in ratios of national labour costs shows that the terms of international competition have varied widely for reasons unrelated to changes in physical production or developments in domestic prices and wages.

ASSESSMENT OF EXCHANGE RATE SYSTEM

An assessment of Pakistan's exchange rate experience uptil the mid 1990s, compares favourably with that of many developing countries. Like Thailand, India, and Sri Lanka, Pakistan has historically been a low-inflation country, and a solid exchange rate regime, with its commitment to exchange rate stability, in combination with conservative monetary policy, helped Pakistan avoid the macroeconomic destabilization that afflicted much of Latin America in the 1980s. By prudent monetary and exchange rate management, Pakistan was spared much of the terrible effects of the adverse linkages between overvalued exchange rates, low export performance, poor agricultural growth, and destabilizing capital inflows seen in some parts of the world, especially in sub-Saharan Africa. Econometric work has shown strong links between countries with volatile exchange rate policies and countries suffering from debt crisis. In Pakistan, devaluation was usually perceived as potentially inflationary and damaging to the economy and was only used as a policy instrument in exceptional circumstances. Despite a series of adverse shocks in the 1970s and 1980s (remittance flows, oil shocks, changes in the terms of trade) the exchange rate system has managed to shelter Pakistan from the spillover effects.

Mohsin Khan, Bijan Aghelvi, and Peter Montiel make the very important point that there is no ideal exchange rate regime, but that the optimal management of the exchange rate depends on the policymakers' economic objectives, the sources of shock to the economy, and the structural characteristics of the economy in question. Furthermore, they argue that developing countries undertaking adjustment need to strike the appropriate balance between restrictive financial policies and exchange rate adjustment in order to improve external competitiveness.

To Pakistan's credit, it has followed such a policy mix since 1982 until recently. However, new macroeconomic crises threaten to erode the gains achieved. It would be fair to argue that Pakistan's current macroeconomic problems have emerged in spite of a solid exchange rate regime, and are due to fiscal indiscipline, not a misguided exchange rate policy. Whether the close association between the real effective exchange rate and the nominal effective exchange rate will continue remains to be seen. The vexing issue remains the stagnant export growth even in the face of very significant currency depreciation. Since 1995,

Pakistan has devalued its currency several time but the impact on export expansion has been minimal. This once again confirms that non-price factors including the bureaucratic procedures and hindrances may be more effective in muting the response and thus generating low elasticities. If the elasticity could somehow be boosted, Pakistan's economy would partly compensate for the fiscal indiscipline which has resulted in such a high fiscal deficit.

TABLE 3.1
TRENDS IN FEDERAL AND
PROVINCIAL EXPENDITURES
(In Percentage of GDP)

	1972-3	1980-1	1985-6	1990-1	1995-6
Current Expenditure	17.8	15.2	18.4	18.8	19.5
1) Defence	6.9	5.5	6.9	6.4	5.5
2) Interest	1.9	2.0	3.8	4.2	6.1
Development Expenditure	6.8	7.8	7.7	6.5	4.3
1) Federal	3.9	6.2	5.4	5.0	3.1
2) Provincial	2.9	1.6	2.3	1.5	1.2
Total Expenditure	24.6	23.0	26.1	25.3	23.9
1) Federal	17.4	18.3	19.4	19.8	17.6
2) Provincial	7.2	4.7	6.7	5.5	6.3
Budget Deficit	2.6	4.7	8.1	8.8	6.3

Source: World Bank, IMF, Pakistan Economic Survey (various issues)

TABLE 3.2
GOVERNMENT CURRENT REVENUES 1994-5:
INTERGOVERNMENTAL DISTRIBUTION
(In Billions of Rupees)

	Amount of Revenue Collected	Per centage Share	Amount of Revenue Retained	Percentage Share
Federal Government	324.3	90.2	222.6	63.1
1) Taxes	249.5	69.3	151.8	42.2
2) Non-tax	74.8	20.8	74.8	20.8
Provincial Government	17.7	4.9	112.0	31.1
1) Taxes	12,531	3.4	9.4	2.6
2) Non-tax	5,180	1.4	4.9	1.3
3) Tax Transfers	-	-	97.7	27.1
Local Government	17,521	4.8	20.8	5.8
1) Taxes	11,538	3.2	111.5	3.2
2) Non-tax	5,983	1.6	5.9	1.6
3) Tax Transfers	-	-	3.1	.8
Other Grants	-	-	0.24	.0

Source: Ministry of Finance data

TABLE 3.3
VERTICAL IMBALANCES IN PAKISTAN

	Revenue Share	Expenditure Share	Surplus/Deficit
National	90.7	67.1	23.6
Provincial	4.9	28.8	-23.3
Local	4.4	4.1	-0.3

TABLE 3.4
SUB-NATIONAL TAX - GDP RATIOS

	Provincial	Local	Total
1980-1	.77	.58	1.35
1984-5	.67	.63	1.30
1989-90	.59	.62	1.21
1994-5	.69	.63	1.32

TABLE 3.5
GROWTH OF MAJOR FEDERAL EXPENDITURE COMPONENTS
(annual growth rates)

	1979-80	1990-1	1995-6
Development	28.1	7.1	2.8
Defence	14.8	14.6	11.7
Debt-servicing	16.3	20.0	18.6
General Admin.	29.8	14.1	19.4

TABLE 3.6
SECTORAL ALLOCATION OF BANK CREDIT
(Percentage of Total Allocation)

Year	Agriculture	Manufacturing	Commerce	Other
1965	6.5	38.8	37.1	17.6
1970	9.6	43.2	30.7	16.5
1975	11.1	40.7	30.3	17.9
1980	12.3	37.5	23.2	27.0
1985	20.1	48.5	21.4	10.0
1990	27.5	41.3	21.0	10.2

Source: Malik, Sohail, *Pakistan's Economic Performance 1947-1993: A Descriptive Analysis*, Sure Publishers, Lahore 1994.

TABLE 3.7
TAX-GNP RATIOS

1949-50	4.7
1959-60	6.1
1964-5	8.2
1969-70	9.1
1974-5	12.3
1979-80	14.6
1984-5	13.3
1989-90	14.0
1995-6	14.1

TABLE 3.8
COMPOSITION OF TAXATION
(Percentage Distribution)

Year	Income and Corporation	Customs	Sales Tax	Excise Tax
1950	16.0	56.8	12.4	7.2
1960	22.8	40.1	12.2	20.4
1970	10.0	35.0	8.2	45.7
1980	16.9	41.0	7.8	31.6
1990	12.6	44.4	13.7	20.2
1995	24.7	29.1	16.9	17.2

Source: *Economic Survey* (various issues), Ministry of Finance, Government of Pakistan, Islamabad

TABLE 3.9
PAKISTAN: CONSOLIDATED FEDERAL
AND PROVINCIAL REVENUE: 1990-1 TO 1995-6
(In Billions of Pakistan Rupees)

	1990-1	1991-2	1992-3	1993-4	1994-5	1995-6
Tax Revenue	130.9	164.4	178.4	208.7	257.5	305.3
Income and						
Profit	19.1	27.7	35.0	41.8	59.2	73.9
Excises	25.1	30.7	35.6	35.1	44.3	51.5
Sales Tax	16.9	20.8	23.6	30.4	43.6	50.8
International						
Trade	50.5	61.8	63.2	95.0	77.7	87.1

Source: *Recent Economic Developments in Pakistan*, International Monetary
Fund Country Report, Washington DC

TABLE 3.10
SELECTED INFLATION RATES

Year	WPI General	CPI General	WPI Food	WPI Raw Mat.	WPI Manufact.	WPI Fuel
1960-9	2.6	3.3	2.6	2.0	3.4	3.3
1970-9	13.5	11.9	13.4	12.9	11.7	17.8
1980-9	7.1	7.5	7.2	6.9	7.0	7.2
1990-1	11.7	12.6	9.0	7.1	17.7	16.8
1991-2	9.3	9.6	10.2	11.0	9.5	4.9
1992-3	7.1	9.3	10.6	8.4	3.3	1.2
1996-7	13.0	11.8	11.8	24.2	11.9	17.4

Source: *Economic Survey*, Ministry of Finance, Government of Pakistan,
various issues

TABLE 3.11
INFLATION RATE IN PAKISTAN

Year	Inflation Rate
1959-60	5.0
1964-5	4.8
1969-70	4.1
1974-5	26.7
1979-80	10.7
1984-5	7.5
1989-90	6.0
1996-7	11.4

Source: Malik, Sohail, *Pakistan's Economic Performance 1947-1993: A Descriptive Analysis*, Sure Publishers, Lahore 1994
Economic Survey, Ministry of Finance, Government of Pakistan, (various issues).

TABLE 3.12
MONEY AND INTEREST RATES—AN
INTERNATIONAL COMPARISON

Country	Average Annual Growth Rate of Money (per cent)		Average Outstanding Money as Percentage of GDP			Average Annual Inflation (GDP Deflator)
	1970-80	1980-93	1970	1980	1993	1980-93
Pakistan	17.1	14.2	41.2	38.7	41.9	7.4
Bangladesh	NA	18.0	NA	18.4	33.1	8.6
India	17.5	16.7	23.6	36.2	44.1	8.7
Indonesia	35.9	26.3	7.8	13.2	48.2	8.5
Sri Lanka	23.1	15.6	22.0	35.3	36.3	11.1
Argentina	143.4	356.7	21.6	19.0	15.0	374.3
Mexico	26.6	57.8	26.9	27.5	31.9	57.9
Brazil	52.7	NA	23.0	18.4	NA	423.4
Korea	30.4	21.9	31.6	31.2	62.7	6.3
Egypt	26.0	21.4	33.5	52.2	95.6	13.6
Turkey	32.9	60.6	27.9	17.2	21.2	53.5

Source: *World Development Report*, 1995, World Bank

Note: Money Stock is broadly defined

TABLE 3.13
FINANCIAL DEEPENING IN PAKISTAN

Year	M2/GDP (Percentage) Average
1961-70	49.5
1971-80	44.2
1981-90	45.6
1991-6	44.6
	Rate (Percentage)
1961-81	-1.0
1982-95	-2.0

M2 is defined as currency in circulation + demand deposits + time deposits

Source: *Economic Survey*, various issues, Ministry of Finance, Government of
Pakistan

TABLE 3.14
INCOME VELOCITY OF MONEY

Year	Income Velocity of M1	Income Velocity of M2
1980-1	3.7	2.7
1989-90	3.4	2.8
1994-5	4.3	2.6
1996-7	4.6	2.5

Source: *Economic Survey* 1997-1998, Ministry of Finance, Government of
Pakistan, Islamabad

TABLE 3.15
STRUCTURE OF CONSOLIDATED EXPENDITURE
(Percentage Share)

	1975-6	1986-7
A. Current	61.8	71.2
Defence	25.1	25.1
Interest	7.6	14.3
Subsidies	9.2	6.2
Others	19.9	25.6
B. Development	38.2	28.8
Current	15.3	18.4
Development	9.5	7.5
Total	24.8	25.9
Overall Deficit	9.6	7.8

TABLE 3.16
OVERALL FISCAL TRENDS
(Percentage of GDP)

Year	Revenues	Expenditure	Fiscal Deficit
1950	6.3	9.4	3.1
1960	9.9	10.7	0.6
1970	15.4	NA	NA
1980	16.8	23.9	7.1
1990	18.6	25.7	6.6
1996	17.5	23.9	6.3

TABLE 3.17
ELASTICITIES OF MAJOR TAXES

	1952-3 to 1963-4	1972-3 to 1979-80	1979-80 to 1992-3
Income and Corporate Tax	1.52	0.83	0.84
Customs Duties	NA	1.26	0.73
Central Excise	1.61	1.28	0.41
Sales Tax on Domestic Goods	NA	0.46	1.97
Land Revenue on Irrigation Charges	0.80	0.32	NA

Source: Ahmed and Amjad (1984); Sohail Malik et al. (1995)

CHAPTER 4

INVESTING IN PEOPLE: EDUCATION, POPULATION, HEALTH, AND POVERTY ALLEVIATION

INTRODUCTION

One of the paradoxes of the Pakistani economy has been the persistence of widening income inequalities and weak social development in spite of high growth rates. The adverse distributional consequences of a capital-intensive trade and industrial policy, coupled with a skewed agrarian land distribution and a political economy based on rent-seeking by a small group of the population, have contributed to Pakistan's high poverty profile. Although incidence of absolute poverty seems to have declined in the 1970s and 1980s, the speed of the decline has not been as rapid as other fast-growing countries. There are indications that the incidence of poverty has risen in the 1990s. High agricultural growth rates have not made an appreciable dent on rural poverty, and the high growth rates in the large-scale manufacturing sector, due to their low employment absorption, have not had a positive effect on the urban poor. The open unemployment and disguised unemployment rates would have been much higher but for the safety valve provided by migration to the Middle East in the 1970s and 1980s.

Poverty alleviation and redistribution of income have been central concerns of development economists since the early 1970s, although the mechanisms to reduce poverty are still debatable. The preoccupation with poverty alleviation and equitable income distribution goes beyond the narrow economic dimension. Social cohesion and stability among and within nations owe a great deal to both the actual and the perceived sense of equity and access to opportunities for production and employment. Lifting out of poverty and a rise in income and consumption provide greater command over commodities for poor households. Furthermore, recognition of the importance of human capital has been one of the key themes in development economics in the last two decades. The idea is that investment in assisting the poor has important spillover effects on the rest of the economy, besides the alleviation of poverty. 'Redistribution with growth' stresses the importance of income equalization as a prerequisite for economic takeoff. In sum, a country's success in the alleviation of poverty is vital not only for its developmental success, but for maintaining political and social stability.

The hypothesis that economic growth and equality are incompatible, at least in the initial stages, advocated by Simon Kutznets, has been challenged in recent years by a large volume of research that has found that policies fostering economic growth are not inconsistent with reducing poverty. The effects of growth on inequality depend on the initial distribution of assets, the nature of imperfections in markets (especially the capital market), the pattern of growth, factor bias in technology, and government policies, especially fiscal, social welfare, and trade (Bardhan, 1995). The theory that growth can have positive effects on the alleviation of poverty is borne out by much recent research. Lipton and Ravallion (1995) report estimates for eight developing countries (Bangladesh, Brazil, Ivory Cost, Indonesia, Morocco, Nepal, and Tunisia) that a 2 per cent annual rate of growth in consumption per person will typically result in a decline in the poverty gap index of 3 to 8 per cent (Lipton and Ravallion, 1995). The East Asian Miracle demonstrates a positive link between growth and more equal income distribution. There is growing empirical evidence that supports the claim that a reasonable degree of equality is good for development.

DIMENSIONS AND TRENDS

From a methodological point of view, most studies on poverty in Pakistan are limited to estimating the headcount ratios for single years based on the Household Income and Expenditure Surveys (HIES). These studies are thus limited by the grouped nature of the published data from these surveys and by the arbitrary basis on which poverty lines have been set up (Malik et al, 1994). S. Malik, in his recent seminal work, has stressed the need to assess the overall gains in welfare in terms of poverty, as measured from private incomes and consumption, and in terms of the levels of public incomes, measured through the trend in social indicators and public expenditures (Malik, 1994). While there is a relative dearth of analysis of poverty in Pakistan, the literature on poverty in India is voluminous and many of those findings are analytically relevant to Pakistan.

Nevertheless, there is a widespread consensus that the poverty profile of Pakistan followed a Kuznetian trajectory. In the early years, the extent of poverty in Pakistan increased, verifying Kutznet's hypothesis of an inverse relationship between economic development and income inequality. In the 1970s and 1980s, the trend had been reversed, in terms of headcount index, but more recent data supports a stagnation of this trend (Table 4.1). Observed income inequality measures have fluctuated widely, but adjusted measures point to a widening gap between the top and bottom quintiles.

A number of papers have analysed the issue of poverty in Pakistan, surveying the trends using different methodologies. Two main bodies of evidence suggest that poverty increased in the early years but declined from the early 1970s (World Bank b, 1995). The first source is the published data on the national accounts, the distribution of household income, and the real wages of unskilled workers. The second is a number of studies that have sought to measure the incidence of poverty based on survey data. While both systems have their relative strengths and weaknesses, the trends are similar, regardless of the methodology used.

In the pioneering work of S. M. Naseem in the early 1970s, an analysis of the trends in rural poverty using the household surveys of income and expenditure showed that the proportion of people in poverty, with poverty being arbitrarily defined as the level of expenditure consistent with the intake of 95 per cent of the minimum caloric requirement, increased during the 1960s in spite of the high growth rates of the rural economy (Naseem, 1977). Since the head-count measure of determining poverty is highly sensitive to definitions of the poverty line, a relaxation of the line shows that the findings of increased poverty do not hold any validity. Thus, the results for the 1950s and 1960s are ambiguous.

The trends from 1970 to the present time tell an entirely different story. Consumption poverty has declined since the mid-1970s due to a combination of factors. While GDP per capita increased in real terms by about 70 per cent between 1972-3 and 1993-4, private consumption per capita increased by about 50 per cent. Given the difficulties in estimating poverty based on income declarations, the consumption poverty measure is the best index of poverty in Pakistan. Moreover, this result is also substantiated by other complementary indicators. The data on the real wages of unskilled urban construction workers and of agricultural workers show that average real wages have increased annually by 1.1 to 2 per cent (depending on location) for the former and 3 per cent for the latter since the mid-1980s (World Bank b, 1995).

The evidence for this reduction in poverty is corroborated by a plethora of studies that use survey data to measure the extent of poverty. Studies that have measured the incidence of poverty for one, two, or three years using different methodologies, have confirmed the decline in consumption poverty.

Irfan and Amjad (1984) derive estimates of the proportion of people in poverty in 1979, using a poverty line that assumes 2550 calories per day per adult equivalent and actual observations, as opposed to the grouped data analysis of the previous researchers, to determine an income-based poverty line of Rs 109 per capita in 1979 prices. Their finding is that the incidence of poverty increased from 32 per cent in 1963-4 to over 43 per cent in 1969-70 and then declined to 29 per cent in 1978-9 (Irfan and Amjad, 1984).

Malik, using grouped data from the Household and Expenditure Surveys from 1963-4 to 1984-5, sees an increase in the per centage of poor households in the 1960s and a decline in the 1970s and 1980s (Malik, 1988). Ahmad and Ludlow, attempting to avoid the arbitrariness involved in the construction of the poverty line, use several different lines to measure poverty, and then take the medium line to find that poverty declined by about 20 per cent between 1979 and 1985 (Ahmad and Ludlow, 1989). Ercelawn, using a very strict concept of undernourishment to define absolute poverty, finds that the incidence of poverty on the whole has been quite modest, and regards Pakistan as fortunate in relation to acute poverty and its risks of malnourishment and starvation (Ercelawn, 1990).

Malik (1993) finds that, on aggregate, monthly expenditures of Rs 185 per adult equivalent were required in 1984-5, Rs 241 in 1987-8 and Rs 320.42 in 1990-1 to meet the minimum calorie requirement of 2550 calories per adult equivalent per month, with considerable variation across regions. Moreover, the finding that the expenditures of the poor grow at rates higher than that of the overall price level in order to maintain the same minimum calorie requirement is a conclusion with disturbing implications.

Further statistics confirm these findings. The national head-count ratio, which measures the incidence of poverty, fell from 46 per cent in 1984-5 to 37 per cent in 1987-8 and then to 34 per cent in 1990-1, using the reference poverty line of Rs 296 per capita monthly expenditure in 1991-2 rural prices and Rs 334 in urban prices (World Bank b, 1995). Between 1990-1 and 1993-4, a 3 per cent growth in private per capita consumption reduced the incidence of poverty from 34 per cent to 22 per cent, but the findings must be taken with a degree of scepticism given the scarcity of data on the distribution of household consumption at the time.

A comparison with other countries for the period 1984-5 to 1990-1 shows that, while the average annual compound rate of decline in Pakistan's head-count ratio was 4.9 per cent, a comparable East Asian figure was 8 per cent (World Bank b, 1995). However, combined poverty head-count ratios for sub-Saharan Africa and Eastern Europe remained constant during 1985-90, while the combined poverty head-count ratio for the Middle East and North Africa increased during the period, as did that for Latin America and the Caribbean. Thus, Pakistan performed well in the 1970s and 1980s when compared to its international competitors, with the exception of East Asia. The more recent slowdown in the economy since the early 1990s does suggest that the incidence of poverty may have risen. Although there is no corroborative empirical data, a number of observers have used the secondary and collateral information to arrive at this conclusion. The results of the next household survey will reveal if this hypothesis is borne out by the evidence.

The migration of a significant proportion of unskilled workers to the Middle East after the oil price boom and their remittances, averaging $2 billion annually, equivalent to 6-7 per cent of GDP, played an important role. The home remittances accrued to the families belonging to the levels closer to the poverty line, and these income flows enabled them to be lifted out of poverty.

URBAN AND RURAL PROFILES

Generally, urban and rural poverty trends have followed an identical pattern to the national trends, with an increase in the first two decades followed by a decline since the mid-1970s. However, the magnitudes of change have varied more. While in the 1950s and 1960s the poverty growth rates were higher in the rural than in the urban sectors, in the 1980s the incidence of poverty fell more in urban areas than in the rural area (World Bank b, 1995). Poverty incidence has, nevertheless, been significantly higher in rural areas than urban areas, both in absolute terms and in relative terms, although the higher cost of living in urban areas reduces that gap significantly (Table 4.2). A variety of different indices reach identical conclusions about the geographical distribution of poverty. In the Household Income and Expenditure Survey of 1990-1, while 28 per cent of the urban areas are poor, the rural figure is 36.9 per cent, leading to a national average of 34.0 per cent, since 70 per cent of people live in rural areas and 30 per cent in urban areas.

Currently, of the urban poor, 44 per cent are wage earners, 36 per cent are self-employed, and 20 per cent are either inactive or undetermined (World Bank b, 1995). Poverty head-counts correspond well with the level of asset holdings in both the wage-earner and self-employed category; among wage-earners, white-collar workers have the lowest poverty head-count of 22 per cent, while casual and manual labour have the highest incidence, at 38.8 per cent in the self-employed sector. The highest incidence of urban poverty was found, among those whose assets are valued at less than Rs 1,000. The poverty head-count ratio for this group was 51 per cent. This group, consisting of about 10 per cent of the urban sample, together with the industrial proletariat, compose the backbone of urban poverty in Pakistan.

In the rural sector, where the bulk of Pakistan's poor reside, tenants constitute a sizable group of 14 per cent and have a poverty head-count at 44 per cent, while agricultural labourers, making 7 per cent of the population, have a poverty head-count of 56 per cent (World Bank b, 1995). Among non-agricultural rural households, the groups with the highest poverty head-counts are casual workers (at 45 per cent) and the self-employed with less than Rs 1,000, having a headcount ratio of 46 per cent. Asset ownership in the rural areas corresponds to the urban pattern and is inversely proportional to poverty incidence. In the agricultural sector, a highly unequal land distribution creates large differences in wealth and income.

The poverty profile of Pakistan therefore leads to the following picture. Poverty is more widespread among the rural population, and the groups that are likely to fall below the poverty line are landless agricultural labourers and casual workers. In the urban areas, the poor are the self-employed with assets valued at less than Rs 1,000.

INCOME DISTRIBUTION TRENDS

The inequitable agrarian structure, the industrial bias of Pakistan's development strategy, the alternation of economic regimes, the import substitution trade strategies, and the political economy of rent-seeking and absence of strong countervailing forces that could challenge the power of the elites have all influenced the extent and intensity of income distribution in Pakistan. The links between economic policies and income distribution have been well-documented in the development literature, and Pakistan presents an interesting test case of the linkages.

The hypothesis that income inequality increases with economic growth is very plausible in Pakistan's case. The argument that the shift in the structure of production from agriculture to industry will result in higher capital-labour ratios in the expanding sector and a consequent rise in profits relative to wages and a further widening in income differentials due to rapid growth in demand for skilled labour bears merit for Pakistan. The household income Gini Coefficient, the leading indicator of income distribution, declined in the 1960s from 0.356 in 1963-4 to 0.345 in 1971-2. But it has gradually risen since the early 1970s to 0.407 by 1990-1 (Table 4.3). Except for a decline in the mid-1980s, the overall trend for the last two decades indicates growing income inequality. While in 1971-2 the ratio of the household income share of the highest 20 per cent of the population relative to the lowest 20 per cent was 5.4 per cent, by 1985-6, it increased to 5.8 per cent, and by the early 1990s it had reached 6.1 per cent. Thus, income distribution had clearly worsened.

In an international comparison, Pakistan's performance was respectable compared to Latin America countries, which clearly have the most skewed income distribution, but was inferior to many of the countries in Asia in the 1980s. Estimates for the early 1970s do not show much difference between Pakistan and other Asian countries, but by the 1980s, Pakistan had lagged behind. The high growth performance of East Asian countries was accompanied by both poverty reduction and decline in income inequalities. However, Pakistan joins the rank of the 50 per cent of developing countries whose inequality has worsened with economic growth, especially in the last two decades. By contrast, countries such as Indonesia, Korea, Taiwan, the Philippines, and Sri Lanka have all had appreciable improvements in income distribution.

A recent study by Deininger and Squire calculates the ratio of the top quintile's share of income to the bottom quintile's share for a large number of developing countries (Deininger and Squire, 1997). This average ratio, that spans a twenty to thirty year period, in many cases looks quite favourable for Pakistan. But it masks the fact that the higher inequality of the 1980s and 1990s is offset by the low inequality of the 1970s (Table 4.4).

Thus, Pakistan presents the paradoxical picture of a country with both worsening income distribution and improved poverty alleviation. These contradictory findings can be reconciled when it is seen that, while economic growth did much to reduce the number of absolute poor, it did not result in an increase of the ratio of their income relative to the richer segment of the population.

DETERMINANTS OF INCOME INEQUALITY

A. AGRARIAN STRUCTURE

Being the mainstay of the economy and the area where most of the poor reside, the rural sector has been both the beneficiary and the victim of technological progress. The effects of agricultural change on rural poverty have been mixed as Pakistan has embarked on a whole series of policies to increase agricultural productivity. Thus, Pakistan provides a good background for an analysis of the effects of the pace and pattern of agricultural growth on poverty and income inequality.

The key factor affecting income distribution in the rural sector is the nature of the agrarian structure: the land tenurial system and the institutional climate. A large number of models have stressed the importance of the distribution of endowments and the potentially large increases in social welfare gained by an initial redistribution of assets (Banerjee and Newman, 1994). Bourguignon and Morrisson (1990) have found that, in a typical cross-sectional regression for a sample of developing countries, the distribution of land explains about 17 per cent of the variance in inequality (Borguignon and Morrisson, 1995). In this context, the impact of land reform policies must be assessed. Land reforms can have important direct and indirect effects on tenurial status and land distribution, thus influencing income levels of the bottom quintile in the rural areas. By providing security of tenure through land redistribution in favour of small peasants, tenants, and landless labourers, and by contributing to self-cultivation of land, land reforms can play a part in alleviating rural poverty. Both the Martial Law Regulations of 1959 and the 1972 Land Reforms were aimed at improving the rural distribution of income by instituting ceilings on landholdings and providing incentives to tenants to crop. However, given the meagre amounts of redistributed land, these reforms have not been far-reaching—they have provided benefits to about 10 per cent of the tenants, about 300,000 farm families, thus failing to make an appreciable dent on the inherited agrarian structure.

Compounding the failure of land reforms, thin credit markets have persistently been heavily biased towards the large landlords. Chenery, has argued that, without a redistribution of at least the increments of capital formation, other distributive measures are not likely to have a lasting impact on the poverty problem (Chenery, 1974). Despite increases in credit in recent years, credit in terms of sectoral GDP has been below 10 per cent. These imperfections, in credit and insurance markets, and the usually costly private adjustments to these imperfections, are the key to understanding the important distinctions between transient poverty, caused largely by relatively short-term income variability, and chronic poverty (Bardhan, 1995). Given the fragmentary and weak nature of the rural money markets in Pakistan, the dearth of credit from official sources to small farmers meant that the poor in rural areas could not overcome the critical credit shortages needed to buy important inputs to boost agricultural productivity as well as make productive investments in human capital, especially education. Bourguignon and Morrisson (1990) find that educational difference explains about one-fifth of the variance in inequality. Pakistan is a prominent example of a country where skewed land asset distribution, severe credit market imperfections, and differentials in educational attainments combine to negate the effects of high growth rates on improved income distribution.

Another factor influencing income inequality outcomes in the rural sector has been the technological change in agriculture. While in the 1950s, Pakistan's agricultural growth rate remained very low due to the industrial bias of the development strategy, the situation in the 1960s changed radically with the introduction of new technologies in seed, fertilizer, tubewells, and tractors, which dramatically boosted growth. In the 1950s, while the rural poor stagnated with little in the way of new employment or productivity gains, the number of landless workers had increased by 350 per cent between 1951 and 1961 (Naseem, 1977). The absence of any policies to improve the agricultural sector in the 1950s, and the intersectoral transfers from rural to urban sectors, had laid the foundation for a worsening urban-rural income gap.

By the mid-1960s, the Green Revolution in agriculture had resulted in spectacular increases in yields of wheat and rice. Although there is substantial evidence for the hypothesis that the biological and chemical innovations that generated this rapid growth in Pakistani agriculture have been scale-neutral in terms of cost per unit, mechanical innovations have had an adverse effect on income distribution because they have been capital-using and labour-displacing (Khan,Mohsin, 1991). Many small farmers participated in the seed and fertilizer revolution, perhaps lagging a year or so behind the large farmers in adopting the new techniques. The absence of significant scale economies meant that the fruits of agricultural research could be shared by all. The reduction in time required for land preparation and the increase in cropping intensity due to technological progress had a beneficial effect on agriculture.

However, in the two critical areas of tubewell technology and tractorization that accompanied the seed-fertilizer technology, the effects on income distribution were visibly negative. With regard to tubewells, subsidized credit was more readily available to large farmers because they possessed greater familiarity with administrative procedures. According to the Farm Mechanization Survey of 1968, 70 per cent of the tubewells in Pakistan were installed by farmers having more than 25 acres, while only 4 per cent were installed by the group possessing 0-13 acres (Naseem, 1977). Tractor mechanization has been perhaps the most income-redistributing of Pakistan's agricultural policies. Although the main rationale for the introduction of tractors was to improve cropping intensity, the big-farm bias of the tractorization programme has been strong, with estimates suggesting that the labour force per acre in mechanized areas has decreased by more than 50 per cent. According to a joint survey by the World Bank and the Agricultural Development Bank, of the farmers who received ADBP loans to purchase tractors, there was a 140 per cent increase in the average size of farms, from 25 acres to 109 acres per farm, with 80 per cent of the new land acquisition coming from land already in use (Naseem, 1977). Thus, the increase in large farm size meant a displacement of tenants and small farmers. Overall, the total labour used per cropped acre, made up of family, regular, and casual workers, dropped by 40 per cent, meaning a net destruction of five jobs per tractor; thus the total displacement effects of the 40,000 tractors introduced in the late 1960s and early 1970s has been about 200,000 workers. A variety of indirect effects of the farm mechanization programme on small landowners and wage labourers, such as the effects of tractorization on farm eviction rates, demand for land, and general level of wages, suggests that mechanization has had a much more negative effect on income distribution than the numbers show.

In a critical decomposition analysis using three-year panel data from 727 households, it was found that returns to labour and crop profitability in Pakistan were as important, if not more important, sources of agricultural income inequality than unequal landownership, as measured by land rent (Alderman, 1993). The policy implications of this are that, from the standpoint of the government, it is far easier to improve the productivity of land through subsidies, technology transfers, and sound pricing policies, as well as through the technologies of crop production, than to alter the distribution of land. Since Pakistan's strong feudal land tenure system is highly obstinate to change, perhaps the best way to alleviate rural poverty is through measures to create higher returns for labour and enhance the profitability of crops.

In sum, although technological progress resulted in some poverty reduction due to the spread of new varieties of inputs to small farmers, sharecroppers, and tenants, the less than uniform diffusion of technology in the critical areas of tractors and tubewells has resulted in worsening income distribution in the rural areas. Policies to promote high and sustained agricultural growth that favours small-scale farmers and landless labourers represent the best measures to improve the plight of the rural poor. Exploring the relationship between growth and poverty in rural India, Ravallion and Datt have found that measures of absolute rural poverty responded elastically to changes in mean consumption, but agricultural growth had no discernible impact on the share of total consumption going to the poor (Ravallion and Datt, 1995). Their finding that the rural poor can gain from agricultural growth, with about half of the long-run impact coming within three years, holds considerable promise for Pakistan. Major policy changes that address ways to improve the technical efficiency of inputs as well as cropping intensity are the best hope for improving rural income distribution. A sound land reform policy that reduces the power of the large landlords is also important, given the important role the skewed agrarian structure plays in fostering income inequality. The increase in the Gini Coefficient of the distribution of land from 0.52 in 1972 to 0.58 in 1991 needs to be reversed. Thus, it is vital to formulate a new agrarian reform policy.

B. TRADE AND INDUSTRY

Pakistan's industrial policy has been a major factor explaining the incidence and intensity of poverty and income inequality. The import substitution industrialization strategy followed for the first three decades of its existence have had a pronounced impact through a variety of channels and mechanisms. Firstly, the favourable treatment of industry was achieved by discrimination against agriculture and an underinvestment in agriculture, where most of the poor reside. The high intersectoral transfers from agriculture to industry, the turning of the terms of trade against agriculture, and the bias in agricultural exports due to overvalued exchange rates maintained to allow sustained industrial output and access to cheap capital imports, have militated against the agricultural poor.

Furthermore, within industry, the capital-intensive pattern of industrial development has led to a redistribution of income away from the urban poor and to the large industrialists. The perceived inequalities of the Ayub years and the high industrial concentration figures prompted the reforms of the Bhutto years. The preference for import-substituting manufacturing industries, supported by a high degree of effective protection, such as industrial chemicals, iron and steel, and petroleum products, and the neglect of the small-scale industries, in areas as diverse as sporting goods, leather manufactures, and surgical instruments, with their higher-than-average labour-intensive production, has translated into lower or declining incomes for those who did not participate in the large-scale manufacturing sector. The low absorption of labour force by the large-scale manufacturing sector exacerbated urban unemployment. Furthermore, poor labour legislation in the manufacturing sector, with unionization protecting few workers, did not help to improve the expansion of employment opportunities. Most of industrial profits were reinvested in labour-saving plant and equipment or absorbed by industrialists for conspicuous consumption. Industrial workers' wages also rose, albeit at a lower rate than the profits earned by the owners.

In order to improve the urban distribution of income, casual labourers and the self-employed with very small asset holdings must become the beneficiaries of government job-creation programmes and of targeted income and subsidy schemes. A system of providing basic social services to urban slums, in collaboration with NGOs, represents an important channel by which these issues can be addressed.

C. FISCAL POLICY

In many countries, government tax and expenditure policies have been instrumental in combating poverty and improving income distribution. The case of Pakistan stands on the other extreme— the tax system was highly regressive, based on indirect taxes, and the expenditure pattern favoured the well-to-do segments of the population. The low coverage and poor collection of direct taxes have meant that a large proportion of earned incomes is virtually exempt from any payment of taxes on income or property. The reliance on indirect taxes results in an unfair burden on lower deciles, thus having adverse effects on the poor and lowering their purchasing power.

The weakness in resource mobilization efforts has pushed Pakistan's fiscal deficit to 8 per cent of GDP in recent years, forcing the government to indulge in extensive borrowing to finance this deficit. Finance has not been available for important social welfare programmes that could assist the poor. The importance of lowering the deficit in order to have sustained economic growth has been well-recognized. Furthermore, the onset of structural adjustment programmes, under the sponsorship of the IMF and the World Bank, has caused Pakistan to focus more on the importance of maintaining its macroeconomic fundamentals in order to achieve long-term growth.

D. SOCIAL PROTECTION

Social protection in Pakistan is basically a composite of private and voluntary transfers and government arrangements. Since the social welfare system in Pakistan suffers from all the chronic weaknesses of such systems in developing countries, private transfers are currently the main means of protecting the economically disadvantaged.

The private social safety net in Pakistan is supported by large private, voluntary, inter-household transfers. Forty per cent of all households nationwide were part of the network of private transfers in 1991, with 30 per cent of these households net recipients of transfers and 10 per cent, net donors (World Bank b, 1995). Transfers have been especially important for the poor, with 48 per cent of households in the lowest income strata net recipients of transfers. These households have used the transfers to finance half of their development expenditures. The positive effect of private transfers on the poor can be gauged from the fact that the average consumption in households without transfers was only 64 per cent of the average consumption of households who were net recipients of private transfers (Rs 15, 617 compared with Rs 24,413) (World Bank b, 1995).

At the government level, two targeted income transfer programmes provide the rudiments of Pakistan's welfare state— the *zakat* and *ushr* programme and the *Bait-ul-Maal* programme. Together, they complement private flows to redistribute income.

Zakat and *ushr* are basically Islamic charity programmes of special taxes and transfers instituted in the early 1980s to assist the poor. Basically, these schemes finance income transfers to the poor specifically widows, orphans, and disabled individuals—with direct cash payments to 400,000 carefully selected nationwide beneficiaries at a rate of Rs 225 per beneficiary allowance. While *zakat* taxes are levied on a range of financial assets at a rate of 2.5 per cent annually, *ushr* taxes are levied on the produce of landowners that exceeded 948 kilograms of wheat or other crops of the same value. Organizationally structured at a multi-tier level, with central and regional offices, total *zakat* receipts are first apportioned between funds to be retained at the federal level and funds to be transferred to the provinces. However, in spite of all the strengths, in 1993-4 total *zakat* revenue amounted to Rs 2.844 million, which translated into a negligible 0.2 per cent of GDP; similarly, the total amount of *ushr* tax collected amounted to an insignificant Rs 200,000.

A wide range of criticism has raged in recent years over the efficacy of the programmes and their operational weaknesses (World Bank b, 1995). The misuse of *zakat* funds has been so patent that in 1991, although 50 per cent of benefits went to the poor, about 28 per cent went to people who cannot be considered poor. Furthermore, the number of direct beneficiaries of subsistence allowances exceeded 1.5 million in 1993, thus diluting the impact of the scheme. An average monthly payment of Rs 38 per direct beneficiary has done little to reduce the incidence of poverty. Theoretically, the current subsistence allowance of Rs 225 monthly should be adequate to finance the poor's income gap of Rs 84, defined as the average shortfall in the consumption of the poor relative to the poverty line. In practice, however, the presence of dependents and multiple beneficiaries has thinned the gains to any individuals. A third line of attack has focused on the inadequacy of revenue collection. Two prevailing practices, the withdrawal of deposits in the days before the collection dates and the false declaration of oneself as non-Muslim, have substantially reduced the *zakat* revenues, with Rs 1,767 million collected on savings accounts (Rs 3,494 million available) and Rs 527 million on fixed deposits (Rs 1,268 million available). These discrepancies suggest that violation of the codes is pervasive.

Another federal government programme, established in 1992 to help the poor that are not among *zakat's* target group, the

Bait-ul-Maal programme has several components, with the Food Subsidy Scheme (FSS), targeted to non-*zakat* recipient households whose monthly income is less than Rs 1,500, and the Individual Financial Assistance (IFA), targeted to widows, orphans, and disabled persons who also have monthly incomes of less than Rs 1,500 (World Bank b, 1995). While the IFA families receive Rs 300 monthly for a household head, and Rs ·50 monthly for each child up to a maximum of four, FSS benefits are Rs 150 monthly for each household. Unfortunately, like the *zakat* and *ushr* programmes, the *Bait-ul-Maal* has been strongly criticized for its use of household income ceiling as a screening device, given the problems associated with income assessment, and for its limited coverage, with only about 400,000 households receiving FSS benefits and 10, 280 receiving IFA benefits, thus ignoring more than 1.2 million households that are eligible beneficiaries. Thus, the programme does not seem to have made a major dent in poverty alleviation.

Although social welfare programmes are prominent and directed credit schemes popular, the impact of all government programmes on both rural and urban poverty is quite small. Only through sounder targeting, an improvement in coverage, and a repair of leakages and abuses of the system can these programmes improve Pakistan's income distribution. The delayed trickle-down effects of high growth rates has been so slow that a pro-poor policy action is vital. However, in the wake of the government's structural adjustment programmes and the consequent reductions in budgetary subsidies, these transfers will be increasingly difficult to expand, given the high political and administrative costs.

REGIONAL EQUITY

The gains from Pakistan's industrial development and agricultural growth have not been evenly distributed around the country (Pasha, and Hasan 1982). While Sindh and Punjab have been relatively prosperous, Balochistan and NWFP have remained relatively backward. The geographical location of much of Punjab and Sindh—around the Indus and its tributaries—as well as the large populations of those areas, has meant that development has been concentrated in that area. The choice of Karachi as capital, the ISI regime's capital-intensive industrial strategy, and the Green Revolution have all contributed to the development of Punjab and Sindh as leading regions of the country.

Estimates of poverty incidence show that Sindh is the most prosperous province and has a lower poverty incidence than Punjab. The Green Revolution was predominantly focused in the Punjab, and the adverse distribution consequences of mechanization seem to have been most prominent in Punjab. Rural South Punjab has a high incidence of poverty, with 50 per cent of the population below the poverty line, in comparison to rural North Punjab (26-32 per cent) and rural Sindh (31-6 per cent). While Punjab is richer than the other provinces, intra-provincial disparity is most prominent there. The NWFP is considerably poorer than the national average, with different estimates ranging between 20 and 40 per cent poverty incidence. Finally, Balochistan's poverty estimates waver between 22 and 41 per cent.

In an attempt to quantify the level of development of different districts using a wide variety of development criteria such as agricultural growth, industrial presence, housing, and human resource indicators it was found that Karachi, Lahore, Rawalpindi/Islamabad, Quetta, and Peshawar were the first five districts in terms of level of development (Pasha, and Hasan 1982). On the second rung, a large group of districts from Punjab, including Multan, Jhelum, and Sargodha, were found to show the broad-based character of regional development in Punjab. Of the country's 23 most underdeveloped districts, 9 are in Balochistan, 6 from Punjab, 5 from Sindh, and 3 from NWFP. Thus, while Balochistan is clearly the poorest region in the country, Punjab has not managed to redistribute its wealth and the fruits of the Green Revolution. While many of these findings are conventional wisdom, other findings of intra-provincial disparity show the presence of highly concentrated pockets in backward regions like Balochistan and NWFP, and large pockets of poverty in rural Sindh and rural Punjab. 15 per cent of the population of Punjab and 24 per cent of that of Sindh live in underdeveloped districts.

Many factors explain both inter-and intra-provincial disparities in income distribution. Literacy, housing, transport, basic municipal services, and sexual equality indicators have been found to be highly correlated with the overall level of development of a district, while income and wealth indicators are less important.

In conclusion, while Sindh and Punjab are the most advanced provinces, a district-level analysis reveals a more nuanced picture.

POPULATION

Rapid rates of population growth have emerged in recent years as the single most important factor thwarting the economic achievements of the less developed countries. The demographic decline witnessed in most parts of the world is beginning to reach South Asia, where high growth rates have eroded many of the positive achievements of development policy. Higher fertility has translated into lower per capita incomes and increased the burden on society. The economic costs of feeding, clothing, and educating a larger and larger population have been substantial, and the pressures on infrastructure and scarce resources have exacerbated.

Pakistan, together with Sub-Saharan countries, has been conspicuous in the persistence of population growth rates above 3 per cent. The economy's dependence on agriculture and the weak investment in education and health show the pernicious effects of high growth rates on the economic, political, and social structure of the society. The reductions in both current welfare and that of future generations is a factor that has to be taken seriously.

Despite an ambitious population planning programme begun with much fanfare in the mid-1960s, myriad public pronouncements on the importance of reductions in the population growth rate, and a host of policies and schemes to assist in fertility decline, the growth rate has not changed significantly since Partition. The rapid population growth rate in Pakistan has been responsible for a host of maladies—inability to spread the economic gains, difficulties in the absorption of labour by industries, and exacerbation of ethnic tensions. Despite repeated claims about the importance of human resources, population growth has been detrimental to Pakistan's economic performance. The human capital endowment in Pakistan, notwithstanding its quantity, has been qualitatively weak.

CHARACTERISTICS OF PAKISTAN'S POPULATION

Pakistan's population has been growing at a rate of over 3 per cent since the early 1970s, in comparison to a rate of 2 per cent in the first two decades of its history (Table 4.5). The current population of Pakistan, estimated at around 130 million, makes Pakistan the seventh most populous country in the world. The population growth rate has been so rapid that the population has quadrupled since the early 1950s. Although the accuracy of these figures is subject to the degree of coverage and accuracy of the censuses, there is an unmistakable acceleration of the growth rate since 1960 (Sathar, 1991).

The increase can be attributed to the decline in mortality rates from 31 per 1,000 in 1941 to less than 10 per 1,000 by 1998 (Table 4.5). This is mainly due to the curtailment of infectious diseases, especially cholera and smallpox, and the introduction of antibiotics (Sathar, 1991). Furthermore, there has been a marked increase in levels of sanitation. By contrast, the crude birth rate has decreased very slightly, from about 45 per 1,000 in 1941 to 36 per thousand in 1998. The total fertility rate, the number of children a woman bears during her reproductive span from 15 to 49, is estimated 5.6 births per woman. A large body of evidence has brought out the lack of decline of fertility rates in the last two decades (Sathar, 1984; Population Welfare Division, 1986). In spite of controversies, there is a consensus that fertility decline in Pakistan has not been significant.

Thus, mortality decline represents the greatest victory, in spite of the persistence of high rates of mortality in infants and in women—the infant mortality has stabilized at a relatively high level of 100 infant deaths per 1,000 live births, while female mortality exceeds male mortality, at least during the reproductive period (Sathar,1987; Irfan, 1986).

An analysis of the population data for Pakistan reveals a series of interesting trends. The most noteworthy is the increasing urbanization of the country. (Table 4.6). While 17.2 per cent of people lived in urban areas in 1951, by 1998 the figure had reached 32.5 per cent, with a corresponding decline in rural population. Due to a combination of high rates of natural increase and significant rural-urban migration influenced by the search for higher wages and the desire for a better life, the urban growth rate in the last two decades has been more than 4 per cent, with the urban population increasing more than sevenfold between the early 1950s and the late 1990s, in contrast to the less than fourfold increase of the rural population. Interestingly, and in contrast to other countries, urban fertility in Pakistan has not been found to be lower than rural fertility (Sathar, 1979; Casterline, 1984). The growth of large urban metropolises like Karachi, Lahore, and Faisalabad represents the triumph of the principle of urban agglomeration. It is important to note that in spite of its large index of urbanization, Pakistan remains a predominantly agrarian society, in explicit contrast to Latin American countries, where the majority of the population lives in the urban areas.

A second trend has been the larger male population as a percentage of the total population. Although the ratios of males to females has remained relatively constant over the last forty years, the larger male population at Partition has resulted in a significant difference in the magnitudes of the two populations.

Estimates for 1996 suggest that there are 6 million more males than females in Pakistan, a non-trivial sum with important implications for the economy and society.

Thirdly, Punjab has the lion's share of the population, with 55.6 per cent according to the latest census in 1998 (Table 4.7). The shares of Sindh, NWFP, and Balochistan are 23.0, 13.4, and 5.0 per cent respectively. While the Punjab rate has decreased from 60.8 per cent in 1951, the shares of Sindh (17.9 per cent in 1951) and Balochistan (3.5 per cent in 1951) have increased significantly. Meanwhile, the share of NWFP has remained relatively constant over the last four decades. Moreover, population density has been the highest in Punjab, with 230 people per sq. km. followed by NWFP, Sindh, and Balochistan. Although there has been considerable variation of population densities across the provinces, there has been no population policy directed at the redistribution of population (Sathar, 1991).

Thus, the picture of Pakistan is of an overpopulated country with large geographic, regional, and gender differentials in population, stubbornly high growth rates, unchanging crude birth rates, and declining mortality rates.

REASONS FOR HIGH GROWTH RATES

A variety of factors explain the persistence of high fertility rates in spite of social and economic modernization in Pakistan. Economic, cultural, and social phenomena shed considerable light on the South Asian population debacle.

One major factor in explaining the high total fertility rates is the early marriage of females in Pakistan. More than 50 per cent of Pakistani women marry before the age of twenty— lending truth to the demographic truism that the earlier the marriage age the more likely the chances of conception.

A second factor is the low schooling of women. Data from the 1991 PIHS indicate an inverse association between women's schooling and children borne by women between the reproductive years of 15 to 49 (Berhrman, 1995). There is abundant evidence internationally that well-educated women have fewer children since they have access to many more economic opportunities, and thus have less time for bearing and raising children.

Thirdly, and related to the poor education of women, is low access to contraceptive use. The poor organization of the family planning organizations, the low outreach component, and the cultural suspicion about outside intervention in private areas of sexuality have conspired to produce a low incidence of contraceptive prevalence. Only two-fifths of Pakistani women in a 1991 survey knew of major contraceptives, and less than a quarter of those who knew about these used them. Reasons cited for nonuse included husband preference, religious reasons, cost, and lack of knowledge (PIHS, 1991). Interestingly, there are vast differentials in contraceptive use recorded by the educational attainment levels of women, with 30 per cent of college graduates reported using contraceptives compared to 8.5 per cent of uneducated women (PWD, 1986). Since the increased use of contraception is directly linked to fertility decline in almost all countries of the world, an increase in use of birth control in Pakistan would translate into lower fertility levels. Furthermore, related to this is the lowered rate of breast-feeding. Breast-feeding, which demographic consensus holds to be one of the best natural birth-interval-spacers, has declined in Pakistan for a variety of reasons. Like in India, Indonesia, Korea, and Thailand, reductions in breast-feeding have reduced fertility decline significantly.

Fourthly, the poor income levels of Pakistani society have resulted in an increased demand for children. The demand for child assistance in the agricultural sector, the social prestige of children among the poor, the alternative uses of time that come with wealth, and the importance of children to support the elderly in poor families, all provide the scenario for higher fertility in lower socio-economic classes. Survey and research studies are conclusive in establishing this link in Pakistan.

Fifth, cultural and religious norms have associated high fertility with success and achievement. The high incidence of son-preference has had the unfortunate effect of increasing the fertility rates. The dishonourable bias against female offspring has been an important but neglected factor in explaining the high growth rates.

For a variety of reasons, demand for children has remained high in Pakistan and has proven invulnerable to a series of demographic, economic, and social shifts.

INTERNATIONAL COMPARISON

Pakistan compares very unfavourably with a broad spectrum of developing countries with regards to population growth and labour force (Table 4.8). While the average annual population growth rate for Pakistan is estimated to have been 3.1 per cent for 1980-92 and projected to be 2.7 per cent for the rest of the decade, the corresponding figures in low-income countries are 2.0 and 1.7 per cent (Behrman, 1995). This figure shows the large lacuna that is present between the success stories like Indonesia and Malaysia and the laggers like Pakistan and Kenya. Furthermore, while the Pakistani crude birth rate (CBR) was significantly above the developing country average of 28 per 1,000, the total fertility rate of 5.6 was higher than the 3.4 average for low-income countries. By contrast, the crude death rate of 10 per 1,000 has been at par with the rate of other developing countries, suggesting that improvements in sanitation and vaccination have had a nondifferentiated global impact. Perhaps the most telling statistic has been the extremely low rates of contraceptive prevalence in Pakistan—just over 10 per cent in the last decade, in contrast to the 25 per cent of developing countries. This one statistic alone tells the unfortunate story of the nondecline of fertility rates in Pakistan.

The statistics for the labour force tell a similar story. The labour force growth rate is estimated at 2.9 per cent for 1980-92 and projected to increase at the same rate for the rest of the decade, in contrast to the respective means of 2.2 and 1.7 per cent for all low-income countries (Behrman, 1995). Moreover, the female share of the labour force in 1992 was 30 per cent in contrast to the mean of 46 per cent for low-income countries. A combination of high proportion of children with low proportion of women means that the share of the labour force in the total population was 30 per cent, far below the mean for low-income countries of 46 per cent (Behrman, 1995).

This has adverse implications for the dependency ratio, implying that for each working person, the number of dependents (young, women, sick, etc.) is increasing over time.

IMPACT OF POPULATION GROWTH

The theoretical literature on population is vast and complex. The linkages between population growth rates, economic development, and human capital formation are quite ambiguous. Growth remains much of a mystery in the neoclassical formulation, and a variety of conflicting hypotheses contest the terrain. Nevertheless, a series of tentative conclusions mark the contours of the research. Numerous efforts to use aggregate country data to examine the possibility of empirical evidence for a significant relation between population growth and per capita income growth have yielded few significant results (Behrman, 1995). The influential East Asian Miracle study found no statistical relations between the average rate of real per capita income growth and population growth rates. In spite of some research suggesting that slower population growth would be beneficial to economic development, a large arsenal of econometric work has not resolved the issue in any significant way.

Nevertheless, it is abundantly evident that population growth has had a detrimental impact on developing countries through its adverse impact on the quality of human resources and through the pressures on government resources and infrastructure.

Firstly, population growth in Pakistan has had an adverse effect on food security. High growth rates have constrained government policies to provide food for all and forced the country to embark on an expensive wheat import policy. It is obvious that population growth has resulted in an exacerbation of rural poverty and an increase in landless labourers, identified as the most vulnerable group in a series of poverty assessments. One important study suggests that high population growth rates in Pakistan, by affecting the poor disproportionately since they bear more children than the rich, has perpetuated the intergenerational transmission of poverty by lessening the resource investments of the children of the poor (Birdsall, 1994).

Secondly, population growth has had a negative effect on the quality of human resources by lowering investments in education, health, and nutrition, and thus on overall macro-economic performance. A large annual increase in population has created pressure on a constrained government exchequer and reduced per capita allocations to health and schooling. It is argued that had Pakistan had lower growth rates, it could have enrolled far more children than it did, thus following the East Asian 'virtuous circle' of linking the elimination of the gender gap in basic education with the increase in primary enrolments (Birdsall and Sabot, 1994). Part of the success of the East Asian societies was attributable to the rapid rise in the educational level of women contributing to the sharp decline in fertility rates, which in turn increased the affordability of expanding educational opportunities. The pressures on Pakistan government have been strong, however, making it difficult to finance the investments in education and infrastructure that would have insured sustained economic growth.

Thirdly, high growth rates have had a negative effect on the urban economy. A combination of anecdotal evidence and survey research shows that urbanization in Pakistan has led to an exacerbation of unemployment, air pollution, congestion, social disturbances, and crime. The complex cluster of services—housing, traffic, sewerage, and water—that provide the foundations for a vibrant urban economy have been badly affected by the 3 per cent growth rate. The impact of migrants to the urban areas has been mixed. While the skilled and educated among them have contributed positively the same cannot be said about the unskilled migrants. The low employment generation capacity of the industrial sector has not allowed many of these unskilled migrants to find productive work. In turn, this impoverishment and uprootness has translated into resentment and frustration which was easily channelled into riots and violence. The ethnic problems in Pakistan's major cities are partly attributable to this migration. The pressures on urban infrastructure in Karachi, Lahore, Peshawar, Quetta, Faisalabad, and Hyderabad have been tremendous.

The fourth pernicious effect of population growth has been a detrimental impact on women. According to an influential PIHS Survey in 1991, women of childbearing age cited the refusal of the husband as the major reason for not using contraception. While the number of children desired by women was 3.9, those desired by the spouse was 4.3 (Behrman, 1995). Thus, it stands to reason that a reduced population growth rate would improve the choices for women and reduce the current burden on them.

Although part of the population difficulties have been reduced by the emigration of about 2 million migrants to the Middle East in the last two decades, resulting in large inflows of remittances, their impact on population has not been significant. Similarly, the 3 million Afghan immigrants do not seem to have substantially changed the structure of the society nor affected the demographic problems.

Thus, population growth in Pakistan has had a deleterious effect on macroeconomic performance, on food policy, on government investment in education and health, on urban infrastructure, and on the status of women. The economic and social losses to Pakistan have clearly outweighed the gains of high growth rates.

FAILURE OF POPULATION CONTROL

By almost all tokens and standards, Pakistan's family planning programme and population control policies have failed resoundingly, even in spite of some achievement in recent years in the attainment of targets. For a variety of reasons, the broad array of policies have failed to make any appreciable dent in Pakistan's population growth rate. Despite much fanfare and widely touted schemes, the programme has been disastrous, with rates of contraceptive prevalence stubbornly clinging to around 10 per cent. The fact that the population growth rate has worsened during the implementation of the programme speaks volumes about its ineffectiveness.

Firstly, administrative *ad hoc*ism has crippled the programme. Ambitious schemes were launched amidst much excitement and fervor and then quickly abandoned in favour of some new untested approach. A clinical system involving the use of rural midwives to disseminate contraceptive information was abandoned in 1969, after three years, to be replaced by an outreach-based system, in which a team of male and female motivators would visit the homes of prospective clients to explain the merits of family planning; this in turn was abandoned because of the 1971 War and replaced by a plan to inundate society with contraception under a USAID-sponsored scheme. Throughout, the family planning programme has been bereft of proper evaluation. No system has been left in place for a significant stretch of time and then properly evaluated and its consequences understood. In the early 1980s, the controversial decision to reintegrate the programme with the health ministry led to a significant downsizing of the staff and a demoralization that eroded any earlier gain.

Secondly, the programme has been starved of funding. The budgetary difficulties of the Pakistani economy, the importance of defence and debt expenditure in the government budget, and the low interest and investment in the human resource side have severely weakened the programme. While foreign interest and investment has been sporadic, public expenditure has been substantially below the one per cent of GDP mark. Uncertainties over allocation of funds have delayed new projects and schemes that would otherwise have yielded successful returns.

Thirdly, related to the financial constraints, there has been poor quality and low deployment in the outreach component. The ratio of family planning workers to population has been very low in Pakistan, especially in comparison to international success stories like East Asia. A weak network of poorly trained, underpaid workers in populations of high density has not served the programme well. Since its inception, it has been plagued with recruitment problems. While in the late 1960s only a seventh of the midwives assigned as fieldworkers believed in the efficacy of modern contraceptives, in the early 1970s the army of unmarried female motivators from urban areas could not gain the confidence of the villagers.

Fourthly, the low status of women has been a critical factor delaying the adoption of contraception. The gender-bias of Pakistan society, shown by a wide array of indicators, has not provided enough education and confidence for women to practice the techniques of family planning. The high rates of female illiteracy and low access to health and schooling, and male indifference have compounded the problem, as has male resistance to any outside supervision of a personal matter.

Fifthly, religious opposition to the programme has made its acceptance difficult. Allegations that family planning is contrary to the dictates of Islam have abounded, and little attempt has been made by the political elites to incorporate the local *ulema* in the programme, as was the case in successful societies such as Indonesia and Malaysia.

Finally, political commitment to the programmes has been minimal. In explicit contrast to countries in East Asia such as Thailand, Malaysia, and Korea, the Pakistani political elites have had greater interest in short-term financial gains and in horse-trading. The oscillation between military and civilian rule has not provided that element of political stability that is central to the success of any programme.

In sum, for a wide variety of reasons—organization, financial, religious, cultural—the family planning programme in Pakistan has been quite ineffective in reducing the growth rates. While in the past such factors could be tolerated, this high population growth could be the demographic timebomb that wrenches apart the Pakistani polity unless remedial measures are taken soon.

EDUCATION

A high level of illiteracy is one of the most prominent features of the Pakistani economy and society. The negative effects this has had on economic productivity, performance, and growth are still being spelled out. Crucial deficiencies in both primary and secondary schooling, as well as large gender and regional inequities in the distribution of educational services, plague the Pakistani economy. Internationally recognized as a crucial component of a nation's success, a sound and educated workforce can be the critical factor that explains why some nations fail and others succeed. While the importance of education in fostering development has been a prominent theme in both academic and policy circles for many years, the role of educational quantity and quality has lately been mentioned as perhaps the single most important factor in helping a country rise out of poverty.

Pakistan's educational performance during its fifty years of history has, in spite of the much touted quantitative expansion at all levels, been dismal, with both the quantity of education barely keeping pace with the population growth and the quality deteriorating significantly. The fact that Pakistan has managed to obtain such high growth rates in spite of such a fragile educational base is one of the central paradoxes of the Pakistani economy.

THEORETICAL INSIGHTS

In the early years of development planning, investment discussions were dominated by plans to increase the physical capital stock. The Harrod-Domar model, which guided developing country thinking and planning in the 1940s and 1950s, was based on the idea that production and output of an economy were crucially dependent on the physical capital stock, which in turn was dependent on the savings rate. The higher the savings rate, the greater the growth rate of output generated by productive investment. While other models recognized the importance of other inputs, only by the 1970s and 1980s did many statistical investigations in the growth accounting tradition find that output had increased at a higher rate than could be explained by an increase in only the inputs of labour and physical capital. This 'residual' difference, total factor productivity, between the rate of increase of output and the rate of increase of inputs, was explained by an improvement in the quality of the inputs. Foremost among the input qualities was the level of education of the workforce. Economic backwardness was highly linked to low labour efficiency and training, deficient supplies of entrepreneurship, and slow growth in knowledge. Much empirical work along these lines linked popular clichés about the importance of education for economic success with sound statistical proof that the quality of the labour force was as important as the stock of physical capital in contributing to economic growth. A whole new 'human capital' school has emerged, whose main contention is that the quality of the labour force, in terms of education and health, is a very important ingredient for a nation's success (Romer, a 1986).

This work has spawned a voluminous body of research that analyses the role of education in the process of economic development (Maier, 1990). A combination of factors— increased evidence that educational levels are the best proxy for human capital accumulation, the proliferation of high quality microeconomic data sets in developing countries, and the importance the 'new growth theory' places on education in the development process—have made this new research possible. Furthermore, the remarkable success of the East Asian economies and the prominent role assigned to education as a leading factor in their success has motivated other countries to replicate their experience. The effects of educated labour in raising the level of output and rate of growth, the effect of education on the productivity of rural workers, the rates of return on different levels of education, the gender biases in education and the implications of these biases have all been leading topics of research.

With the benefit of the insights offered by this research, it is easier to understand the characteristics of Pakistan's education sector and to offer explanations for the low education-productivity link. Much of the discussion on education in Pakistan has been dominated by clichés that lack a rigorous analytical framework. The new 'human capital' theories attempt to provide that framework.

CHARACTERISTICS OF PAKISTAN'S EDUCATION

Pakistan's adult illiteracy has historically been high, both in absolute terms and in comparison to other countries (Table 4.9). Pakistan's adult illiteracy rate in 1990 was 65 per cent and was high in comparison to a broad spectrum of developing countries. When compared with a broad variety of countries with differing per capita incomes and geographic locations, Pakistan is consistently at the bottom.

Comparisons of indicators of schooling investment, including enrolment rates, pupil/teacher ratios, and cohort persistence to certain grades yield similar conclusions. By most aggregate indicators, basic schooling investments in Pakistan are low and have been growing less rapidly in recent decades than on the average for low income countries (Behrman, 1995). For Pakistani primary and secondary schooling, 1991 enrolment rates were 46 and 21 per cent, respectively, of the relevant age groups—only about half the average for all low-income countries; between 1970 and 1991 they increased by 6 and 8 per cent respectively, much less than half of the increase in the averages of all low-income countries which came to 27 per cent and 20 per cent. Only about half of those who enrol in school stay on until the fourth grade in Pakistan, in comparison with an average of about two-thirds for all low-income countries. Finally, while the primary pupil ratio of 41 in Pakistan was higher than the South Asian average of 57, it was substantially below East Asia's 24 and below both low-income country average of 38 and the middle-income average of 25. By all criteria, Pakistan's educational system is at the bottom of the international ladder.

Historically, the literacy rate has increased from 13.2 in 1951 to 21.7 by 1972 to 38.8 by 1996 (Table 4.10). This tripling of the rate suggests that there was a significant improvement since independence. There has been a substantive quantitative expansion at all levels; however, given the high population growth rates, the number of illiterates has continued to grow from 3 million at Partition to 20 million by the early 1980s to 49 million by 1996.

The key factor behind this poor performance has been the low investment and attention given to education. Public pronouncements and ambitious plans notwithstanding, expenditure on education since independence has remained 1-2 per cent of GNP, lagging considerably behind most developing countries, which spend 3-4 per cent of their GNP on education. Budgetary shortfalls, large military expenditure, huge fiscal deficits are all responsible for this meagre allocation of resources to education. The problem is compounded by the weak demand for education. Consistently, households spend less than 2 per cent of their income on education.

Besides these important statistics, a whole series of additional numbers and evidence points to a system that is inadequate in quantity, deficient in quality, and inequitable in structure, and needs considerable overhauling. A group of disturbing trends emerges when considering the stylized facts.

Firstly, one prominent feature of Pakistan's schooling system has been the relative emphasis on tertiary education. Historically, Pakistan has placed greater emphasis on tertiary education than on basic primary and secondary education (Behrman, 1995). Compared to many low-income countries, the percentage of people at higher levels of education is similar, but the figure for primary and secondary levels is far below any international mean. Central government expenditure has mostly been concentrated on colleges and universities, with 27 per cent of public expenditure on tertiary education in Pakistan in 1985-6, compared to 16 per cent in Malaysia and 9-11 per cent in Indonesia and Korea. This share increased between 1965 and 1985-6, although the tertiary enrolment rate declined during this period. The bias in favour of colleges and universities can be gauged by the fact that the net current expenditure per student on public education in 1990-1 was 1,379 rupees for college as compared to 792 and 841 rupees respectively for primary and secondary education. Amidst a plethora of international economic evidence that suggests that the rate of return on investment in primary education is much higher than that on tertiary education, the Pakistani bias shows an inadequate understanding of the dynamics of educational policy.

A second prominent feature of the educational sector, one which has drawn considerable international attention, is the large gender gaps in schooling (Behrman, 1995) (Table 4.11). In 1990, female adult illiteracy in Pakistan was 79 per cent, in contrast to India's 66 per cent, China's 38 per cent and Sri Lanka's 17 per cent. One has to search very deeply through international statistics to find other countries that have neglected female education as much as Pakistan.

All available indicators suggest relatively large gender gaps favouring males in Pakistani schooling in comparison with the average experience of all low-income countries. Pakistan's 1991 female primary and secondary schooling enrolment rates were 15 per cent and 8 per cent below the total enrolment rates, while those for low-income countries were 8 and 6 per cent, respectively. Furthermore, while mean schooling for males 25 years or older in Pakistan in 1992 was the same as for other developing countries in the same income level, that for females was only 70 per cent of the mean (Mahmood and Zahid, 1992). In addition access to educational facilities has been quite limited for women, with school/population ratios being quite low. Although primary enrolment rates increased more for women than for men between 1970 and 1996, the change has been too marginal to have any overall impact.

A third feature has been the large regional and rural/urban disparities (Behrman, 1995) (Table 4.12). The ramifications of Pakistan's pro-industry trade and macroeconomic policy on the distribution of educational facilities throughout the country have been considerable. Primary enrolment rates for males in 1991 were over 80 per cent in urban areas of Punjab and the NWFP, but below 50 per cent in Balochistan and barely above 50 per cent in rural areas of Sindh. Similarly, the gender gaps in these enrolment rates ranged from less than 3 per cent in urban areas of Punjab and Sindh to more than 35 per cent in the rural areas of the NWFP and 30 per cent in rural areas of southern Punjab and Balochistan. An examination of the statistics shows a consistent pattern of higher literacy of males in urban areas followed by females in urban areas, with the lowest literacy rates among females in rural areas. With the exception of Punjab, the literacy rate for females in rural areas has remained stubbornly below 10 per cent.

A fourth factor has been the level of waste and inefficiency in the system. Of the various forms of educational waste, such as inability to provide sound facilities to students and inefficiency in the achievement of objectives, dropout has historically been the most important and has resulted in a large number of illiterates. Dropout rates from primary school from 1975 to 1995 were above 50 per cent for males and above 60 per cent for females. While the dropout rates were higher for males at the secondary level than at the primary level, the reverse is true for females. Furthermore, dropout rates are more prominent in the rural areas, where a combination of poverty, low socioeconomic status, and indifference reduce interest in education.

IMPACT OF SCHOOLING ON ECONOMIC PRODUCTIVITY

In recent years, a large body of academic research under the rubric of 'human capital' economics has examined the linkages between schooling and productivity (Psacharopoulos, 1994). Although the precise chain of causality is unclear, there are abundant indications of a strong causation and influence. The mainline consensus is that primary education continues to be the main investment priority in developing countries; the returns decline by the level of schooling and the country's per capita income; investment in women's education is more profitable than that for men; returns in the private competitive sector are higher than those in the public sector. Two assumptions which underlie the orthodox view have been questioned. Firstly, formal schooling has been taken as the best indicator of human capital accumulation, neglecting informal education and on-the-job training. Secondly, production-relevant skills are assumed to be embodied to a greater extent in those individuals who have acquired a greater quantity and quality of education, with a 'skills hierarchy' rising from the primary to the tertiary levels. The human capital model has been challenged by the signalling and credentialist schools, with the argument that, while formal education does not give the relevant skills, it signals to the labour market that the individual possesses the capacity to function as a productive member of the market. Part of the controversy between the two schools regards whether the associations between years of schooling and earnings underlying these estimates reflect the causal effect of schooling or whether factors such as unobserved ability, motivation, and family background play an important role. Furthermore, it has been argued that there is a considerable equity-productivity tradeoff, and that gains may be greater from concentrating resources among fewer students with higher quality. In this view, schooling quality is an important part of an educational strategy, and the current bias towards tertiary and against primary schooling is partially justified. This debate involves a contest between egalitarian and elitist models of schooling.

The bulk of the literature supports the 'human capital' argument. A surfeit of statistics backs the claims that human capital in Pakistan is weak. A number of empirical studies show that the returns to expanding years of education in Pakistan are still considerable i.e. about 20 per cent compared to the average of 35 per cent for low-income countries (Behrman, 1995) (Table 4.13). The implications of these findings is that Pakistan has lost considerable earnings due to underinvestment in education. A higher rate of return on schooling would considerably boost earnings of the population. However, these rates of return vary depending on the level of schooling. Academic studies have found that the social rate of return of 13 per cent for primary school would, with reinvestment, lead to a doubling of assets within six years (Shabbir, 1994). The private rates of return for tertiary schooling are the highest because of the large subsidies at that level. Because the gaps between the social and the private rates of return are higher at the university and college level, it follows that public educational expenditure has been too concentrated at the higher level and would help increase productivity if concentrated at the primary levels.

In one influential work, an attempt to characterize the cost to Pakistan of having low schooling and a relatively large gender gap by a series of simulations based on pooled estimates of the dependence of economic growth on initial schooling investments, the authors find that Pakistan's 1985 income would have been 25 per cent higher if Pakistan had had Indonesia's 1960 primary enrolment rate, and about 16 per cent higher if female enrolment rates had been at the same level as for boys (Birdsall, Ross and, Sabot, 1993).

The gender gap in educational opportunity in Pakistan suggests that the country has foregone a great opportunity by not capitalizing on the large rates of return of female schooling on economic productivity. In a study of estimates of wage relations for males and females separately over several time periods using Household Income and Expenditure Surveys, it was found that females had higher rates of return than their male counterparts during both the late 1970s and the mid-1980s (Ashraf and Ashraf, 1993). Some estimates suggest that that the return on getting more girls into schooling may be over 20 per cent. An assessment of the empirical magnitude needs to be taken with some caution because the spillover effects of higher female literacy on female health and family planning use have not been precisely quantified. The externalities of knowledge that lie at the heart of the 'new growth theories' are nevertheless important factors to consider when deciding an educational policy.

With regard to regional disparities, the finding is the opposite. Estimates for males in different regions find that the rate of return in Punjab has been slightly higher than in the other provinces, leading to the unfair implication that there has been too little schooling in Punjab and too much in Balochistan (Shabbir, 1994). Thus, the efficiency-equity tradeoff presents a policy dilemma.

With regard to the rural-urban divide, estimates in 1988 for males in rural areas place the social rates of return to improving primary school quality to 16.4 per cent, at expanding low-quality primary schools at 13.7 per cent, and to expanding middle schools at 3.4 per cent (Behrman, 1995), thus reiterating the conventional finding that rural primary education should be the main economic priority of developing-country policymakers.

EDUCATIONAL POLICY

In view of the growing criticism of Pakistan's educational policy and its inadequate attempts to boost literacy, the Social Action Plan, under the guidance of the World Bank and a whole new policy package under the Eighth Five-Year Plan (1993-8), were designed to improve educational performance. Major components of the plans are to improve basic education, particularly for female children in the rural areas, and to increase the quality of education through better training of teachers and provision of sufficient non-salary current budgets. According to the planners, the total primary enrolment ratio for boys would rise to 95 per cent from the current 85 per cent, that for girls would rise from 54 per cent to 82 per cent, and the overall literacy rates increase to 50 per cent by 1998.

In spite of these ambitious proposals, a number of caveats remain. Firstly, the present concerns may not be properly targeted, in respect either of the individuals of interest (enrolment and retention of girls, residents of remote rural areas) or the bottlenecks in the schooling process (shortages of textbooks and other materials). A diffuse plan without proper targets risks becoming ineffective.

Both questions of school availability and school quality must be addressed. It has been found that the availability of a school nearby accounts for one third of the gender gap in rural Pakistan (Behrman, 1995). Furthermore, studies show that the specific schools that students attend have important effects on cognitive achievement and labour market outcomes, but considerable controversy rests on which school indicators—teacher education, teacher/pupil ratio, expenditure per pupil—are important. In the absence of proper criteria to gauge schooling quality, a dense deployment of schooling facilities in rural areas may represent the best hope for educational policy reform in Pakistan.

Secondly, the bulk of educational reforms are targeted at the primary levels, reflecting the mainline consensus that investment in primary education creates the highest social returns for society. However, the inefficiencies of both secondary and higher education are legion, with their inadequate facilities and poor teaching levels. Given the abundant linkages between tertiary schooling quality and international competitiveness, some measures need to be undertaken to remedy the neglect of the tertiary levels.

A third weakness of current proposals and policies has been a predominant concern for improving the supply of schooling, with little attention given to demand (Behrman, 1995). A plethora of academic studies, both internationally and with regard to Pakistan, find household demand factors as important in determining school enrolments, retention, and cognitive achievement as are supply factors. Some estimates suggest that these demand factors account for about two-thirds of the gender gap in cognitive achievement in rural Pakistan.[1] Thus, educational reform that focuses on improving household demand for schooling needs to be thought out and implemented.

Lastly, pilot projects that incorporate the introduction of voucher systems for all schools, the collection and dissemination of information regarding the value-added of individual schools, the extension and increase of merit awards for teachers and students, the increased empowerment of parents and community members, decentralized procurement of nonsalary materials and staff, and the collection of information about the effectiveness of these projects must be undertaken. These additional features can help improve the informational base of future public policy.

HEALTH

The health and nutritional status of a population in the developing world are not only useful indicators in determining the success of a country's development strategy in alleviating poverty, but they are means to other objectives, such as the increase in labour productivity through income-generating activities. While considered marginal in the early years of development theorizing, their importance has increased since the early 1970s, when it was recognized that a sustained effort to satisfy the 'basic needs' of the population was essential.

---

[1] According to another study, estimates on the predicted probability of boys and girls aged 7-14 in 1991 to enrol yield positive associations with household income, mother ever enrolled, and father literate, suggesting an intergenerational spillover. The association with girls is stronger than with boys, suggesting that the returns to investing in girls is higher than for boys.

Systematic work has shown large correlations between per capita income and indicators measuring health and nutritional status. The development trajectory of the rich countries has consistently led to higher life expectancies and lower mortality rates.

Pakistan's performance with regard to the health and nutritional status of the population has been quite negative, with a whole array of statistics showing that Pakistan is on the bottom rung of the development ladder.

THEORETICAL INSIGHTS

In recent years, the 'human capital' school has found that investments in health and nutrition are perhaps as important for increasing economic output as increases in physical capital stock (Behrman, 1995). Although a part of the 'residual' difference can be explained by education, a significant part of economic output can be explained by the health status of the population.

A large body of academic literature has found that the health and nutritional status of the population has strong consequences on the productivity of the workforce. Debility and malnutrition translate into significant efficiency losses and productivity shortfalls. From estimates of daily caloric need in different occupations, shortfalls in work capacity can be calculated for different levels of shortfall in caloric intake. For many low-income countries, these shortfalls are almost always very substantial, often as high as 50 per cent. Furthermore, another cost of malnutrition is the reduced number of working years resulting from early death. The age structure and life expectancy rates of developing countries indicate that reductions in adult mortality would not only add years to income-generating lives and reduce the dependency ratios that measure the burden of the older members of society on the younger ones, but also increase the yield on education and other investments in workers. Contrary to the prevailing wisdom that the developing countries suffer from a mass of idle workers whose improvement in health and nutritional status will not increase labour productivity, the 'human capital' school has found that human energy is a critical factor influencing productivity and that it would be simplistic to dismiss the productivity value of nutrition because of the existence of idle adults (Romer, b 1994).

Moreover, an additional benefit of a nutrition programme is the medical costs that can be saved as the demand for medical services decreases. Estimates suggest that about one-third of the sick in developing countries are victims of nutritional disorders. Given the well-known fact that it is much cheaper to prevent malnutrition than to cure it, developing countries' exchequers could be spared a huge financial burden through the encouragement of nutrition education. The literature suggests that the magnitude of money thus made available could be utilized for a range of alternative programmes.

Although certain links between diet, performance potential, and economic returns are ambiguous and the chain of causation not entirely clear, it has become a truism that the health and nutritional status of a population are one of the crucial factors determining its productivity. An unhealthy and malnourished population is a sure ingredient of failure.

CHARACTERISTICS OF HEALTH AND NUTRITION

The health and nutritional status of Pakistan's population is among the worst in the developing world, according to several indicators (Table 4.15).[2]

---

[2]The infant mortality rate (IMR) per 1,000 live births in 1992 for Pakistan was 88, in contrast to China's 33, India's 65, Sri Lanka's 15, Egypt's 53, and Philippines' 37. Considerably higher than the mean for low-income countries which is 76, Pakistan's IMR is only higher than certain of the poorest Sub-Saharan countries. In part, the relatively high IMR may reflect the fact that 30 per cent of the babies were reported to have low birth weight, in contrast to the 23.5 of other low-income developing countries (Behrman, 1995). Furthermore, the relatively high IMR is an important component of low life expectancies at birth in Pakistan, although the drop in Pakistan's IMR between 1970 and 1996 has helped increase the life expectancy rate in the last two decades.

The data on under-5 mortality rates per 1,000 live births reveals similar trends.[3]

In addition to these high infant and neonatal mortality rates, maternal mortality rates are relatively high, with differing sources giving different rates.[4] Thus, Pakistan has the paradoxical combination of lower life expectancy and higher disease prevention.

An analysis of another important indicator—the prevalence of malnutrition among children under-5—presents unfavourable comparisons for Pakistan. In an evaluation of malnutrition from 1987 to 1992.[5]

An analysis of the data on life expectancy produces a more balanced record (Table 4.14). Pakistan's 1992 life expectancies at birth were four years and two years below the means for low-income countries for males and females (Behrman, 1995). Though there was no gender gap in life expectancies within Pakistan, the shortfall in comparison with means for all developing countries were twice as large for females as for

---

[3] The 1996 Pakistani under-5 mortality rate of 123 is high in comparison with other developing countries. China's 39, India's 85, Kenya's 57, Sri Lanka's 15, Philippines' 37 and, Jordan's 30 once more put Pakistan near the bottom of the international ladder, with the poorest Sub-Saharan economies. The Pakistani rates are higher than the respective means of 102 and 114 for all low-income countries (Behrman, 1995). These high under-5 mortality rates are important components of Pakistani lower life expectancy, but their substantial favouring of females means that mortality rates for other ages must favour males for there to be this equalization of life expectancies at birth.

[4] The World Bank presenting a figure of 340 per 100,000 live births in 1996. By contrast, morbidity rates for Pakistan present a better picture, with the incidence of tuberculosis and malaria significantly below international comparisons.

[5] Pakistan's figure of 40.4 per cent of children with a deficiency or an excess of nutrients that interfere with their health and their potential for growth is high compared to China's 21.3 per cent, Kenya's 18 per cent, Sri Lanka's 36.6 per cent, Honduras' 20.6 per cent, and Egypt's 10.4 per cent. Poverty and poor eating patterns have consigned Pakistani children to the bottom of international figures.

males.[6] The considerable rise in average life expectancy over the last three decades has resulted in a diminishing of the gap between Pakistan and the developed countries to about 16 years. Thus, Pakistan has made a considerable improvement when compared to the pace of change of other developing countries. The levelling of gender differences seems especially noteworthy.

In terms of health and nutrition inputs, the Pakistani record is mixed (Table 4.15). Population per physician in 1994 in Pakistan was 2,000, and population per nursing person was 3,500, the former far below the mean for low-income countries and the latter significantly above the mean for low-income countries, suggesting that there was a much higher availability of physicians per person and physicians per nursing person than on average in low-income countries. The comparable figures for a broad sample of low-income developing countries gives Pakistan a mixed record. Thus, while higher-level medical care seems more easily available in Pakistan, the weak deployment of nursing services diminishes the good physician/patient ratio. However, the fact that 90 per cent of Pakistanis had access to health services in the last decade implies that a respectable patient/doctor ratio has been reached. Combined with a high availability of safe water (74 per cent), pregnant women receiving prenatal care (70 per cent), use of oral rehydration salts to combat diarrhoea (97 per cent), and high immunization rates among one-year-olds (75 per cent), Pakistan's health system does have a few prominent positive measures that dilute the impact of the more grisly statistics.

In terms of government expenditure on health, the share of GDP has historically been low in Pakistan. In 1990 this came to 3.4 per cent of GDP, low in comparison to the international

---

[6]In 1992 Pakistan's life expectancy was calculated as 59 which put it significantly below most countries in Asia. However, it was above, Ethiopia, Sierra Leone, Nigeria, and Congo. On a more positive note, the increases in Pakistani life expectancy between 1970 and 1992 were substantial (12 and 10 years, respectively, for females and males) and larger than the means for all low-income countries, more so for females than for males.

average for low-income countries which is 4.9 per cent. This share has not increased in recent years because of a combination of high military spending, recurrent fiscal deficits, and low prioritization of health issues.

PRODUCTIVITY IMPACT OF HEALTH AND NUTRITION

Although the literature on Pakistan is sparse, a considerable body of international work on countries with similar endowments allows one to make inferences on Pakistan. There is considerable evidence that the low health and nutritional status of the population has a deleterious effect on labour productivity and economic growth through both direct and indirect channels of causation.

Health and nutrition have effects on the rest of the economy through their influence on three different variables—labour productivity, schooling productivity, and human fertility (Behrman, 1995). Although it is difficult to quantify these effects because of a series of measurement and analytical problems, the impact is substantial.

Better health and nutrition can increase labour productivity directly by making workers stronger and more energetic. Both weight-for-height and caloric intake have a significant effect on farm output. Micro studies consistently show that farm labour is a consistent function of caloric intake (Behrman, 1995). The quality of labour is an important component of the agriculture production function, and productivity enhancement is critically linked to food supply. An estimate of the impact of caloric consumption on agricultural productivity in Pakistan that distinguishes explicitly between the planting and harvest stages on agricultural production, found that there was no effect on the harvest stage, when food was relatively abundant, but there were significant positive effects of caloric consumption on agricultural production during the planting season. On a more macro level, better nutritional intake leads to higher wages in both the peak season (when greater sustained energy expenditure is required for tasks such as harvesting) and the planting season (where innate strength is important). The main point is that cross-country associations between health and per capita incomes are abundant. Pakistan's low life expectancies and health have not allowed any dramatic boost in agricultural labour productivity.

Secondly, health and nutrition have a considerable negative impact on schooling productivity in Pakistan. Studies of experimental and socioeconomic survey data on the indirect effects of health and nutrition on cognitive achievement, schooling, and pre-school ability show that there is a strong link between the two. The consensus is that better endowed children do better at schools and have better health than others.

A whole series of informal linkages shows the interaction between health, socioeconomic status, and productivity. In a series of cross-tabulations from the 1991 Pakistan Integrated Household Survey (PIHS), it was found that infant mortality rates are a third higher for the households in the bottom quintile of expenditure/income distribution than for other households, a fifth higher in rural than in urban areas, almost two-thirds higher if mothers had no schooling versus some schooling, and over two-fifths above the national average in Balochistan. The reported incidence of diarrhoea for children aged five or younger is about a quarter independent of expenditure or sex of the child, but is lower in urban areas. Urban households are closer to all types of health facilities than their rural counterparts.

UNEMPLOYMENT

A clear understanding of the trends, level, and changes in the unemployment situation of Pakistan is marred by a number of conceptual and empirical problems. The definitions of labour force and unemployment—open, reported, disguised, underemployed—are in themselves highly contentious, but in the case of Pakistan it is further compounded by serious measurement problems.The more comprehensive coverage is provided by the census data for 1951,1961,1972 and 1981.Since then, the pieces have been put together by combining disjointed data from the Demographic Survey and the annual Labour Force Surveys. In recent years the coverage and definitions of these surveys have themselves changed, and thus a comparable time series is hard to construct.

Even if the estimates derived from these sources are accepted at face value with no questioning, the picture that emerges is highly blurred and does not provide hard empirical facts. These data do not suggest the existence of any structural unemployment problem in Pakistan over the long term, and indicate. only a slight worsening of the situation in recent years.The average rate of unemployment, according to these sources, hovers around 5-6 per cent of the labour force in the 1990s, having risen from 1.7 per cent according to the 1961 census. Urban unemployment estimates place the rate at about 7 per cent.

The biases in these estimates arise from different factors and it is not obvious where they finally end up. First, the labour force itself may be underreported due to the exclusion of both women and those working in the informal sector as well as non-agricultural self-employment in the rural areas. For example, the labour force estimates indicate that the labour force participation rate (LFPR) for females is less than 8 per cent. For the sake of comparison, the same rate in India is 30 per cent. The gender bias in measurement and recording is known to be skewed in favour of males, and thus the underreporting of female LFPR could be significantly high. Second, there is a lack of consistency between the sample frames used and the adjustment for undernumeration made in the Demographic Survey and those used for the Labour Force Survey.Third, the labour force surveys have improved the quality of the questionnaires as well as their coverage over time. There appears a tendency to smooth out large variations.[7]

The data presented in Table 4.17 confirm the conventional wisdom about discrimination against females in employment. Notwithstanding all the problems that have been adduced above, the female unemployment ratio in its reported and unadjusted form is unacceptably high—between 14 and 16 per cent. This compares to 5 to 6 per cent for the aggregate and 4 per cent for males. Some of the high incidence may result from the statistical improvement of the labour force survey, but casual empiricism strongly suggests that the barriers to female employment— social, cultural, and religious—remain formidable. Discouraged but involuntary unemployment rates may in fact be much higher.

The above estimates do not include child labour, which has become a burning social issue internationally and which is hurting Pakistani exports of carpets, leather and sports goods etc. A recent survey has estimated that about 8.3 per cent of children between the ages of 5-14 years were economically active. Three-fourths of them were boys and one fourth were girls. As a significant proportion of child labour is employed in export industries, alternative arrangements have to be made urgently to remove children from these industries if Pakistan wants to retain access to markets in the EC and North America.

Attempts to establish a quantitative relationship between economic growth and employment in Pakistan thus suffer from

---

[7]According to the most recent estimates (Table 4.16), 37.1 million people participate in the labour force, yielding an aggregate LFPR of 27.4 per cent. According to the 1951 census, the LFPR was 30.5 per cent. The reason why the rate has declined is not clear. The employment estimate based on the current LFPR is 35.1 million; consequently the unemployment rate is 5.37 per cent. If on the other hand, it is assumed that the LFPR remains unchanged at 30.5 per cent as it was in 1951, the true labour force would be 41.2 million and the true unemployment rate could be as high as 15 per cent maintaining the employment numbers at 35.1 million. It may be argued that, for the sake of symmetrical treatment, the reported employment numbers should also be adjusted upwards. If such an adjustment is made the unemployment figure could be close to 10 per cent. The range therefore is wide—betwen 6 to 15 per cent. This exercise demonstrates the highly tenuous nature of officially-reported unemployment figures.

the weak and unsatisfactory basis of the employment data. This has not, however, precluded a number of analysts from estimating the output elasticity of employment for the aggregate as well as for various sectors. Table 4.18 summarizes the various estimates for the different periods. There are serious methodological problems in the estimation of these coefficients and they should be treated with extreme caution, but, if it is assumed that these problems remain constant across various time periods, some tentative conclusions may be offered.

First, there seems to be a decline in the aggregate elasticity over time. By the end of the 1980s, the elasticity was almost halved from the level of the 1960s. In other words, the capacity of the economy to generate the same level of employment required that the growth rates of GDP should at least be twice those attained in the 1951-61 period. Second, despite serious fluctuations in the elasticity of the agriculture sector, the coefficient for the 1980s is extremely low. Whether the rates of GDP growth themselves have much to do with the size of these coefficients is a question that needs to be explored before any serious inferences can be drawn. Third, the services sector, whose share in GDP has risen from one-fourth to one-half and which normally absorbs most of the labour force, does not exhibit significant capacity to do so. This may also be partly due to underreporting in the self-employment and informal sector.

The above picture, if accurate, indicates that the scope for absorbing future additions to the labour force and maintaining socially acceptable unemployment rates is limited even if output growth maintains its high trend rate. The situation may get out of control if unemployment among educated youth rises as a result of greater emphasis on education. This sobering conclusion requires further investigation and policy response if it turns out to be substantiated by careful analysis.

International experience does suggest that in low-income developing countries, small scale agriculture, small and medium enterprises, and, more recently, knowledge-based enterprises are the main avenues for productive employment. This is a strategy which merits serious consideration by the policy makers in Pakistan.

TABLE 4.1
ESTIMATES OF POVERTY IN PAKISTAN (per cent)

	Rural Poor	Urban Poor	Total
1963-4	42.6	48.89	40.24
1966-7	49.6	45.99	44.50
1969-70	50.7	42.55	46.53
1979	35.1	30.95	30.68
1984-5	49.3	38.2	46.0
1987-87	40.2	30.7	37.4
1990-91	36.9	28.0	34.0

Source: Economic Survey, 1997-98 Finance Division, Government of Pakistan, Islamabad. World Poverty Assessment 1995

TABLE 4.2
DISTRIBUTION OF THE POOR BY
REGION AND SECTOR

	1984-5			1987-8			1990-1		
	P	%P	%Pop	P	%P	%Pop	P	%P	%Pop
Pakistan	18.3	100	100	16.6	100	100	17.2	100	100
Urban	11.1	83	72	8.7	15	28	9.8	18	57
Rural	21.1	17	28	19.6	86	72	20.6	83	119
Punjab	19.0	62	59	19.9	73	61	19.0	69	110
Urban	12.8	11	16	11.9	11	15	11.4	11	66
Rural	21.3	51	44	22.6	62	45	21.9	58	127
Sindh	15.3	18	22	9.5	13	22	12.3	16	71
Urban	7.0	4	11	3.1	2	10	6.7	4	39
Rural	22.2	14	12	14.6	11	12	17.6	12	102
NWFP	9.6	7	13	15.5	12	13	20.2	13	117
Urban	7.5	1	2	12.4	2	2	14.3	2	83
Rural	9.0	6	11	16.0	11	11	21.4	12	124
Balochistan	27.5	9	6	9.3	3	4	7.1	1	41
Urban	17.0	.5	.5	4.4	.2	1	4.5	.0	26
Rural	28.5	9	6	10.0	2	4	7.7	1.1	45

Source: Malik, Sohail, *Pakistan's Economic Performance, 1947-1993: A Descriptive Analysis*, Sure Publishers, Lahore, 1993

P — Poverty ratio
Pop — Population

TABLE 4.3
HOUSEHOLD INCOME DISTRIBUTION

Year	Gini Coefficient	Ratio of Highest/ Lowest 20%
1971-2	0.345	5.4
1979	0.373	6.1
1984-5	0.369	6.2
1990-1	0.407	6.1

Source: *Pakistan Poverty Assessment*, Country Operations Division, World
Bank (1995)

Note: These officially estimated Gini Coefficients and other measures of
income inequality in Pakistan are partial and incomplete as they do not
incorporate the incomes generated in the parallel economy. The parallel
economy is estimated at 30-40 per cent of GDP, and if this adjusted
GDP, after adding the parallel economy, is taken as the base and 80 per
cent of the incomes in the parallel economy accrue to the top income
quintile, the Gini Coefficient moves closer to 0.5 rather than the current
0.4. The ratio of the highest/ lowest quintile would then be almost 10
instead of the officially estimated 6.

TABLE 4.4
INCOME DISTRIBUTION:
(International Comparison)

Country	Ratio of Top Quintile's Share to Bottom Quintile's Share
China	5.17
Indonesia	5.22
Malaysia	4.21
Philippines	4.67
Vietnam	5.51
Pakistan	4.68
India	4.98
Sri Lanka	7.98

Source: Deininger and Squire (1995), 'Income Distribution and Development,'
mimeo, World Bank.

TABLE 4.5
POPULATION

Census Years	Popula- tion (Millions)	Labour Force Partici- pation Rate	Civilian Labour Force	Emp- loyed Total	Crude Birth Rate	Crude Death Rate	Com- pound Growth Rate
1941	28,282	31.3	8.9	..	45.0	31.2	1.9
1951	33,817	30.7	10.4	..	..	..	1.8
1961	42,978	32.4	13.9	14.7	..	..	2.4
1972-3	65,321	32.7	19.5	18.6	..	..	3.7
1981	84,254	27.8	25.8	24.7	43.3	11.8	3.1
1998	130,580	28.0	36.5	34.3	36.0	9.0	2.6

Source: *Economic Survey* (Various Issues), Ministry of Finance, Government of Pakistan, Islamabad

TABLE 4.6
POPULATION AND ITS GROWTH BY SEX AND RURAL/URBAN AREAS
(Thousands)

Year	Total	Rural	Urban	Male	Female
1941	28,282	24,267	4,015	15,400	12,900
1951	33,817	27,797	6,019	18,191	15,626
1961	42,978	33,324	9,654	23,017	19,961
1972	65,321	48,727	16,594	34,840	30,481
1981	84,254	60,413	23,841	44,232	40,021
1991	113,780	77,939	35,841	59,734	54,046
1998	130,580	88,141	42,440	67,901	62,678

Source: *Economic Survey* (Various Issues), Ministry of Finance, Government of Pakistan, Islamabad

TABLE 4.7
ENUMERATED POPULATION OF PAKISTAN
BY PROVINCE, LAND AREA, AND PERCENTAGE
DISTRIBUTION: 1951-98

	Area (Sq.Km.)	1951	1961	1972	1981	1998
Pakistan	796.095	33,816	42,978	65,321	84,253	130,580
(per cent)	100.0	100.0	100.0	100.0	100.0	100.0
NWFP	74,521	4,587	5,752	8,392	11,061	17,500
(per cent)	9.4	13.6	13.4	12.8	13.1	13.4
Punjab	205,344	20,557	25,500	37,612	47,292	72,500
(per cent)	25.8	60.8	59.3	57.6	56.1	55.6
Sindh	140,914	6,054	8,374	14,158	19,029	29,900
(per cent)	17.7	17.9	19.5	21.7	22.6	23.0
Balochistan	347,190	1,187	1,385	2,433	4,332	6,500
(per cent)	43.6	3.5	3.2	3.7	5.1	5.0

Source: *Pakistan Economic Survey* (various issues), 1998–Preliminary census results

TABLE 4.8
PAKISTANI POPULATION AND LABOUR
FORCE IN INTERNATIONAL PERSPECTIVE: 1992

	Pakistan	South Asia	East Asia	Low- Income	Middle- Income
Average annual	3.1[1]	2.2	1.6	2.0	1.8
growth rate	2.7[2]	1.9	1.2	1.7	1.5
Crude birth rate	40	31	35	28	24
CBR change 1992-70	-8	-11	-14	-11	-11
Crude death rate	10	10	8	10	8
CDR change 1992-70	-9	-8	-1	-4	-3
Total fertility rate	5.6	4.0	2.3	3.4	3.0
TFR change 1992-70	-1.4	-2.0	-3.4	-2.6	-1.6
Average annual	2.9[1]	2.1	2.1	2.2	2.2
labour force growth	2.9[2]	1.9	1.8	1.7	2.8
Labour force partic. rate	30	36	55	46	31
Female share of labour force	13	22	42	35	32
Change in female share 1992-70	4	-4	1	-1	2

Source: Behrman, Jere, *Pakistan: Human Resource Development and Economic Growth into the Next Century*, Background Paper for *Pakistan 2010*, World Bank, Washington DC (1994)

[1] 1980-92
[2] 1992-2000

TABLE 4.9
ILLITERACY—INTERNATIONAL COMPARISONS

Country	Adult Illiteracy (Percentage)	Female Illiteracy
Pakistan	65	79
India	52	66
China	27	38
Kenya	31	42
Ghana	40	49
Sri Lanka	12	17
Egypt	52	66
Peru	15	21
Thailand	7	10
Turkey	19	29
Iran	46	57
Brazil	19	20
Malaysia	22	30
Morocco	51	62
Colombia	13	14
Mexico	13	15
Spain	5	7
Argentina	5	5

Source: *World Development Report*, 1994, World Bank, Washington DC

TABLE 4.10
LITERACY RATE

Year	Percentage
1951	13.2
1961	18.4
1972	21.7
1981	26.2
1996	38.0

Source: Economic Survey, Government of Pakistan, various issues.

TABLE 4.11
PAKISTANI SCHOOLING IN
INTERNATIONAL PERSPECTIVE

	Pakistan	South Asia	East Asia	Low-Income	Middle-Income
Enrolment Rates 1991					
Primary-Total	46	89	119	101	104
Female	31	76	115	93	99
Secondary Total	21	39	50	41	55
Female	13	29	47	35	56
Tertiary Total	3	NA	5	3	18
Changes in Enrolment Rates 1970-91					
Primary Total	6	22	31	27	11
Female	9	26	NA	NA	12
Secondary Total	8	14	26	20	23
Female	8	15	NA	NA	30
Tertiary Total	-1	NA	1	NA	NA
Primary Pupil/ Teacher Ratio	41	57	24	38	25

Source: Behrman, Jere, *Pakistan: Human Resource Development and Economic Growth into the Next Century*, Background Paper for *Pakistan 2010*, World Bank, Washington DC (1994)

TABLE 4.12
REGIONAL DIFFERENCES IN PRIMARY SCHOOLING
ENROLMENT RATES AND LITERACY RATES, 1991

Province	Male Primary School Enrolment Rate	Female Primary School Enrolment Rate	Male Literacy Rate	Female Literacy Rate
Punjab				
Urban	81.1	78.5	62.9	36.8
Rural North	70.8	52.9	44.6	13.6
Rural South	61.0	31.2	34.5	8.9
Sindh				
Urban	63.3	63.3	61.5	41.3
Rural	51.5	24.1	43.2	6.6
NWFP				
Urban	81.3	53.5	53.8	20.9
Rural	47.3	19.8	29.1	3.2
Balochistan				
Urban	44.9	34.0	52.0	16.5
Rural	47.3	19.8	29.1	3.2

Source: Behrman, Jere, *Pakistan: Human Resource Development and Economic Growth into the Next Century*, Background Paper for *Pakistan 2010*, World Bank, Washington DC (1994)

TABLE 4.13
RATES OF RETURN TO SCHOOLING

Country	Primary	Secondary	Tertiary	Overall
Low-Income Country				
Private	35.2	19.3	23.5	
Social	23.4	15.2	10.6	
All Countries				
Male	20.1	13.9	13.4	11.1
Female	12.8	18.4	12.7	12.4
Pakistan				
Private	20.0	11.0	27.0	
Social	13.0	9.0	8.0	

Source: Behrman, Jere, *Pakistan: Human Resource Development and Economic Growth into the Next Century*, Background Paper for *Pakistan 2010*, World Bank, Washington DC (1994)

TABLE 4.14
MORTALITY RATES AND LIFE EXPECTANCY 1996

Country	Infant Mortality Rate (per 1000 live births)	Under-5 Mortality Rate	Maternal Mortality Rate (per 100 000 live births)	Life Expectancy (Female)
Pakistan	88	123	340	65
China	33	39	115	71
India	65	85	487	63
Kenya	57	90	650	60
Egypt	53	66	170	67
Sri Lanka	15	19	30	75
Philippines	37	44	208	68
Jordan	30	35	150	72
Thailand	34	38	200	72
Brazil	36	42	160	71
Malaysia	11	14	43	74
Mexico	32	36	110	75
Korea	9	11	30	76

Source: *World Development Indicators*, 1997, World Bank, Washington DC

TABLE 4.15
PAKISTANI HEALTH AND NUTRITION IN INTERNATIONAL PERSPECTIVE

	Pakistan	South Asia	East Asia	All developing countries
Life Expectancy 1994				
Female	63	61	71	63
Male	63	60	67	61
Infant Mortality Rate	80	73	41	64
Population per Physician	2,000	3,704	NA	5,833
Population per Nursing Person	3,448	5,468	NA	4,691

Source: UNDP, Human Development Report 1997

TABLE 4.16
LABOUR FORCE AND EMPLOYMENT ESTIMATES

	1951	1961	1972	1981	1990	1997
Labour Force (mill.)	10.3	13.9	19.5	25.8	31.8	37.1
Urban		2.9	5.1	7.3	8.6	10.2
Rural		11.0	14.4	18.5	23.2	26.9
Employment (mill.)		13.6	18.5	24.7	30.8	35.1
Urban		2.8	4.8	7.0	8.2	9.5
Rural		10.8	13.7	17.7	22.6	25.6
Unemployment Rate (per cent)		1.6	4.6	4.5	2.6	4.8
Urban		3.0	6.1	3.4	4.6	6.9
Rural		1.6	4.6	4.5	2.6	4.8

Source: Census of Pakistan (various issues), Labour Force Surveys and Statistical Appendix, Economic Survey of Pakistan

TABLE 4.17
TRENDS IN FEMALE EMPLOYMENT

	1982-3	1990-1	1994-5
Female Population (mill.)	42.9	54.9	61.8
Female Labour Force (mill.)	3.1	4.5	4.7
Female LFPR (per cent)	7.2	8.2	7.6
Female Employment (mill.)	3.05	3.75	4.05
Unemployment Rate (per cent)	1.6	16.7	13.7

Source: Author's Calculation from Labour Force Survey data

TABLE 4.18
OUTPUT ELASTICITIES OF EMPLOYMENT

	1951-61	1961-72	1972-78	1978-87
Agriculture	1.62	0.48	1.27	0.42
Mining and Manufacturing	0.77	0.28	0.80	0.35
Construction	0.47	1.30	0.55	0.39
Electricity, Gas and Water	0.21	0.41	1.04	0.43
Transport and Communications	1.71	1.26	0.36	0.43
Trade	0.86	0.92	0.73	0.48
TOTAL EMPLOYMENT	0.94	0.45	0.56	0.41

Source: ILO/ARTEP

TABLE 4.19
TRENDS IN HUMAN DEVELOPMENT

	1960	MRY	Change Over Period
Life Expectancy at Birth	43.1	61.8	+ 43 %
Infant Mortality Rate	163	189	+ 46 %
Population with Access to Safe Water	25[1]	79[2]	+ 316 %
Underweight Children under Five	47[3]	40[4]	+ 15 %
Adult Literacy Rate	21[5]	36	+ 71 %
Gross Enrolment Ratio for All Levels	19[6]	24	+ 26 %
Human Development Index		0.442	

Source: *Human Development Report*, 1996, UNDP, N. Y., 1997

CHAPTER 5

PHYSICAL CAPITAL: INFRASTRUCTURE

Physical capital in any country is its economic infrastructure; it includes services from public utilities—power, telecommunications, piped water supply, sanitation, and sewerage, solid waste collection and disposal, and piped gas; public works—major dam and canal works for irrigation and drainage; roads and other transport sectors—urban and interurban railways, urban transport, ports and waterways and airports.

Infrastructure can contribute to economic growth, poverty alleviation, and environmental sustainability, but only when it provides services that respond to effective demand and does so efficiently. The adequacy of infrastructure helps determine a country's success or failure in diversifying production, expanding trade, coping with population growth, reducing poverty or improving environmental conditions. Good infrastructure raises productivity and lowers production costs by making better use of underutilized materials and human resources, enabling more efficient tradeoffs among factors of production, increasing economic efficiency due to reduced costs and expanded markets within and outside the country. But it has to expand fast enough to accommodate growth. It has been empirically estimated that a 1 per cent increase in the stock of infrastructure is associated with 1 per cent increase in GDP across all countries. And as countries develop, infrastructure must adapt to support changing patterns of demand, as the shares of power, roads, telecommunications in the total stock of infrastructure increase relative to those of such basic services as water and irrigation.

Pakistan has invested $3 billion a year, or 5-6 per cent of GDP, in creating, operating, and maintaining its infrastructure. An analysis of development expenditure patterns shows that transport, power, water, sanitation, telecommunications, and irrigation have consistently claimed one-half to two-thirds of the total outlays. There have been some gains, particularly in irrigation water availability, access to clean water, and power generation. Irrigation water availability has almost doubled since 1947; the share of households with access to clean water has risen to almost 70 per cent; and generation capacity has reached 7 KW per 1000 population.

Despite these impressive gains, shortages and deficiencies—in maintaining the existing stock, operating it efficiently, and expanding the assets in relation to income and population growth—have become apparent. The main culprit in this respect is not the level of investment or expenditure, but the deteriorating management capacity of the institutions that have been traditionally responsible for infrastructure services. There has been a historical evolution that has moved the locus of responsibility from government departments to autonomous corporations such as WAPDA, NHA, PTC, etc., but the outcomes in terms of indicators of efficiency, access, or financial profitability have not improved. The inadequacy of Pakistan's infrastructure remains one of the weakest elements of Pakistan's development experience. While the economy has maintained reasonable rates of growth in agriculture, trade, and industry, the provision of infrastructural facilites has lagged far behind the country's needs. In critical sectors of the economy—power, transport, telecommunications, waste disposal and management—Pakistan has lagged behind many developing countries.

In Pakistan the supply of infrastructure is inadequate in all sectors except irrigation, where a strong and vibrant canal system has tremendously helped the agricultural sector. A comparison with countries representing the range of per capita incomes and growth rates that encompass Pakistan's current and potential future experience shows that, relative to its level of income,

Pakistan lags behind in terms of asset supply or service quality in most infrastructure sectors. This inadequacy combined with weak human capital base is a serious constraint to Pakistan's long-term growth.

Historically, after a sluggish performance in the early decades, in the 1970s the public sector undertook large investments in infrastructure. However, due to the nationalization policies, the economy had a low performance in the 1970s so that the infrastructure shortages were not felt. However, the past neglect of investment became apparent in the form of infrastructural shortfalls when the economy once again began to grow rapidly after 1978. In the 1980s and early 1990s, infrastructural investment had to be curtailed in order to alleviate the growing budgetary deficits. However, a whole series of policies have been instituted in the 1990s to encourage the private sector and foreign investors to assist the government in overhauling the infrastructure system and improving service delivery.

The stylized facts yield depressing conclusions. Low access of the population to water and sanitation (74 per cent and 30 per cent respectively), overcrowded traffic and low percentage of roads in good conditions (18 per cent), the sharp decline in the railway system's volume of passenger and freight handling (30 to 60 per cent since the late 1970s), electricity shortages (20 per cent of peak-load demand), and the length of the waiting list for telephones (16 per cent of lines in service) are. empirical indicators of the weakness of Pakistan's infrastructure provision.

HISTORICAL AND COMPARATIVE PERSPECTIVE

The best method of assessing Pakistan's international performance in the provision of infrastructure is through comparison with a relatively large sample of developing countries. A group of countries was chosen to reflect the diversity of the developing economies, including countries from Africa, Latin America, and Asia, as well as including low-income, middle-income, and high-income countries. Since these sectors are nontraded, the conventional methodology employed to compare infrastructural capital stock across countries, used in the World Bank's *World Development Report*, is a comparison based on inputs: the supply of infrastructural assets mixed with some measures of quality and efficiency (Isfahani 1994). Secondly, in order to assess the present infrastructure of Pakistan, it is necessary to examine the historical evolution of these sectors.

ROADS

In terms of the road network, Pakistan ranks above average, but the road density of 0.23 km. is relatively low. The generally accepted standard for developing countries with similar topography and level of economic development is 0.5 km. (Table 5.1). The paved road network has about 123,000 km., and this translates into a service ratio of 73 km. per 100,000 population, substantially higher than many of the low-income sub-Saharan countries but significantly behind some fast-growing economies like Indonesia (86.0), Brazil (105.0) and Malaysia (149.0). However, in terms of the quality of its roads, Pakistan ranks with the rest of the South Asian economies in having the world's highest percentage of poor roads. Only 20 per cent of Pakistan's roads are in good condition, compared to 50 per cent for Thailand and 75 per cent for Ivory Coast. The road infrastructure in Pakistan consists of aging and obsolete roads that have neither the geometric capacity nor the structural strength to carry the traffic loads (Faiz, 1992). Unless there is some modernization and renovation, Pakistan's road infrastructure will remain one of the world's worst.

Historically, there was very slow growth in the transportation sector in the early years, but a surge in the second half of the 1980s resulted in a huge increase. The kilometres of roads expanded from 16,860 in 1960 to 24,776 in 1970 to 38,035 in 1980 to 86,839 by 1990. This acceleration of the growth rate reflects investments carried out in the late 1970s and early 1980s to revamp the road network. However, in recent years, growth has slowed down, accident rates have increased, and maintenance has been deficient. This has deterred the private sector, both domestic and foreign, from undertaking important investments. In fact, firms that were surveyed for the World Bank's Private Sector Assessment Project ranked road quality second only to power supply problems as the main factor hindering their investments (Isfahani, 1994). Unfortunately, the National Highways Authority, which manages the maintenance of most of the roads, has not been able to involve the private sector beyond the partial financing offered to construction contractors.

The initiative taken by the Nawaz Sharif government to involve the foreign private sector in B.O.T. for constructing a major highway between Islamabad, Lahore and Peshawar will bear some fruit in the near future. The six-lane, 335 km. motorway project between Islamabad and Lahore, constructed at an estimated cost of $ 725 million, was completed early in 1998. The second leg of this project, between Islamabad and Peshawar was cancelled for some time but has recently been revived. Tolls will be levied on these new highways, which offer improved level of service.

ENERGY SECTOR

Per capita energy use in Pakistan has risen much faster than growth in incomes or poulation (Table 5.2). Starting from an almost insignificant level in 1947, current consumption has reached 243 kg. It has doubled since 1980, when the level was only 139 kg. The annual growth rate of the consumption of commercial energy has been spectacular—8 per cent—during the most recent decade.

The total commercial energy consumption in 1996-7 was 38 million tons of oil equivalent (MTOE), while the domestic production is only 20 million tons. In 1980, domestic sources

provided only 7.2 million tons but the consumption level was
11.2 million tons. The dependence on imported energy was
limited to 35 per cent of the total requirements. By 1997 the gap
had widened to 18 million tons, and imports provided almost
one half of the total consumption.

Out of the total commercial energy supply, oil accounted for
45 per cent, natural gas 34 per cent, hydel power 15 per cent,
and coal 5 per cent. Non-commercial energy consumption,
largely in the rural areas, is currently estimated at 23 MTOE.

As oil accounts for almost one half of the total energy supply
and domestic oil production meets only 7 per cent of the total
oil demand, imported crude and petroleum products have
remained the single largest import item on the country's list.
The oil import bill has been one of the contributory factors to
the pressures on the balance of payments and, despite
moderation in international petroleum prices, has doubled in
less than a decade; it now accounts for 25 per cent of the total
value of merchandise imports.

In 1947, when Pakistan became independent, the country
possessed only two small hydroelectric power stations, with a
total installed capacity of electricity generation of 57 MW,
accounting for about 3 per cent of the total generating capacity
of undivided India. Due to the political and administrative
problems of the early years, only 46 MW of additional power
capacity had been brought onstream by 1958 (Ebinger, 1981).
The development of hydel power generation was confined to
the utilization of canal falls and tunnel water, partly due to the
country's inability to finance the large-scale dams needed to
generate commercial power. This inability to develop the power
sector was a critical constraint to growth during the period, as
revealed in the very low GDP growth rates of the period. Thus,
the early years witnessed a significant neglect in the expansion
of hydroelectric power.

In the late 1950s, India's curtailment of water supply to West
Pakistan's large irrigation system led the Pakistan government
to conduct a major inventory of the national potential for
hydroelectric power development (Ebinger, 1981). In 1958, the

government, in order to facilitate the growth of power generation, as well as its transmission and distribution, created the Water and Power Development Authority (WAPDA). It was only after the formation of this statutory autonomous corporation that efforts were stepped up to expand this capacity.

The 1960s saw a large expansion in Pakistan's hydroelectric capabilities. During the Second Five-Year Development Plan (1960-5), hydroelectric capacity rose from 66.7 MW in 1959 to 267 MW in 1964-5. At the same time, installed thermal capacity rose from 39 MW in 1959 to 560.5 MW in 1965 (Ebinger, 1981). International assistance played a pivotal role in constructing a number of large hydroelectric projects: Warsak (1961), Mangla (1968), and Tarbela (1973). Thermal power plants using natural gas were also set up in the Upper and Lower Indus Basin.

During the 1970s, the Bhutto government gave high priority to the power sector and increased power-sector investment from Rs 684 million to $2.4 billion annually, representing a more than threefold increase in a span of five years (Ebinger, 1981). The government formulated a strategy for dealing with long-term energy requirements by minimizing the importation of oil for power generation. The available options included stepping up the pace of exploration for oil and gas, setting up nuclear power plants (the 137 MW plant at KANUPP based on natural uranium heavy water is the most prominent), and the exploration of hydro potential in the upper reaches of the Indus and Jhelum. By 1973, the generating capcity had increased to 2180 MW— one-third supplied by the hydro projects and two-thirds from thermal.

The 1980s witnessed a regime change and a consequent reallocation of sectoral priorities. The power sector was relegated a lower priority. During this period investment in this sector increased from Rs 2.6 billion to Rs 5.1 billion—percentage wise this represented only a hundred per cent increase as oppossed to the threefold increase within half a decade during the Bhutto years. The situation worsened during the 1980s, when load-shedding became a prominent feature of economic life, resulting in diminished industrial production and agricultural development, and a plethora of other maladies.

Since the creation of WAPDA in 1958, the intervening three decades have seen more than a twenty-five fold increase in the number of electricity consumers and a sixty-five fold increase in power generation capacity in the country (Azhar B.A., 1991). The annual growth rate of electricity produced in the first twenty-five years was 20 per cent. The average annual energy consumption per consumer in 1970 was 2,636 KWH. The domestic (residential) sector consumed about 430 KWH. Per capita electricity consumption rose from 10 units in 1955 to 75 units in 1970. In the most recent period, 1980-95, the annual growth in electricity production was 9.6 per cent. Per capita electricity production was 450 KWH (Table 5.2), which is still lower than the average for low income countries.

The combined power generation capacity of WAPDA and KESC is 12,851 MW (Table 5.3) with 4,825 MW of hydro and 6,288 MW of thermal with the remainder coming from nuclear power. The actual generation of 46,226 million KWH in 1995-6 was produced equally through hydel and thermal sources. The annual growth rate of electricity generation between 1960 and 1995 has averaged about 10 per cent—more than three times the rate of increase of population and twice the growth rate of the economy.

Pakistan is one of the few developing countries where residential or household consumption of electricity has outstripped that of the industrial and agricultural sectors. While the latter's consumption has declined from 63 to 47 per cent in the last two decades, domestic consumption has more than doubled, from 18 to 40 per cent.

Power losses by WAPDA and KESC of more than 25 per cent are relatively higher than most developing countries. The reduction in these losses to manageable proportions would improve the financial position of the two organizations and ease the burden on the honest consumers who have to pay higher charges than are warranted in order to offset the losses.

The energy sector, which comprises the extraction and exploitation of primary energy sources, especially hydropower, oil, natural gas, and petroleum, currently absorbs one-third of total development expenditure. On the demand side, Pakistan's per capita energy consumption is broadly in line with the country's income per capita, but it could increase rapidly with industrialization and rising incomes (Faiz, 1992).

In terms of power generation capability, Pakistan's 76.6 kilowatts per 1,000 population ranks above average compared to the low-income countries (Table 5.4) but stands weak in comparison to many of the higher-performing economies, like China (118.6) and Egypt (214.6). While Pakistan tripled its kilowattage from 1980 to 1990, greater demand has resulted in prolonged load shedding during the dry season since the early 1980s. Use of the current generating capacity is so intense that the generation capacity factor of 61 per cent is the highest among developing countries. Meanwhile, its power system losses (25 per cent) are relatively high compared to countries of similar per capita incomes like India (19 per cent) and Sri Lanka (18 per cent).

While Pakistan has great potential for hydropower, currently only 18 per cent of this potential has been developed (Faiz, 1992). Since this accounts for about 50 per cent of the country's total generation capacity, there is tremendous scope for domestic hydropower expansion and for supplementing foreign oil and petroleum products with local sources.

In recent years, in order to combat public criticism of the inadequate energy policy and to combat the problems of energy shortage, the government identified power as the industry most in need of foreign investment. The Benazir government in 1994 launched an ambitious attempt to create an economic and legal environment to encourage private investment in infrastructure. It articulated a concise long-term energy development plan involving new public and private investments to increase the growth rate of generation capacity. Under the new plan, increased private-sector participation was encouraged in power generation through financing and operational know-how. The policy, aimed primarily at attracting foreign investors, established a universal tariff structure guaranteeing operators an inflation-adjusted equivalent of 6.5 US cents per kilowatt/hour in the first ten years of the project (Euromoney, 1995). This was designed to provide annual returns of between 18 and 25 per cent. Moreover, a combination of tax concessions and free repatriation of profits provided added incentives to foreign investors.

The policy had paid handsome dividends, with Pakistan moving to the forefront of infrastructural development after so many years of inactivity. In 1996 the government issued letters of support to thirty projects worth around $7 billion. The most well-known success story has been the $1.6 billion Hub power project, hailed by international investors as a blueprint for infrastructural financing of power projects. The Hub Power Project, a Build-Own-Operate scheme to provide 1,292 MW, is the first of a series of projects to increase Pakistan's long-term energy production. It is expected that about 3000 MW additional generating capacity will become available by 1998 from the power projects in the private sector. The total investment in these projects will be about $3 billion. The Nawaz Sharif Government has, however, started re-negotiation with these Independent Power Producers (IPPs) on the delivered price of electricity. It has also initiated an investigation into the corrupt practices of some of these IPPs. This action has caused a considerable setback in the efforts to attract private investment in Pakistan's infrastructure.

The private sector's involvement in power generation will, however, create increased pressures on the balance of payments in the form of increased imports of fuel, debt-servicing, and payments of dividends and remittances. The guaranteed tariff level of 6.5 cents has also caused a controversy in Pakistan about the likely impact of the high-cost electricity on the competitiveness of domestic industry, especially that of tradable goods.

As domestic savings are likely to play a bigger role in financing private infrastructure projects in the future, domestic capital market development and instruments such as buyers' credits, equity sales, and cofinancing arrangements will be critical. In addition, the development of domestic capabilities to manage, participate in, and mobilize private infrastructure projects will be quite important in the near future (International Finance Corporation, 1996).

While commercial risk can be minimized, country risk is harder to control. The low level of reserves could be a serious disincentive to financiers interested in seeing a timely repayment of their loans. Given the magnitude of Pakistan's infrastructural needs, there is a constant need to take measures that can mitigate the perceived country risk. A lower negotiated tariff structure along with lower spreads on debt financing raised in the international markets by the independent power producers will go a long way towards improving the cost structure of the industrial and commercial users of power in the country.

Although Pakistan needs less money than China and India, the infrastructural requirements are colossal (Euromoney, 1995). In power, Pakistan has an average peakfall of some 20 per cent and will need another 14,500 megawatts of new generating capacity in the next five years to keep pace with the projected demand, thus necessitating the doubling of existing capacity and an investment of $15 billion. The slowdown of the economy in the 1993-6 period has reduced the demand for power somewhat, but if the past trend growth rate of GDP is restored, the past demand projections will become valid.

In sum, Pakistan's past record of power generation and delivery has been adversely affected by weaknesses in service standards, but the new energy policy that seemed extremely promising in terms of revamping Pakistan's power generation capability is currently on hold.

Pakistan did discover substantial natural gas reserves that helped in meeting the country's energy requirements. Despite an almost doubling of gas production from 951 to 1806 MMCFD, its share in overall energy has not increased. The gas reserves are depleting fast, and it is estimated that at the current rate of production they will last another fifteen years. Most of the future energy needs will have therefore to be met from imported oil, as the recoverable reserves of oil are extremely low. More than three-fourths of the natural gas is consumed by three sectors—power (30 per cent), fertilizer (26 per cent), and general industries (22 per cent). A major initiative has also been taken to privatize public-sector gas transmission and distribution companies. Gas exploration and development has traditionally been the domain of the private sector. Privatization will lead to improved efficiency and reduced losses in transmission and distribution.

TELECOMMUNICATIONS

In the important area of telecommunications, the coverage of telephone services increased from about 3 lines per thousand population in 1978 to nearly 18 lines per thousand in 1996 (Table 5.7). Pakistan has a higher telephone availability than most Asian nations, but this has been weakened by a high fault line. This is perhaps the single worst rate in the entire world. Countries as diverse as Indonesia, Egypt, Turkey, Brazil, and Malaysia all have faults of less than 10 per 1000, an amount smaller than one-tenth of Pakistan's. Furthermore, the telecommunications sector has a high urban bias, like Pakistan's other infrastructure, with over 90 per cent of the users and beneficiaries in the urban areas.

The telecommunications sector grew very sluggishly in the first three decades, but it has accelerated in the 1980s and 1990s due to increased demand. In similar fashion, service quality has been improving, with both domestic and long-distance access expanding. However, complaints about the unresponsiveness of the telecommunications utility to the demands of the users are perennial.

While the public sector retained a monopoly under the Telegraph and Telephone (T&T) Department of the Communications Ministry until 1990, in recent years there has been a mushrooming of private companies supplying cellular phones and data transmission (Isfahani, 1994). In response to growing criticism that the telecommunications sector was overregulated, the government has converted the T&T into the Pakistan Telecommunications Corporation (PTC), to be funded from internally-generated funds. The eventual privatization of PTC should reduce the serious overstaffing and inactivity that hindered the performance of T&T. One interesting phenomenon is that PTC's tariff structure is considerably skewed, allowing long-distance calls to subsidize local calls.

In recent years, with the globalization and integration of the economy, telecommunications is becoming more and more profitable. Telecom privatizations in Venezuela, Mexico, and Argentina have reaped huge windfalls for private investors and led to better services for domestic users. The deregulation and eventual privatization of Pakistan Telecom is an attempt to replicate the experience. The reforms in this sector are described later in this chapter.

RAILWAYS

Pakistan Railways, with over 130,000 employees, operates the fourth largest railway system in Asia (8,800 line km.). It is largely a passenger-oriented service, with more than two-thirds of train mileage devoted to passenger service; and it has one of the lowest rates of rail tracks in the world, with a meager 2.6 km. per 100,000 population. This pales into insignificance when compared with the high rates of countries like Turkey (14.8) and Malaysia (31.0), and compares unfavourably with many of the lowest-income economies (Table 5.8). To make matters worse, the railway system has been running at a financial loss for several years, with wages and pensions accounting for two-thirds of expenditures (Faiz, 1992). Thus, there is little money left for productive investment in trains and tracking facilities.

Historically, after a rapid building of tracks in the 1950s, the sector remained stagnant for twenty years. In 1960 there were 8,574 km. of track; by 1980 the figure was only 8,815km. Since the late 1970s the number of locomotives, wagons, passengers carried, and amount of freight handled has declined by about 30 to 60 per cent. The condition of assets is highly unsatisfactory as the over-aged locomotives, rails, and sleepers have not yet been replaced and account for the bulk of the operating assets. The combination of serious overmanning and severe overaging of operating assets has created intractable financial difficulties for the Railways. An open-access policy has been adopted to allow private investment in railway to operate freight and passenger trains by paying rail track access charges to the Railways. It is hoped that this will help improve the operational efficiency of the system.

WATER AND SANITATION

The main sources of drinking water in Pakistan are surface water, primarily drawn from the Indus River, and water drawn from shallow wells, with both these sources being currently used to levels approaching sustainable capacity. Unfortunately, the poor quality of the water, with high levels of contamination, as well as a weak delivery system, with sporadic supply, have created huge problems (World Bank, 1990). Thus, in this sector, infrastructural deficiency is acute. It is estimated that water supply facilities are available to 80 per cent (36 million) of the urban (45 million) population. The main problem arises due to poor and unreliable distribution mechanisms in urban areas. For instance, distribution leakage has been estimated at 20 per cent of Karachi's water supply. A comparison with other countries is not flattering to Pakistan. While 75 per cent of Pakistanis have access to drinking water, 98 per cent of Bangladeshis, 81 per cent of Indians, and 93 per cent of Koreans have that same access (Table 5.9).

In similar fashion, sanitation facilities (piped sewerage, septic tanks, and soak pits) are available to 53 per cent of the urban population and 12 per cent of the rural population. Unfortunately, when compared to most developing countries,

Pakistan fares badly in indicators relating to sanitation. In Ethiopia, the comparable figures are 97 and 7 per cent for urban and rural sectors, in China, 100 and 81 per cent, in Philippines 79 and 63 per cent, and in Brazil 84 and 32 per cent.

Given the importance of water and sanitation services for public health and the welfare of the population, this represents a critical shortcoming. The links between water quality and health have been abundantly documented in the development literature. A plethora of maladies from cholera to typhoid are water-borne, and diarrhoeal diseases, the major cause of child mortality in Pakistan, accounting for 300,000 deaths in 1986, can be reduced by 60 per cent given proper sanitation.

In the 1970s water and sewerage systems expanded, but they have not kept pace with the overall demand. Unlike other infrastructure sectors, water and sewerage are primarily the responsibility of the provincial and local governments rather than the federal government (Ahmed, 1994). Given the lack of resources and autonomy of most municipal operators, they cannot administer and maintain water supply systems. In 1993, under the auspices of the World Bank, a Rural Water Supply and Sanitation component of the Social Action Plan (SAP) was started in an attempt to involve local communites in water supply development, but changes have not materialized. Access to water and sanitation continues to be one of the weakest parts of Pakistan's infrastructure.

IRRIGATION

The one infrastructural area where Pakistan enjoys unqualified success is irrigation. Its 17.0 million hectares of irrigated land have few competitors internationally, with the sole exception of India and China, which have a much larger landmass (Table 5.10). In terms of the relative availability of irrigated land compared to both the size of the population and the size of the economy, Pakistan tops the list in all countries. The huge system bequeathed by British colonial rule has remained operational, in spite of inadequacy of drainage and poor maintenance.

To sum up, in comparison to a large sample of countries from the developing world, Pakistan has the best irrigation system, a slightly above average power generation and natural gas availability, an expanding transportation sector, and an improving telecommunications industry, but poor rail, water and sanitation systems. In the last two decades, there has been a large change in the composition of infrastructure capital, with telecommunications, power, and gas on the rise and railways and public irrigation infrastructure in decline, road infrastructure growing in terms of quantity, not quality, and water and sewerage systems experiencing uncertain growth. Unfortunately, extremely poor service delivery and chronic breakdowns continue to make the Pakistani infrastructure quite poor in terms of overall performance.

CONSTRAINTS AFFECTING INFRASTRUCTURE DEVELOPMENT

INSTITUTIONAL CONSTRAINTS

The efficient provision of adequate infrastructure depends critically on a country's institutions and the capacity of those institutions to deliver services at least cost to the consumers. By the institutions we mean the entire apparatus of constitutional division of powers between the Federal, Provincial and local governments for infrastructure development, the respective roles of the public and private sector in the provision, the long term planning for investment in the sector and the inter model priorities and the policy and regulatory framework. The organizations actually managing and operating the various services and facilities are discussed separately under administrative constraints. In Pakistan, given the fact that the characteristics of infrastructure development, both in terms of the response to demand growth and the distributional biases of the investments, do not have any clearly defined technological and economic rationale, one has to look to the country's institutions in order to understand the government's sluggish implementation of much-needed reforms in this sector. The division of powers within the Pakistani polity, the nature of decision-making, the relative demarcation of powers and responsibilities between the public and the private sector, and the administrative structure are the main institutional variables that affect the country's ability to provide adequate infrastructure. Unfortunately, Pakistan has had a great deal of instituional uncertainty in these areas.

The first source of institutional uncertainty has been the constant oscillation in Pakistani politics between democratic rule and military dictatorship. A series of regime changes since the mid-1950s created unfavourable and erratic conditions for the regulation and management of long-gestation investment. Given their short time horizons, none of the governments developed a long-term perspective across different infrastructure sectors, prioritized government investment decisions, or developed the regulatory framework in a consistent manner. One prime example of this with regard to infrastructure provision is the non-establishment of politically autonomous regulatory agencies for telecommunications, power, and railways.

A second source of institutional weakness has been the unequal distribution of power between the different layers of government. The Pakistani polity, especially when compared to other developing countries, has been a very centralized political structure, with relatively weak provincial government and very weak local and municipal government. Under both the 1973 and the 1985 Constitutions, the federal government is responsible for allocating infrastructure for power, transportation, communications, social welfare, and a host of other activities, whereas provincial governments are responsible for water and sanitation systems, health, and basic education. Unfortunately, local governments in Pakistan do not have any distinct constitutional status. They are established by provincial governments and maintained by provincial statutes. This top-heavy system does not allow for any positive role to be played by strong local bodies, such as efficient municipalities, in improving the quality of public service delivery. A decentralized service delivery mechanism would be more effective since the local authorities would have access to much better information and beneficiary participation in the design and delivery of services than their federal counterparts. In the critical areas of water and sanitation and in road building, the current institutional setup is overcentralized and reflects the inability of both federal and provincial governments to oversee and monitor a vast system of infrastructure delivery.

A final source of weakness is the administrative system under which many of the public enterprises operate. The predominance of organizations with a lack of clear and coherent goals focused on delivering services, a lack of financial and managerial autonomy and accountability, and, finally, a lack of financial independence has characterized Pakistan's public sector and its infrastructure service delivery capability. There is a vital need for adminstrative institutions that provide the government with low-cost means to accurately assess the cost structure of infrastructure operations, to apply appropriate delivery criteria, and to monitor the performance of private operators in natural monopoly services. Unfortunately, lack of both competence in the bureaucracy and appropriate incentive structures has made the Pakistani administrative system in the 1990s much weaker than it was in the 1950s.

Since Partition in 1947, Pakistan's institutions have changed in several ways, with differing effects on infrastructure. In the early decades of Pakistan's existence, an exemplary Civil Service installed a highly capable administrative culture, but the weakness of political institutions and the lack of commitment in the executive branch due to frequent instability and regime changes dampened the power of the institutions (Isfahani, 1994). Thus, given this managerial and administrative capability, it was natural for the public sector to run infrastructure policy through its network of public enterprises. In the last two decades, this administrative edge has been lost due to political encroachment into the bureaucracy; paradoxically, political commitment has become much higher as governments face increasing pressure and demands from both local and international sources to revamp the infrastructure. Under the current institutional setup, Pakistan stands to gain substantially from greater private-sector participation in infrastructure sectors. While the private-sector cannot replace the public sector in the provision of infrastructure with high capital costs and long-term commitments, such as irrigation and transportation facilities, it can supplement public financing; in other sectors where efficient service delivery is of key importance, as in telecommunications and water supply systems, the private sector can play an important role (World Bank, 1990).

In sum, the current institutional setup needs substantial revamping in order to create better infrastructural policies. Although institutions are by no means the sole determinants of commitment and administrative capabilites (other factors include resource endowment, technological advancement, economic growth), strong institutions foster good policies. Political uncertainty, overcentralized government structure, and a poor adminstrative framework do not provide a good recipe for success.

FINANCIAL CONSTRAINTS

Financial constraints have prevented Pakistan from undertaking critical investments in infrastructure. Historically, the federal government spearheaded the industrialization drive in Pakistan and was responsible for large engineering public works projects and the construction and supply of the large networked delivery system designed to serve a multitude of users, including public utilities such as piped water, electric power, telecommunications, gas, and sewerage.

For a variety of reasons, the private sector has stayed away from infrastructure provision. These sectors required large commitments of capital in the early stages which were unavailable to the private sector. The presence of natural monopolies, economies of scale, and a large overhead have been the main considerations that kept the government from inducting the private sector. Recent advances in technology and the successful experiences of countries in Latin America have opened new avenues of private sector participation, and Pakistan has been one of the early leaders in this respect through the Hub and Uch power projects. One of the difficulties that persist in the context of poor countries is the cost recovery from users, because the services are viewed as basic needs (water, energy, etc.) and exclusion of non-paying users is too costly (World Bank 1990). The dilemmas in the provision of public goods, and the twin features of non-rivalness, in which an increase in one person's consumption does not affect another's, and non-excludability, where everyone can use the asset without payment, have further deterred the private sector from contributing to infrastructure development.

Thus, the Pakistan government was solely responsible for infrastructure provision until the early 1990s. The combined expenditures of federal and provincial governments have increased, from Rs 44 billion in 1980-1 to Rs 500 billion in 1997-8. However, the share of infrastructure in the combined current expenditures declined sharply, from 7.5 per cent in 1982-3 to 5 per cent in 1997-8. The decline in federal spending has led to a deterioration of federal highways, public buildings, and power generation and distribution facilities, while low spending at the provincial level has primarily affected the maintenance of irrigation works.

Pakistan's development expenditure has been substantially reduced in the recent years. Since the 1980s the government has been making attempts to curtail its development spending in light of the alarming levels of the overall fiscal deficit, which averaged more than 6 per cent of GNP per year throughout the 80s. The share of development expenditures in GNP fell from 8.6 per cent in 1980-1 to 3.4 per cent in 1997-8, with total devlopment expenditures rising from Rs 26 billion in 1980-1 to

Rs 96 billion in 1997-8, but unable to keep pace with the rising inflation. This comparison is not perfectly valid, however, as the development expenditures of the power, telecommunications, and gas and oil sectors are no longer included in the federal budget. Most of the development investments by WAPDA, PTC, and OGDC in recent years were financed by heavy borrowing. Thus, owing to the financial constraints imposed by debt service, it has not been possible to maintain and expand physical infrastructure at the needed levels, with the result that shortages of electricity, gas, and transport are emerging as major bottlenecks to economic growth.

Infrastructure investment has maintained a central position in development expenditures throughout the last five decades. In the Second plan period, when the Indus Basin works were being built, 43 per cent of the public sector development programme was allocated for water resources. The total outlay for infrastructure including irrigation in that period was at a peak— 78 per cent. It was maintained as high as 75 per cent for the next ten years, but with the completion of Tarbela Dam, the level was down to 64 per cent in the 1980s. The average for the 1990-6 period is estimated at 60 per cent of a much smaller overall allocation for development expenditures.

Unfortunately, a combination of a low level of gross investment in infrastructure (averaging about 4.8 per cent of GNP throughout the 1980s) and a heavy dependence on external loan disbursements which did not follow the original disbursement schedules has not boded well for Pakistan's infrastructure. To give an empirical assessment of the delays in implementing infrastructure projects, the World Bank's project portfolio shows that infrastructure projects have the poorest annual disbursement performance—a disbursement rate of 7 per cent compared to 14 per cent for energy projects and 21 per cent for agriculture and industry projects (Isfahani, 1994). Thus, the twin problems of adequate financing in the face of budgetary cuts and implementation delays in the projects suggest that a critical barrier and constraint to infrastructure development is financial in nature.

ADMINISTRATIVE CONSTRAINTS

Another set of constraints on the performance in infrastructure is the poor organization and administrative calibre of the executing agencies entrusted with the operation and maintenance of the facilities built. Government organizations operating in infrastructure such as WAPDA, KESC, and Pakistan Railways did a remarkably good job in the earlier phases of their functioning, but over time infrastructure became generally inefficient, overstaffed, poorly managed, and also underfunded for maintenance. Four basic problems plague these organizations.

Firstly, many of these organizations have unclear, diffuse, imprecise organizational mandates. They are burdened with social objectives that are not quantifiable. As they do not have a clear mandate or detailed sets of policy targets to be achieved, the organizational incentives in which outputs and inputs are closely monitored are conspicuously absent.

Secondly, a lack of managerial and financial autonomy and accountability cripple the institutions and enterprises. Financial problems, overemployment, and poor goals occur because the managers do not have control over day-to-day operations or over decisions on prices, wages, employments, and budgets (Isfahani, 1994). One area where financial problems are common is in the power sector, where politically-motivated tariff adjustments frequently lag behind cost increases. In this situation, infrastructure providers do not have sufficient funds to maintain existing infrastructure and invest in new projects.

Thirdly, the pressures of wage compensation and employment constraints are a further burden on these agencies. The majority of expenditures in Pakistan's public-sector organizations go towards meeting wages and pension, which are not linked to productivity. For example, two-thirds of the expenditure on railways goes on wages and benefits of the employees, leaving very little finance available for new investments in modernization (Faiz, 1992). Furthermore, the infrastructure utilities are overstaffed in Pakistan because the government uses them to create public-sector jobs, passing on the additional cost to the taxpayer and consumer.

Fourth, the rampant corruption in public-sector organizations has led to collusion between unscrupulous customers and dishonest staff. Heavy commercial losses in power, water, and railways can be directly attributed to the leakage of revenues. As the revenues collected fall short of the cost of production, there are continuing pressures to raise tariff rates. The escalation of tariff rates, in turn, creates further incentives for evasion of dues and increases opportunities for further collusion between the staff and the payers. In some instances, revenues are not adequate to meet even the recurrent expenditures for operation and maintenance of the facilities. In these circumstances, the existing infrastructure is poorly maintained and resources for expansion and investment are no longer forthcoming. The congestion and bottlenecks in basic infrastructure facilities in Pakistan are the product of this vicious circle of revenue leakages, higher tariff setting, evasion in payments, and underinvestment.

POLICY REFORM

In recent years, successive governments have attempted to come to grips with the above constraints by instituting a series of limited reforms aimed at improving the operational efficiency of the enterprises and departments involved in the provision of infrastructure services and encouraging the private sector to participate in this area.

The current main reform focus of the government is through large-scale privatization in the telecom and power sectors and increased private participation in parts of railways, interurban highways, and water and sewerage in large metropolitan areas. Several approaches are now under way aimed at reducing the organizational, financial, and managerial constraints to successful performance.

Firstly, corporatization—the process of giving public enterprises independent status and subjecting them to the same legal requirements as private firms—is an important step (Faiz, 1992). Along with this separation of public sector entities from the general budget, measures are needed to provide them with necessary financial autonomy to raise their own resources, through such measures as user charges, cost-based tariffs, and bond issues.

Secondly, a series of public-private partnerships under the Build-Operate-Transfer (BOT) schemes seems promising. In BOT projects, private sector sponsors, usually international construction contractors, heavy equipment suppliers, and plant and system operators, together with local partners, make equity investments (usually 10 to 30 per cent of the total project cost) in a private company that will build the project, operate it long enough to pay back the project debt and equity investment, and then transfer it back to the host government (Augenblick and Custer Jr., 1990). Under this setup, the company is financed from commercial sources and international donors to complete the project within an allocated timeframe and takes the entire commercial risk burden from the public sector. This is a new area where the private sector can involve itself in fields that it has historically shied away from. These policy reforms have affected different sub-sectors in a varied manner. The discussion in the following paragraphs is therefore organized to highlight the progress made in each sub-sector.

TELECOMMUNICATIONS

One area where policy reform is quite advanced is in the telecommunications sector. In 1994, the Government of Pakistan issued a Telecommunications Ordinance that detailed the privatization process for PTC. Basically, PTC will be transferred to a strategic investor under a twenty-five year licence with an exclusivity period of seven years. The tariffs are to be set under a formula that sets a price-cap that rises with inflation, thus increasing the current low rates. The proposed agreement does not encourage an unbundling or increase of competition in the long-distance market because in this market the call tariffs have historically been priced high in order for PTC to earn reasonable profits.

In order to strengthen the new arrangement, a new regulatory body, the Pakistan Telecommunications Authority (PTA), has been created to issue licences and enforce regulations. This organization, an independent body with both organizational and financial autonomy from the government, will lend credibility to the government's policies. After the initial seven years, when the PTA will be working with a single profitable entity, substantial competition will be introduced to encourage alternative providers of long-distance facilities and to involve the private sector in the telecommunications business.

Currently, the main examples of private-sector participation in the last years have been the entry of three cellular telephone operators and the contracting of a Build-lease-transfer (BLT) operation for PTC. While in the cellular contract, the government issued fifteen-year exclusive licences to two operators, and set a series of rates and sharing rules, as well as requiring the cellular operators to set a nationwide network, under the BLT contract, the private sector had to install 500,000 telephone lines under a system in which it would build the infrastructure and then return it to the public sector. There have been a few attempts to sell the shares of the PTC to private investors. A successful launch was made through a GDR floatation and an IPO in Pakistani stock markets. About $ 1 billion was collected by selling 10 per cent of the shares and a benchmark price was established for subsequent sale to a strategic investor. Since then, the progress in finding a strategic investor for PTC has stalled.

POWER

The private sector has also become involved in the generation of electricity, especially the 1300 MW Hub Power Project. This project, with a total cost of $1.8 billion, represented uncharted territory for Pakistan, with a combination of commercial lenders, sponsors, and the Government having to deal with a cluster of legal and administrative complications. However, the guaranteed returns from the project seem to considerably outweigh the costs.

Other policy reforms in the private sector include the privatization of the thermal generation, transmission, and distribution networks of WAPDA in order to make each section more accountable, and the creation of a new regulatory body to ensure compliance with the new system. The Kot Adu Power Station was sold to a private British power company. Unfortunately, the unbundling of WAPDA services, dealing with overstaffing and labour issues, and setting up organizational arrangements that co-ordinate dispatch activities while ensuring competition among generators are very difficult policy measures that will take years to implement and administer (Isfahani, 1994).

One key difficulty will be the ability of the government sector to attract the private capital to finance the new projects in transmission and distribution. A combination of low electricity price recovery rates, a high imbalance of these prices in favour of residential and agriculture users at the expense of industrial enterprises, and the inability of the power sector to earn foreign exchange all suggest that private investment in transmission and distribution may not prove to be as attractive as generation. But the government has decided to experiment by putting one of the Area Electricity Boards up for transfer to the private sector.

OTHER SECTORS

Reform in other sectors of infrastructure—roads, railways, water, and sewerage—has moved at a much slower pace than in the telecommunications and power sectors, but the momentum of encouraging greater private sector participation should spill over to these other sectors. The railway sector has received some attention in recent years regarding possible use of rail tracks by private operators. Actual progress has, however, been unimpressive. Similar initiatives are under way for some of the port operations at KPT and Port Qasim.

Depending on the nature of the sector and its technical characteristics, a reform process that ensures extensive private sector participation can come to fruition. The unbundling of railway services, port handling operations, and a series of BOT and joint ventures in the road system seem to be the best measures for improving efficiency.

In the water and sanitation sector, concessions, i.e., financing arrangements in which a private company contracts with the government to build and operate an infrastructure system for a period of time under full commercial risk and then hand over all fixed assets of the system to the public authorities, seems to be the most effective policy.

FUTURE REQUIREMENTS

In order to fill in the gaps and meet the challenges of future growth, Pakistan must complete reforms in the power and telecommunications sectors while making further headway in railways, roads, water supply, ports, and shipping. These reforms and institutional changes will draw new investment, improve the productivity of investment and thus affect the rate of economic growth.

In order to assess the impact of reforms in infrastructure on growth in Pakistan, the performance requirements and infrastructure financing of two macroeconomic scenarios were contrasted: a high scenario in which the GDP growth rate is 6.5 per cent per year during 1995-2005 and accelerates to 8.0 per cent thereafter, and a base scenario in which the growth rate remains at 5 per cent per year (Isfahani, 1994). In the high scenario, the government's macroeconomic reforms to reduce the budget deficit, trade reforms to liberalize the sector and make it more competitive, and public-enterprise reforms that enable the private sector to play a more productive role in the provision of infrastructure, allow the economy to have an accelerated growth. By contrast, the base scenario represents a continuation of policies adopted in the last couple of years, without any attempt to improve the present situation.

The conclusions are interesting (Isfahani, 1994). Under the high-case scenario, the infrastructure asset formation index rises to. 46 by 2001 and then to. 47 after a couple of years. In the base scenario, by contrast, the index reaches. 45 by 2001 and remains there. In the high case, the infrastructure investment-GDP ratio rises to 6.5 in 2010 as GDP growth accelerates, while in the base scenario, the share of infrastructure investment in GDP remains close to the current level.

In both cases, Pakistan will have large investment requirements. During the next fifteen, years Pakistan will need about $99 billion in the high case and $70 billion in the low case. In the high case, the sectoral shares of investments are: power and gas 58.7 per cent, telecommunications 19.6 per cent, irrigation 4.6 per cent, water and sewerage 4.6 per cent, railways 2.8 per cent, and roads and transport 9.6 per cent, while the shares of power and gas in the base years are somewhat lower and the other shares somewhat higher.

In a similar vein, in order to understand the public sector's financing gap, two scenarios are constructed. It is assumed that in the base year the government reduces its deficit by 2.5 per cent to make it barely sustainable, while in the high case it reduces its deficit by 5 per cent (Isfahani, 1994). The results show that in the base case, budgetary development expenditures on infrastructure decline to 2.3 per cent of GDP, self-financing remains around 1.6 per cent, and the private sector's contribution amounts to about 1.5 per cent of GDP until 2000 and then declines to 1 per cent. If the economy is to grow vigorously, the flow of new private-sector capital will be three times the amount needed in partial reforms. Under the high scenario, the power sector, the transport sector, the irrigation sector, and the water and sanitation sector will need only 1 per cent of GDP in future years to sustain themselves.

The lessons and policy implications are starkly clear. If the government succeeds in reducing the deficit by 5 per cent, the infrastructure development expenditures—which will be 1 per cent of GDP will easily cover the road and irrigation investments. Thus, private investment in telecommunications and power, as well as a limited role in railways, water and sanitation systems, and highways, is a crucial necessity.

Finally, if the government can succeed in improving the economy's creditworthiness, infrastructure projects are likely to attract the 20 per cent equity needed to begin the financing process. That would represent an order of the magnitude of $1 billion by 2010.

In sum, a series of macroeconomic reforms, including deficit reduction, trade liberalization, and public enterprise reform, as well as policies to allow both the private sector and foreign investors to bring in much-needed capital and expertise, will be crucial for the success of Pakistan's infrastructural facilities.

Although lack of infrastructure is only one of the factors that will affect Pakistan's growth, it is a vital ingredient to success, and neglect of this sector can doom Pakistan's chances of becoming a prosperous nation.

TABLE 5.1
PAVED ROADS (km per 100,000 pop.)

Country	Level (1990)	% in good condition
Pakistan	73.0	18
Ethiopia	24.1	48
Tanzania	13.5	25
Nepal	14.1	40
Bangladesh	5.8	15
India	86.0	20
Nigeria	30.4	67
Egypt	26.7	39
Indonesia	63.2	30
Peru	33.5	24
Thailand	68.8	50
Brazil	105.0	30
Korea	78.3	70

Source: *World Development Report 1994*, World Bank, Washington, DC

TABLE 5.2
ELECTRICITY INDICATORS

Year	Per Capita Electricity Generation (GWH) (Per Million People)	Per Capita Electricity Consumption (GWH) (Per Million)
1960	NA	NA
1970	95	63
1980	185	123
1990	342	261
1996	450	350[1]

Source: Economic Survey (various issues), Ministry of Finance, Government
    of Pakistan, Islamabad
[1] estimate

TABLE 5.3
COMMERCIAL ELECTRICITY SUPPLIES

Year	Installed Capacity (MW)	Percentage Change
1947	57	
1955	161	182
1960	731	354
1965	1135	55
1969	1920	69
1973	2185	14
1980	3518	61
1985	5615	74
1990	7449	33
1996	1285	72

Source: Economic Survey (various issues), Ministry of Finance, Government
    of Pakistan, Islamabad

TABLE 5.4
ELECTRICITY-GENERATING
CAPACITY (KW/1000 POP.)

Country	Level (1990)	% of Houses with Electricity	% of Power System Losses
Pakistan	76.6	31	24
Bangladesh	22.0	N.A.	30
India	86.0	54	19
China	118.6	N.A.	15
Sri Lanka	74.1	15	18
Indonesia	62.3	14	21
Thailand	167.6	43	11
Malaysia	270.8	64	16
Korea	550.5	100	N.A.

Source: *World Development Report 1994*, World Bank, Washington DC

TABLE 5.5
COMMERCIAL ENERGY CONSUMPTION
AND PRODUCTION

Year	Production (000 MTOE)	Consumption (000 MTOE)	Net Oil Import	Per Capita Consumption (Kg. of oil equivalent)	Energy Imports as Percentage of Merchandise Exports
1960	NA	NA	NA	97	17
1970	3,860	6,932	375	110	15
1980	7,217	11,698	621	142	23
1990	16,419	25,508	NA	233	21
1995	20,000	33,000	1055	254	28

Source: *World Bank Database*, Industry and Energy Department, Washington DC

TABLE 5.6
GROWTH IN ENERGY PRODUCTION
AND CONSUMPTION
(Annual Average Rates)

Year	Energy Production	Energy Consumption
1960-74	9.2	4.8
1974-81	9.1	7.8
1980-90	12.8	8.0
1990-5	5.0	6.4

TABLE 5.7
TELEPHONES (INSTALLED LINES/1000 POP.)

Country	Level (1996)	Waiting times (years)
Pakistan	18	0.7
Bangladesh	3	6.6
India	15	1.0
Egypt	50	5.0
Indonesia	21	0.2
Turkey	224	0.7
Brazil	96	NA
Malaysia	183	0.4
Mexico	95	0.5
Korea	430	0.0

Source: *World Development Indicators 1998*, World Bank, Washington DC

TABLE 5.8
RAILWAYS (KM PER 100,000 POP.)

COUNTRY	LEVEL (1990)
Pakistan	2.6
Bangladesh	2.5
India	8.5
Kenya	10.3
Nicaragua	8.5
Indonesia	3.8
Thailand	6.8
Malaysia	11.9
Mexico	31.0
Korea	7.1

Source: *World Development Report 1994*, World Bank, Washington DC

TABLE 5.9
WATER ACCESS

COUNTRY	% of Population with Access to Safe Water 1990-96	Per Capita Water availability (*cu m*)
Pakistan	74	1678
Bangladesh	97	10,940
India	81	1,896
Kenya	53	696
Sri Lanka	57	2,341
Thailand	89	1,845
Turkey	84	3,074
Brazil	73	31,424
Malaysia	78	21,259
Mexico	83	3,729
Korea	93	1,434

Source: *World Resources 1998-99* (World Resources Institute, Washington DC)

TABLE 5.10
IRRIGATED LAND AREA

COUNTRY	LEVEL (1990)
Pakistan	16,960
Bangladesh	2,936
India	45,500
China	47,403
Philippines	1,560
Malaysia	342
Mexico	518
Korea	1,345

Source: *World Development Report 1994*, World Bank, Washington DC

CHAPTER 6

FOREIGN TRADE, EXTERNAL DEBT, AND RESOURCE FLOWS

FOREIGN TRADE: TRENDS, POLICIES, AND PROSPECTS

By many standards, Pakistan has been very successful in its trade strategy since 1947. Its trade growth has been strong, the structure and direction of trade have diversified, international linkages have evolved soundly, and its strategy seems to have paid many handsome dividends. But the radically changing nature of the global economy and increased competition from other developing countries pose serious challenges for the future. The stylized facts and empirical evidence are impressive. Exports have multiplied by a factor of 14 in constant US dollar prices from 1947 to the present. (Table 6.1). The foreign trade-GDP ratio has more than doubled, from 15.2 in 1960 to 34.5 by 1996, (Table 6.2), reflecting the nation's growing integration in the international economy. The growth rate of trade has averaged over 6 per cent annually since 1947 to the present (Table 6.3).

From being a meagre trading nation, Pakistan has developed a reasonably strong export sector. The share of primary commodities, which accounted for 99 per cent of Pakistani exports in 1947, was less than 20 per cent in 1996. By contrast, manufactured goods, which were almost negligible in 1947, accounted for more than 60 per cent of exports in 1996. The share of semi-manufactures, although fluctuating in recent years, has managed to reach the 22 per cent mark. The import statistics tell a similar story. The import of consumer goods, which was approximately 40 per cent in 1947, dwindled to 15 per cent by 1996, while the share of capital goods which was about 10 per cent in the early years, increased to about 40 per cent by 1996. The economy has made strides in domestic production of consumer goods, but the record in the capital goods sector so far has been disappointing. Tables 6.4 and 6.5 document these changing trends. In confirmation of its trade strategy, the share of Pakistan's economy in the world market has increased from an insignificant figure in 1947 to 2 per cent in the last decade (Table 6.6).

These are no mean accomplishments, given the fears at Partition that Pakistan would be unable to develop a strong industrial sector or evolve as a major trading partner. Several factors stand out in any positive evaluation of the Pakistani strategy.

Firstly, Pakistan, in spite of all the criticisms has managed to build a competitive export sector. The spectacular shift in the commodity composition can best be characterized as a movement from the export of raw materials to products reflecting higher domestic value-added. Although cotton accounts for about two-thirds of merchandise export earnings, shipment of raw cotton for processing abroad has given way to the exports of processed cotton, textiles, garments, and other manufactured products based on this material (Riordan and Srinivasan, 1996). Table 6.7 presents substantial evidence of the phenomenal boom in the production of cotton manufactures and textile exports.

Furthermore, there has been a strong growth in non-traditional exports in recent years. Pakistan has successfully diversified its export portfolio, but it is still limited in the number of items that are exported. It has been able to find a comparative advantage in a few areas, such as leather goods, surgical goods, carpets, and sports goods, in an increasingly competitive world economy. Table 6.8 shows the change in the composition of manufactured exports. Cotton textiles account for 60 per cent of manufactured exports, but other new, non-traditional exports have emerged since the 1980s and are growing much faster than the traditional exports. Table 6.9 shows the spectacular growth rates of these non-traditional exports since the 1970s.

Secondly, the ISI strategy pursued by Pakistan was successful in developing 'infant industries' and in sheltering these industries from international competition in the early years. A high rate of effective protection, which later became a serious liability, did sustain Pakistani industrial development in the early years. This facilitated the switch from import substitution to export orientation to be completed in case of textiles.

Thirdly, Pakistan had sheltered itself sufficiently from the international economic environment to avoid many of the exogenous shocks that other developing countries have suffered. The one advantage of the ISI trade regime historically has been a relative invulnerability to strong shocks, such as a decline in the terms of trade or a global recession. The 'excess profits' thus earned from the protected import substitute industries were wisely reinvested in export-oriented industries. This laid the foundation for the industrial culture of the country.

In spite of the manifest successes, there were several weaknesses in Pakistan's trade strategy.

Firstly and most importantly, Pakistan has not had the phenomenal export-led growth of the East Asian 'Tigers'. There was discrimination against most non-traditional exports and, as a result, Pakistan has lagged significantly behind other Asian countries in generating foreign exchange, employment, and income from labour-intensive, manufacture-based exports. The high-tech revolution has passed Pakistan by, and it has not managed to achieve a strong comparative advantage in any of the higher value-added manufacturing products. Its trade has been too cotton-based, and this overdependence on cotton has created a textile sector with low value-added.

Secondly, it has been extremely slow in its approach to trade liberalization (Winters and Ingco, 1995). The cumbersome web of administrative controls, stifling bureaucracy, and licensing system still, delays Pakistan's rapid integration into the world economy. The widespread prevalence of quantitative restrictions, high tariff levels frequently averaging 60 per cent, export restrictions, and discretionary quotas have provided a hindrance to trade expansion. High effective protection rates continue to plague the Pakistani economy, with industries sheltered from the world market at a big cost to Pakistani consumers.

Thirdly, the economy has experienced chronic balance of payments problems, and in recent years it has become evident that these are unsustainable (Mohsin Khan, 1990). There has been a continuous secular increase in the current account/ GDP ratio since 1947, with the ratio hovering around 4-5 per cent in the last two decades (Table 6.11) and reaching 6.5 per cent in 1996. Furthermore, complementing this shift has been some worsening of the terms of trade (Table 6.12). An increasing dependence on imports of food and oil militates against the idea of self-reliance that has been so widely touted in recent years. The current account deficits arising out of a relatively faster growth of imports are sustainable over an extended period of time if they can be financed out of foreign aid, direct foreign investment, portfolio flows, etc. Many Asian countries, including India, in the last five years have demonstrated that this is a viable proposition provided the overall economic and political environment is conducive. Whether Pakistan can achieve this objective is an issue that will be analysed in other chapters.

In sum, the foreign trade record of Pakistan has been nurtured on a very narrow base that has made it increasingly vulnerable to exogenous shocks. For example, the vagaries of weather, pest attacks, and international demand fluctuations play a decisive role in the determination of outcomes on growth, exports, government revenues, and foreign exchange reserves. This narrow base, in turn, is the reflection of the elitist growth strategy, whereby the government's incentive policies to provide cotton at subsidized prices (much below world market prices) and cheap loans from development financing institutions and nationalized commercial banks to well-connected and influential members of this group spurred overinvestment in the cotton ginning industry. The allocation of quotas under the MFA by the government assured steady returns without much entre-preneurial effort or competitive pressures. The large loans also allowed opportunities for overinvoicing in the import of machinery, and the loan payments fell into arrears.

On the import side, the licensing system created the many billionaires and multimillionaires which Pakistan has today. The lack of depth in the manufacturing industry did not permit the development of an industrial infrastructure with strong backward and forward linkages.

TRADE POLICY REGIME

The trade policy inherited by Pakistan in 1947 was marked by two distinct features—it was part of the unified economic structure of undivided India, and it was linked to the colonial interests of the British. The British departure from the subcontinent had been speedy and chaotic; Pakistan did not have any remnants of the institutions that are normally required for regulating international trade. Nor did it have such tools as exchange rate, monetary policy, or tax and tariff structures that could affect the direction or speed of trade. The private actors involved in trade and exports were primarily Parsi and Hindu merchants based in Karachi, the latter fled Pakistan at the time of Partition. A strong Muslim merchant class had not developed for a variety of reasons. Thus the early years after partition were devoid of any deliberate policy or institutional support. Demand and supply of goods and services were the prime determinants of the flows. To meet the basic needs of the country, the majority of the imported goods consisted of consumer goods and cotton textiles. Five major commodities— raw jute, raw cotton, raw wool, hides and skins, and tea— accounted for about 99 per cent of export earnings in 1948-9. Trade accounted for about one-fourth of the economy's total output.

The best way to characterize Pakistan's trade strategy for the period from 1947 to 1958 is to say that the policies of the government were restricted to the management of short-term crises and reactions to various developments in the foreign trade sector (Amjad and Ahmed, 1984). Administrative *ad hoc*ism became the rule of the day. As mentioned above, Pakistan had neither the institutions nor the expertise to tackle the intricacies of foreign trade.

The first serious crisis for Pakistani policymakers came in September 1949, when the pound sterling, along with a host of other currencies, including the Indian rupee, was devalued by almost a third. Pakistan decided not to follow suit for a variety of reasons, of which the main reason seemed to be the fear that devaluation would raise the import bill without an offsetting increase in export earnings (Amjad and Ahmed, 1984). The prevailing belief at that time was that export receipts would remain unaffected because export demand was assumed to be inelastic and because returns to principal export crops in terms of domestic prices were seen as adequate to obtain increasing supplies; import demand was assumed to be inelastic because of Pakistan's heavy dependence on imports of capital goods and manufactured consumer goods. The higher price of imported goods would fuel inflationary pressures which Pakistan wanted to avoid (Islam, 1981). India responded to this decision by suspending trade, thereby, damaging the Pakistani economy. The Indians felt that Pakistan's dependence on the Indian economy was too strong and that the severing of economic ties would motivate Pakistan to change its decision.

The Korean War of 1950 came to Pakistan's rescue. There was a huge upsurge in demand for Pakistani export commodities, and export receipts doubled from $176 million (constant price) in 1950 to $346 million by 1951. The balance of payments position became very strong in just one year, and the foreign reserves substantially increased. Furthermore, Pakistan diversified its exports to regions of the world besides India and the United Kingdom.

However, within a year the situation changed dramatically. The start of negotiations to resolve the Korean War led to a plummeting of the price of raw materials, namely raw cotton and jute, and Pakistan's balance of payments position was severely affected. Exports fell to $226 million (in constant prices) in 1952, and imports increased to $806 million, leading Pakistan to a substantial deficit for the first time in its history. The government did not respond to the crisis by adjusting the exchange rate, which had become clearly overvalued, but instead adopted a stringent system of import controls, supported by direct controls on prices, production, and distribution, and by a series of different incentives to individual exports (Islam, 1981). This represented a historic departure from liberal import policies and paved the way for a whole new trade regime based on import substitution.

From July 1950 to December 1952, Pakistan's import policy was known as the Open General Licence (OGL) system. Under this system, licences were issued for the import of certain commodities, but there were virtually no restrictions on source or quantity. With the end of the Korean War and the consequent recession, this policy was abandoned and replaced with a whole new import licensing framework.

The import licensing system was matched by a parallel system of discretionary controls, i.e., foreign exchange allocation system (Thomas, 1966). A centralized Foreign Exchange Budget controlled by the Ministry of Finance allocated the available foreign exchange to the public or private sector. Government imports were determined as part of the budgetary process itself, and capital imports for industry were determined as part of the broader industrial policy of the government. The licences for imports such as consumer goods, raw materials, and spare parts, were issued by the Chief Controller of Imports and Exports (CCI & E). Under this rigid system, the government decided for every six-month 'shipping period' the total value of licences to be issued and the allocation of licences by commodity and by importer. Moreover, although initially almost all the imports were handled by commercial importers for resale, the new industrialists were given industrial licences for their raw materials and spare parts. It was hoped that this would accelerate the process of industrialization. But overall, the rationale for this policy was that imports had to be limited to prevent a further weakening of Pakistan's balance of payments and foreign exchange position. This policy, by artificially curbing demand, led to a decline in the value of imports over the short term. But the longer-term consequences of the new trade regime on the economy were by no means benign. Firstly, import trade became largely concentrated in the hands of the holders of 'categories' and 'quotas' (Naqvi, 1970). Hence, a narrow group of importers earned monopoly rents. Corruption became rampant as a black market in licences developed. Secondly, the interpretation of 'essentiality' in the allocation of import licences was such as to give the lowest priority to consumer goods, particularly luxury items, and high priority to raw materials, spare parts, and machinery. This resulted in a very protected and profitable market for the domestic production of consumer goods, with the highest protection given to the least essential consumer goods industries. Thirdly, the system perpetuated the differences between West Pakistan and East Pakistan, with West Pakistani importers receiving the larger portion of the licences.

On the other front, efforts were also made to promote exports. Export duties on agricultural commodities were reduced on wool, tea, and raw cotton, although the duty on jute remained unchanged. An export incentive scheme went into operation in 1954-5 that allowed exporters of a specified list of primary and manufactured goods to receive a uniform entitlement of 30 per cent of their export proceeds. However, all these measures did not do much to help Pakistan's export regime. With the exception of 1951, exports were low during most of the decade, creeping below $100 million(const. price) by 1957-8. This sluggishness was beginning to have an adverse effect on the balance of payments, with deficits becoming more common in the latter years of the decade. Coupled with adverse price ratios for jute and cotton in relation to the competing crops, this was enough for Pakistani policymakers to devalue the rupee.

In 1955 Pakistan undertook a devaluation of the rupee by 33.5 per cent. Three major reasons were cited by the authorities to justify their devaluation (Islam, 1981). Firstly, Pakistan had established a range of manufacturing industries that could enter the export market, having high elasticities of export demand.

Secondly, devaluation would not hurt the standard of living because imports supplied a smaller portion of consumer goods than in 1949. Thirdly, the large profit margin of the importers would be squeezed without causing an increase in prices. Devaluation was intended to give a boost to exports and not establish a new equilibrium exchange rate.

Unfortunately, the devaluation did not prove strong enough to boost exports. Export performance remained sluggish, and Pakistan could not draw on accumulated foreign reserves as it had in the past. The exchange rate adjustment that Pakistan undertook in 1955 was merely a delayed reaction to the earlier devaluation undertaken by the trading partners in 1949, but the circumstances of the mid-50s involved a rapid rise in costs and in prices. In a way, it can be said that Pakistan had moved too little, too late.

In sum, it can be said that the period from 1947 to 1958, characterized by *ad hoc* reactions to short-term crisis, laid the foundation for a highly inefficient system of administrative controls and the allocation of imports and foreign exchange required to finance it, it also saw the emergence of a new elite deriving monopoly rents from the foreign trade sector. The output and efficiency losses resulting from this trade regime have been quite severe.

1958-69

The accession of Mohammad Ayub Khan in 1958 resulted in a change in the economic policy and structure of the country. Ayub assumed power in the name of improving the living conditions of Pakistan, and he felt that accelerating the pace of industrialization would be the means of achieving this objective. Pakistan's trade regime would have to be altered to meet the needs of the industrial sector.

The main thrust of reforms was to liberalize domestic trade by removing price controls. In April 1960, controls were taken off the movement and price of wheat and its products in West

Pakistan. An arrangement made with the United States through PL-480 to augment the supply of wheat to Pakistan enabled the decontrol to succeed without raising the general price level. By 1963 the prices of only twelve commodities were controlled.

As the 1955 devaluation had not helped boost Pakistan's exports, the option of devaluation to boost exports was rejected in 1959. As an alternative, an Export Bonus Scheme (EBS) was introduced to provide monetary incentives to exporters.

Basically, the system allowed the exporter of a 'bonus commodity' to earn a market-based premium over and above the rupee equivalent of his foreign exchange earnings in the form of a bonus voucher (Islam, 1981). This voucher could be traded openly in the market or used to import a large number of consumer goods, industrial raw materials, and capital goods. Over time, the range of goods eligible for premium under the bonus voucher scheme was extended to cover all but a few export goods.

One line of criticism against the Export Bonus scheme was that the system was basically a multiple exchange rate system where exports were subject to more favourable exchange rates than the official rate at which imports were imported (Islam, 1981). It was argued that the export bonus system distorted the pattern of resource use towards a less efficient allocation. Furthermore, it was empirically demonstrated that the differential patterns of bonus caused a loss of foreign exchange because they distorted the pattern of exports and resource use in favour of commodities which earned relatively less foreign exchange.

A second policy, the Export Credit Guarantee Scheme (ECGS), was formulated in order to encourage exports by underwriting financial risks in the buyer's country that were beyond the control of exporters and were not covered by normal insurance guarantees. Besides this measure, a whole array of policies, ranging from special rebates to cheaper loans, were instiued.

At the institutional level, an Export Promotion Bureau was formed in order to provide information to exporters, settle trade disputes, and advise the government on commercial policies affecting exports.

The policies did seem to bear the desired results, and Pakistan's exports peaked during the 1960s. By 1968, exports more than tripled to $338 million (constant price) in eight years ($106 million in 1959). In contrast to the stagnation of exports during the previous period, this represented an average annual growth rate of exports of more than 10 per cent throughout the Ayub years (Table 6.13).

The export sector in the 1960s was also characterized by diversification and the rapid growth of manufactured exports. Ninety-two per cent of the total average increase in overall exports between the first and the second half of the 1960s was due an increase in manufactured exports. The three most important manufactured exports, cotton textiles, jute textiles, and leather manufactures, were based on domestic agricultural raw materials in accordance with the country's comparative advantage.

Changes in the import licensing system were also implemented to complement the reforms in the export sector. Although the import licensing system was retained in 1961, a new OGL system was introduced which eroded the monopoly of category holders by granting commercial licences. In 1964 liberalization was continued; industrial raw materials and spare parts were placed on the Free List and could be imported without requiring a government licence. By the end of 1965, imports had increased to $812 million (constant price) from $479 million in 1960. However, since import growth was faster than export growth, Pakistan's balance of payments position was worsening in this period.

The outbreak of hostilities between India and Pakistan in 1965, coupled with consecutive bad harvests and a slowing down of external assistance, retarded the liberalization efforts. Quantitative restrictions were reimposed on imports, and tougher measures were introduced to regulate large conglomerates, industrial companies, and interlocking financial and trade interests.

The trade policy pursued by Ayub during the 1960s has attracted considerable attention by academic researchers (Balassa, 1971; Little, Scitovsky, and Scott, 1970; Noman, 1994). While the export strategies of that period were touted as being models for successful export-led growth and liberalization, the continuation of an import substitution trade strategy was found to be seriously problematic.

On the positive side, the Ayub years have been hailed as leading to large growth rates in the export sector and reorienting Pakistan's export portfolio away from primary commodities and into manufactured exports. For some experts, the success of Ayub's liberalization policies was due to their self-funded nature, the multistaged approach, and the spread over a couple of years (Guisinger, 1981). The sequential introduction of reforms was viewed as a vital ingredient to the success of the trade strategy. Furthermore, the reforms were self-funded in the sense that increased imports were only permitted when firm commitments for increased foreign exchange availability were possible. Given Pakistan's scarce foreign exchange earnings over the period, this was a very sound policy.

The success of the Ayub reforms can be attributed to the response elasticity of export supply to various export incentive schemes, and to the positive relationship between export performance and improvements in the effective exchange rates. The export promotion schemes, although haphazard and fluctuating, did succeed in improving the effective exchange rate by narrowing the differential between the effective exchange rate for exports and for imports. Furthermore, the response of export supply and demand to price incentives was favourable. Thus the export incentive schemes, in spite of their overly adminstrative nature, their delayed sequencing and timing, were found to produce favourable results.

Pakistan's import substitution industrialization (ISI) has been studied extensively and used to discredit this particular strategy, which was widely prevalent among developing countries in the 1950s and 1960s. The argument is complex and merits considerable elaboration.

The intellectual foundation of the ISI was the premise that developing countries, as exporters of primary products, would face declining demand for their products in the world market. What became known in development literature as the Prebisch-Singer model, after its two leading proponents, was based on this idea of export pessimism (Maier, 1984). Moreover, the theory of the 'secular decline in the terms of trade', which implied that the ratio of export prices to import prices would continuously decline for primary commodities, prescribed that developing countries in order to survive had to diversify their export portfolios in favour of manufactured goods. With these ideas in mind, Pakistan, like many other newly independent poor countries attempting to improve its economic conditions, embarked on import-substitution industrialization.

In the first stage of ISI, there was the replacement of imports of non-durable consumer goods, such as clothing and household goods, with domestic equivalents. In the second stage, there was the replacement of the imports of intermediate goods and producer and consumer durables by domestic production. Pakistan had completed the first stage in the 1950s and was following the second-stage trajectory. By many tokens the degree of import substitution was impressive. In the early 1950s, about one-quarter of the total supply of industrial goods was provided by domestic industrial production; by the end of the 1960s, the share of domestic production had increased to about 73 per cent. The leading performers were the consumer goods sector, with growth in cotton textiles, sugar, tobacco, and matches, and the intermediate goods sector, with strong production of jute textiles and leather goods.

The criticism of Pakistan's ISI strategy during the Ayub years was manifold. Firstly, it tended to progressively worsen the balance of payments. From a current account deficit/ GDP ratio of 2.8 per cent in 1959, the balance of payments position worsened to a ratio of 3.3 per cent by 1964. This is a paradoxical result, since ISI was meant to reduce imports. The increase in imports of machinery and raw materials expanded more than the gain in exports. Secondly, the high rates of effective protection reduced consumer welfare by forcing him to buy low-quality domestically produced goods at prices relatively higher than border prices (Islam, 1981).

Many studies have estimated that the average effective protection rate was excessively high in Pakistan in the 1960s, and that it varied from negative to more than 1000 per cent in different industries (Little, Scitovsky, and Scott, 1970; Islam, 1981; Kemal and Naqvi, 1981). Moreover, capital goods were protected less than intermediates, and intermediate goods less than final consumption goods. Third, the reallocation of resources towards highly protected but inefficient industries, (with domestic resource costs exceeding), generated a production structure that could not compete internationally.

Anne Krueger has made the useful analytical distinction between export promotion strategies, defined as a general bias towards exports, and a package of specific measures to encourage the selective exports of particular items themselves induced by a bias toward import substitution (Krueger, 1978). The critics of Pakistan's trade strategy have argued that Pakistan followed the latter course, not the former. I.M.D. Little has criticized countries, such as Pakistan, that 'promoted' exports (Little, 1970). He argues that these policies were only used to offset overvalued exchange rates, and that export subsidization was too selective to militate against the general bias against exports.

The period of the 1960s can be divided into two sub-phases. The first phase, which lasted until the war with India in 1965, was focused on relaxation of controls on prices and distribution, and an intense effort was made to liberalize the economy, but this effort received a setback in the period 1966-70 due to the costs imposed by the war, bad harvests, and a slowing down of external assistance.

1971-7

After the secession of East Pakistan in 1971, a profound change in Pakistan's trade strategy and orientation became necessary.

Historically, the two countries had been important trading partners. West Pakistan's exports to East Pakistan amounted to $ 169 million in 1969-70, which constituted about 50 per cent of its exports that year, while imports from East to West Pakistan amounted to $124 million in 1969-70, which was only about 18 per cent of Pakistan's total imports for the period. Commodities such as rice, raw cotton and tobacco, as well as manufactured goods such as cotton fabrics and machinery, had to find alternative markets.

This exogenous shock of the disruption of inter-wing trade was accompanied by a radical change in the overall economic policy stance of the new government that came to power in Pakistan in 1971. One of the key planks of the ruling Pakistani People's Party was the attack against the concentration of wealth and economic privilege that had accumulated during the Ayub years. It was widely percived that the Ayub system of import licensing and exchange rate policy had spawned massive inequalities, in the country—both regional and inter-personal. Thus nationalization of industries, banking, insurance, etc., were needed to correct the situation.

In May 1972, the rupee was devalued by about 58 per cent in an attempt to unify the multiple exchange rates that had developed in the 1950s and 1960s as a result of the Export Bonus Scheme. The justification for devaluation was the perception in official circles that the rupee had once again become overvalued and that a boost was needed for exports after the loss of the East Pakistani market (Amjad and Ahmed, 1984). It was also argued that the EBS had distorted the allocation of resources towards the industrial sector and against the agricultural sector. A second reform of the Bhutto administration was the removal of the EBS, which had been a pillar of the export policy in the 1960s. The rationale for the elimination of the EBS was to unify the effective exchange rate system for exports thus, eliminating the multiple exchange rates which had been prevalent in recent years.

The effects of devaluation on Pakistan's export performance proved short-lived as the oil price increases in 1972 plunged the world economy into recession. Between 1970-1 and 1973-4 exports more than doubled, from \$420 million to \$1 billion. However, when judged at constant dollar prices, Pakistani exports decreased from \$393 million to \$234 million. The fears that the loss of the East Pakistan market and the consequent disruption of interwing trade would severely jeopardize Pakistani exports proved to have some merit. By 1974-5 the performance of Pakistani exports had suffered due to poor agricultural production resulting in small export surpluses, as well as a recession in the world economy. Furthermore, there was a sharp deterioration in the terms of trade in this period. The index, which had appreciated to 106 in 1973-4, was down to 76 by 1976-7. Exports of traditional goods, such as raw cotton, cotton yarn and cloth, leather products, and hides and wool, all declined in real terms in the last years of the period. The effects of devaluation were also neutralized by cost increases in the domestic production of manufactured goods, erratic supplies due to repeated crop failures, and the value of exports remained stagnant between 1974 and 1977. At constant dollar prices, exports continued to record a decline in value terms. The ratio of exports to GDP, which had jumped to over 12 per cent soon after devaluation, fell to about 8 per cent by 1977. With this in mind, the government began to offer a series of export rebates on textiles and other goods.

In the area of import policy, the Bhutto government simplified and liberalized the import system by abolishing all diverse categories and entitlements in imports and regrouping imports into only two categories (Guisinger, 1981). The first category was a free list containing 327 items importable on cash as well as loans and credits from worldwide sources. A second list, a tied list, covered items that could only be imported from tied sources. The rationale was to facilitate industrial expansion by making imported raw materials and capital goods easily accessible to businessmen.

In spite of the audacity of the reforms, several criticisms were made. Firstly, the reforms in the import licensing system were not matched by reforms in the foreign exchange allocation system, which continued to be administered in a highly discretionary manner. The free list of imports permitted unlimited imports only to those buyers who held foreign exchange; consequently, importers without foreign exchange had to line up to obtain foreign exchange in the black market. Secondly, the reforms were viewed as incongruous with the Bhutto government's nationalization of industry and attack on private sector investment. The exportable surplus capacity did not keep pace with the demand from the foreign markets in response to a more liberalized trade policy, as new private investment had completely dried up in the aftermath of the massive nationalization of industry.

By 1973, the OPEC oil price shocks had had a strong adverse effect on the Pakistani economy, which lingered on until the late 1970s. The formation of the OPEC oil cartel resulted in a fourfold increase in the price of oil within just a few weeks. Pakistan, being an oil importer, suffered tremendously. The petroleum and oil import bill rose from $59 million in 1972-3 to $374 million in 1975-6 and $862 million in 1979-80. This new exogenous shock was exacerbated by bad harvests and a sharp deterioration in the terms of trade. The import/GDP ratio increased from 7.0 per cent in 1972 to 20.5 per cent by 1980.

The composition of exports and imports was also changing as Pakistan diversified its export portfolio and import needs. By 1971-7, the share of primary commodities, had dwindled to less than 43 per cent, while the ratios of semi-manufactures decreased and manufactured goods increased. By the end of this period, more than one-third of exports were manufactured goods. Cotton textiles and leather goods were replacing raw cotton and raw skins and hides as important exports, and leather garments, sporting goods, and carpets became progressively more important. In spite of the attempts at industrial diversification, traditional exports continued to dominate Pakistan's trade, and their high concentration, in terms of both commodities and geographic regions, was responsible for the large fluctuations in aggregate export earnings during this period (Naqvi and Sarmad, 1984). Interestingly, the share of manufactured goods in total exports remained more or less the same in the base and final years of the Bhutto period, reflecting the wide fluctuations and low productivity of domestic manufacturing activity from 1971 to 1977.

A similar change was occurring on the import front. The share of capital goods decreased from 52 per cent of total imports in 1971 to 38 per cent by 1977, while the share of consumer goods increased from 11 per cent to 16 per cent during the same period. The stagnation in manufacturing activity and the resulting low rate of investment during the early 1970s induced lower imports of capital goods and of raw materials for capital goods (Naqvi and Sarmad, 1981). On the other hand, the decline in both agricultural and manufacturing production led to a greater demand for consumer goods.

In terms of direction, there were important changes (Table 6.13). On the export side, the detrimental effects of high commodity concentration were to some extent offset by increased exports to non-traditional markets (Naqvi and Sarmad, 1981). The Middle East replaced East Pakistan as an important market for exports. The share of the five major OPEC trading partners increased from 8.7 per cent in 1971 to 23.9 per cent by 1977, while that of the traditional trading partners (US, Western Europe, Japan, China, Russia) decreased from 54.5 per cent to 41.5 per cent. On the import side, the share of the United States and the other industrialized economies decreased from 73 per cent in 1971 to 53.8 per cent by 1977, while the share of the Middle East OPEC partners increased from 4.0 to 17.3 per cent over the same period. Pakistan became more dependent on the Middle East for imports of oil and on Japan for imports of capital goods and raw materials, while its dependence on the US and Western Europe was beginning to decline.

The 1970s also marked Pakistan's economy's growing dependence on foreign sources of finance to balance the growing trade deficit. As the accounting identity clearly states, the capital and current accounts must move in opposite directions. Thus, the Pakistani economy became dependent on large flows of foreign capital, which translated into a growing debt burden for the economy. Although foreign resources helped to ease the constraints, the external debt problem became quite serious in terms of. four dimensions: a sharp escalation in the net outstanding debt, rising debt-service payments, an increase in the cost of borrowing, and the multiplication of sources of external assistance (Naqvi and Sarmad, 1981).

The one strong positive factor for the economy during this period was the spectacular increase in remittances as Pakistani workers flocked to the Gulf in the aftermath of the oil boom (Khan, 1990). During the seventies, workers' remittances increased from $82 million in 1970-1 to $883 million by 1976-7. This helped to ease pressure on the balance of payments position.

It is true that the Bhutto years were characterized by a series of exogenous shocks that adversely affected Pakistan's balance of payments position. The civil war of 1971, the OPEC oil shocks of the early 1970s, the deteriorating terms of trade, poor agricultural harvests, and related factors caused an exacerbation of balance of payments difficulties for Pakistan. The initial gains of a large devaluation, redirection of inter-wing trade to world markets, and a more streamlined and liberal import policy were partly offset by these exogenous shocks. But the effects of the radical change in the orientation of domestic economic policy had equally strong adverse effects. In order to sustain the volume of exports and promote new non-traditional sources of exports, investment in new profitable activities was necessary to expand the production and exportable surplus. But the large scale acquisition of private assets by the government generated an adversarial relationship between private business and the government. The result was stagnation in production and consequently, a deterioration in the balance of payments. The lesson that can be drawn from the Bhutto era in Pakistan is that a liberal trade policy cannot produce favourable results over the long term in the absence of supportive macroeconomic policies and a market-friendly environment for investment.

1977-88

The period from 1977 to 1988 was marked by relative stability. General Zia's policies were based on a reversal of the Bhutto policies of nationalization and a strategy to encourage the private sector to invest and contribute to Pakistani economic expansion.

The accession to power of General Zia coincided with a sharp increase in export performance, due to an upswing in world trade. The value of Pakistani exports increased from $1.1 billion in 1977 to $3.0 billion by 1981. In constant dollar terms, this was an increase of over 70 per cent. Not only did exports of rice and raw cotton grow faster in this period in comparison with earlier periods, but exports of non-traditional goods, such as leather, sports, and engineering goods, performed remarkably well (Khan, 1990). Unfortunately, by 1981-2, an international recession and the consequent declining terms in trade made export earnings fall sharply. An appreciation of the exchange rate by about 10 per cent did not do much to make matters better.

On the import front, the second OPEC oil shock further hurt Pakistan's economy, with the import bill increasing rapidly. Imports were clearly becoming excessive, and the government reversed the policy of import liberalization in 1979 by raising substantially the margin requirements for import letters of credit, tightening the import licence procedure, and stopping the mushroom growth of importers by imposing a registration fee of 2 per cent of the value of the licence. However, in spite of these changes, the growth rate of imports continued to outpace the growth rate of exports. These policies proved to be of little avail as Pakistan's balance of payments position deteriorated over time. Strong action was needed to forestall an imminent crisis.

In January 1982 the exchange rate was removed from its peg to the US dollar, where it had been since 1972, and put on a managed float. The rationale given for this change was the traditional one, i.e., the balance of payments situation was worsening year by year. From a current account deficit/ GDP ratio of $235 million in 1972, the balance of payments (BOP) position had deteriorated to $545 million by 1977 and to $795 million by 1982, i.e. 5 per cent of GDP. This BOP position was becoming unsustainable, and there was considerable pressure to devalue. Pakistan finally decided to experiment with flexible exchange rates and adopted the managed float system.

In 1979, the Soviets invaded Afghanistan, and Pakistan became a front-line state. This attracted a huge inflow of foreign aid to Pakistan during the 1980s. The combination of foreign financial assistance with remittances from expatriate Pakistani workers gave the policymakers some breathing space. The remittances had reached the peak of $3 billion in 1983. This new source of foreign exchange earnings would not have been possible if the exchange rate had remained overvalued. Most of the remittances would have found their way in the form of 'informal' transfers in the absence of exchange rate adjustments.

The large remittances and foreign aid flows allowed the policymakers to pursue a relatively easy, soft-option growth (Noman, 1994) without addressing the problems underlying the balance of payments. The narrow base of the country's exports remained unaltered during this period, while import expansion continued unabated.

1988-96

The period from 1988 to 1996 can best be characterized as a time of political consensus on the nature of the country's trade policy, although changes of administration and leadership have resulted in constant administrative *ad hoc*ism. Although both Benazir Bhutto and Nawaz Sharif have been committed to trade liberalization, the policies have been so variable that the period has been characterized as a 'muddle-through' scenario.

By 1990, a series of sweeping reforms had been introduced in order to liberalize the economy (Noman, 1994). Exchange and payments reform were fundamental parts of the new policy to mobilize the private sector to play a greater role in the economy. Capital accounts were liberalized, and privatization and deregulation measures were introduced. In just a couple of years, the number of items included in the Negative List was reduced from 300 to 75, tariff rates were cut from 77 to 50 per cent, industrial licensing was abolished, and the foreign investment regime was liberalized. On the export front, export taxes were reduced and incentives provided in the form of duty and tax concessions, export processing zones, and additional methods of export financing.

The reforms did seem to work—exports surged during the period. Although the share of Pakistani exports in global GDP had remained around the 0.2 per cent mark since 1970, the late 1980s and early 1990s were marked by a growth of about 10 per cent per annum. Interestingly enough, a contributing factor to this new growth was the shift in Pakistani market orientation from developing country markets to industrial markets. Industrial countries now absorb about 60 per cent of Pakistan's exports, up from 40 per cent in the earlier period; the decline in the importance of developing countries is due to the drop in purchasing power of the oil-exporting countries since the mid-1980s, the breakup of the CMEA, and the deep recession accompanying the transition (Riordan and Srinivasan, 1996).

This period was the only one in Pakistan's history where exports grew at a faster pace than imports, and that despite a terms of trade decline, floods, and viral attacks. Most of the decline in the period beginning 1988 in the terms of trade was due to the decrease in the prices of traditional exports like rice, cotton, cotton yarn, carpets, and fish. A sluggish international demand was the principal factor behind this decrease. The import price index increased by 5.5 per cent between 1988 and 1992 due to increases in wheat, crude oil, and POL product prices. Exports of cotton-based goods increased in volume and thus compensated for the adverse price movements. The composition of exports changed significantly: manufactured goods accounted for almost 60 per cent of total exports during the period, and primary commodities for less than 20 per cent. A strong factor boosting export performance over the period was the strong growth (at a 12 per cent annual average) of nontraditional exports, especially leather and sporting goods (Khan, 1990). Non-traditional exports more than doubled in a span of five years. If this growth can be sustained, it will have positive repercussions for the diversification of Pakistani exports. But the heavy reliance on cotton-based exports has not diminished in the 1990s, and Pakistan's vulnerability to domestic supply shocks and external market developments therefore remains intact. The stagnation in 1997 and 1998 attests to this vulnerability.

On the import side, the growth rate of imports average about 6 per cent during the period. The composition of imports has changed surprisingly since the earlier years, with capital goods imports and raw material for consumer goods accounting for more than 80 per cent of imports and consumer goods accounting for a bare 15 per cent. The rise in capital goods imports is probably tied to advances in Pakistan's fixed investment spending and stronger demand for consumer durables (Khan, 1990). Meanwhile, declining oil prices in the early 1990s as the OPEC cartel's power has waned, have reduced the import bill significantly.

Private transfers in the form of remittances have declined and averaged about $1.5 billion in this period, which, although a half of the peak in the early 1980s, still represents a significant amount, especially when compared to the dwindling amount of official aid, which averaged half a billion dollars during the same period. Although these remittances have traditionally funded trade deficits, the structural changes in the economies of the Gulf countries and the consequential depressed demand for foreign labour do not augur well for a continuation of the past trend. However, as official aid has declined in recent years, and as there has been a shift from concessional to non-concessional sources, as well as a change from bilateral to multilateral forms of aid, it would seem appropriate that export penetration in the growing markets of East Asia and burgeoning markets of Central Asia should become an integral part of the trade strategy of Pakistan.

The declining volume of official aid is being replaced by increased private capital flows. But these flows, particularly short-term flows, are highly volatile, and any hint of macroeconomic instability results in an abrupt outflow of private capital. The overall quality of economic management has become a critical variable in attracting these flows.

PAKISTAN'S EXTERNAL DEBT AND RESOURCE FLOWS

Pakistan is one of the group of developing countries which have relied heavily on external sources of financing for their development. This strategy has helped Pakistan to achieve reasonable growth in per capita incomes and consumption. A combination of propitious factors has enabled Pakistan to attract a relatively high level of external resources in the past (more than 10 per cent of GDP), but it is becoming clear that this level is untenable over the long run. The costs of this heavy dependence on external resource flows have started manifesting themselves in various forms, and questions are being asked as to whether it is in the collective national interest to continue this strategy unabated.

There appears to be an emerging consensus that the country would be better served by reducing this heavy dependence. This is a welcome development which deserves serious consideration. The implications of this option, and particularly the trade-offs involved, have to be examined. It must be recognized, for example, that it is not feasible to cut external resource flows while maintaining the present level of consumption and imports.

The option for Pakistan in eschewing large capital flows and maintaining reasonable growth in per capita income can be realized only if domestic saving rates are at least doubled from their present level. This goal is not at all unrealistic as almost all the countries in Asia, with very few exceptions, have saving rates around 25 per cent. In Pakistan's case this can be attained if there is willingness, political commitment, and tenacity in taking some hard decisions which may not be popular in the short run. But even with a doubling of saving rates and efficient use of resources, there is no question that low-income countries such as Pakistan would continue to require external resources to support their development. The issue is, what should be the desirable sources and characteristics of these flows.

Historical experience suggests that it is only the countries which have been able to raise and maintain high rates of domestic saving that have achieved impressive growth rates on a sustainable basis. In short, countries which help themselves emerge as winners in the long term. Recent empirical research amply shows that foreign aid of the right type and quality can have a positive impact only if the macroeconomic policies are right, macroeconomic incentives are not distorted, and the supporting institutions are in place. In the absence of these preconditions, foreign aid only helps countries to postpone the tough decisions required for prudent economic management. Under those circumstances, foreign aid is a curse which should be avoided.

HISTORICAL OVERVIEW

Pakistan in its present geographical form emerged as a separate political entity after 1971, and most of the meaningful analysis will therefore have its focus on the period covering the last two decades. But it is useful to provide a historical context by looking at the external capital inflows of the 1950s and 1960s.

During the period 1947-58, Pakistan's GDP growth rate was 3.1 per cent per annum—slightly ahead of the population growth rate. Foreign resource inflows were insignificant and mainly provided for technical assistance. Domestic savings and investment rates were also low due to the very low levels of per capita income, the pressing need to assist the millions of people displaced by partition, and the imperative of creating the basic administrative apparatus and institutions required to run a new country.

The 'heyday' of Pakistan's economy remains the decade of the 1960s, when the GDP growth rate averaged 6.8 per cent annually. The investment rate reached a peak of 23 per cent in 1964-5, and foreign savings financed almost half of this investment. The 1965 war with India led to a setback, and the level of aid declined from 10 per cent of GDP at its peak to 4 per cent by 1970. The higher incomes generated during this period boosted the domestic savings rate, which reached almost 12 per cent.

The separation of East Pakistan, the two oil shocks, and a fundamental change in the economic philosophy of Pakistan accentuated pressures on the external finances of the country in the 1970s. Had it not been for the liberal policy of manpower exports to the Middle East, the upsurge in the demand for Pakistani goods in these countries, and generous assistance from the newly rich Islamic countries, Pakistan would have found itself in an extremely difficult position. Even so, in 1974 the country was forced to reschedule its bilateral debt to the western creditors. GDP growth rate took a downward dive and averaged 3.9 per cent between 1971 and 1978. It would not be correct to blame external events for the poor outcome in the 1970s. As pointed out in Chapter 1, the nationalization of industries and financial institutions, a shift towards more long-gestation, capital intensive, public-sector investment, and the ensuing uncertainty created by the change in the ground rules for economic management, were potent factors accounting for slower growth and low investments in this period.

The rising trend of workers' remittance which came to Pakistan's rescue in the 1970s continued into the 1980s and surpassed merchandise exports in 1983-4. The Afghan War brought an unexpected windfall in the form of increased assistance from the US. This allowed the government to avoid the need to restructure the economy and eliminate imbalances on fiscal and external accounts. Thus, although GDP growth rates picked up in the 1980s, the cumulative effect of emphasizing short-term objectives for too long (i.e., maintaining growth in income and consumption) impaired the country's long-term capacity to generate sustainable growth, reduce poverty, and achieve equitable income distribution.

The economic and social costs of this strategy have gradually begun to surface. Physical infrastructure such as irrigation, electricity, roads and highways, telecommunications, railways, and other capital assets have been poorly maintained and have neither been replaced nor have they been expanded to keep up with the growing demand. Social services and human sector development have been neglected and the social indicators have worsened, leaving Pakistan at par with some of the poorest African countries. Pakistan ranks 120th in the Human Development Index constructed by the UNDP. Public sector imbalances have worsened and non-wage components of recurrent expenditure are being squeezed. Saving rates have remained low—not much above the level reached in the 1960s— and the trade gap has widened. This happened at a time when almost 50 per cent of Pakistan's external resource requirements were being met through foreign aid, borrowing, and workers' remittances. In fact, this amounted to more than 12 per cent of GDP in 1980—a situation that is hardly tenable in the long run (Table 6.16). Merchandise exports provided only 40 per cent of the total external financing requirements in 1980.

By 1995 the performance of merchandise exports had improved somewhat, financing 59 per cent of external sector requirements, but the situation is still fragile. The composition of external finance has also changed remarkably. External borrowings, official aid, and workers' remittances have declined in their relative importance, while foreign investment and foreign assets of Pakistanis provide a much larger volume in the 1990s.

PRESENT SITUATION

Pakistan's debt situation has continued to deteriorate in the 1990s. By the mid-1990s, debt servicing was consuming more than half of the country's annual revenues, leaving little space for social and developmental expenditures. The twin problems of high fiscal deficits and high current account deficits have become more problematic in the 1990s than in previous decades. A combination of lacklustre export performance and consistently upward-moving import demand led to a gradual worsening in the current account deficit by 1996. While the secular long-term trend shows a widening of the current account deficit, the year-to-year variations merely reflect the instability in export earnings. Nevertheless, the greater current account deficit translates, from an accounting viewpoint, into greater dependence on foreign capital inflows to finance the difference. The 1990s have been characterized by a series of important shifts in the nature of capital flows to the Pakistani economy; the implications of these changes for the country's debt profile are equally important.

Pakistan received an average $2.3 billion in aggregate net flows from all external sources during 1990-95. Net transfers, on the other hand, are about $1.6 billion annually (Table 6.17). Net flows equalled about 4.1 per cent of GDP in 1995, compared to 5.3 per cent in 1980. Aid dependence indicators (Table 6.18) show the trend of reduced dependence on aid (defined as external loans and grants together) as workers' remittances substituted for most of the slack in foreign aid flows. Aid finances only 13 per cent of imports and 16 per cent of the total investment. These ratios were much higher at the beginning of the 1980s.

The major change in Pakistan's debt profile has been a sharp change in the composition of external financing—away from bilateral grants and concessional lending towards multilateral and non-concessional flows. While grants covered 35 to 50 per cent of external financing requirements during the 1970s and 1980s, by 1995 they accounted for under 5 per cent of flows. This shift, motivated by changing political orientations and 'donor fatigue' on the supply side, has led to a sharp increase in Pakistan's interest and debt service cost over the 1990s.

A second key shift has been in the composition of the debt stock. A decade ago, bilateral debt accounted for two-thirds of official financing. By 1996, the share of bilaterals had declined to less than 35 per cent, while the international financial institutions supplied the bulk of the finances (Table 6.20). Among bilateral donors, Japan has emerged as Pakistan's largest bilateral aid donor, supplanting the US. Of the total stock at the end of 1995, almost 80 per cent was related to long-term projects and commodity aid, while the remainder consisted of credits by the commercial banks and the International Monetary Fund (IMF, 1996).

An analysis of the composition of net flows for five-year periods since 1970 shows that while the share of grants has decreased, the rise in the share of non-concessional loans has hardened the debt profile. The average terms of new commitments in 1996, i.e., interest rate, maturity, grace period, and grant element, are harder than a decade ago. Concessional flows have declined from 74 per cent of total flows in 1971-5 period to less than 20 per cent during the last five years, while non-concessional flows have risen to one-half of the total flows. Foreign Direct Investment (FDI) flows are gradually increasing and have reached 16 per cent of all flows.

Total debt stock has risen sharply, from $3.1 billion in 1970 to almost $10 billion in 1980, to $30 billion at the end of 1995 (Table 6.21). The World Bank classifies Pakistan as a 'moderately indebted' country, but the vulnerability coefficients (Table 6.21) are all moving in the wrong direction. Non-concessional debt as a share of total debt is close to 50 per cent—up from 24 per cent ten years ago. Variable interest-rate denominated debt has risen to 20 per cent from almost zero. Multilateral debt which enjoys the status of preferred credit and has to be serviced first, has risen to two-fifths, while debt servicing on multilateral debt is close to one-third of the total debt servicing obligations (Table 6.22). The stock of interest-sensitive debt, composed of variable-rate long-term and short-term debt, has been rising rapidly and currently comprises about 30 per cent of total external debt and 15 per cent of GDP, while the shift toward non-concessional debt has widened interest rate spreads (on private flows) above London Inter Bank Offer Rates (LIBOR). Short-term debt, which is highly volatile, is 13 per cent of the total debt and has more than doubled in the last fifteen years.

Almost all debt indicators show a worsening situation. Debt-export and debt-GNP ratios have both worsened despite the impressive growth of exports and GNP. Debt servicing now claims more than one-third of the country's foreign exchange earnings. The debt/GNP ratio worsened from 50 per cent to 57 per cent over the last five years. The interest-to-export-ratio rose, from 8 per cent in 1980 to 11 per cent by 1997. The empirical magnitude of the future debt payments is so daunting for Pakistan that debt payments of more than $4 billion were paid by the end of June 1997 (IMF, 1996). Interest payments alone made up 11 per cent of exports (Table 6.23). These indicators are all alarming, and the long-term trends based on existing flows are not very encouraging. The main sources of official grants have been the USA and Japan, but technical assistance grants, which do not directly help the balance of payments position, form a significant proportion.

On a more optimistic note, there has been an increase in private capital inflows as both foreign direct investment and portfolio equity flows are moving in to Pakistan to replace the traditional sources of official capital. In 1985, foreign private flows supplied an insignificant portion of Pakistan's external finances. By 1996, its share had risen to almost 50 per cent of net resource flows. Foreign portfolio investment has taken place through the stock market whose capitalization jumped from $1.8 billion in 1990 to $12.6 billion in 1996 (Table 6.23). Foreign direct investment has increased from negligible amounts in the 1980s to over $500 million by 1995. FDI now represents about 7 per cent of private fixed investment in Pakistan, contrasting very favourably to India's 1.5 per cent, but still considerably lagging behind East Asian rates (Nabi, 1992). More than one half of FDI during 1990-4 had flown mainly into commerce and manufacturing (Table 6.25). But this has changed dramatically since 1995 when independent power producers (IPP) brought in significant amounts of FDI for investment in electricity generation. Similarly, portfolio equity inflows have averaged

$100 to $200 million per year (the $1.1 billion received in 1995 was due to a one-off $900 million in privatization proceeds). As financial and economic integration is occurring globally, Pakistan is starting to benefit from international capital movements.

The gain in FDI and foreign currency deposits has been achieved at the expense of remittances, which had been instrumental in financing a large part of the current account deficits in the 1970s and 1980s. Diluting the effects of poor macroeconomic policies and financial repression, the remittances helped give Pakistan's macroeconomic indicators some respectability. The reduced demand for labour in the Middle East has led to a reduction in remittances from the $3 billion average in the 1980s to about $1.5 billion by the mid-1990s. This shortfall is expected to become permanent, as the relative returns on foreign currency deposits and the ability to borrow in domestic currency against these deposits have made remittances less attractive.

The net inflows of foreign currency deposits in the wake of the government's exchange and payments liberalization measures reached $ 11 billion by 1998 from a meagre base of less than $0.5 billion at the beginning of the decade. Foreign exchange bearer certificates (FEBCs) are currently about 10 per cent of GDP. These inflows reflect both investor response to the higher domestic interest margin offered on these accounts and the ease of movement of deposits in and out of the country. These FEBCs represent a very critical attempt to reverse the capital flight which has been the bane of the Pakistani economy since the 1970s. However, the combination of widening deficits and episodes of transitory loss of confidence in international markets has led to intermittent outflows from these accounts. Thus, the fragile nature of this 'hot money', to borrow a term from international financial parlance, does not bode well for the Pakistani economy and exposes its vulnerability to exogenous shocks of any nature, both domestic and external.

A final change in the 1990s, one of the most pernicious trends for the Pakistani economy, has been the sharp fluctuations in currency reserves and their falling to dangerously low levels in recent years. Despite the inflows of foreign exchange deposits and investment flows, the reserve situation has always remained precarious. Reserves have plummeted on several occasions. During 1992-3 they fell to about two weeks in imports. At their peak, they had increased to $2.7 billion, financing 13 weeks of imports. In October 1996, reserves had plunged to less than $800 million and in July 1998 again they had plunged to less than $600 million. This low level reflected an ebbing in the confidence of investors and was caused by lack of credibility of economic policies.

Pakistan's external debt and foreign aid cannot be discussed in isolation from its macroeconomic policies and performance. Future inflows, especially from the major official creditors—World Bank, IMF, ADB, and Japan—will be driven from this angle. The underlying sources of difficulty are quite well-known and documented. These have implications for external debt. The revenue base is inelastic, relying mainly on international trade taxes on a limited range of commodities. Government consumption expenditure has almost doubled in the last ten years, while development expenditure has been cut drastically. This reduction in public investment, in turn, has exacerbated the infrastructural deficiencies and edged social services out of reach for a large segment of the population, especially in the rural areas. The investment budget needs to include only the highest priority projects, given the backlog of needs in the social sectors, operations and maintenance, rehabilitation, etc. Pakistan could increase its domestic saving rate dramatically if the 7 to 8 per cent of GDP which is diverted to the public sector for meeting its budgetary deficits could be left in the hands of the private sector for investment purposes, and the budget balanced by curtailing consumption expenditure and mobilizing additional revenues from untaxed or low tax incidence activities.

Public sector deficits in the 1980s were financed through a combination of concessional external borrowing, foreign aid, and domestic debt from the non-banking sector at low and subsidized interest rates, thus avoiding inflation. But this was done at the expense of crowding out private investment, and implied slower growth than would otherwise have been observed. The recent liberalization of the foreign exchange regime and the auctioning of government debt will eliminate the implicit subsidy enjoyed by the government so far, and force it to borrow at market interest rates, as domestic savers now have other attractive alternatives such as foreign exchange deposits to invest in. The recourse to short-term and commercial borrowing on hard terms, along with continued depreciation of the rupee, will require larger budgetary outlays on external interest payments. If an adequate primary surplus is not generated to take care of this increased cost of interest payments, the fiscal deficits will have to be monetized, resulting in high inflation rates. The threshold of tolerance for inflation in Pakistan is quite low, and high inflation rates may further heighten social tensions. In summary: achieving a radical improvement in the fiscal balance is the imperative; it will also lead to reduced external borrowing requirements.

In order to alleviate its fiscal deficit and improve efficiency in the use of resources, the government has embarked on an ambitious privatization programme. The attempt to privatize industry has been quite successful, with over 70 units sold to the private sector by the middle of 1996. This has partially relieved the government's burden by providing over $2 billion in revenue. To the extent that these proceeds have been generated by the sale of profit-making enterprises, the net gain to government finances will depend on the tax receipts and expansion in investment and output by the newly privatized enterprises. If the loss-making industries are also sold off, the budgetary impact is likely to be positive. The choices in the use of the privatization sale proceeds will have a bearing on the debt situation, too. If these proceeds are used to pay off high-cost domestic or external debt, there will be net savings in the fiscal account when the rate of return on these proceeds (if they were invested) is lower than the interest rate on the debt that is paid off. While privatization represents an important short-term stopgap measure, more comprehensive fiscal reforms will be needed to address Pakistan's high fiscal deficits and consequent reduction in the debt burden.

FUTURE PROSPECTS

The weak economic prospects of the OECD countries, their burgeoning fiscal deficits and budgetary cuts, political pressures to assist the former Soviet Union and Eastern Europe financially, and a growing sense of aid fatigue, do not bode well for any higher allocation of foreign aid by the industrialized countries. On the demand side, whatever amounts are likely to be available will have to be shared by a larger pool of claimants, as some middle-income countries in Africa and Central America have become eligible for concessional assistance due to the continuous decline in their per capita incomes. African countries poorer than Pakistan and undergoing structural adjustment programmes are on the preferred list of the donors. Rich OPEC countries such as Saudi Arabia and Kuwait are faced with their own internal financial difficulties. The largest single bilateral donor to Pakistan was the USA. Even if the contentious issue of the Pressler Amendment is amicably resolved, it is unlikely, in view of other pressing claims, that the US will be able to commit the same levels of allocations as Pakistan received in the 1980s.

Commercial banks in North America, Europe, and Japan, having been severely hit by the debt crisis of 1980s, and caught in the web of new capital adequacy guidelines, are wary of lending to marginally creditworthy countries such as Pakistan. Its own prudential considerations indicate that, it would not be in Pakistan's best interest to contract commercial loans at market terms. The country's debt indicators and vulnerability coefficients hardly permit taking this kind of risk.

Workers' remittances have almost stabilized, and the spending spree of the 1980s is unlikely to be repeated in the Middle East. Barring any unforeseen mishap in that region, the present level of remittances is the maximum amount that should be assumed for the coming decade. Any expectations of growth in this source of financing are unrealistic.

This leaves three sources which were earlier identified as desirable and healthy from Pakistan's viewpoint. Incentives for export expansion need to be strengthened so that the existing narrow base outside cotton-based products can be broadened. World trade volumes have invariably increased faster than world output growth. As Pakistan has a very low share in the international market, it should not be too difficult to increase both the volume as well as the share of manufactured exports. Within the 'cotton group' itself there is considerable scope to double the value of exports by moving vertically towards high value-added products.

Foreign direct investment and portfolio investment flows are still meagre by both international standards and from the regional perspective. Pakistan attracted $350 million annually in the last five years compared to an average $1.5 billion by Thailand. Worldwide flows of FDI have soared to a record $325 billion in 1995, while the inflows to developing countries have surpassed $100 billion, with China, Mexico, and Brazil taking the lion's share.

The opening up of the stock markets to foreign investors and the launching of the Pakistan Fund have already produced very positive results. There is no reason why the changed economic policies should not be fully used to maximize these flows— Pakistan is starting from a low base and has certain advantages of location, labour costs, and raw materials to offer. But there are other prerequisites which are missing. Studies of determinants of FDI have shown that a stable political and economic environment, enforcement of laws and contracts, a trained, skilled, and disciplined labour force, critical support services, and availability of quality infrastructure are the key factors for potential investors in making investment choices. Tax holidays, fiscal concessions, subsidies, and import tariff protection are the wrong means to promote investment if the goal is to develop competitive and efficient industries. As a matter of fact, FDI should not be encouraged in countries where effective rates of protection are high. Pakistan will not be able to maximize social benefits from FDI unless the present high tariff structure is dismantled.

The recent fierce competition for foreign investment among the developing countries is motivated less by the capital flow aspect and more by the transfer of technology, managerial skills, and export market considerations. Two major arguments have been advanced in the academic literature on the causes of foreign direct investment (Krugman and Graham, 1994). One explanation, the 'industrial organization' theory, argues that foreign firms invest abroad in order to capitalize on some firm-specific knowledge (research and development, production-management skills, etc.) that the domestic firms do not possess. The 'cost of capital' explanation suggests that the main motivation for FDI is the movement of resources in search of the highest return; the cost of a firm's capital determines the discount rate of the investment project that it considers. The consensus in the academic literature is that FDI is seen as a means to extend control for reasons of corporate strategy rather than as a means to shift resources from one country to the other. The flow of FDI into Pakistan seems to fit predominantly into the former category, with multinational investors hoping to consolidate a large foreign market and using the Pakistani market as a part of that strategy. Nevertheless, regardless of the rationale for the flow of FDI, the movement toward Pakistan has been slow compared to other developing countries.

East European countries, due to their geographical, ethnic, and historical ties, are in a better position to attract foreign investors; but the countries of East Asia and Latin America are also strong candidates. India has also emerged since 1991 as a big contender for foreign investment. There is some concern that other South Asian countries, including Pakistan, and Africa will be left behind in this race unless corrective measures are taken and some fundamental changes take place in their thinking and attitudes.

LESSONS OF EXPERIENCE FROM OTHER DEVELOPING COUNTRIES

The desirable change in the composition of external resource flows to Pakistan towards merchandise exports, FDI, and reflow of assets held by Pakistanis abroad can be effected through a number of measures, none of which are easy. It may be useful to recount the experience of other developing countries which were once at the same crossroads as Pakistan is today, but which have made great strides since. There are always those who argue that conditions in Pakistan are unique and that lessons from other countries cannot be applied or are not relevant. While it is true that each country has different resource endowments and historical, cultural, and administrative traditions, these countries also faced a set of similar economic problems and issues. It is instructive to probe and ascertain how they handled those problems, learn from their successes and avoid their mistakes. The neighbours of Pakistan in the region to the east have done extremely well in attracting capital flows and expanding exports. What can be learned from their experience? A recent study of the comparative experience of successful Asian countries with that of Latin America highlights the following factors common to the Asian countries:

- stability, credibility, and continuity of economic policies over an extended period of time;

- outward orientation policies that promoted export expansion, reduced levels of protection, and maintained realistic exchange rates;

- prompt adjustment to adverse external shocks by avoiding recourse to borrowing in order to maintain consumption;

- cautious and prudent macroeconomic management that ensured price stability, financial liberalization, and non-expansionary fiscal policy;

- industrial and trade policies geared to enhancing domestic competition, import competition through lower tariffs, and removing non-tariff barriers and price controls.

East Asian countries were able to avoid the debt crisis in the 1980s, despite their heavy debt burden, because they made productive use of borrowed external funds that eased infrastructural bottlenecks, focused investment on human resource development, expanded the productivity base, and did not allow public enterprises to run up massive financial deficits. External flows were diversified over time, with export earnings and FDI being the main vehicles for raising external finance. Empirical work on the sources of growth corroborate this evidence on efficient use of resources, both domestic and foreign, in these countries. For the period 1973-80, total factor productivity (TFP) accounted for one-fifth of the growth in East Asian countries, while its contribution to both Africa and Latin America was strongly negative. This study also found a strong and positive association between aggregate growth and productivity growth.

East Asian countries not only invested the borrowed resources productively, but had a balanced portfolio of capital flows. Asia and China relied heavily on FDI flows. FDI has contributed to growth both by augmenting resources available for capital formation and by improving the efficiency of investment. FDI is thought to possess four advantages over borrowing. First, equity financing requires payments only when the investment earns a profit, while debt requires repayments regardless of whether an economic return was earned or not. Second, payments on FDI can be regulated by the host country, while debt repayments are outside its control and are affected by interest rates set in the international markets. Third, because much of the FDI consists of reinvested earnings, only a portion of the returns on investment is repatriated, as opposed to the need to repay interest and principal on loans. Fourth, FDI permits a closer match between the maturity structures of the earnings from an investment and that of the required payments to the capital used to finance it.

Finally, an important lesson that needs to be reiterated is that stronger and persistent efforts in increasing domestic saving rates were the driving force in East Asia and financed a large proportion of their overall investment. For the period 1973-80, Asia's domestic saving rates exceeded 25 per cent while investment was 26 per cent. In the subsequent period these ratios were 27 and 28 per cent respectively. Thus, external capital flows were of marginal nature and provided 1 to 1.5 per cent of GDP despite two oil shocks and an adverse external environment. Empirical studies have shown a stronger correlation between growth rates in GDP and domestic saving rates than between investment rates and growth rates in GDP.

The main thrust of the East Asian experience is that foreign aid, of the right type and form, is highly efficient in stimulating growth and equitable income distribution when it is accompanied by appropriate economic policies. Asian countries made greater use of IMF facilities in the 1970s than did the Latin American nations. The recent positive developments in Mexico, Chile, and Venezuela tend to confirm that the policies pursued by East Asia in the 1980s are equally valid in their case. The post 1997 crisis in Thailand, Indonesia and Korea does not, in any way, detract from the lessons ennunciated above. The causes of this crisis were different and deserve a separate discusssion.

CONCLUSIONS

Pakistan has achieved relatively high growth rates in income and consumption since independence. Foreign aid and external borrowing made it easier to avoid hard policy choices and trade-offs. Frankly speaking, Pakistan has lived beyond its means for the last two decades, and has been fortunate in bridging the gap between domestic savings and investment through heavy reliance on foreign savings and current income transfers from abroad. The external financing strategy pursued so far has placed a greater emphasis on foreign aid, external borrowing, and workers' remittances.

Pakistan would be better served by increasing those sources of external financing that are stable, sustainable, have positive effects on growth, and are largely within the policy control of the Pakistani authorities, rather than continuing to depend on the traditional sources, which have been found to be volatile, less stable, overly dependent on the whims and caprices of external policy makers, and make a questionable contribution to growth performance. These desirable sources are: export of goods and non factor services, foreign direct investment (FDI) and portfolio investment, and foreign assets of Pakistanis and non-resident Pakistanis in the former category; while foreign aid, external borrowing, and workers' remittances (the traditional sources) are in the category of less stable sources. Although the boundaries between the two categories are not always clearly demarcated, empirical evidence provides corroboration to this hypothesis. The external economic environment does influence the demand for exports, supply of FDI, and foreign assets of Pakistanis. But it has been found that, in general, despite their short-term fluctuations, these sources of finance are influenced relatively more by domestic policy variables and hence can be relied upon to a much greater extent for long-term development financing than workers' remittances, official aid, or external borrowing. At a later stage of development, when the credit-worthiness of a country is well established in the financial markets, commercial borrowing assumes a more stable role. Pakistan, however, has yet to reach that stage.

It is valid here to seek the rationale for proposing this new financing strategy for Pakistan. A detailed analysis of the theoretical and empirical foundation for this argument can be found in Husain and Jun (1991), but it may be useful to summarize here the empirical results. A simultaneous equation model consisting of a growth equation and a savings equation, where the former is the traditional export-augmented neoclassical production function, and the latter the traditional Keynesian-type saving function augmented for several variables, was estimated. Regression results for the growth equation, based on pooled cross-section and time-series annual data for nine Asian countries during the sample period 1970-88, suggest that economic growth in the region has been most significantly related to exports and foreign direct investment. Both parameters are positive and statistically significant. It is also interesting to note that official flows, i.e., aid, were found to be an insignificant explanatory variable. In the savings equation, domestic savings were negatively related to official flows and the coefficients were significant statistically. In contrast, FDI was found to be an insignificant factor in explaining saving rate. The results were found to be robust when separate regressions were run for ASEAN and South Asian country sub-samples.

This study confirmed other previous studies (*see* for example, Lee, Rama, and Iwasaki (1986) that export performance has contributed more to economic growth than aid. A study by Aslam (1987), which estimated the impact of foreign capital inflow on savings and investment in Pakistan for the period 1963-4 to 1984-5 came to similar conclusions: it found that private capital inflow exercised a complementary effect on investment whereas public capital inflow played no significant role in increasing investment. On the savings side, public capital inflow exerts a negative effect on savings while private capital inflow is neutral in this respect.

On the basis of the above findings and the discussion of the experience of other Asian countries reported in the previous section, there is ample justification for suggesting that Pakistan should bring about a shift in its present external financial strategy by moving towards increased reliance on domestic savings, using external flows only to supplement these savings, and making greater use of types of flows which are more stable, less volatile, have more beneficial effects on growth, and are within the control of Pakistan. It is not suggested that by adopting this strategy the country should completely discontinue borrowing on concessional terms from various bilateral and multilateral sources for productive investment, physical infrastructure, or social services, nor that it should refuse offers of official aid that help to further the country's development objectives. Neither is it implied that the liberal policy of manpower exports and attracting workers' remittances should be abandoned. There is no question that, for a long time to come, prudent borrowing on appropriate terms and conditions and for the right purposes, official aid, and workers' remittances will be required to support the external financial position, and these flows should not be affected, except for the following two caveats. First, instead of passively accepting or actively soliciting all types of aid or borrowing indiscriminately, there should be greater selectivity in choosing the kind of assistance that makes sense from the national perspective; offers that do not make any positive contribution but only increase the debt burden should be refused. Second, a more pro-active policy should be pursued in promoting the kind of capital flows that are part of the alternate strategy proposed here.

The policies required to bring about these changes in the composition of external flows—placing greater emphasis on exports, FDI, and long-term foreign assets of Pakistanis, and increasing domestic savings—are quite consistent and complementary. It may be recalled that the current account balance is the mirror image of the domestic saving-investment balance, and a faster increase in export earnings than imports will improve the current account balance and hence reflect itself in higher domestic savings.

The changing geopolitical situation, global capital shortages, competition from other low-income countries for limited amounts of concessional aid, increased attention to the former Soviet Union and Eastern Europe, and the rising debt burden of Pakistan call for a gradual shift in strategy in the 1990s. The experience of other successful developing countries, taking into account the peculiar characteristics and initial conditions of Pakistan, suggests an alternate strategy of external financing. The basic elements of this strategy are an increase in domestic saving rates, merchandise export earnings, FDI and portfolio investment, and reflow of foreign assets held by Pakistanis abroad.

A number of important first steps have already been taken by the government in recent years, and a shift is taking place towards a more liberal, outward-oriented economic environment, but there are additional, equally essential, measures that have to be taken. Some of these proposed changes are extremely difficult to accomplish and require drastic alterations in attitudes, ingrained habits and beliefs, and ways in which business is conducted. It is obvious that this transformation has begun to take root. It must be recognized, however, that the alternative is a decline or stagnation in living standards, incomes, and consumption, or high rates of inflation. The country can no longer postpone the hard decisions and continue to live on soft options.

The strategy outlined above is feasible—it has been tried out and found to work elsewhere—and there is little doubt that it would also work in Pakistan, but the costs should be clearly recognized and there should be a willingness and readiness to bear these short-term costs. Whether Pakistan enters the twenty-first century as a secure, stable, and economically well-off country, or joins the ranks of the struggling, poor, and stagnant or declining economies will crucially depend upon the choices made today.

In the light of the evolution and globalization of the world economy, Pakistan's foreign trade faces a series of new challenges. These major changes in the world economy are the impact of the Uruguay Round on developing countries, the phasing out of the Multi-Fibre Agreement (MFA), the tremendous growth of world trade as countries liberalize and privatize, and increased competition between developing countries. The implications of these changes on the Pakistani economy are unclear, as they represent both incredible opportunities and serious risks (Winters and Ingco, 1995). The reaction of Pakistan to these changes may well spell out the future of its economy.

The Uruguay Round of trade negotiations is the most comprehensive set of trade negotiations ever negotiated. Areas that have traditionally and historically not been included in the GATT negotiations are now included; liberalization tackles areas such as agriculture, services, and non-tariff barriers. The effects of the Round on the international economic environment and the regimes and institutions which support it will be very marked in the years to come. A voluminous body of literature has sprung up over the effect of the Uruguay Round on the economies of developing countries (Winters and Martin, 1995).

Preliminary estimates of the impact of the Uruguay Round on Pakistan are positive. Pakistan stands to gain significantly from the Uruguay Round commitments to tariff reductions and elimination of non-tariff barriers facing its major exports; however, it is committing to only a minor degree of liberalization in its own schedule of tariff concessions. This may mean that Pakistan could miss crucial opportunities to benefit from the Round. Countries with liberal trade regimes gain most from overall trade liberalization as well as from the liberalization and restructuring of other economies. In fact, Pakistan's diffidence in pushing ahead with its trade liberalization will lessen the welfare gains to be obtained from improved access opportunities in the markets of its trading partners.

In general, Pakistan was very cautious with its offers under the Round (Winters and Ingco, 1995). In agriculture, the most common tariff rate was 75 per cent, which accounted for more than 40 per cent of all tariffs, while in agriculture, the average tariff was 55 per cent. This is extremely high, even when compared to developing country or South Asian standards. The Pakistani response to pressures to reduce these high tariffs was not encouraging. While in agriculture, it offered very high ceiling bindings (100-150 per cent), in manufacturing, it committed to bind only 25 per cent. This failure to reduce about 75 per cent of its tariffs in manufacturing and making no commitments to reduce protection in agriculture means that Pakistan lost an important opportunity to achieve potential gains from a more efficient resource allocation and lower costs resulting from lower average and variability of protection (Winters and Ingco, 1995). It must be said that, in the area of agriculture, the trade liberalization is not predicted to have a major impact on world prices.

One area where Pakistan stands to gain is from the trade liberalization of its major trading partners, which should allow Pakistani exports greater market access. In terms of total developing countries' exports to industrial countries, the reduction in average tariff is 30 per cent. Overall, Pakistan's total merchandise exports to OECD and developing countries will benefit from a weighted tariff reduction of 2.4 per cent and 6.9 per cent respectively.

The phasing out of the Multi Fibre Agreement (MFA) seems to have the best consequences for Pakistan. The MFA, an agreement that had its roots in the 1950s, sought to avoid disruptions in the world textile market due to oversupply by forcing countries to voluntarily restrain exports at times of glut in world markets. Covering over 75 per cent of textile trade, the MFA also allows quantitative import restrictions in order to manage trade. The criticism against this agreement is that it represents a major departure from the GATT principles of nondiscrimination and reciprocity. The Uruguay Round agreement on textiles and clothing provides for a phasing out of non-tariff restrictions under the MFA in three stages over the next ten years. The effect on Pakistan will be a significant expansion in market access in three major markets for textiles and clothing due to an increase in export quotas over ten years.

Thus, in the post-MFA world, there will be increased competition among developing countries in textiles and clothing. Pakistan's success in the export of cotton and textiles will depend crucially on its ability to maintain competitiveness with respect both to other developing countries and to its South Asian neighbours. Unfortunately, a recent analysis of unit labour costs within South Asia shows that Pakistan's competitiveness in producing cotton yarn and T-shirts compares unfavourably with India; in fact, Pakistani labour is three times more expensive than India's in producing cotton yarn and four times more expensive than Bangladesh in producing cotton T-shirts (Riordan and Srinivasan, 1996). Thus, Pakistan must make its workforce both more efficient and productive if it wants to maintain its international competitiveness. Moreover, appropriate cotton policies must be formulated so that Pakistani domestic prices are aligned with world prices. In sum, the phasing out of the MFA represents a two-edged sword that could potentially either strengthen or damage the economy, depending on Pakistani policy reforms.

In conclusion, the main effects of the Uruguay Round on Pakistan will be in the liberalization of manufacturing and in the phasing out of the Multi-Fibre agreement. Estimated gains for Pakistan vary from $0.2 billion to $3.4 billion, depending on the assumptions of the simulation model (Riordan and Srinivasan, 1996). One-fourth of these gains will be attributable to trade policies abroad, such as tariff reductions and the abolition of the MFA, but three-fourths of the gains should come from the region's own reforms, a cut in tariffs, and other import liberalization measures. However, the conclusions are extremely tentative.

Another factor that has been of increasing importance to the Pakistani economy has been the growth of world trade. One of the great differences between this and previous periods has been the greater integration of the Pakistan economy in the international economy. The combined import and export share of GDP amounts to almost 34 per cent in the period, compared to 11 per cent in 1970. The effects of this increased integration on the Pakistani economy have been the subject of great controversy. The consensus in the literature is that increasing globalization can lead to tremendous advantages for Pakistan. The main lines of agreement are that the evolution of Pakistan's international linkages has better positioned the country to take advantage of increased growth in world trade, an opening of the markets for textiles as a result of the phasing out of MFA, significant potential in the area of 'long-distance' services trade and an accompanying reduction in pressures for migration, and increased availability of external finance from private sources, especially foreign direct investment and portfolio equity flows

(Riordan and Srinivasan, 1996). The growing globalization of the international economy should help Pakistan to end its inward-looking economic strategy and pursue new policies of export-led growth.

On the negative side, there are immense risks involved in Pakistan's growing integration. Firstly, the increased regionalism of the world economy (NAFTA, APEC, the enlarged EU) confronts Pakistan with the risk of being marginalized from the larger blocs (Riordan and Srinivasan, 1996). The tendency to build free trade areas creates its own momentum, and any country that does not fit into a bloc can be deprived of the maximal trading and foreign investment that it can otherwise enjoy. Secondly, as international capital is flowing to only those developing countries that have sound and stable macroeconomic policies and a predictable environment, there is the risk of being marginalized from international capital markets if Pakistan does not put its internal house in order (Cline, 1995). External financing mechanisms that are stable, self-financing, and have positive effects on growth will be needed for Pakistan (Husain, 1992). Thirdly, in spite of the phasing out of MFA restrictions, the long-run income elasticities for textiles and related products are low, especially when compared to the higher-technology manufactures. Pakistan, unlike India and East Asian countries, hasn't even touched the fringes of technology-intensive exports. Fourthly, the pace of import liberalization and tariff reforms should be matched with the phased reduction in the fiscal deficit so as to avoid the recurrence of macroeconomic instability (Noman, 1994). The argument that liberalization will not conflict with the imperatives of alleviating the balance of payments deficit is not a powerful one. Lastly, the risk of escalation in oil prices, food and raw materials can increase Pakistan's import bill.

As times change and the intellectual case for protectionism becomes weaker and less compelling than it was in the heyday of development thinking in the 1940s and 1950s the Pakistani economy will have to change to adapt itself to the emerging forces of the 21st century—globalization, integration and liberalization.

TABLE 6.1
EXPORTS, IMPORTS, AND TRADE BALANCE
AT CURRENT AND CONSTANT PRICES OF 1969-70
($US Million)

Years	Exports (Current Prices)	Exports (Constant Prices)	Imports (Current Prices)	Imports (Constant Prices)	Trade Balance CurrentP)	Trade Balance ConstantP)
1949-50	171	176	276	595	-105	-419
1959-60	160	176	379	479	-219	-303
1969-70	338	338	690	690	-352	-352
1979-80	2365	855	4740	1,714	-2375	-859
1989-90	4954	1,167	6935	1,634	-1981	-467
1995-96	8,707	2,509	11,805	3,402	-3,098	-893

Source: *Pakistan Economic Survey*, Government of Pakistan, Islamabad, (various issues)

Note: 1995-6 figure at constant 1988-9 price

TABLE 6.2
FOREIGN TRADE RATIOS (per cent OF GDP)

Year	Exports/GDP	Imports/GDP	Total Trade/GDP
1950	10.4	9.0	19.0
1955	3.4	5.4	8.8
1960	4.5	10.7	15.2
1965	4.5	10.6	15.1
1970	3.7	7.6	11.3
1975	9.8	20.0	29.8
1980	10.2	20.5	30.7
1985	8.0	19.0	27.0
1990	13.0	18.1	31.1
1996	14.7	19.8	34.5

Source: Sohail Malik et al., *Pakistan's Economic Performance, 1947-1993* (Sure Publishers, Lahore) *Pakistan Economic Survey*, Government of Pakistan, Islamabad (various issues)

TABLE 6.3
EXPORT AND IMPORT GROWTHS
(Average Annual Rates of Growth)

Decade		Exports		Imports	
		Current Price (US$)	Constant Price (US$)	Current Price (US$)	Constant Price (US$)
1947-8 to 1959-60		-5.0	-3.0	2.0	-2.4
1959-60 to 1969-70		11.1	10.1	5.5	3.8
1969-70 to 1979-80		16.8	-3.1	20.9	-1.2
1979-80 to 1990-1		8.1	1.0	3.4	5.3
1989-90 to 1996-7		4.4	-6.6	4.8	-4.8

Source: Sohail Malik et al, op. cit., *Economic Survey*, various issues

TABLE 6.4
COMMODITY COMPOSITION OF
PAKISTAN'S EXPORTS

Year	Primary Commodities	Semi-Manufactures	Manufactured Goods
1950	NA	NA	NA
1960	NA	NA	NA
1970	33	23	44
1980	44	11	45
1990	19	24	57
1996	16	22	62

Source: *Pakistan Economic Survey* (various issues), Government of Pakistan, Islamabad

TABLE 6.5
COMMODITY COMPOSITION OF
PAKISTAN'S IMPORTS

Year	Capital Goods	Raw Material for Capital Goods	Raw Material for Cons. Goods	Consumer Goods
1950	NA	NA	NA	40
1960	NA	NA	NA	NA
1970	50	11	29	10
1980	36	6	42	16
1990	33	7	41	19
1996	35	5	43	15

Source: *Pakistan Economic Survey* (various issues), Government of Pakistan, Islamabad

TABLE 6.6
SHARE IN WORLD MARKET

Year	Percentage Share
1950	0
1960	0.11
1970	0.34
1980	0.21
1990	0.20
1996	0.20

Source: International Monetary Fund: *International Financial Statistics*, January 1953, March 1963, January 1973, March 1983, February 1993, December 1996.

TABLE 6.7
MAJOR TEXTILE EXPORTS BY VOLUME

Year	Raw Cotton (000 MT)	Cotton Yarn (MKG)	Cotton Clothes (MSQ.M.)	Synthetic Textiles (MSQ.M.)
1950	NA	NA	NA.	NA
1960	NA	NA	NA	NA
1970	84	72.8	297.7	10.9
1980	251	99.8	545.8	5.1
1990	295	377.4	1,018.0	338.2
1996	263	578.5	1,046.8	875.2

Source: *Pakistan Economic Survey,* (various issues), Government of Pakistan, Islamabad

TABLE 6.8
COMPOSITION OF MANUFACTURED EXPORTS
(% Share in Total Manuf. Exports)

Goods	1950	1960	1970	1980	1990	1995
Cotton Manuf.	3.5	43.9	70.0	44.8	57.8	60.0
Chemicals, Drugs	29.2	.1	-	1.1	2.5	0.6
Jute Manuf.	1.4	43.1	16.2	-	-	-
Leather Manuf.	-	2.9	10.4	12.0	10.2	5.2
Footwear	-	-	-	0.8	0.6	-
Sporting Goods	-	-	-	1.8	3.9	4.4
Carpets	-	-	-	17.2	8.3	3.1
Surg. Instr.	-	-	-	1.8	2.4	2.2
Postal Articles	16.8	-	-	-	-	-
Others	26.3	8.6	3.4	20.3	14.3	24.6

Source: *Pakistan Economic Survey,* (various issues), Government of Pakistan, Islamabad

TABLE 6.9
NON-TEXTILE EXPORTS
(Annual Growth Rates %)

Goods	1969-70 to 1979-80	1979-80 to 1990-1	1989-90 to 1994-5
Leather	24	18.9	-1.2
Surg. Instr.	22.4	11.2	10.5
Carpets	34.5	9.6	-1.3
Sports Goods	14.6	15.9	15.0

Source: Sohail Malik et al., *Pakistan's Economic Performance, 1947-1993* (Sure Publishers, Lahore) *Pakistan Economic Survey*, Government of Pakistan, Islamabad. (various issues)

TABLE 6.10
COMPOSITION OF IMPORTS
(Percentage Share)

	1970	1980	1990
Edible Oil	5.7	6.9	8.3
Petroleum	1.4	40.0	25.0
Chemical fertilizers	8.8	7.1	4.4
Machinery	40.0	20.0	31.6
Iron, steel	12.3	7.3	7.0
Transport equipment	11.2	12.3	8.4
Chemicals	22.6	6.3	15.3

Source: *Pakistan Economic Survey,* (various issues), Government of Pakistan, Islamabad

TABLE 6.11
CURRENT ACCOUNT DEFICIT/ GDP RATIO

Year	Ratio
1950	.1
1960	1.9
1970	3.3
1980	3.7
1990	4.8
1996	6.5

Source: International Monetary Fund: *International Financial Stastistics*, January 1953, March 1963, January 1973, March 1983, February 1993, December 1996

TABLE 6.12
UNIT VALUE INDICES FOR IMPORTS AND EXPORTS
AND TERMS OF TRADE
(1980-81=100)

Year	Exports	Imports	Terms of Trade
1981-82	98.4	110.8	88.2
1986-87	132.0	136.9	96.5
1991-92	209.6	253.3	82.7
1996-97	401.0	433.5	92.5

Source: 1996-7, Government of Pakistan, Islamabad.

TABLE 6.13
DIRECTION OF EXPORTS
(Percentage of Total Exports)

Country	1960	1972	1980	1990	1996
USA	13.8	4.0	5.1	13.2	15.5
W.Europe	25.6	25.0	25.0	39.2	27.2
Middle East	-	9.0	22.8	11.4	11.5
Japan	13.9	18.2	7.7	9.2	6.6
Hong Kong	-	11.2	7.8	4.2	9.1
Others	46.7	32.6	31.6	22.8	30.1

Source: *Pakistan Economic Survey* (various issues), Government of Pakistan, Islamabad

TABLE 6.14
PAKISTANI COTTON PRODUCT EXPORTS
IN RELATION TO WORLD EXPORTS

Year	World Exports Cotton Yarn (Metric Tons)	Pakistan's Exports	Pakistan's Share in World Exports
1972	461,487	160,700	35.0
1979	626,300	88,800	14.1
1989	1,474,070	331,320	22.5
1995	1,788,690	506,980	28.3

Year	World Exports Cotton Fabric (Metric Tons)	Pakistan's Exports	Pakistan's Share in World Exports
1972	725,207	56,910	7.0
1979	923,700	58,707	6.3
1989	2,251,740	139,040	6.2
1995	2,781,900	160,800	5.8

Source: *Cotton-World Statistics, Quarterly Bulletin of the International Cotton Advisory Committee* Vols. 35, 45, 48

TABLE 6.15
COMPARISON OF LABOUR COMPETITIVENESS
IN PRODUCING COTTON YARN AND T-SHIRTS, 1994

	Unit Labour Cost ($/Unit)	Wages ($/Year)	Productivity (Units/Worker)
Cotton Yarn			
Bangladesh	.46	780	1699
India	.15	1622	10745
Pakistan	.53	1208	2296
Cotton T-Shirts			
Bangladesh	.11	290	2536
India	.26	668	2592
Pakistan	.43	1343	3100

Source: Riordan and Srinivasan, 'Pakistan's International Linkages: Evolution and Prospects,' *Background Paper for Pakistan 2010*, World Bank, International Economics Department, 2996

TABLE 6.16
TRENDS IN FINANCING
PAKISTAN'S DEVELOPMENT
(Percentage of GDP)

	1970	1980	1990	1995
Gross Domestic Investment	15.8	18.5	18.0	18.5
Gross Domestic Savings	9.0	5.8	9.3	14.4
Net Current Transfers[1]	2.0	7.4	4.8	4.0
Foreign Savings[2]	4.8	5.3	3.9	3.9

Note: Gross domestic savings are derived as a residual in this table and may not correspond with other published data.

1.   Net current transfers equal workers' remittances.
2.   Foreign Savings equal aggregate net resource flows.

Source: World Bank data base

TABLE 6.17
FINANCING PAKISTAN'S EXTERNAL SECTOR
(Percentage Share)

	1970	1980	1990	1995
Merchandise Exports	44	41	50	59
Workers' Remittances	5	31	20	13
Official Aid	3	8	5	1
External Borrowing	36	17	19	10
Foreign Investment	1	1	2	3
Foreign Assets of Pakistanis	-	-	3	14
Others	-	2	1	
Total	100.0	100.0	100.0	100.0
Memo: Amount of foreign exchange required (US$ million)	1,515	5,707	9,832	16,391

Note: The amount of foreign exchange required equals imports of goods and non-factor services and debt-servicing payments.

Source: World Bank data base

TABLE 6.18
AGGREGATE NET RESOURCE FLOWS TO PAKISTAN
(In Millions of $)

		1980-89	1990-95	1996
A.	OFFICIAL	876	1281	1647
	Official Loans	557	997	1447
	Multilateral	372	714	866
	BILATERAL	185	177	581
	Official Grants	319	283	200
B.	Private	160	1000	2377
	FDI	108	335	700
	Portfolio Equity	0	401	200
	Debt Flows	52	263	1477
	Commercial banks	57	185	1123
	Bonds	0	32	240
	Others	-5	46	114
	Total	1036	2281	4024

Source: World Bank data base

TABLE 6.19
AID DEPENDENCE INDICATORS
(Percentage; annual averages)

	1971-5	1976-80	1981-5	1986-90	1994
Aid as percentage of GDP	6.1	4.6	2.6	3.0	3.1
Aid as percentage of total investment	49.0	24.9	13.9	16.6	15.8
Aid as percentage of imports	33.6	20.1	10.6	12.3	12.6
Aid as percentage of budget expenditures	5.2	14.7	7.3	NA	14.9
Aid as percentage of development expenditures	72.5	36.8	28.4	NA	NA
Aid per capita (US dollars)	8.4	10.4	8.6	10.4	13.0

Source: World Bank data base

TABLE 6.20
COMPOSITION OF PAKISTAN'S EXTERNAL DEBT
(Percentage Share)

	1971-7	1976-80	1981-5	1986-90	End 1995
OFFICIAL	93.4	95.0	92.6	93.8	80.0
Multilateral	20.3	23.7	33.0	38.6	45.0
ADB	.7	2.8	5.1	10.6	14.4
World Bank	15.2	12.7	13.7	20.1	21.0
IMF	4.4	7.7	12.7	5.9	5.0
Others		.5	1.5	2.0	4.6
BILATERAL	73.0	71.3	59.6	55.3	35.0
Islamic countries	10.0	14.2	10.6	4.9	2.0
USA	35.6	28.0	23.3	18.4	9.2
Japan	5.2	5.6	7.3	12.4	10.8
Others	22.3	23.5	18.4	19.6	13.0
PRIVATE	6.6	5.0	7.4	6.2	20.0
Commercial banks	.3	.6	4.1	3.9	6.0
Suppliers	4.6	2.2	1.5	1.3	1.0
Others (Short term)	1.4	2.2	1.8	1.0	13.0
Total	100.0	100.0	100.0	100.0	100.0

Source: World Bank data base

TABLE 6.21
VULNERABILITY COEFFICIENTS OF
PAKISTAN'S DEBT
(Annual Average)

	1971-5	1976-80	1981-5	1986-90	1991-5
Current account deficit/ GDP	5.1	4.4	2.7	2.6	4.4
Non-concessional debt/ Total debt	25.9	22.2	31.4	31.4	46.0
Variable interest rate debt/Total debt	-	.3	4.2	7.5	19.3
Multilateral debt service/ Total debt service	36.7	37.7	29.3	40.3	38.5
Short-term debt/Total debt service	0	3.8	7.8	14.3	12.2
Aggregate net resource flows/GNP	6.2	4.8	2.9	3.5	4.7
Interest payments/ International reserves	18.2	23.6	24.8	52.7	38.1

Source: World Bank data base

TABLE 6.22
COMPOSITION OF PAKISTAN'S DEBT SERVICING
(Percentages; annual average)

	1971-5	1976-80	1981-5	1986-90	End 1997
OFFICIAL	76.6	83.1	68.0	83.4	72.4
Multilateral	37.9	39.9	31.5	45.1	40.6
ADB	.9	3.4	4.5	6.5	N.A.
World Bank	21.8	10.9	7.1	11.0	13.6
IMF	15.2	22.6	19.1	22.8	10.7
Others	-	3.0	.8	4.8	N.A.
BILATERAL	38.7	43.2	36.5	38.3	31.7
Islamic countries	2.5	8.5	11.1	7.7	N.A.
USA	11.8	13.4	11.5	13.0	N.A.
Japan	6.4	4.8	3.5	5.9	N.A.
Others	18.0	16.5	10.4	11.8	–
PRIVATE	23.4	16.9	32.0	16.6	27.6
Commercial banks	1.5	2.0	22.5	11.0	11.8
Suppliers	6.7	7.1	3.8	2.2	-
Others	15.2	7.8	5.7	3.3	15.8[1]
Total	100.0	100.0	100.0	100.0	100.0

Source: World Bank data base
[1] Short term debt

TABLE 6.23
EXTERNAL DEBT INDICATORS
(Annual Averages)

	1971-5	1976-80	1981-5	1986-90	1997
Debt-GNP ratio	48.8	46.6	40.3	48.4	57.0
Debt-export ratio	397.7	276.6	200.3	241.5	277.8
Debt-service ratio	20.2	19.3	18.8	24.6	30.8
Interest-export ratio	7.6	7.7	7.5	9.4	11.1

Note: A debtor country is classified as severely indebted when three out of the above four key debt indicators exceed the critical values. These critical values are debt to GNP (50 per cent); debt to exports (275 per cent); debt service to exports (30 per cent), and interest to exports (20 per cent). Moderately indebted means three of the four key indicators exceed 60 per cent of, but do not reach, the critical levels. Present value of debt to export ratio is 196 per cent and present value of debt to GNP ratio is 37 per cent in the case of Pakistan.

Source: World Bank data base

TABLE 6.24
STOCK MARKET CAPITALIZATION
(US $ Billion)

	1990	1991	1992	1993	1994	1995	1996
Emerging Markets	611.2	854.8	883.4	1586.8	1921.4	1895.7	2425.6
India	38.6	47.9	65.1	98.0	127.5	127.2	135.0
Pakistan	1.8	7.3	8.0	11.6	12.2	9.2	12.6
India as Multiple of Pakist.	21	6.5	8.1	8.4	10.4	13.8	10.7

Source: International Finance Corporation

TABLE 6.25
SECTORAL DESTINATION OF FDI NET INFLOWS
(Percentage Share)

	1990	1991	1992	1993	1994	1990-4
Agriculture	0	0	0	0	0.3	
Mining	34.4	45.5	4.1	9.9	4.6	13.1
Manufact.	8.7	16.2	11.9	11.1	35.0	21.6
Construct.	10.7	5.2	36.3	17.4	10.7	15.2
Utilities	0	0.1	9.6	0	31.7	15.0
Commerce	38.9	33.2	34.4	61.2	13.5	31.5
Others	7.4	0	3.6	0.5	4.1	3.6

Source: *Pakistan Economic Survey* (various issues), State Bank of Pakistan, Annual Reports (various issues)

TABLE 6.26
NET FOREIGN DIRECT INVESTMENT:
INTERNATIONAL COMPARISON
(As a ratio of GNP)

	1990	1991	1992	1993	1994	1995	1996
All Developing Countries	0.6	0.8	1.0	1.5	1.8	1.8	1.9
South Asia	0.1	0.1	0.2	0.2	0.3	0.3	0.5
Low-Income Countries	0.5	0.7	1.4	3.2	3.4	3.0	3.0
Low-Income Countries (excl. China)	0.2	0.5	0.5	0.8	0.9	0.8	0.9
Pakistan	0.6	0.6	0.7	0.7	0.8	0.7	0.3

Source: World Bank data

TABLE 6.27
PORTFOLIO EQUITY INVESTMENT:
INTERNATIONAL COMPARISON

	1990	1991	1992	1993	1994	1995	1996
All Developing Countries	3,225	7,207	11,012	44,987	32,688	32,088	45,700
Low-Income Countries	351	874	1,659	5,930	11,081	5,612	NA
South Asia	105	23	380	2,025	6,223	2,341	5,400
Pakistan	0	23	139	185	1,335	729	700
Pakistan (as per cent of South Asia)	0	100	36.6	9.1	21.4	31.1	13.0

Source: International Finance Corporation

CHAPTER 7

EXPLAINING PAKISTAN'S ECONOMIC PERFORMANCE

Economic growth has been the consistent goal of Pakistan's planners and policy makers since independence. While the critical importance of economic growth in lifting societies out of poverty cannot be denied, an examination of the experience of developing countries during the past fifty years suggests that economic growth is just one critical component of sustainable development. The other components are environmental protection, equity, and social justice. This broadening of the concept of sustainable development from mere economic growth to incorporating environmental and social concerns has serious repercussions for the evaluation of development strategy in Pakistan.

The processes driving sustainable economic and social development can best be learnt from accumulated experience and comparative analysis. This chapter analyses this experience in four different ways: (a) Pakistan's development experience over time; (b) Pakistan's experience against the best-practice countries' performance, i.e., East Asia; (c) Pakistan's experience in relation to the closest comparator, i.e., India; and (d) Pakistan's development in the context of South Asia. The final section explores the dynamics of the elitist model as it has evolved in Pakistan over the last five decades.

PARADOXES IN ECONOMIC PERFORMANCE

The economic and social outcomes in Pakistan over the last fifty years have turned out to be a mixture of paradoxes. The economic growth rate during the last fifty years has averaged five per cent annually—a feat achieved by very few countries in the world—but almost all social indicators are below the average for low-income developing countries. Domestic savings and investment ratios have remained in the mid-teens but the productivity of investment has been high, with incremental capital output ratios of around three (Table 7.1). Fiscal deficits have hovered around eight per cent for the last fifteen years, but the inflationary pressures have remained subdued. Most of the institutions have gone through a process of decay, but a handful of them have succeeded in maintaining standards of excellence. Indices of human capital formation place Pakistan on the bottom rung of the developing countries, but it is one of the select group of nations that have acquired nuclear capability. The hold of a narrow, self-centred elite on the economy and on politics is much stronger than in some other countries in the region, but episodes of popular revolt by the masses are few.

The persistence of poverty, large income inequalities, severe rural-urban disparities, gender discrimination, endemic ethnic rivalries, and political instability suggest that the benefits of economic growth have not been spread evenly. Unlike some countries where rapid growth has been accompanied by a reduction in the incidence of poverty and improved distribution of income, rapid growth in Pakistan has led to some reduction in poverty but also promoted greater income inequalities and accentuated social and ethnic tensions.

The pattern of growth is as important as the speed of growth. The sectoral and regional pattern of development strategies can have a major influence on income distribution and poverty reduction. If public policies favour labour-intensive activities such as labour-intensive exports, small-scale industries, and agriculture, and assist the development of neglected, highly-populated regions, poverty is reduced faster than otherwise. Faster poverty reduction is correlated with dynamic agricultural growth rates, and in no case has poverty declined when agricultural growth was slow.

Greater equality in wealth, human capital, and political power is likely to promote the evolution of broad and deep markets through the institutions conducive to greater commercialization and technological change. Greater densities of potential users and beneficiaries raise the projected returns on investment and facilitate the mobilization of necessary political and financial backing. In the early development stages of the United States, without the substantial numbers of small businesses, farms, and households seeking better access to product and capital markets, there would have been less potential for realizing the substantial scale economies characteristic of transportation and financial intermediation. Greater equality in economic circumstances among the US population not only encouraged investment in financial intermediation and transportation through the structure of demand, but also through a legal framework that was conducive to private enterprise in both law and administration. Not only is it likely that the greater equality in human capital accounted partially for the high rates of invention in the US overall, but also the more general concern with opportunities for extracting the returns from invention.

Explaining the paradoxical trends and outcomes of Pakistan's development experience of the last fifty years is both analytically difficult and empirically intractable. The conventional tools of economic analysis are inadequate to disentangle the relative contribution of factors that cannot be measured quantitatively. Dummy variables can be used to proxy some of the qualitative indicators, but the changes in magnitude or intensity are hard to capture.

DETERMINANTS OF ECONOMIC PERFORMANCE

Economic performance is affected by initial endowments, external factors, including exogenous shocks outside the control of policymakers, and domestic policy and institutional factors. The evolution of the Pakistani economy has been shaped largely by a constellation of factors under domestic control. Unlike many other developing countries which have suffered serious external shocks such as adverse terms of trade, disruption of access to world markets, debt crisis, or the collapse of the Soviet bloc, external factors have played a more favourable role in the case of Pakistan.

The terms of trade facing Pakistan remained favourable in the 1980s and early 1990s. Unlike many developing countries which have seen a decline in this terms of trade, this index in the case of Pakistan has either risen or remained unchanged. The terms of trade index (1987=100) was 112 in 1985 and 101 in 1994. The export concentration index has also remained unchanged while the composition of exports has shifted dramatically towards manufactured and semi-manufactured goods. In the decade of the 1970s, the terms of trade changes were also positive. The aggregate net resource flows averaged more than six per cent of GNP annually. Official development assistance was the main source of external financing, accounting for five per cent of GNP in 1980, but has been replaced by workers' remittances and private capital flows.

The large volume of foreign aid in the 1960s, the remittances from the workers in the Middle East in the 1970s, the Afghan war in the 1980s, have all benefited the Pakistani economy. It may be argued that these exceptional sources of external financing in fact did not impose a hard budget constraint on Pakistan and allowed the country to postpone the required adjustments when they were needed. The current economic difficulties can, in fact, be ascribed to the cumulative effects of the incomplete, or in some instances, postponed adjustment in the last three decades.

The empirical framework for explaining the economic per-formance of any country is to examine the relative contribution of capital, labour, and total factor productivity, controlling variables such as initial resource endowments, public policies, political and social stability, institutional capacity, and external environment. As the external environment has been favourable for Pakistan, the economic performance can be explained largely in terms of domestic factors.

DOMESTIC FACTORS

Cross-country regressions to explain growth have revealed that countries with greater financial development, larger fiscal surpluses, and lower black-market exchange rate premia grew significantly faster than countries with more shallow financial systems, larger fiscal deficits, and sizable black market premia. The regressions also indicate that political instability is negatively correlated with long-run growth, while educational attainment is positively linked to growth. Countries with better educated workers should have greater growth opportunities than countries with less educated citizens.

Studies aimed at explaining the slow long run growth in Africa compared with East Asia found that low school attainment, political instability, poorly developed financial systems, large black-market exchange rate premia, large government deficits, inadequate infrastructure, poor property rights, and an inefficient bureaucracy account for about half of the growth differential between the countries of Africa and East Asia.

In pure economic terms, the estimates of annual growth of total factor productivity (TFP) for the period 1970-85 places Pakistan among the high achievers. The rate of growth of TFP was three per cent annually, and the contribution of TFP to output growth exceeded the contribution of capital stock growth. In other words, despite relatively low investment ratios compared to other Asian countries, the rate of output growth was respectably high. But this neglect of investment in physical and human capital is not without a cost to sustained high growth in the long-term.

How has Pakistan utilized its resource endowments and institutional capacity? How has it pursued public policies during the last fifty years, and can these support the maintenance of past productivity gains and poverty reduction in the future?

RESOURCE ENDOWMENTS

Pakistan's critical natural resources are the large reservoir of irrigation water and the fertile land of the Indus Valley. The availability of this irrigation network has made it possible to extend the coverage to 70 per cent of Pakistan's cultivated area—a high proportion by any standards. The resource utilization of this valuable commodity has, however, been less than optimal as efficiency considerations have been overtaken by claims of equitable and fair distribution of water between the two major provinces. The increasing waterlogging and salinity problem has also surfaced due to poor management. With better management capability, the returns from these valuable resources would have been much higher for two reasons: first, the composition of crops grown would have been directed toward high value crops that could be domestically consumed as well as exported, and second, the productivity of irrigated land would have been at least 50 per cent higher than past and current trends suggest. The mispricing of water, the political economy of water allocation, and inefficient management of the system have not allowed either a change in composition or a rise in productivity. The same four major crops that occupied the space in 1947 still dominate, and, after a spike in the post-Green Revolution days, productivity is stagnating.

ROLE OF THE MARKET

Competitive markets are the best way yet found for efficiently organizing the production of goods and services. Domestic and external competition provides the incentives that unleash entrepreneurship and technological progress. But markets, to work efficiently, require a legal and regulatory framework that only governments can provide. And markets fail or prove inadequate at many other tasks such as investing in infrastructure, providing essential services to the poor, and maintaining security, law and order, and a judicial system that is fair and enforces private contracts promptly. The roles of the markets and the state should therefore be analysed in this framework of complementarity. If markets can work well, and are allowed to, there can be a substantial gain. If markets fail, and governments intervene cautiously and judiciously in response, there is a further gain. When markets and governments have worked in harness, the results have been spectacular, but when they have worked in opposition, the results have been disastrous.

The public policy posture, except during the brief period of 1972-7 when the populist policies of Zulfikar Ali Bhutto led to the acquisition of private property by the state and where the state played an interventionist role, has been, at the surface, market-oriented. But a closer analysis reveals that the roles of the market and state that are essential elements for the success of the market-friendly strategy of development leading to equity and sustainability have in fact been reversed in the case of Pakistan.

Large scale private entrepreneurs in Pakistan have been protected from the forces of market competition and have been provided ample rent-seeking opportunities by government policies. In the 1950s, a highly restrictive trade policy relying on high tariffs and quantitative restrictions conferred huge windfall gains on a small group of import licensees. The import-substitution strategy that provided a highly-protected environment for the domestic manufacturing industry in consumer goods and textiles insulated the industry from market tests of efficiency and competition. The industrial licensing schemes, investment allocation by the government, subsidized interest rates, and overvalued exchange rate led to a capital-and import-intensive pattern of production, with high private returns to investors but low and in some instances negative social returns. The Little-Scott-Scitovsky studies and the Krueger-

Bhagwati volume on industrialization and trade policies in Pakistan have amply documented the evidence of high rates of effective protection, negative value added at world prices, and high domestic resource costs.

The external competition which would have had beneficial effects on the diffusion of technology and innovation, efficient use of resources, and managerial and organizational skills, was conspicuously absent and left Pakistan's industry lagging behind its competitors.

The Bhutto government, on assuming power in 1971, nationalized all major sectors of industry, banking, and financial services in the name of de-concentrating economic wealth and dispersing ownership. But the actual results of this experiment were disastrous. Private investment flows virtually dried up, and expansion of industries in the public sector was motivated by non-economic considerations such as control of the commanding heights of the economy, heavy industry orientation, self-reliance, etc. The management of the nationalized industries was de-professionalized, and large numbers of ill-equipped, technically unqualified political workers were inducted into the labour force of these industries in the guise of promoting employment. Lack of competitive pressures, and large subsidies, both hidden and explicit, from the exchequer to absorb the losses of the state-owned enterprises, led to further deviations by industry and the financial sector from the path of competitive efficiency. The overthrow of the Bhutto government in 1977 arrested the trend of nationalization, but the ownership of the industrial assets and financial sector remained in the hands of the state until the 1990s. The weaknesses and deficiencies that had become apparent in the Bhutto era remained unchecked, and the financial losses and losses to consumer welfare arising out of the quasi-monopoly or oligopolistic market structure remained unabated. This inefficient resource use by state-owned enterprises run by a small group of bureaucrats made a major contribution to the evolution of fiscal imbalances, an accommodating monetary policy, and the build up of an exploding domestic debt burden.

An unfortunate, potentially devastating, trend started emerging in the 1980s. The nationalized commercial banks and development financial institutions were increasingly employed as a source of political patronage—to reward the loyal followers of the government or to win over the adversaries. This large expansion of credit, engineered by considerations other than the viability of the projects or proper appraisal of the credit risk, had four deleterious effects. First, it promoted overinvoicing of imported machinery and equipment whereby the inflated price was used to finance the sponsors' equity contribution out of the loan proceeds. Second, it resulted in a serious infection of the portfolio quality of the financial sector as the loan recipients, many of them not genuine businessmen, failed to repay the interest and principal on their loans. Third, it crowded out the small and medium entrepreneurs who were efficient and competitive in their production of goods and services from access to credit. Finally, the substantial increase in administrative expenses of these institutions and a large proportion of non-performing assets raised the pricing of the loans and increased the spread between the deposit and lending rates.

While a small group of import licensees, big trading houses, large-scale private industrialists, recipients of loans from NCBs and DFIs, and managers of state-owned enterprises were protected from domestic and external competition, the agriculture sector, which employed the largest proportion of the country's population and the poor, was penalized by the government policies. A combination of forced procurement of agricultural commodities by the government at prices much lower than import parity prices, an overvalued exchange rate, export taxes, and a government monopoly on the sale of inputs and outputs led to significant inter-sectoral transfers from rural to urban areas. In the 1970s, these trends were reinforced by the takeover of export trading of cotton and rice and the import acquisition of edible oils, fertilizers, etc., by the state corporations. The dismal record of these corporations in incurring huge financial losses and paying lower prices to the farmers was one of the principal disincentive effects in the stagnation of agriculture production. The large farmers, on the other hand, were able to obtain higher prices for sugarcane, rice, and other commodities due to their political connections and influence. They also misused their tax-exemption status as agriculturalists to channel their earnings to industrial and services sectors. Moreover, in the irrigated zones, these influential landlords diverted water to their holdings in collusion with officials of the Irrigation Department, thereby depriving the small cultivators of their due share of irrigation water. Users of canal water pay only one-fifth of its social price.

The effective rates of protection for 1991-2 for four major crops grown in Pakistan show that farmers growing wheat, rice, and cotton were facing negative effective rates i.e., they were being implicitly taxed and thus penalized relative to the high positive effective rates of protection enjoyed by a large number of manufacturing industries. Sugarcane was the only crop that earned a high rate of protection and it is a crop grown disproportionately by large farmers. A recent World Bank report calculated that the trade-weighted mean, all-inclusive import tax rate, of manufacturing was 73.8 per cent and for agriculture 46.7 per cent. Consumer goods industries enjoy an average rate of 92.4 per cent.

The most recent estimate of the transfer from agricultural producers for the four major crops is about Rs 19 billion in 1992-3, or just over 6 per cent of agricultural gross product. Thus there has been some decline from the 14 per cent of agricultural gross product estimated for the period 1984-7.

The argument, however, remains unchanged. To the extent that this discriminatory policy has reduced overall agricultural growth and the distribution of the burden of the resource transfer within the agriculture sector is regressive, the impact on poverty alleviation and income distribution has been negative.

This wide gap between large-and small-scale farmers was further accentuated by the generous subsidies and loans at lower than market interest rates provided by the ADBP for tractors and mechanization. The recovery rate of ADBP loans has been, on average, 25-30 per cent. The beneficiaries of this implicit subsidy, through interest rate differential and non payment of the principal on these loans, along with the recipients of the subsidies for large tubewells and tractors, have been large farmers.

The above analysis demonstrates that the 'markets' in Pakistan were manipulated by public policies and the parasitic behaviour of big business and large farmers to suppress external and internal competition and to create opportunities for rent-seeking by a small segment of population. This is in complete contrast to the beneficial and assigned role of the market, i.e., to promote competition so that resources are used efficiently, innovation and risk-taking is encouraged, and new technology is adopted, thus lowering production costs and benefiting the consumers.

ROLE OF THE STATE

How has the state performed in relation to the role assigned to it? As the markets, if allowed to function well, can promote efficiency but not equity the state, has to step in to fill this gap. The first issue therefore has to do with the overall capacity of the public institutions to deliver the goods and services to its citizens. This encompasses the entire spectrum ranging from the executive, legislative, judicial branches of the state to the scientific and educational institutions, financial institutions, etc.

The public sector can play a crucial role in lowering the transaction costs to farmers and firms by supporting them with investments, infrastructure, and institutions. Publicly provided goods such as agriculture research and extension, farm to market roads, human capital formation, power, small-scale and rural credit can be particularly beneficial. Markets for goods, inputs, labour and capital need to be better integrated: from the farm to the town, from the city to the market abroad. Entrepreneurs need access to appropriate infrastructure and to research and extension services; these foster the integration of markets and help to spread new technology. Businesses also need a legal and contractual framework for their activities—one that protects property rights, facilitates transactions, and lets firms enter and exist.

In addition to the above elements of state support in helping private economic activity, there are some other functions that can only be performed by the state. Investing in health, education, nutrition, family planning services, water supply and sanitation are some of the activities where the social returns may exceed the private returns. Government can provide these services to the poor so that their productivity is raised and they are able to lift themselves out of poverty. Alternatively, government can enter into partnerships with non-governmental organizations and the for-profit private sector where financing and the provision of services are separated.

After independence, Pakistan struggled to carve out institutions, almost from scratch, that were basic to the running of the economy and the administration of law and order, justice and security. Over time, and for various reasons, principally the threat from neighbouring India, the defence forces were strengthened more than other institutions affecting civilian life. Although the civil services, the superior administrative arm, remained quite powerful until 1973, the relative strength of the armed forces as an institution led to the various periods of military rule beginning in 1958. The civil services, which had had the edge until then, decided to act in cahoots with the military rulers, and this collusion between the civil and military bureaucracy retarded the growth of political parties and set back the process of democratization in the country. This slow process of institutional decay had serious repercussions on the activities that the state was able to carry out.

Despite the modest progress in human and physical capital that is catalogued in Chapters IV and V, the current status of the social indicators and infrastructure index is not very satisfactory. Without going into the details of the various social indicators here as they are presented later in this chapter, suffice it to say that the human capital base of Pakistan is much weaker in relation to its economic growth performance and, compared to its neighbours in the region, disappointing relative to the best performing developing countries and constricting the potential for economic development.

The rapid growth of population in general, and the increased share of urban population—from 17 per cent in 1947 to almost 40 per cent in 1996—has created bottlenecks for infrastructure. Traffic congestion in the major cities has taken a heavy toll on the efficient movement of people and goods. Inter-city highways are unable to cope with the growing volume of traffic, and their maintenance is highly inadequate. There are now 18 vehicles per kilometre of paved road, compared to 3 in the 1950s. The poor performance of the railways has contributed to this large expansion of traffic volumes on the inter-city highways.

Not only is the level of infrastructure attainment low, the distribution of infrastructure facilities is also uneven. Fewer than a third of Pakistan's 45,000 villages have access to wholesale trading centres through the network of all-weather roads. Overall rural road length increased by 70 per cent between 1981 and 1991, but over half of the road network is still unpaved and more than two-thirds of the paved arterial roads do not have enough carriage-way width for two lanes. It is estimated that poorly maintained roads are raising transport costs by 30-40 per cent.

In addition to the poor outcomes in human capital and physical infrastructure—the traditional areas of responsibility of the state—the deteriorating law and order situation in the country and the ineffective and protracted legal system have impaired the overall environment for economic activity for the majority of the population. The taxation system, which relies heavily on indirect taxes, has large discretionary concessions and exemptions, and the poor collection machinery is also regressive in nature. The inequities created by distortionary economic policies and institutional failure could not be rectified by a progressive tax system.

The above analysis of the roles of the market and the state leads to the conclusion that there has been an overall perverse effect. The markets were non-competitive in structure and conferred enormous rents to a small group of the influential and well-connected while the state, was unable to perform the basic functions that are normally assigned to it—access to basic social services, provision of infrastructure, maintenance of law and order, and an effective judicial system.

The paradoxes that characterize the Pakistani economy can thus be explained in this framework of the perverse roles of the market and the state. As the market was rigged and distortions were rampant the country did not achieve the efficiency and productivity gains that it ought to have done, both—in relation to its potential and compared to other countries. The instruments of the state were also directed to benefit the same small group rather than correcting the inequities created by the market forces.

GROWTH EXPLAINED

How could Pakistan achieve reasonably high rates of growth— 5 per cent per annum—over a fifty year period under this perverse role of the market and the state and inspite of low human capital and lacklustre investment rates?

First Pakistan's record in private sector development, liberal trade regime and deregulation was relatively better than that of the neighbouring countries. By and large small and medium entrepreneurs and farmers operated efficiently, used the right factor proportions and received prices for their products which reflected their scarcity values. Public policies favoring large scale businesses, industrial houses and big landlords, generated the rents for these groups by means of selective interventions and discretionary measures.

Second, agriculture productivity achieved through the combination of a large investment in Indus Basin Works and the Tarbela Dam, ground water tubewells, tractorization and high yielding varieties raised the incomes in agriculture and non-farm sectors and increased the demand for labour in the economy. The spill-over effects of these productivity gains in agriculture also benefited the trade and transportation sectors. The biological and mechanical revolution in agriculture was spearheaded by large landowners and farmers with more education. But it was soon diffused and adopted by small farmers who were persuaded by the demonstration of benefits gained by the large landowners.

Third, the migration of unskilled labour to the Middle East in the 1970s and 1980s, eased the pressure on the domestic labour market, provided a social safety net to their families and enabled the country to earn foreign exchange through remittances. At one point in time, the remittances were financing more than 50 per cent of the country's imports expanding the productive capacity beyond what it could achieve through domestic savings.

Fourth, Pakistan has relied heavily on foreign savings— official aid in the 1960s and 1980s, and private flows in the 1990s—to finance its investment needs. For example, Official Development Assistance (ODA) to India never exceeded more than 1 to 2 per cent of GDP. On the other hand, Pakistan regularly received ODA equivalent to 6 to 7 per cent of GDP. This additional financing combined with the remittances in the 1970s, and 1980s and foreign currency accounts of residents and non-residents enabled Pakistan to maintain higher level of private consumption.

So it is not so much the rate of growth that is at the centre of this issue but how the benefits from this growth were distributed. It is the concentration of economic and political power that has given rise to the social exclusion of the majority from the benefits of this growth. The sobering lesson to be drawn is that the direction of public policies and institutions exacerbated the inter-personal, inter-regional, and gender inequities.

POLITICAL ECONOMY HYPOTHESES

The question that needs to be addressed is: what were the underlying political and non-economic factors that led to this state of affairs? There are many possible answers to this question. Our main hypothesis is that failure of governance and the consistent domination of political power and state apparatus by a narrowly based elite seeking to advance their private and family interests to the exclusion of the majority of the population lies at the root of the problem. Although there have been several regime changes—nominated, self-appointed, military, elected—the same small group, or its associates has always been well-placed. The poor quality of economic and political governance and the reversed role of the basic economic institutions—the state and the markets—(which is explained below) have grown worse over time. The continued lack of accountability by the policy makers to the public has been one of the important characteristics of the weak governance structure in Pakistan. This, in turn, has allowed varying rules, regulations, and policies to govern the distribution of patronage to supporters or to penalize the opponents. The regulatory orders issued by the tax authorities, State Bank, Ministry of Finance and Commerce have been used liberally to serve particular interests, creating socially inefficient and inequitable outcomes for the economy but large personal gains for the individuals concerned.

Instead of striking at the roots of these economic disparities created by the market due to differences in initial distribution of endowments and defusing the bomb of potential ethnic conflicts, arising out of regional disparities the ruling coalitions in Pakistan have put all their energies into playing the musical chairs of retaining or assuming power by the use of extraordinary measures to oust each other. This preoccupation with keeping hold of power—and this applies to both the military rulers and the elected regimes alike—and fending off attacks from the opposition by co-opting them through state patronage or by bribing or otherwise pleasing the elected or nominated members of the national and provincial assemblies, has led to a laxity in fiscal and monetary policies and to the concentration of economic and political power. The excessive use of discretion in case-by-case policy making by this narrow interest group has derailed the institutionalized decision making that was based on well-established rules, transparency in transactions, and professional management. Relaxation of rules of business and regulations has been resorted to on a large scale by successive governments seeking to win or sustain political support from key players of this group. This arbitrary exercise of power benefited a select few at the expense of the majority of the population, and has made institutionalized decision-making irrelevant. The resulting decay of institutions, particularly the judiciary and the financial and educational institutions, and the short-term, opportunistic, and *ad hoc* nature of decision making, has given rise to untenable long-term policies, low provision and poor maintenance of infrastructure, and low levels of human development. The large amounts of external aid and the substantial inflow of workers' remittances allowed the country to accommodate these unsustainable policies, but the drying up of external aid and the return of migrant workers to Pakistan have already created difficulties and will no longer cover up these fundamental deficiencies.

There is some theoretical and empirical support to the hypothesis advanced above. Alesina recently argued that 'society's polarization and degree of social conflict' are key factors underlying policy decisions. Political economy models suggest that polarized societies will be prone to competitive rent-seeking by the different groups and have difficulty agreeing on public goods. Easterly shows that high levels of ethnic diversity in Africa are strongly linked to poor policies, low provisions of infrastructure, and low levels of education, even when more violent expressions of ethnic conflict are absent. Thus, the evidence suggests that ethnic diversity is an underlying cause of poor economic growth and that extraordinarily high levels of ethnic diversity in Africa help explain a substantial amount of Africa's growth tragedy. Indeed, after accounting for the effects of ethnic diversity on growth through policies and public goods, ethnic diversity alone accounts for about one-third of the growth differential between the countries of Africa and East Asia. The data also support the proposition that countries with efficiently operating institutions eliminate the negative effects of ethnic diversity.

The poor policies, low provision of infrastructure, and low levels of education that characterize Pakistan in the 1990s can, on the above parallels, also be ascribed to the behaviour of the coalition between the landed aristocracy, industrialists and big businesses, civil and military bureaucrats, and the professionals who have found ethnic diversity a useful tool for promoting their self-interests. This coalition is drawn from all the ethnic and regional groups and has come together, at different points of time, purportedly to protect the interests of their respective constituencies that are 'threatened' by the excesses of the state or the excesses of one ethnic group or the other. Military dictatorships came to power to 'save' the country or Islam, the popular forces struggling to overthrow the military rulers were to 'save democracy' from the excesses of authoritarianism.

In a multi-ethnic society, the very perception of exclusion from, or non-participation in the decision-making process leads to suspicion, lack of trust, and non-co-operation on the part of the minority ethnic groups, and this perception is promoted by the elite belonging to the various ethnic groups for their own self-interest. This is exactly what happened in Pakistan during the periods of military rule that spanned 1958-71 and then 1978-88. In the first period, the inter-wing economic disparities between East and West Pakistan became the rallying point for the confrontation by the East Pakistani populace against the predominantly West Pakistani military rulers. The civil servants belonging to East Pakistan saw better opportunities for rapid advancement in their careers in an independent Bangladesh than in a united Pakistan, and the big businesses perceived that the rents from import licences, foreign aid, and other economic controls in an independent Bangladesh could be captured by them exclusively and not shared with the elite of West Pakistan. The second period accentuated the tensions and rivalries between the ethnic groups in the remaining provinces of Pakistan. The Movement for the Restoration of Democracy against the Zia regime was instigated by elites of the three smaller provinces who felt that the benefits of state patronage were accruing to a small group belonging to the majority province. They created tensions and fostered resentment against the regime in order to to preserve and promote their own and their families' interests.

The history of political parties and elected governments substantiates this hypothesis of coalition making and alliances by the elite class drawn from different ethnic groups to protect and serve their narrow personal and familial interests. The 1947-58 period was notorious for the frequent demise and re-formation of governments under different parties but with the same cast of individuals. Iskander Mirza was able to create a completely new 'Republican Party' overnight out of the ruling Muslim League. Once Ayub Khan decided to legitimize his regime by instituting 'Basic Democracies', the same people who had formed the Republican Party reconstituted themselves as the Convention Muslim League under Ayub. When Z. A. Bhutto, Ayub's Foreign Minister, saw a weakening of the Ayub government in the post-1965 war period, he formed a new political party, the 'Peoples' Party of Pakistan'. Except for a handful of dedicated workers who truly believed in the socialist principles espoused by the PPP, most of those elected on its ticket in 1970 were former members or supporters of Ayub's Muslim League. The circle was fully completed at the time of the 1977 elections, when almost all the tickets were awarded by the PPP to former Muslim Leaguers, the majority of whom had by now crossed over to the party in power. The list of PPP candidates was almost indistinguishable from those who had supported Ayub Khan.

The Junejo government, nominated by Ziaul Haq in 1985, came to power initially on a no-party basis, but a large number of PPP leaders, either directly or through their 'proxies' joined the government. Some of them kept their options open as they felt that Benazir Bhutto would initiate a popular movement against the military-supported regime and they would be better off if they remained on the fence and did not openly align themselves with the Junejo government.

The post-1988 period, when the tradition of elected governments was restored, resulted in the emergence of two major political parties—the Pakistan Muslim League and the PPP.

There have been floor-crossings, shifting of party loyalties, formation of dissident factions within the parties, and a spate of short-lived and unstable governments. The fierce bickering and rivalries among the two major parties do not stem from differences in ideological stances, economic policy, or other matters of principle. They are motivated purely and simply by lust for power, which can be profitably employed to make further economic gains for themselves and their families. There are many examples of the family members joining different political parties to ensure that they are always represented on the ruling party of the day.

Pakistan has witnessed nine different governments in the last ten years and four general elections. None of the elected governments could complete their tenure of office and were dismissed by the President in each instance. The spectre of Martial Law always looms large on the political horizon. The emergence of the ethnic and regional political parties such as the Awami National Party (ANP), the Balochistan National Party (BNP) and the Mohajir Qaumi Movement (MQM) has added to this political instability particularly in the smaller provinces. They have aligned themselves, in different configurations with the two major parties at various points of time not on the basis of any stated principles but to articulate the interests of their leaders in capturing cabinet positions. The other indicator of political instability apart from the electoral politics is the spate of ethnic, religious and sectarian riots which have engulfed Karachi and the province of Punjab.

What is the evidence that Pakistan suffers from macro-economic instability? Since 1988, Pakistan has negotiated successive agreements for achieving macroeconomic stabilization with the IMF. None of the agreements have been completed as the process went off-track or the agreed targets could not be achieved. The economic outcomes for this period—lower growth, stagnant exports, high rates of inflation and serious debt burden—are the manifestation of this phenomenon. These, in turn, have resulted from the policies pursued by the successive governments in the past.

It is thus obvious from the above that the cycle of political instability has engulfed the Pakistan scene in the last decade with consequent implications for macroeconomic stability. Recently, there has been some investigation of the political conditions that give rise to certain types of macroeconomic policy. Roubini finds a significant negative correlation between the frequency of government change and the average fiscal balance for 77 countries over the period 1971-82. Dornbusch and Edward have identified the phenomenon of macroeconomic populism in a number of Latin American countries. They define this as 'an approach...that emphasizes growth and income distribution and de-emphasizes the risks of inflation and deficit finance, external constraints and the reaction of economic agents to aggressive non-market policies'. Because these policies are misconceived, they end in economic crisis and, in many cases, increasing political tension. Not surprisingly, countries which have experienced 'populist' episodes score poorly in the measures of macroeconomic management. The authors emphasize that the causation runs from macroeconomic policy to political instability rather than the other way around. Like a number of other authors, they tend to identify structural features of the society as the ultimate factor giving rise to populist economic programmes, and they see the failure of these programmes as a potential source of political instability.

However, it seems likely that political instability is itself an independent source of macroeconomic instability. In a struggle for power, politicians become focused on extremely short-term goals, and this does not make for sound macroeconomic management. To this extent, there is likely to be a causal relationship between political and macroeconomic instability.

BREAKING THE VICIOUS CYCLE

How can this vicious cycle of instability—originating from political insecurity leading to macroeconomic unsteadiness and back to political uncertainty be broken? In many progressing countries the instrument that has broken this unending cycle is a high rate of literacy among the population at large. But in the case of Pakistan, this instrument is not available. The low rates of literacy among the population have actually played into the hands of the elite and helped to reinforce the tendency of concentration of economic and political power.

Under the military regimes the members of this elite convinced their respective ethnic groups that the absence of democratic institutions meant the denial of opportunities for these groups to participate in the affairs of the state and the usurpation of power by those groups that dominated the armed forces. They deliberately fanned a sense of disillusionment and deprivation among the residents of the minority provinces, which were backward to start with.

The low rate of literacy and the strong tradition of *mai-baap* (paternalistic behaviour) or subservience arising out of the feudal relationships and bureaucratic domination did not allow the majority of the ethnic groups to see through the game of their well-to-do leaders, and they never challenged the entrenched vested interests in any meaningful way. Zulfikar Ali Bhutto, who came to power with the popular mandate of uprooting these interests and who could have made a difference, also succumbed to their pressures and, in his quest to retain, the Prime Ministership, finally yielded by co-opting them.

The ruling elites therefore found it convenient to perpetuate low literacy rates. The lower the proportion of educated and literate people, the lower the probability that the ruling alliance could be displaced. Among the more traditional tribal societies of Balochistan, rural Sindh, rural southern Punjab, and the tribal areas of the NWFP, the overall literacy rates and female literacy rates, in particular, are among the lowest in the world. The feudal landlords who dominate these societies feel threatened by the spread of education and communication as within their areas they fear that this will erode their monopoly over power.

The effects of low literacy are also apparent in the composition of the labour force and the skill base. Non-wage work, self-employment, and unpaid family helpers still dominate the

employment scene in Pakistan. Half of the labour force is still
employed in the agriculture sector, where informal modes of
employment persist. The open unemployment rate of 5-6 per
cent reported officially is an underestimate, as it excludes a
large proportion of disguised unemployment and under-
employment. The skill base in Pakistan is fairly narrow since
the mean educational attainment level of the labour force is
only a few years of schooling. The absence of organized trade
unions, which could have become an alternative source of
challenge to the traditional focus of power, is also a direct result
of the low literacy among the population.

The full extent of income inequalities cannot be discerned
from officially recorded national accounts. The large unrecorded
or parallel economy does not figure in official calculations.
Estimates of Gini Coefficients and other measures of income
inequality in Pakistan are, therefore, incomplete. Recent studies
place 30-40 per cent of the GDP in the parallel, undocumented
economy. The combined formal and parallel GDP of Pakistan is
thus $75 billion, compared to $60 billion in the official economy.
The parallel economy is largely fuelled by the economic rents
created by government favours and interventions, including
smuggling of goods and currency, drug trafficking, evasion of
taxes, overinvoicing, bribery, etc. The main actors involved in
the parallel economy are a relatively small proportion of the
income recipients in the top decile. It is true that the multiplier
effect of conspicuous consumption would have helped other
economic actors too, but the concentration of assets—foreign
currency deposits, real estate, stock market shares, capital flight
overseas—clearly indicates that the major beneficiary of the
parallel economy in Pakistan has been this small class of asset
holders. It would thus be fair to ascribe 80-90 per cent of the
incomes in the parallel economy to the top income decile. If
this adjustment is made to the official national income statistics,
then all measures of income distribution for Pakistan turn out to
be among the worst in the developing countries. This 'adjusted'
income distribution measure, therefore, explains most of the

discrepancy between high income growth and poor social progress in the case of Pakistan.

The only viable way in which this vicious cycle can be broken is by intensification of efforts at all levels—government, private sector, non-governmental organizations and the local communities—towards human capital development particularly where accelerating literacy rates are concerned. The targeted areas for this effort are well known and the techniques for outreach have been applied in practice sporadically. The recent measures taken by the Chief Minister, Punjab show some enlightened thinking by a group of politicians. But the success of this effort can only be achieved by the non-government sector, at gross roots level in rural Sindh, Balochistan, rural Southern Punjab and the tribal areas of NWFP.

HOW HAS PAKISTAN COMPARED TO THE BEST PERFORMING DEVELOPING COUNTRIES, I.E., EAST ASIA?

Both Pakistan and East Asian countries achieved high economic growth rates during 1960-90 period. While in East Asia, the incidence of poverty declined significantly and income distribution improved dramatically, leading to social cohesion and political stability, the opposite was the case in Pakistan.

How can this differential outcome in terms of equality, distribution, and economic performance be explained? Comparisons and analogies are at best approximations, for no historical situations are exactly similar, but Pakistan and Korea started out with very similar economic conditions, yet their paths diverged in drastically different ways. Pakistan's per capita income rose from $ 95 in 1960 to $ 460 in 1996, while Korea, which had a per capita income of $100 in 1960, has become, the eleventh largest economy in the world, joining the OECD with a per capita income of over $ 8,000 in 1995. Korea was not alone; almost all the other countries in East Asia traversed the same path. What did these countries do so differently?

The East Asian governments provided political stability, stable macroeconomic conditions, appropriate legal systems, a high level of human capital, attractive enabling environments for business, and a basic infrastructure that fostered growth. Governments intervened in markets both in East Asia and Pakistan to create economic rents. In the former, rents were reallocated by the governments to participants on the basis of performance-based criteria. Firms which were able to increase exports and thus expand employment opportunities and incomes in the domestic economy were rewarded through allocations of credit and foreign exchange. These incentives, in turn, encouraged the adoption of international standards, accelerated the diffusion of technology, and helped the exporting firms in capturing a growing share of a much larger world market. Government support to industry, by establishing research and science centres and quality control standards, was important both in attracting foreign investment and in encouraging domestic investors. Government interventions helped to realign private and social profitability together, and thus economic growth and social justice moved hand in hand.

In the case of Pakistan, government controls on the allocation of resources and interventions in the markets were equally strong, but the institutional and political character of the successive governments was entirely different. The power relationship in Pakistan has been characterized by a 'feudal' mind-set and behaviour. The 'feudals', or the narrow class of ruling elites that moved in and out of power at various intervals of time, captured most of the rents for themselves and their families. This class of elites, which includes politicians, big businessmen, bureaucrats, military officers, and landlords, was attuned to the patron-client relationship. The economic rents created through import licensing, industrial permits, foreign exchange allocations, credit by government development banks or nationalized commercial banks, discretionary tariff concessions, award of contracts, subsidized agriculture credit, cheap urban land, evasion of taxes, and a host of other government policies, in fact widened the discrepancy between private and social profitability. The ratio of cumulative private benefits to social benefits could be high—ten or twenty in many instances. Though economic growth was stimulated but as the allocation of these rents was not guided by any performance-based criteria, the benefits of growth were concentrated disproportionately among a very small segment of the population—the top five per cent of income distribution—neglecting the general population.

The fiscal budgetary space in East Asia was created deliberately to provide safety nets to and broaden the benefits of growth. In contrast, the fiscal space in Pakistan was squeezed and crowded out, making it difficult to invest in basic social services or infrastructure that could bring about a wider distribution of the benefits of growth. The taxation system was a regressive tool that further perpetuated income disparities and allowed large-scale tax evasion.

The other factor that shows divergence between East Asia and Pakistan is that the former pursued policies ensuring universal literacy while only one-third of the adult population in Pakistan was literate. Universal literacy both increased productivity and promoted greater equality. The emphasis on female education led to reduced fertility, thus mitigating the adverse effects of population pressure, and directly increasing the supply of educated labour. The education of women can be thought of as a roundabout but high-return way of enhancing labour force productivity. In Pakistan, female education rates remained dismally low, with the attendant problems of high fertility rates, high population growth rates, and a low-productivity labour force.

In Korea, Japan, and Taiwan, land reforms were important in the initial stages of development. They had three effects: they increased rural productivity and income and resulted in increased savings; higher incomes provided the domestic demand that was important in these economies before export markets expanded; and the redistribution of income contributed to political stability, an important factor in creating a good environment for domestic and foreign investment. In Pakistan, half-hearted attempts at land reform did not unleash the productive forces of the small and landless farmers, which could have had similar beneficial effects.

The cultural, social, and economic barriers erected during the last fifty years have effectively excluded most of the population from full involvement in the economy and have reinforced the policy that perpetuates inequities and skewed distribution of economic and political power. The phenomenon of 'social exclusion' applies to Pakistan more aptly. In many countries, social relationships have proven to have a positive impact on the quality of development by enhancing collective action, mitigating risks, promoting accountability, and reducing transaction costs. In Pakistan, on the other hand, social relationships have been used by a small elite to control and acquire publicly owned resources for private enrichment, and to exclude the majority of the poor from the benefits of development.

Economic performance and social relations are shaped by the degree to which accountability and participation characterize governance; by the way in which information is generated and disseminated within the society; by the legal environment within which contracts are drawn and executed; by the transaction costs associated with trust within the group or society. The weak governance which characterized every form of government in Pakistan, whether military, democratically elected, or nominated, is linked to political factors.

The unending contest for power has not allowed the roots of democracy to find solid ground. The periods of military rules, totalling over twenty-five years in all, did not help either. The more recent experience of democratic rule (1988-to date) has been one of instability, fragility, and shakiness. The confidence of the common masses in the electoral system has been badly shaken and social cohesion has been upset.

At the time of independence, state power was predominantly in the hands of the bureaucracy and the military. The leading political party, the Muslim League, was unable to organize itself at the grassroots level and thus found it difficult to counter the more sophisticated and educated members of the civil service and the army. The Muslim League needed them badly, to consolidate the power of the new state and to lay the foundation of an administrative machinery and a security apparatus. The weakness of the Muslim League leadership and the rivalries and factions within the party did not allow the party to strengthen its hold on the state machinery. The protracted negotiations on the constitution, the erosion of the popular mandate, and the growing chasm between the East and West political leaders provided further opportunities to the non-elected elites to exercise power both formally and informally.

The Martial Law under Zia was an attempt at *ex post facto* rationalization of the action taken by the military to oust the democratically elected government of Bhutto. The Zia regime's justification for continuing in power after the November 1979 elections were indefinitely postponed was the 'Islamization of society'. This consisted of the adoption of Islamic Shariat laws, establishment of Shariat courts, enforcement of *zakat* and *ushr,* and the abolition of *riba*. The consumption of alcohol was banned, traditional dress became mandatory for government officials, and many other rituals were promoted in the name of Islamization. A hand-picked *Majlis-i-Shura* was inaugurated, and a Prime Minister was appointed by Zia, although as soon as he started to assert himself, he was dismissed from office.

The state sponsored 'Islamization' campaign created another powerful elite, i.e., the religious oligarchy that has since played a major divisive role in the country's polity and society. By fanning the differences between various sects—Shias and Sunnis, Deobandis and Barelvis, etc.,—this elite sowed the seeds of further polarization and friction that has engulfed the country during the decade since the death of Zia. These forces have also put a brake on any modernization of the society on the lines adopted by two East Asian Muslim countries, Indonesia and Malaysia. The emergence of this new but powerful group has introduced a new dimension into the debate about the kind of development strategy Pakistan should follow in the future—

isolationist, cut off from the technological and scientific revolution, and self-sufficient internally.

HOW HAS PAKISTAN FARED IN COMPARISON TO INDIA?

As both countries inherited a common historical, cultural, geographical, and institutional heritage with almost identical levels of economic development at the time of their independence, it is fair to ask the question: How have the two countries fared during the last fifty years? The comparative performance indications are summarized in Tables 7.2 and 7.3.

On the surface, the claims that Pakistan has pursued a more liberal and market-oriented development strategy may be valid relative to India. But this assertion is highly superficial, as the above analysis shows. At best it is only a matter of degree and the relative speed of change that distinguishes the two countries.

The fundamental characteristics of the economic policy regimes in the two countries were more or less identical. These involved industrial licensing under which the scale, technology, and location of any investment project other than relatively small ones were regulated and permission was needed to expand, relocate, or change the output and input mixes of operating plants. Second, there was an all-pervasive exchange control system which required exporters to surrender their foreign exchange earnings to the Central Bank at the official exchange rate and allocated the exchange earnings to users through import licensing. Third, the capital issues controls required permission to be granted by the government before domestic equity markets and debt finance could be accessed by potential investors. The prices of the initial offerings were determined by the Controller. Fourth, price controls were imposed on some vital consumption goods and critical inputs, and any changes in price levels for these items had to be approved by the government. Fifth, made-to-measure protection from import competition was granted to domestic industries in many 'priority' industries. Sixth, the agriculture sector was forced to sell most of its output at fixed prices, normally below world market prices, to the state and was provided subsidies on irrigation, fertilizers, and electricity. Seventh, since 1972, the nationalized commercial banks were subject to directed and selective credit controls and controls on deposit and lending rates, and had to lend substantial amounts of their loanable funds to the government at below market rates of interest.

Despite this similarity in policies, the initial endowments of human and physical capital, institutional base, and political environment differed markedly. The enforcement of these controls was more strict and vigorous in India's case. A strict comparison is also made problematic because of the separation of East from West Pakistan in 1971. But it is possible to draw some valid conclusions from the experience of the past fifty years.

First, both countries have shared some common successes. Despite the prophecies of gloom and doom on both sides of the fence, both India and Pakistan have succeeded in more than doubling their per capita incomes. This is a remarkable feat considering that the population has increased fourfold in the case of Pakistan and threefold in India. Leaving aside the countries in East Asia and China, very few large countries have been able to reach this milestone.

- The incidence of poverty (defined as $1 per day) has also been reduced, although the number of absolute poor remains astoundingly high.
- Food production has not only kept pace with the rise in population but has surpassed it. Both countries, leaving aside annual fluctuations due to weather conditions, have attained self-sufficiency in food. (Pakistan exports its surplus rice but imports wheat).
- Food self-sufficiency has been accompanied by improved nutritional status. Daily caloric and protein intake per capita has risen by almost one-third, although malnourishment among children is still high.

- The cracks in the dualistic nature of the economy—a well-developed modern sector and a backward traditional sector—are appearing in both the countries. A buoyant middle class is emerging, albeit threatened by the undercurrents of religious fundamentalism. The use of modern inputs and the mechanization of agriculture have been a levelling influence in this direction, but public policies have not always been consistent or supportive.

Second, the two countries have met common failures. Their relatively inward-looking economic policies and high protection of domestic industry did not allow them to reap the benefits of integration with the fast-expanding and much larger world economy. This has changed, particularly since 1991, but the control mind-set of the politicians and the bureaucrats has not changed. The centrally-planned allocation of resources and 'license raj' has given rise to an inefficient private sector that thrives on contacts, bribes, loans from public financial institutions, lobbying, tax evasion, and rent-seeking rather than on competitive behaviour. If both the control mind-set of the government and the parasitic behaviour of the private industrial entrepreneurs do not change drastically, the potential of an efficient economy will be hard to achieve. This can be accomplished by promoting domestic and international competition, reducing tariff and non-tariff barriers, and removing constraints on entry for newcomers.

The weaknesses in governance in the legal and judicial system, poor enforcement of private property rights and contracts, preponderance of discretionary government rules and regulations, and lack of transparency in decision-making act as brakes on broad-based participation and sharing of benefits by the majority of the population.

In terms of fiscal management, the record of both countries is less than stellar. Higher fiscal deficits, averaging 7-8 per cent of GDP, have persisted for fairly long periods of time and have crowded out private capital formation through large domestic borrowing. Defence expenditures and internal debt servicing continue to pre-empt a large proportion of the tax revenues, with adverse consequences for the maintenance and expansion of physical infrastructure, basic social services, and other essential services that only the government can provide. The congested urban services such as water, electricity, and transport in both countries are a potential source of social upheaval.

The state of the financial sector in both countries is plagued with serious ills. The nationalization of commercial banking services, the neglect of credit quality in allocation decisions, lack of competition, and inadequate prudential regulations and supervision have put the system under severe pressure and increased the share of non-performing assets in the banks' portfolio. The role of financial intermediation in mobilizing and efficiently allocating domestic savings has been seriously compromised and the banking system is fragile. Both countries are now taking steps to liberalize the financial sector and open it up to competition from foreign as well as private banks.

Third, there are several areas where India has surpassed Pakistan. There is little doubt that the scientific and techno-logical, manpower, and research and development institutions in India are far superior and can match those of western institutions. The real breakthrough in India's export of software after the opening up of the economy in 1991 attests to the validity of the proposition that human capital formation accompanied by market-friendly economic policies can lift developing countries out of the low-level equilibrium trap.

Indian scientists working in India excel in the areas of defence technology, space research, electronics and avionics, genetics, telecommunications, etc. The number of Ph.Ds produced by India in science and engineering every year—about 5,000—is higher than the entire stock of Ph.Ds in Pakistan. The premier research institutions in Pakistan, started at about the same time as India, have become hotbeds of internal bickerings and rivalries rather than generators of ideas, processes, and products.

Related to this superior performance in the field of scientific research and technological development is the better record of investment in education by India. The adult literacy rate, female literacy rate, gross enrolment ratios at all levels, and education index of India have moved way ahead of Pakistan. A rapid decline in total fertility rates in India has reduced the population growth rate to 1.8 per cent compared to 3.0 per cent for Pakistan.

Access to health care and infant mortality rates are also better in India and thus the overall picture of social indicators, although not very impressive by international standards, emerges as more favourable to India. The two most important determinants of Pakistan's dismal performance in social development are its inability to control population growth and the reluctance in the rural areas to educate girls.

Fourth, there are areas where Pakistan has performed better than India. The economic growth rate of Pakistan has been consistently higher than India's. Starting from a slightly lower level in 1947, Pakistan's per capita income today in US nominal dollar terms is one-third higher (430 versus 320), and in purchasing parity dollar terms, two-thirds higher (2,310 versus 1,280). The latter suggests that the average Pakistani has enjoyed better living standards and consumption levels in the past, but the gap seems to have been narrowing since the early 1990s. Had the population growth rate in Pakistan been slower, equalling that of India, this gap would have been much wider; the per capita income in Pakistan today would have been twice as high and the incidence of poverty further down.

Although both India and Pakistan have pursued inward-looking strategies, the anti-export bias in the case of Pakistan has been comparably lower and integration with the world market faster. The trade-GDP ratio in Purchasing Power Parity (PPP) terms is twice that of all South Asian countries. Pakistan's export growth over the 50-year period has been stronger and the composition of exports has shifted from primary to manufactured goods, albeit the dominance of cotton-based products has enhanced its vulnerability.

Domestic investment rates in Pakistan have remained much below those of India over the entire span, primarily due to the relatively higher domestic savings rates in the latter. But the efficiency of investment as measured by the aggregate incremental capital-output ratio or total factor productivity has been higher in the case of Pakistan and has, to some extent, compensated for the lower quantity of investment.

What is the bottom line then? The overall record looks mixed. Pakistan scores high on income and consumption growth, poverty reduction, and integration with the world economy. India has done very well in developing its human resource base and excels in the field of science and technology. Both countries face a set of common problems—the inherited legacy of a control mind-set among the government and rent-seeking private sector, widespread corruption, poor fiscal management, weak financial systems, and congested and overcrowded urban services. But there is an important and perceptible positive shift in most of the indicators for India since 1991. Export growth rates have almost doubled, GDP growth is averaging 6 to 7 per cent in recent years, the current account deficit is down, and foreign capital flows for investment have risen greatly. The edge that Pakistan had over India in most of these indicators before 1990 is fast eroding. Pakistan, on the other hand, has made greater progress in the privatization of state owned enterprises and in attracting foreign investors to expand power-generating capacity in the country.

What does the future look like? Since 1991, both India and Pakistan have embarked on a policy of liberalization, outward orientation, and faster integration with the global economy. The initial responses have been very positive. As outlined earlier, portfolio and foreign direct investment flows in the last few years have surpassed those accumulated over the last twenty to twenty-five years. Indian exports have recorded an increase of 50 per cent since 1991, while Pakistan's, despite a setback due to the failure of successive cotton crops, have expanded by two-thirds since 1990. The political uncertainty in India has not threatened the agenda of economic reforms which was adopted by the Congress Party in 1991, although the speed of the reforms may have been affected during the coalition-led governments. This combination of political maturity, economic policy credibility, and a well-developed human resource base places India at an advantage today. The imperatives of globalization and integration with the world economy dictate that countries that are not agile and do not seize opportunities at the right time are likely to be losers.

PAKISTAN'S DEVELOPMENT IN THE CONTEXT OF SOUTH ASIA

The large size and diversity of India may raise some questions about the validity of comparisons between Pakistan and India. It may, therefore, be useful to place Pakistan in the context of South Asia and extend the comparative analysis to include Bangladesh and Sri Lanka. Bangladesh was part of Pakistan until 1971 and has a significant number of similarities— population size, historical evolution, institutional structures, initial conditions, etc. Sri Lanka is a much smaller country in size but enjoys ethnic diversity. This broad-based assessment covering all the four countries may provide better insights than the bilateral comparison between India and Pakistan.

The data in Table 7.4 once again confirm the lagging nature of the social indicators of Pakistan relative to its neighbours in the region. Two-thirds of the population is still illiterate, compared with one-half for South Asia. The population growth rate is the highest in the region and has added 104 million people to the population of 30 million inherited in 1947. Pakistan's infant mortality rate is 90 when, for its level of development, it should be no more than 30. Not only has this explosive growth of population created severe capacity strains in the availability of social services, but rapid urbanization is fuelling environmental degradation. The maternal mortality rate—600 women die during childbirth for 100,000 live births— is one of the highest in the world. The female literacy rates in most rural areas are still in the 10s and 20s. The gender

disparities in terms of participation in the labour force, legal
rights, access to credit, land tenure, etc., are still huge. The
lower attainment of females in education has a domino effect—
lower participation in the labour force, high fertility rate, and
limited access to publicly provided services. The much lower
achievements of women in literacy, health, etc., bring down the
values of the aggregate social indicators for the country as a
whole. The legal and regulatory constraints are further
impediments in the way of women's participation in economic
and social life. The inequalities between women belonging to
the elite classes and the rest of the population are much sharper
than income, class and regional inequalities. The example of
Bangladesh—a fellow Muslim country sharing the same
historical and political background for the first twenty-five
years—amply shows the potency of benign and sensible public
policy interventions in upgrading the status of women and
thereby improving the aggregate social indicators. Bangladesh
had similar population growth rates—about 3 per cent per
annum—at the time of separation from Pakistan. Two and a
half decades later, it has emerged as one of the international
success stories in population control and microcredit to women
farmers, workers and entrepreneurs. These two stories, always
told in isolation of each other, are in fact mutually reinforcing
and form a single strand. Educated and healthy women, when
provided access to credit, increase their participation in the
labour force. This, in turn, leads to wider child-spacing and
reduced fertility rates, thereby lowering the population growth
rate. The gross female enrolment ratio of 105 and the female
labour force participation of 42 are the highest in South Asia
and low income countries.

The best overall record of social development is, of course,
that of Sri Lanka. Very few low-income countries in the world
can excel this record. Not only is the population highly literate,
the health status is equally impressive. For example, the infant
mortality rate and life expectancy are more akin to those in the
developed countries. However, recent experience does suggest
that this high investment in human capital cannot have the

expected payoff unless the economic environment is also conducive. It is the complementarity between sound economic policies and investment in human capital that produces opportunities for employment, growth, and improved living standards for the majority of the population. A stagnant economy imposes serious difficulties on sustaining the gains from investment in human capital. On the other hand, economic growth is not sustainable unless there is adequate improvement in human capital.

An analysis of the economic indicators of the four countries (Table 7.5) shows that, by and large, Pakistan fares better than its neighbours on most counts. Sri Lanka is the only one that has a higher per capita income, higher per capita consumption in terms of purchasing power, and a higher investment ratio. Sri Lanka is also a more open and outward-oriented economy, although smaller economies do invariably enjoy higher trade ratios.

Pakistan's per capita income is twice as much as that of Bangladesh and almost 30 per cent higher than India's. Poverty incidence is lower than Bangladesh and India but higher than Sri Lanka. The indirect indicators of economic performance, such as energy use per capita, electricity production per capita, and telephone lines per 1,000 people, also favour Pakistan compared to the other three countries. (Table 7.6)

Rapid population growth and the lower status of women acted as a strong brake on Pakistan's development. Had Pakistan succeeded in containing the population growth rate at the level of Bangladesh (2 per cent instead of 3 per cent per annum) and continued to achieve 6 per cent growth in GDP, it would have doubled its per capita income every 17 years instead of every 23 years. In addition to population growth as a constraining influence, the lower social and economic status of women—one half of the country's population—plays an equally debilitating role. A more enlightened environment and a public policy posture that encourages female education would remove many of these constraints, including the high population growth rate that is slowing down the growth momentum and impairing the quality of growth. A more equitable outcome would result from greater participation of women in the economic, political, and social life of the country. Most of these gains would accrue not due to factor accumulation but through total factor productivity. Investment in female education and the removal of other barriers in the way of their participation in the labour force are good for both social and economic development.

DYNAMICS OF THE ELITIST MODEL IN PAKISTAN

This section attempts to offer some concluding observations as to why the elitist growth model was successful in Pakistan and what can possibly be done to weaken the grip of the elites and thus change this past pattern of growth. These observations are rooted in the literature on the political economy of developing countries.

How does one know that an elitist growth model is in fact being pursued? Although there are no direct indictors or precise quantifiable parameters, a number of characteristics can be identified that make this type of model work in practice. The essential ingredients are:

(a) a strong leader or succession of leaders who enjoy almost regal powers and implement their own agenda with few or almost no checks and balances;

(b) a powerful bureaucratic class that implements the wishes of the leader without questioning their legality or relating them to the larger public interest, and in the process arrogates to itself the task of defining the goals of the State, which are made to coincide with its own; and

(c) a dormant and subservient population that is passive and indifferent to the actions of the leaders and bureaucracy.

For almost half of its fifty years Pakistan was governed by strong military leaders, and for the other half by strong civilian leaders who, unwittingly, adopted the same military leaders as their role model. Although the Eighth Amendment introduced checks on the powers of the Prime Minister, in actual practice this had little effect. The elected governments were dismissed four times between 1988 and 1996 on charges of corruption and excesses.

The bureaucratic class was a powerful ally of the strong leaders until 1973 and played a major role in advising and implementing the agenda of their political masters. After 1973, when they lost their security of tenure, the nature of the alliance shifted to that of a docile, subservient, and unquestioning group of functionaries who diligently carried out the orders of the politicians—right or wrong.

Until recently, freedom of expression, freedom of association, and freedom of the Press were severely curtailed. The majority of the population was uneducated and illiterate and used to a tradition of a paternalistic way of governance inherited from the colonial period and cemented by the subsequent autocratic rulers. Agitations against the government were seldom triggered by economic issues.

This combination of strong autocratic leaders, a pliant bureaucracy, and a subservient population made it possible for the benefits of growth to be unequally distributed and concentrated.

The relationship between economic growth and income . inequality in developing countries has been the subject of numerous empirical investigations as well as speculative discourses. The inverted U curve discovered by Simm Kuznets, based on the cross-sectional study of a sample of developing and developed countries, has remained the predominant strand of thinking on this subject. The literature on 'redistribution with growth' which appeared in the mid-1970s confirmed the tendency for the benefits of growth to be concentrated in the early stages and to spread only slowly. Those developing countries which have taken positive action such as improvements in modern sector employment through education and the rapid growth of demand for labour or redistribution of land and, redirection of public investments have witnessed the poor sharing equitably in income growth.

In the case of Pakistan and a number of other countries, the poor have been prevented from sharing equitably in the general increase in output by a number of specific disabilities that can be summed up as lack of physical and human capital and lack of access. In the political economy of growth in Pakistan, a narrow minority of influential elites drawn from the landlords, political parties, the military, civil servants, big business and the professional class dominated the scene throughout the past five decades and maximized their rent-collecting activities. As demonstrated earlier this was the main stumbling block in securing access to public services by the poor and their acquisition of physical and human capital.

PRODUCTIVE SECTORS

The distribution of land—the most important asset in the first two decades of the country's history—was highly skewed, with large landholdings and *jagirs* concentrated in the hands of a few thousand families. These land titles were not earned; they were conferred on the beneficiaries by the British for the loyalty demonstrated by these classes in keeping the British raj intact. This particular incentive, i.e., to acquire wealth not through hard work or productive means but by winning the favours of the ruling classes, formed the basis for the subsequent evolution of Pakistan's economy.

In the 1950s, import licensing, overvalued exchange rates, and subsidized capital made available by a succession of politically unstable but bureaucratically entrenched governments provided ample opportunities for a small class of robber barons to enrich themselves and their families. Although they laid the foundation for industrial growth in Pakistan, the efficiency and equity dimensions of this growth were never seriously considered.

The Ayub decade of reforms, with its overt emphasis on 'liberalization', was anything but 'liberal'. Under high rates of effective protection, working in almost monopolistic or oligopolistic market structures with interlocking interests in financial and banking houses, a few hundred industrial families were able to capture enormous gains from the industrialization policy. While the social benefits, i.e., value added at world prices, were insignificant, or in many cases negative, the private benefits, i.e., value added at distorted market prices, were exceptionally high. Several empirical studies of the industrialization of Pakistan by Lewis, Amjad, Whitehead, and Islam, and research articles in the *Pakistan Development Review* have sufficiently documented the concentration of economic assets resulting from the economic policies pursued in the 1960s.

The Green Revolution of the late 1960s and the 1970s did make a significant difference in raising the overall level of wheat and rice production and the productivity of land in Pakistan, but the nature of the technology favoured the irrigated areas rather than rainfed areas. As irrigated land in Pakistan is more unequally distributed—owned or operated mostly by large landholders—while the poor subsist on the rainfed areas, the differential impact of this new technological breakthrough further accentuated the income disparities. Reinforcing this tendency were two other public policy-induced developments. First, private tubewells to tap sweet groundwater reservoirs were encouraged and subsidized, and second, generous amounts of subsidized credit by the Agricultural Development Bank were granted to large farmers to purchase tractors and other mechanized equipment. The expansion in the number of owner-operated farms was paralleled by a decline in the demand for hired labour in the rain-fed areas. The consequent migration of rural labour from the *barani* areas to the urban areas created further pressures on the environmental and general conditions under which the poor lived.

The revolt against the pro-rich economic policies of Ayub Khan that culminated in the separation of East Pakistan brought into power the populist regime of Zulfikar Ali Bhutto. It was felt that the past trend of economic concentration would be reversed under this type of political regime and a more egalitarian economic order would be established. The nationalization of large-scale industries, banks and financial institutions, and agro-processing industries was considered the key element of this strategy. But the record of the 1970s shows that the country not only slipped badly in maintaining its high economic growth performance, but that the income distribution effects were equally disastrous. Instead of expanding investment for productive purposes, large private businesses resorted to speculation, trading, and obtaining contracts from the state-run corporations. While these corporations suffered financial losses which were financed by the exchequer, the business classes prospered by co-opting the managers of the corporations to their side. Although a number of exogenous shocks make it difficult to disentangle the harmful effects of the policies pursued during this period, the migration of millions of workers to the Middle East after the oil price boom and their remittances did act as a safety valve to what would otherwise have been a period of high unemployment, high inflation, stagnant output, and worsening income distribution.

The reversal of the Bhutto policies in the 1980s and early 1990s brought an end to the uncertainty, but by then a new source of rent-seeking had been discovered by the elites. As pointed out earlier, the nationalized commercial banks and the development finance institutions suddenly became major conduits of industrial capital flows. The loans sanctioned by these financial institutions not only allowed the equity portion of the sponsors to be paid off through overinvoicing of machinery and equipment, but the loan applications were never subjected to rigorous appraisal to establish the financial viability of the underlying project. The mushrooming of spinning units that produced low value-added yarn brought enormous grief to export expansion efforts. Unlike other Asian countries, the higher value-added, labour-intensive garment and other ancillary industries never took off, making Pakistan's policy makers hostage to the powerful lobby of spinners and making the country highly vulnerable to fluctuations in the external cotton yarn market. By forgoing an excellent opportunity for expanding employment and incomes in the textile sector, the country once again fell prey to the machinations of a small group of industrialists who earned their profits by processing domestically produced cotton procured at subsidized prices, i.e., below international market prices, and selling yarn at world prices.

Not only did the country get stuck in a low-level export equilibrium, but the financial institutions themselves accumulated a large portfolio of non-performing assets. The non-servicing of these loans has created a serious problem for the health of the financial system, the pricing of new credit, and the access to credit by newcomers. The concentration of written-off or non-accruing credit in the hands of a few thousand individuals and firms exacerbated the inequality trend.

FISCAL POLICY

While the main productive sectors of the economy—agriculture and manufacturing—promoted a pattern of growth that benefited a small minority of the population disproportionately, the contribution of this class to the tax-generating capacity of the country was almost negligible. In many developing countries, taxation has been used judiciously to finance the priority investment needs of the country and as an instrument for promoting equity. In Pakistan, unfortunately, taxation has not only been inadequate in relation to the needs but has also been regressive. The tax-GDP ratio of 14-15 per cent is the lowest among countries of identical income levels. More importantly, it is derived largely from indirect taxes—customs duties, excise taxes, and sales tax—whose incidence falls proportionately on all income classes. Direct taxes account for 2-3 per cent of GDP and the coverage extends to only one million people. Most income tax payers are salaried or wage-earning employees, importers, contractors, or others whose taxes can be withheld at source. The autonomous taxpayers, i.e., those whose incomes are assessed by the tax authorities outside the withholding tax system, account for a very small fraction of the total income tax collected. Tax evasion, exclusion from the tax net, and collusion with the tax collectors have given rise to a *nouveau riche* class of tax officials and businessmen who have made millions at the expense of the State. This tacit arrangement between a small class of tax evaders and unscrupulous tax officials has reinforced the widening gulf between those at the top and the bottom of the ladder. The successive 'whitening' of black money or tax evaded money and its round tripping through foreign exchange bearer certificates has not made it any easier to promote the culture of tax payment in the country.

Another set of fiscal policy instruments that was used throughout the fifty years was an excessive use of selective tax incentives, discretionary exemptions from customs duties and income tax credits, etc. These concessions deprive the State of income that is transferred to the firm or the entrepreneur who makes the investment. The source of the investment was at least partly money that belonged to the government in the form of tax payments, but the income produced by that entire investment belonged to the investing firm or the entrepreneur. The firm did not care if the investment yielded positive economic returns as long as it got good returns on that portion that was its own capital. If part of the investment capital was borrowed from a government-owned financial institution, the expected financial return was even lower. The history of sick industries in Pakistan is replete with several thousand episodes of industrial firms borrowing heavily from government-owned financial institutions, receiving generous tax holidays and exemptions from customs duties, etc., overinvoicing the value of imported machinery, making a fast buck in the process, and abandoning the plant. The economy ended up with inefficient allocation of scarce capital, but the individual firm or entrepreneurs made substantial financial gains at the expense of the State. This *modus operandi* has resulted in Rs 135 billion of non-performing assets in the hands of financial institutions and more than Rs. 60 billion of tax income forgone annually. The beneficiaries of these transfers are no more than one thousand individuals and firms. A small portion of this Rs 60 billion would suffice to provide basic social services to the poor.

The public expenditures, on the other hand, do not show any explicit bias towards the poor. Defence expenditure and debt servicing pre-empt a very significant proportion of the budget leaving very little for redistribution purposes. Subsidies on fertilizers and other agricultural inputs accrue mainly to the large operators or inefficient firms. The wheat subsidy benefits mostly the flour-mill owners. The implicit and explicit losses of state-owned corporations and enterprises such as the railways, steel mills, cotton and rice trading, heavy machinery, and WAPDA have put serious constraints on the manoeuvrability of the government in redirecting public expenditures. Even assuming that there was a benign and willing government that was prepared to invest in pro-poor programmes, it is not obvious that the administrative machinery, given the way in which it is organized, and which has traditionally been beholden to the powerful interests, would be capable of reaching the intended beneficiaries.

The fiscal policy, normally a powerful tool aimed at improving equity, has ended up being an instrument for private wealth accumulation at the expense of large segments of the population. As productive sectors and fiscal policy have failed to spawn equalizing tendencies, the burden for improvement falls on the human resource development strategies. But it has been widely documented that the indicators of human development in Pakistan are among the worst in the developing countries. The reasons for this outcome are not surprising.

HUMAN DEVELOPMENT

The educational system has been torn between the religious *madrassahs* and the modern school system. A large majority of children, particularly in the rural areas, attend the *madrassahs* where they are taught the Koran and Islamic precepts. A minority ends up in the modern school system, which is again subdivided into English medium and Urdu medium schools. As the official working language of the country is still English, this initial choice of schooling bears heavily on subsequent status and achievements in life. Those coming from well-to-do and affluent families invariably go to English medium schools which are run privately and charge exorbitant fees. Children from poor families either do not attend school or, if they do, their place is the poorly-run government schools where Urdu is the medium of instruction. The quality of education is poor in such schools because the appointment of teachers and school administrators is based on political connections, influence, or money. A recent study found that three-fourths of the teachers could not pass the tests administered to their students. The output from such schools is ill-equipped to meet the demands of modern life and is relegated to the ranks of the unemployed, or becomes petty clerks, messengers, or go into similar jobs. Those educated at the best private institutions in the country, such as the Karachi Grammar School or Lahore Aitchison College, go on to the Ivy League institutions in the US or Oxbridge in England and often come back to largely occupy the top professional jobs in the country or inherit political offices occupied by their families. So, unlike other progressive countries where education has promoted access and equality of opportunity across income classes, the education system in Pakistan has in fact strengthened and reinforced segmentation, perpetuated existing divisions among income and social classes, and allowed the benefits of education to be captured by the scions of the already rich.

Access to nutrition and health facilities is also highly differentiated and parallels the story of educational facilities. The government-run hospitals, clinics, and dispensaries are in terrible shape, devoid of basic drugs and equipment. The doctors manning these facilities use these public institutions to further their own personal practices—as patients are encouraged to visit them at their private clinics. The drugs supplied by the government for free distribution among patients are sold in the market to earn private profits, while poor patients have to fend for themselves. The private clinics and hospitals, on the other hand, are well run and maintained and boast of all state-of-the-art equipment, but their fees and charges make them an exclusive domain of the upper income classes.

ORIENTATION OF INSTITUTIONS

The interaction between the initial unequal asset distribution and public policy postures in agriculture, industry education and health further widened the gulf between the top one per cent and the rest of the population. The technological bias of the Green Revolution, the regressive taxation and public expenditure pattern, and the anti-poor nature of the human resource accumulation strategy in Pakistan have all worked in the same direction. The institutional infrastructure was deliberately weakened so that it is no longer capable of delivering services to the poor. The legal, judicial, and contract enforcement mechanisms are so painfully slow that it is almost impossible to obtain any meaningful or timely redress from the infractions committed by state functionaries or members of the elite class.

Underlying the success of the elitist model in Pakistan was the use of power over political resources to acquire power over economic resources. This power was gained either through direct appropriation of state assets or, indirectly, by misappropriating or avoiding paying what was owed to the State. The elite thus had a vested interest in opposing new market liberalizations that might threaten its privileges.

On paper, there have been many attempts to liberalize the economy—right from the days of Ayub Khan. But the system in practice has never worked as it is supposed to. The services of middle and lower levels in the bureaucracy, or agents of the ministers or other influential higher-ups, are always needed if delays, complexities, obfuscations, overlapping jurisdictions, and endless requests for more information are to be avoided. Even if some well-meaning top officials are committed to bringing about reforms and liberalizing the economy, the administrative machinery down the hierarchy is so cumbersome and anachronistic that policy intentions are seldom translated into action.

As if the fiscal, monetary, and trade policies were not stifling enough, politicians, bureaucrats, and military rulers enact a myriad of laws and regulations, rules, decrees, and statutory orders that affect almost every single aspect of running a business. The interpretation of these rules and laws is the exclusive domain of the enforcers, while the appeal and litigation processes are so slow, time consuming, and cumbersome that it makes sense to cut private deals with the enforcing agencies rather than challenge them.

ROLE OF COUNTERVAILING FORCES

In other societies, countervailing forces do emerge that resist and neutralize the parasitic tendencies of the elitist classes, but, in the case of Pakistan, the civil society organizations which could, in principle, have acted as countervailing forces were weak, non-existent, or co-opted. Non-governmental organizations have begun to emerge only in the last five years and are just beginning to make some modest difference. The peasant or farmers' unions are dominated by large farmers and swing into action only when their interests are at stake *vis-à-vis* the manufacturing sector or government agencies. The professional associations, except the Chambers of Commerce and Industry, are either not very active or narrowly focused.

During the Bhutto days, labour unions provided a legitimate voice to the working classes, but there has been a gradual erosion in their power and capabilities. The labour union leaders in the large public-sector organizations such as PIA, the steel mills, railways, and nationalized banks have enjoyed a great deal of perks and benefits and have enriched themselves. In effect, it is widely believed that they had become as much a part of the elite class as the managers of these public sector corporations.

The union leaders have connived with the managers and officials of these corporations in the decapitalization of the assets and incurring of financial losses. Stories of union leaders acquiring millions for themselves or their cronies in 'overtime' and other fictitious payments, or forcing new employment opportunities to be restricted to their own kith and kin, are rampant throughout the country. This is in addition to legal wages, salaries, perks, benefits, social security, health, housing, education for the children, and transport facilities enjoyed as a matter of course by this tiny but privileged faction of the labour force. More than 90 per cent of the country's labour force is self-employed or employed in agriculture small-scale or informal-sector activities and do not belong to any unions. The differential in the income and living standards of the privileged unionized labour and the majority of the labour force, for comparable work, is astoundingly high and is a contributing factor in widening income inequality as well as putting a brake on the expansion of formal-sector employment.

Sick industries are provided tax breaks, debt write-offs, and other life-support instruments to protect the employment of unionized labour. The sick industries have no economic justification and constitute a drain on the country's financial and fiscal system, but every succeeding government has written off or, restructured loans or provided other tax concessions to benefit a small class of inefficient owners and the unionized labour. The massive opposition to privatization of public-sector enterprises is neutralized by generous severance packages, and a portion of the shareholdings is earmarked for union members at below market prices. They then enjoy arbitrage between the initial price of acquiring the share and the market price after the shares are floated on the stock exchange.

In what possible ways could this elitist growth pattern be reversed and their grip broken? The solution clearly lies in the political, judicial, and social forces likely to shape the country.

There are some hopeful signs on the horizon. First, the political transition towards democracy, however faltering or hesitant in the past, has shown signs of consolidation. The

Thirteenth Amendment to the constitution has removed the ambiguity of power-sharing between the President, the Army, and the elected Prime Minister. It has restored the supremacy of Parliament and the elected leaders. Whether this absolute power will be used to maximize overall benefits to the common people of Pakistan or once again be deployed to perpetuate the tyranny of the elites is something which needs to be watched carefully.

Another positive achievement has been the restoration of freedom of expression and freedom of the Press since 1988. There are those who argue that the Press has misused its newly-acquired freedom and has not always acted responsibly, but it is only a matter of time before sanity, balance, and equilibrium, are achieved and 'yellow' journalism will be sifted out from serious, investigative reporting and sober and informed analysis. The Press has played a vital role in consistently highlighting the issue of corruption among those in power and has been a vigilant watchdog.

The third healthy development has been the maturing of the voters themselves. By showing their indifference towards the electoral process they have expressed their indignation over the state of politics in the country. By defeating the corrupt, self-centred or unresponsive representatives or the parties, the electorate has given a signal that it cannot be taken for a ride any more. Although the majority of the voters may be illiterate or uneducated, there is no doubt that they are highly discerning in so far as their choices are concerned. The 1997 elections represent a watershed in the political history of Pakistan, and a loud and clear message has been delivered by the voters. This needs to be interpreted accurately and followed diligently. The foundations of the elitist growth model can then begin to weaken.

The process of accountability, if put in place constitutionally and enforced in practice vigorously, can provide another avenue for the fracturing of the past growth model. If, on the other hand, this process is used selectively only to penalize those from the political parties in opposition or bureaucrats who did not toe the ruling party line, the results will be counterproductive and lead to further cynicism and lack of credibility. If accountability is applied even-handedly and all who are found guilty are punished, irrespective of their political affiliation, then there is a strong possibility that the excesses of the elite class can be contained.

The part likely to be played by an independent, impartial, and honest judicial system in redressing the violation of fundamental rights suffered by the common man in Pakistan, whether at the hands of zealous state functionaries or influential citizenry, and punishing everyone found guilty of illegal acts regardless of their station in life, is the other key ingredient to breaking the monopoly of power enjoyed by the elites. A fair and vigilant judiciary composed of dedicated and competent men and women of the highest integrity can become a countervailing force to the absolute powers enjoyed by the Executive with the assistance of a compliant legislature.

Under the current system, the Legislature, dominated by the majority party which forms the Executive branch of the government, is unlikely to provide any meaningful checks and balances. The inherent conflict of interest between party loyalty and the ability to punish recalcitrant party officials in the government will act as a brake. It is only the judicial arm of the State, which is relatively free from this kind of encumbrances, which can guard and protect against the misuse and abuse of power by those entrusted with the governance of the country or their followers, supporters, affiliates, or cronies in the countryside or the cities.

In addition to the judiciary, there are other potential agents of restraint provided under the Constitution which can make a powerful contribution in dismantling the existing pattern. The offices of the Auditor-General, Chief Election Commissioner, Chairman Federal Public Service Commission, and Chief Ehtesab Commissioner are all protected under the Constitution and can function independent of political pressure by the government. The fact that they have not done so does not detract from the practical possibility that each one of these institutions enjoys the powers to do so. When detecting misuse or misappropriation of government funds, the Auditor-General should be able to refer these cases directly to the Chief Ehtesab Commissioner. The Federal Public Service Commission should make all appointments on pure merit and, if the government does not follow its advice or bypasses the Commission, it should be made known to the public and the Press. The Chief Election Commissioner must insist that the eligibility criteria for candidates contesting elections are fully met and disqualify defaulters of bank loans, taxes, or other government and public utility dues.

The combined effects of the actions taken by these institutions, along with an independent and impartial judiciary which is able to deliver decisions on time, will act as a powerful deterrent to those entrusted with running the affairs of the State. The sum total of these institutional actions is likely to be much greater than the individual parts.

The final blow to the elitist domination of economic and political power will be dealt by vigilance on the part of civil society organizations—the NGOs, the academics, the think tanks and research institutes, the media, the professional bodies. The prerequisite for their effectiveness is that they are themselves cleansed and purged of undesirable elements who are not only part, or natural allies, of the elite classes but act and behave like them. Unless the internal governance and accountability structures of these organizations are satisfactory and made transparent, they will be unable to rock the boat. The emergence of some serious-minded, well-intentioned, and dedicated NGOs in various parts of the country augurs well for the strengthening of this force. But there are many more compelling episodes of NGOs being formed purely in response to the carrots dangled by both foreign and domestic interest groups. These opportunistic and self-serving organizations will become a natural extension of the elitist groups and give a bad name to the whole movement of voluntary organizations.

The professional groups in the country have mostly been busy protecting and preserving their narrow parochial interests. In most instances they have worked hand in glove with the government to derive maximum benefits, privileges, and concessions for their own members. This is quite understandable and happens all over the world, but the distinguishing feature of the Pakistani case is that this symbiotic relationship between the professional groups and the government has gone virtually unchallenged. Interestingly, this co-opting of the professional classes, who are also the chattering class in Pakistan, has not been a blessing for the successive governments. While these bodies extract maximum concessions and benefits for their members, the latter hardly pay any taxes or user charges or other government dues, nor do they disclose their full incomes. At the same time, they are in the forefront of spreading rumours, misinformation, and whispering campaigns to destabilize the government to create uncertainty, or to weaken the ability of the government to take punitive action against them. Alternatively, they win over the income tax, customs, and excise tax officials and other government functionaries by paying them a small fraction of their due obligations and stacking the balance amount in dollar denominated accounts.

Self-regulation, democratization, and, a code of conduct for these professional bodies are the only means through which the unscrupulous elements are weeded out and these bodies become, along with other civic society organizations, a strong pillar for vigilance against the tendencies of the elite groups to acquire political and economic power.

The next chapter extands the above elements and presents an agenda for a shared growth model for the economic and social development of Pakistan in the 21st century. It is always easy to define an agenda but more difficult to implement it. Perhaps the history of Pakistan written in 2047 will tell a completely different story.

TABLE 7.1
INCREMENTAL CAPITAL OUTPUT RATIOS

2ND PLAN	3.04
3RD PLAN	2.63
4TH PLAN	3.45
5TH PLAN	2.40
6TH PLAN	2.41

TABLE 7.2
ECONOMIC PERFORMANCE INDICATORS

	India	Pakistan
Per Capita Income, in US$	340.0	460.0
in PPP$	849.0	1,604.0
GDP Growth Rates, 1950-80	3.6	5.0
1980-94	5.0	5.9
Trade/GDP (PPP) Ratio	10.0	20.0
Per Capita Trade, in US$	44.0	121.0
Average Annual Rate of Inflation, 1980-93	8.7	7.4
Overall Budget Deficit/GDP, 1980-94	-6.5	-7.3
1995	-6.0	-6.9
Current Account/GDP, 1980-94	-1.7	-4.4
1995	-0.9	-3.9
Export Growth Rate, 1980-90	5.9	8.1
1990-4	13.6	11.3

Source: World Development Indicators (World Bank, Washington DC 1998)

TABLE 7.3
COMPARATIVE SOCIAL INDICATORS
(Most Recent Estimates)

	India	Pakistan
Life Expectancy (in years)	62	60
Adult Literacy (per cent)	52	38
Female Literacy (per cent)	38	24
Gross Enrolment Ratio (combined - per cent)	55	37
Access to Health Services (per cent)	85	85
Daily Calorie Supply Per Capita	2,395	2,316
Underweight Children Under Five (per cent)	53	40
Infant Mortality (per '000 births)	68	90
Total Fertility Rate	3.8	6.2

Source: World Development Indicators (World Bank, Washington DC 1998)

TABLE 7.4
COMPARATIVE SOCIAL INDICATORS OF
SOUTH ASIAN COUNTRIES

	Pakistan	Bangla-desh	India	Sri Lanka
Population growth rate	3.0	2.0	1.9	1.3
Life expectancy	62	58	62	72
Infant mortality	88	79	68	16
Child malnutrition	40	84	63	38
Adult literacy	38	38	52	90
Gross female enrolment	49	105	91	105
Female labour force	26	42	32	35
Share of population below $1/day	12	..	53	4
Daily calorie intake	2,618	2,019	2,395	2,275

TABLE 7.5
COMPARATIVE ECONOMIC INDICATORS OF
SOUTH ASIAN COUNTRIES

	Pakistan	Bangla-desh	India	Sri Lanka
GDP growth rate, 1985-95	1.2	2.1	3.1	2.7
GDP per capita US$, 1995	460	240	340	700
Consumption per capita PPP$	1,604	1,049	849	2,373
Trade ratio, 1995	36	37	27	83
Investment ratio, 1995	19	17	25	25
Net private capital flows, 1995 ($ million)	1,443	10	3,592	140
Net FDI/GDP, 1995	0.7	..	0.4	0.5
Mean tariff per cent all products, 1990-3	51	84	56	24
Central Government current revenues as percentage of GDP, 1995	19	..	13	21
Offical aid flows as per cent of GDP, 1994	2.5	6.9	0.8	4.6
Energy use per capita (kg)	254	64	248	97
Electricity production per capita (kwh)	450	83	416	242
Telephone lines per 1,000 people	16	2	13	11
Fiscal deficit/GDP	-6.9	..	-6.0	-8.7
Manufacturing as per cent of GDP, 1994	18	10	18	16

.. N.A.

TABLE 7.6
INDICES OF RELATIVE ECONOMIC
ACHIEVEMENTS (Pakistan = 100)

	Bangladesh	India	Sri Lanka
GDP per capita	52	74	152
Consumption per capita PPP	65	53	148
Net private capital flows per capita	..	35	69
Net aid flows per capita	123	23	253
Trade ratio	102	75	230
Investment ratio	89	131	131
Energy use per capita	25	98	38
Electricity production per capita	18	92	54
Telephone lines	12	81	68
Manufacturing as per cent of GDP	59	117	94

.. negligible

CHAPTER 8

AN ECONOMIC AND SOCIAL AGENDA FOR THE 21ST CENTURY

Pakistan's economic and social record for the last fifty years has been mixed. While its achievements in income, employment, and living standards are by no means modest, the opportunities missed in social progress, equitable income distribution, and regional integration are too numerous to count. The challenges that face the country as it reaches the threshold of the twenty-first century require a governance structure that provides rewards for hard work, initiative, and enterprise, and penalizes those who have behaved like parasites all along.

The problems facing Pakistan at present are no different from those facing other developing countries at a similar juncture in their historical evolution. There is broad agreement as to what the real issues and problems are.

First, there has been a complete breakdown of trust and confidence in the major institutions governing the country. Law and order has broken down and the inability to protect personal life and property has become a recurring nightmare, both among the poor rural areas of the country and the highly advanced metropolitan centres. The judicial system is not only slow, complex, time consuming, and cumbersome, but it has lost the aura of neutrality and impartiality on which it thrived during the early period of the country's history. The common perception that the police and judiciary can be manipulated by those who enjoy power or material wealth at the expense of the ordinary citizenry is getting stronger every day. Drug money, Klashnikovs and private armies have contributed significantly to this state of near anarchy.

Second, the future of the country is being gradually devastated through neglect of the physical infrastructure, and, more importantly, through the decapitalization of the country's human resources. The accumulation of human capital that takes place through the educational institutions and research bodies in any civilized country has been put into reverse gear in this country. The law of the jungle, i.e., 'unfair practices' at examinations, favouritism, nepotism by the teachers, and free use of arms and intimidation have replaced the normal and decent standards of instruction, curriculum development, hard work by students and teachers, inquisitiveness, and search for knowledge. The future generation is not equipped with the skills that are normally demanded by a country in transition to a modern path. Empirically, it has been established that this failure of investment in and nurturing of human resources is the most debilitating factor in the way of economic and social progress.

Third, access by the common citizen to the basic amenities of life—water, power, health services, transport, and communications—has been severely curtailed by a syndrome of short supply, discretionary subsidized prices that benefit the fortunate few, inadequate financing for investment, and further reduction in the supply of output. Many public services are in theory provided free or subsidized on the premise that the poor can have access to them. In practice, because of budget constraints, public services must often be rationed, and the poor people, who have no connection with the administrators of these services, are the ones who fail to get them.

In general, discretionary powers in the hands of regulators and controllers create sources of power and patronage, and an enormous scope for corruption, alienating the general public who derive little or no benefits. A political government that is sensitive to general public opinion and keen to be returned to power would soon discover that the exercise of these discretionary powers for the benefit of the chosen few is likely to be more harmful to their interests. It is true that these controls confer enormous benefits to some powerful memebers of the society, but the common voter in Pakistan is no longer oblivious to these inequities. The defeat of many of these power brokers at the recent elections was the manifestation of this revolt. The society of Pakistan in the next century is not going to be driven by the whims and caprices, orders, or sanctions of a handful of feudal landlords, industrial tycoons, ambitious bureaucrats, or unscrupulous politicians, as in the 1950s or 1960s. The broadening of the middle class and its disproportionately large influence on political events and outcomes in Pakistan, as evidenced by the last four general elections, calls for a different strategy of political survival than the exclusive dependence on traditional power brokers and their machinations. The dismantling of controls and the fostering of competitive forces in the provision of these services have a greater probability of success in the Pakistan of the twenty-first century.

Fourth, the last decade or so has witnessed a dehumanizing intensification of centrifugal and divisive forces in the country. Every conceivable cleavage or difference—Sindhi vs Punjabi, *Mohajirs* vs Pathans, Islam vs secularism, Shias vs Sunnis, Deobandis vs Barelvis, literates vs illiterates, Woman vs Man, Urban vs Rural—has been exploited to magnify dissensions, giving rise to heinous blood baths, accentuated hatred, and intolerance. A religion that prides itself on its message of peace and harmony and tolerance finds itself exploited by a few individuals or groups. A country that was created in the name of Unity, Faith, and Discipline is the epitome of a highly divided, despondent, and indisciplined nation. Ethnic and linguistic jingoism is fast permeating the fabric of the society and corroding the foundations upon which the country was built. The solid pillars of a harmonious multi-cultural society are in danger of developing cracks.

Fifth, the rights of freedom of expression, dissent, and difference of opinion have been curbed for such a long time that ill-founded rumours, speculations, and half-truths have become the handtools of conspirators and vested interests to perpetuate their game. Their favourite pastime of nurturing sectional and parochial suspicions, arousing unnecessary emotions of violence and vengeance, and evoking sympathy for 'oppression and denials of rights' sooner or later becomes a self-fulfilling prophecy. The example of a group of Bangladesh nationalists of the 1960s is still vivid in our memory. They sparked the emotions of the ordinary peace-loving inhabitants of East Pakistan through rumours and whisper-mongering that the export earnings of jute were being used to pave the streets of West Pakistan with gold, and that without access to these earnings West Pakistan would collapse economically. The fact that realities proved different from their rhetoric and that West Pakistan has done economically better during the past twenty-five years is rebutted by the same group arguing that it is drug money which is fuelling the economy of Pakistan.

Sixth, while other countries in Asia have performed economic miracles in recent years with an economic base and endowment much smaller, Pakistan is still struggling to find a few niches here and there. The 'impressive' growth rates so blatantly publicized by every succeeding government have led to an illusion in the national psyche. By consuming 95 per cent of national output and then borrowing from outsiders for a little investment, the nation is clearly living beyond its means, and this situation is not likely to be tenable in the long run. In addition, despite such foreign borrowing the investment level is low in relation to the requirements or in relation to other countries at the same income level, and the composition and pattern of investment are also well behind the times. The technological revolution that is sweeping the frontiers of production in microelectronics, defence, telecommunications, genetic engineering, etc., has hardly touched the fringes of Pakistan's production structure. The increasing dependence on a limited set of agriculturally-based commodities for the manufacturing and export sectors is a cause for serious concern. The managerial revolution that is introducing new techniques and tools of industrial and financial management in other parts of the world seems to be bypassing Pakistan. The intensity of knowledge and skills in the country's output of goods and services is rudimentary. The 'negative equity' and ' negative value-added' type of industrialization has brought about few social gains but enormous private benefits to a handful of families who have been the beneficiaries of the largess made available by successive governments.

The three imperatives that should influence the governance of this country are:

- Restore confidence in the country's institutions— government, legislature, judiciary, universities, etc.
- Initiate and sustain technological change and manage the transition to a modern economy and society.
- Foster stability and trust in social and cultural relationships between various segments of the population.

The implementation of the above goals is intertwined and should be looked at collectively rather than individually or sequentially. Ethnic and cultural cleavages arise primarily because the younger generation graduating from colleges and universities see no hope of employment or a stable career ahead. This is interpreted as a denial of opportunities, discrimination against their particular ethnic group, and usurpation of their rights by other groups. The collapse and paralysis of institutions also implies that only those with connections or riches can have access to public services or the basic amenities of life. The protection and near monopoly provided by the government to a few industrialists and the absence of a technological base in the country means inefficiency, high-cost production, and lack of opportunity for further expansion or job creation. An attack on each of these problems simultaneously is therefore a prerequisite for the achievement of these goals.

The credibility of government policy-making in achieving the goals it sets for itself needs to be restored so that it is taken seriously by everyone concerned. It must be recognized that the administrative division of functional responsibility is not necessarily co-terminus with the sphere of substantive policy changes required. The complex web of interrelationships between the various sectors and policies makes it essential that changes that take place in one particular sector under the control of one ministry are followed up by necessary changes in other affected sectors. Failing this, even the originally initiated changes will not be able to survive in the long run. The problem in Pakistan, unfortunately, has been that policy is designed for each sector separately at different points of time in complete isolation of others. Policies and plans abound in Pakistan. Enormous resources of time and effort have been spent at regular intervals in formulating the industrial policy, agricultural policy, education policy, health policy, science policy etc. These policies have sounded very convincing on paper, but scant regard has been given either to the trade-offs involved among various competing goals, or their resource implications or implementation constraints. In many cases, before the policy could ever be put to serious test, the government of the day has changed or the minister responsible for the original policy has been reshuffled, or some crisis has erupted that has led to a practical abandonment of the policy, so that the credibility of these policies has eroded more quickly than it takes to print the policy papers. There is too much fanfare in announcing the policies and too little monitoring or evaluation of their success or failure, or of their impact on the majority of the population.

In those instances where a policy did survive or made some faltering progress, its life span was short because the complementary policies were never in place. Take, for example, the education policy that aimed to redirect and reorient education towards vocational and technical training. For this objective to be successful, complementary industrial and labour policies are needed that assure the creation of jobs for those who complete such education. As industrial and labour policies remained unaltered, the abundant supply of unemployed technical and vocational graduates produced as a result of the new education policy soon put a damper on the new policy, which soon receded into oblivion and we were back to the *status quo ante*. As a result of this sort of thinking, the policy makers lose credibility and, when a new government or new minister proposes to initiate yet another education policy, there is widespread cynicism and scepticism. Although the bureaucrats and others involved go through the motions and rituals of writing a policy document, there is only a half-hearted or indifferent response as far as implementation is concerned. As results are hard to come by, the political leaders become wary and disenchanted with the civil servants, who they blame for the sabotage of their ideas and initiatives and non-cooperation. The civil servants, on their part, assume a more defensive, unmotivated, and uninspired posture, hoping that the minister or the government will wither away. There is very little thought given to an objective analysis of the factors that led to unsatisfactory results or the failure of a policy. The cycle of policy pronouncements with a big bang and policy failures with a senile shrug has been the history of policymaking in Pakistan.

To give some semblance of respectability to policy formulation, it is essential that sectoral changes are not made in sequence or isolation, but are followed through with the necessary action in other related or affected sectors or fields. It is prudent to initiate only a few strategic policy changes and follow them to their logical conclusion rather than announce a new policy every day of the year which no one takes seriously. Equally important is to ensure that the policy itself is internally consistent and to design its implementation in a realistic way. The tendency of political leaders and ministers to make tall promises and initiate radical changes overnight should be avoided at all costs. In the ultimate analysis, it is the results, i.e., the extent of changes brought about, that counts, not the promises made.

Pakistan inherited and subsequently established a number of solid institutions at various levels in diverse areas of economic policy. However, with the passage of time, the tendencies towards overcentralization, excessive control, increased government interference, and arbitrary instructions from the top made most of them ineffective and impotent, rendering them unable to perform the tasks for which they were set up. The basic configurations which underpin most of these institutions have become fragile. The top-down nature of the administrative fabric, the control mind set of the decisionmakers, and the centrally-commanded ways of doing things are major factors accentuating this fragility.

The agenda for institutional reform is both broad and deep-seated, as decades of neglect and disrepair have done almost irreparable damage. Implementation might be manageable. A real start can be made if a broad political consensus is reached on reforming three key institutions: judicial, educational, and financial. What should be the nature of this consensus? An agreement must be reached between the two major political parties that these three areas—the judiciary and educational and financial institutions—will be completely insulated from the intrusion of political interference and will remain out of bounds as far as the exercise of political patronage is concerned. This should not be interpreted to mean that setting sound objectives, policies, and performance standards and enforcing practices of supervision and accountability should be abandoned, either by the legislature or the ministries concerned, but the areas of discretion should be limited and clearly defined.

Why these three and not others? The beneficial effects of setting right these institutions on other aspects of the economy and policy are so large that each one needs to be examined in turn.

JUDICIAL SYSTEM

Reform of the judiciary requires that the appointment of judges be made on a non-partisan, non-political basis governed strictly by considerations of competence and integrity. Security of tenure and compensation packages must be made so attractive that other temptations become totally redundant. The budgetary costs of paying remunerative salaries to judges at all levels pale into insignificance when compared to the overall benefits that the country will derive from a speedy, fair, and impartial judicial system. For these benefits to be realized, there are many preconditions. Adequate attention must be given to the recruitment of judges on the basis of merit alone, to their proper training, and to their promotion on the basis of seniority.

- No political interference of any kind must be allowed in the appointment, transfer, or promotion of judges. The standards of entry to the Bar need to be strengthened to improve the quality of lawyers.
- Removal of judges should be the prerogative of judicial councils at various tiers, and only on specific grounds, such as incompetence, moral turpitude, corruption, etc.
- The laws governing evidence that are outdated and antiquated need to be revised and the scope for dilatory tactics, a common ingredient of the judicial system need to be eliminated.
- The workload of the courts should be made manageable and time limits enforced for disposal of cases.

If allowed to develop as such, an independent, well-paid, and efficient judiciary is a strong safeguard against state repression, excesses of the law-enforcing agencies, tyranny of the feudal landlords and other influential classes, and against the exercise of arbitrary powers by overzealous politicians and bureaucrats. The common citizen will gain confidence that he or she can obtain due justice from the system and that there will be no discrimination bias in favour of the rich and powerful. This, in turn, will be a source of empowerment for the majority of the population who, under the present system, feel completely detached and disconnected from the apparatus of the state. The behaviour of officials of the executive and that of the legislators will perforce improve for fear of reprisals and accountability for their actions before an independent judiciary.

The vindictiveness and vengeance of the government in power will be restrained by a fair judicial system. For example, the executive will have second thoughts about arresting a dedicated and honest customs collector for doing his job honestly and not yielding to pressure from above. The protection of individual human rights will constitute a new dimension. An understanding in the minds of the citizens that they will be able to obtain relief if wronged by fellow citizens or the state will change the 'psyche' of the nation dramatically. It will alleviate the feelings of insecurity, anxiety, uncertainty, and constant worry and change these to confidence, trust, calmness, and tranquillity.

Occasions will arise when extraordinary circumstances will require exceptional measures to preserve law and order, and the security of the state. Ordinary laws of the land may have to be modified on such occasions, but the expectation that an independent judiciary will interpret and administer those laws in a fair and judicious manner will mitigate the fears of human rights and civil rights activists. In such a scenario, the state will be able to tackle these extraordinary circumstances successfully, with little resistance, criticism, or backlash. The delays in enforcing contracts and obtaining redress of grievances, and the large costs incurred, have a negative impact on the speed and quality of economic transactions. Reduced transaction costs in enforcing contracts through the expeditious disposal of cases will not only improve the efficiency of the markets but also reinforce confidence among the private economic actors. This link between strong judicial institutions and an expansion of the private sector is becoming apparent in a large number of developing countries which are undertaking major reforms of their judicial systems.

The uniform application of the law for all citizens, irrespective of their status and position, triggered by the proposed reform of the judiciary, in place of the present selective application of the law (you show me the person and I will show you the law), will, over time, eliminate the wide gulf in the citizens' access to government services. This will help counter the tendencies that have led to the capture of government by the elites and the well-to-do segments of society, and will nurture a more balanced system in which poorer citizens can also participate and have access to basic government services.

Of course, clear accountability of the judiciary under a pre-specified set of conditions is a *sine qua non* for the success of these reforms; this will help to avoid the conversion of the present 'monopoly of powers by the executive' into a 'monopoly of power in the hands of the judiciary' in the future.

EDUCATIONAL SYSTEM

There is an urgent need to reform the educational institutions including those engaged in scientific research and technology development. The accumulation of human capital that takes place through the educational institutions and research bodies in any civilized society has been put into reverse in this country.

The politically-motivated recruitment of teachers right from the primary school stage, favouritism and partisanship in promotions and appointments at the senior level, strong-arm tactics, intimidation, the use of firearms by a minority of students backed by political parties, and large scale cheating at examinations supervised by some unscrupulous teachers have become normal features of academic life. Quality of instruction, curriculum improvement, hard work by students and teachers, inquisitiveness and the quest for knowledge have all but disappeared from the scene. We are failing to equip our future generation with the skills that are needed in a country if it has to develop along modern lines.

What should be done to salvage the educational institutions from the present morass? First, all the political parties should agree to adopt a hands-off approach and desist from interference in educational institutions, i.e., influencing the administration, teachers, or students. The appointment of teachers should be done in an open, transparent, and merit-based manner. The admission of students to higher education institutions should be based on factors that result in attracting the best and brightest of our younger generations, and the career advancement of teachers should take place according to the highest standards of professional achievement and integrity.

Second, the delivery of educational services should be open to all segments of the society—government, the private sector,

NGOs, community organizations, religious bodies, etc.—but the content and standards must be uniform throughout the country, and the division between the *madrassas* and the modern educational system must be eliminated. This will also eliminate the dichotomy between the children of the rich, affluent, and privileged, who get the best possible instruction at top private schools, and the majority of children who are served poorly by an over-extended and undersupervised public school system.

The opening of access to talented and qualified students from less well-endowed families will ensure a level playing-field where the antecedents of birth, privilege, and connections do not play havoc with the country's economy reinforce the tendencies of worsening income inequalities.

The student unrest in our universities is in fact a symptom of the fundamental malaise that the ordinary and unconnected students feel when they can see no light at the end of the tunnel. They realize that entry into the job market is not dependent on skills, knowledge of the subject matter, or hard work, but on 'who you know'. To compensate for the lack of that familial privilege which is the lubricant for the rich and the affluent, they resort to *goondaism* and hooliganism to attract the attention of the political parties and are thus able to strike the right connections. The more notorious a student leader is in disrupting peace and harmony on the campus, the better are his chances to earn an entry ticket to an important position in one of the main political parties.

Third, the heavy subsidies provided for higher education by the state in the form of ridiculously low tuition fees creates serious distortions and disincentives. Why do the parents of children in private institutions such as the Lahore University of Management Sciences and the Aga Khan University care so much about the standards and quality of education while those at public universities do not? The answer is simple. Those sending their children to the private universities have incurred substantial financial costs and would like to get adequate benefits for their children in return. They therefore insist that classes are held regularly, teachers prepare and present their materials diligently, and students work late into the night in the library and computer labs. The students are aware that if they do well they will succeed in securing good jobs and careers. The management and teachers know that if they do not have satisfactory customers, they will have no one to pay them and may have to close down the facilities. In the public universities, on the other hand, admission is not based on merit and the financial costs to the families of the students are almost zero, the job prospects of graduating students are quite grim, and the reward system for the teachers is not connected with their performance. Is it any wonder that, there is such a tremendous difference in the quality of graduates coming out of these two streams?

Does this mean that higher education should be priced so high that it would be available only to the rich and the affluent? On the contrary, admission to institutions of higher learning should be based purely on the ability of the individual applicant and have nothing to do with the applicant's financial status. In addition to the results of college examinations there should be entrance examinations that are objective in nature. Instead of fully subsidizing each and every university student, adequate financial aid, grants, scholarships, loans, etc., should be provided to those who cannot afford to pay the higher tuition fees.

Finally, the method and content of teaching, the course coverage, and the testing and evaluation procedures should be revised drastically and linked more directly to skill formation and labour market conditions. Theoretical understanding is essential, but neglect of practical and hands-on instruction is criminal. Engineers in Pakistan can talk for hours on the theory of soil mechanics, but they shun jobs requiring them to design engineering projects. Until the relationship between the education they receive and the jobs they obtain at the end of their education is fully visible and transparent the relevance of higher education will always remain questionable.

There is a very legitimate and real role for the government in the education sector. The government should be actively involved in the training of teachers, testing and evaluation, curriculum development, inspection of schools, financing of scholarships, stipends, and subsidies promoting education in backward areas of the country, and providing opportunities to those gifted but less fortunate children who cannot afford access to quality education. But the management and operation of the educational institutions should be entrusted to autonomous boards of professionals, the private sector, NGOs, and community representatives.

In addition to changing the face of these institutions, it will also help in the transition to a modern competitive economy that lifts its population out of poverty and low living standards. Then there is also the need to make intelligent use of science and technology. The disappointing performance of research and technological institutions in the country is related to the weakness of the educational system. The trouble begins with the school and university system, where research and scientific inquiry are shunned like pariahs as there are neither incentives to carry out research nor available adequate facilities. Diffusion and assimilation of technology in a society requires a wide scientific literacy, but this is conspicuous by its absence in Pakistan. The various specialized institutes of research, established since independence are mostly weak and unproductive. Of course, it would be easy to blame the civil service bureaucracy and the low expenditure-GDP ratio (a pet theme with the Ministries of Science and Technology) for creating this sordid state of affairs. But what have such institutions as, PCSIR, the National Science Council, the Pakistan Science Foundation, and other research councils achieved during the past thirty years or so of their existence? These have been manned and managed by scientists, they have collected hundreds of highly qualified personnel and, acquired the latest state-of-the art equipment under various foreign aid programmes. Yet there are numerous complaints of lack of proper facilities. But is this the real problem? In a capital-scarce society rigid compartmentalization between research institutes and universities in the use of equipment and facilities should not be the norm, but it is a matter of fact in Pakistan.

Under-utilized, unutilized and never utilized, scientific equipment which is soon thrown into junk yards is common. It is also true that the fragmented and piecemeal acquisition from abroad, with no sense of purpose and direction, has also contributed to this phenomenon. But the acquisition of technology from abroad without innovating and adapting it to local conditions is a self-liquidating phenomenon. It caters to the particular needs of the day but then disappears from the scene. The export-oriented, technologically advanced industrialization of Pakistan can only take place if artificial protection and government interventions are dismantled and a stronger, more competitive environment is fostered in which only efficient industrial firms can survive.

To participate in the third wave—the information and technological revolution—a much bolder and more imaginative approach will be needed. High schools, colleges, and universities must be provided equipment, computers, apparatus, reagents, scientific journals and periodicals in adequate quantity and numbers. To complement this, science and mathematics teachers have to be retrained and reoriented on a massive scale and given salaries and benefits that are higher than others in the teaching professions.

To make scientific research relevant to the economic needs of the society, the researchers, engineers, and technologists working in the public sector should be allowed to act as consultants in industry, agriculture, energy, defence, communications, etc. This will not only enable them to utilize and apply their knowledge, but also improve their overall compensation. In such a demand-driven system, only those who are capable of working hard and delivering creative and innovative solutions will survive. The salaries and promotions of the scientific cadre should not be dictated by age, seniority, or length of service but by the quality and quantity of their scientific output. A peer review process of evaluating the output and its quality should guide their advancement and promotion, instead of confidential reports written by administrators and heads of organizations.

FINANCIAL INSTITUTIONS

The third set of recommendations relates to the reform of financial institutions. Economic theory and empirical evidence from other successful countries indicate that the efficient mobilization and allocation of resources plays an important role in growth and development. Since the nationalization of commercial banks and the mushrooming of development financial institutions (DFIs), the performance of the financial sector has been not just unimpressive but definitely inimical to capital formation and equitable distribution of the benefits of growth.

Continued interference by political parties in the affairs of the financial institutions gives rise to enormous difficulties in economic management. Not only that, their political interests also suffer considerably as the general unpopularity caused by inflation, unemployment, capital flight, and investor uncertainty is a heavy price to pay for the appeasement of a small and narrow group of party supporters and influentials.

The financial sector reforms should be built on the twin pillars of competition and prudential supervision and regulation. Abandoning policies of mandatory credit targets, subsidizing interest rates and preferential sectors, and privatizating nationalized banks are steps in the right direction, but they do not imply that the government will have no role in the financial sector development.

Competent central bank supervision, enforcement of prudential regulations, and sanctions against undesirable businesss practices are very much an integral part of the new approach to developing banking and non-banking institutions. The capital market authorities also have a major responsibility in ensuring disclosure of full information by entities to the public, for borrowing through long-term bond issues, preventing insider trading, and expediting settlement and delivery of scrips.

But the government must resist the temptation to intervene in individual business decisions made by the financial institutions, and must also stop yielding to interest group pressures seeking special treatment and access to financial resources which they do not deserve on commercial considerations.

Private ownership of financial institutions is by no means an unmitigated blessing unless it operates in an environment of competition and market forces. The trend toward privatizing large state-owned banks is indeed welcome, but entry for newcomers should be based on meeting criteria and standards of financial soundness and professional competence. Once this hurdle is crossed, entry should be relatively easy thus avoiding concentration of market power and the emergence of oligopolistic practices. The beneficial effects of competition can be gauged from Pakistan's own experience of the 1980s in allowing foreign banks to enter the market. The return on equity for the average foreign bank fell from over 30 per cent in 1978 (when there were only a few foreign banks) to around 15 per cent during the 1980s (when their number rose significantly). On the other hand, the lack of competition and market protection allowed to the five Nationalized Commercialized Banks (NCBs) led to a decline in their profitability from 15 to 8 per cent return on equity.

Just as in the educational institutions, student groups backed by political parties have contributed to indiscipline and deviation from academic pursuits. Similarly the unions in the NCBs with political affilitiation and special protection have promoted and influenced unjustified hiring, renumerative bonuses, and other questionable practices that have unduly inflated the expense side of the NCB accounts. This combination of poor credit decisions and strong-arm tactics by the bank unions has led to the malaise in the banking sector.

What kind of reforms are needed to restructure the financial sector? First, the issue of non-performing assets should be resolved. Non-performing assets are normally rolled over. As credit is not withdrawn from defaulters it is not available to new and promising firms. Estimates of non-performing assets vary widely, but it is generally agreed that the figure is close to one-third of total assets. If interest rates on new commercial loans are on average 21 per cent, then an almost 7 per cent increase in volume of credit every year is simply channelled into financing overdue interest charges. Some of these charges are twenty years old and carried on the books as pertaining to sick industries. Such a large infusion of finance to 'unprodutive' and 'unremunerative' businesses is in fact a waste of scarce resources and hampers the expansion of legitimate and economically feasible activities.

Second, the integrity of the original credit decision needs to be preserved by only recruiting qualified and competent staff and allowing them to make decisions on the basis of credit appraisal rather than extraneous considerations. At present, resources are allowed to flow in line with political and non-economic priorities. The privatization of NCBs would at least bring to an end the present state of affairs where the bank managers cannot be held accountable for unwise credit decisions and blame the political leadership for all the bad credit outcomes. But private ownership and management are no guarantee of efficiency if the political heavyweights continue to cajole, coerce, or pressure the new owners to succumb to their wishes.

Third, most of the project financing by the DFIs in Pakistan has been carried out on a non-recourse-basis, i.e., the project is set up as a legal entity and the sponsor's liability is limited to the extent of the project alone. The assumption of such a large part of business risks by the DFIs does not carry correspondingly high rewards as the project loans are not adequately priced. The high rewards are in fact captured by the recipients of these loans, who bear much lower risk. No wonder then that there is so much political pressure involved in the approval of loans by the DFIs. The proliferation of DFIs in the country should have led to intense competition, better risk management, and appropriate pricing of products, but a lack of professional standards and the poor quality of human resources have led to situations of bankruptcy. The sooner the government gets out of the DFI business, the better off the taxpayers in the country will be.

* * *

The reforms in these three categories of institutions are strategic, and, if carried out, will ensure that capital is mobilized and allocated efficiently; human resources are developed and utilized to meet the changing demands of the economy; property rights are enforced; and the rule of law is respected, providing a conducive environment for transactions to take place among millions of economic agents in the country.

These reforms will, in turn, create pressure points in some institutions, or alter the norms and behaviour of participants in other institutions. This agenda is practicable and manageable as it focuses on only three areas of endeavour and thus economizes on the administrative capacity of implementation, but it is also daunting and highly demanding in the sense that it requires a consensus among the major political parties to give up some tools which they are accustomed to without gaining anything tangible for their own narrow interests.

The more enlightened among our political leaders should, however, recognize that broad-based and widely-shared gains do not only promote sustainable and equitable economic and social well-being, but also lay the foundation for a stronger, healthier political system. The choice between pleasing the party influentials and implementing the agenda of institutional reform is by no means easy if the sights are fixed on a five-year election cycle only.

What is needed is the political will and courage to make the right choice—that is, to move away from the corrupt system of industrial production to one that can compete internationally. The pattern of industrial development in this country reflects the low technological bias and heavy domination of low value-added consumer goods: textiles, vegetable ghee, beverages, leather goods, and food products. Technological upgradation will not work by itself unless other impediments are removed. The present financing structure of industrial enterprises in Pakistan, totally dependent on the debt financing provided by government financial institutions with little or negative risk capital from the owners, is an important contributing factor. The financing is so structured that the owners or promoters have no real stake in the long-run viability of the firm, which soon turns into a 'sick industry' with the institutions holding tons of bad debt and the owners, having made quick profits, conveniently exiting the scene. The same owners reappear after a while with a new proposal that is financed by a different set of financial institutions. The legal process is slow and cumbersome, and, as there are no other penalties for those who default on payments, the vicious circle keeps turning. The favours bestowed by the government through price controls, import restrictions, tariff duties, or other forms of licensing are other important determinants. As a result, the country does not develop the comparative advantage it needs to survive in the international market place. Vulnerability to external shocks increases, and any slowdown in economic activity, changes in the tax regime, or macro policies, or other exogenous factors accentuate the risks to the wider economy.

Pakistan cannot achieve a viable human resource, despite a well functioning educational system and an advanced scientific capability, if it continues to neglect 50 per cent of its population—women. The social and cultural obstacles to the advancement of women in Pakistan are aptly reflected in the literacy rates and the labour-force participation rates. While the overall literacy rate is 38 per cent, the female literacy rate in the rural areas is 7 per cent. Roughly 50 per cent of urban boys aged 10 to 14 were in school in 1985, compared with 3 per cent of rural girls in the same age group. Fewer than 1 per cent remained in school by the age of 14. The smaller number of rural girls in secondary education further constricts plans to improve rural primary education for girls because it provides so small a stock of potential female schoolteachers in rural areas. The latest estimates for labour-force participation rates are 30 per cent for the total population, 53 per cent for males and 8 per cent for females. This 8 per cent rate is also heavily influenced by the unpaid female labour-force in rural agriculture. In the periods corresponding to slack agricultural activity, less than 1 per cent of the female population of working age participated in the labour force of Sindh and less than 3 per cent in Punjab.

The wage differentials by gender are high, access to the labour market is restricted for females, and social attitudes toward female education and work are discouraging.

The rights of women have been embroiled in a maze of legal and religious injunctions the interpretation of which may be unclear but whose impact on the initiative and enterprise of women in Pakistan is unsettling. The march of Pakistan towards a modern state of the twenty-first century will be slowed if the progress of one-half of its population is thwarted by a denial of education, skills, and contribution to productive sectors of the economy. Empirical evidence showing a close correlation between lower population growth rate and reduced infant mortality on one hand, and improved levels of education and labour-force participation rates on the other, should act as an eye-opener in a country with finite natural resources but a burgeoning population (adding 3 to 3.5 million persons every year). An educated mother is the cornerstone of a healthy and prosperous family and nation, and the longer we keep women away from schools and the work force, the harder will be our struggle for economic emancipation.

Finally, the ethnic and cultural richness of the Pakistani population should be used to strengthen the country rather than divide it. The major cause for suspicion and mistrust arises when decision-making is centralized and the decision makers represent only a small elite group to the exclusion of the majority. The growing concentration of power in the allocation and distribution of resources arouses feelings of injustice and exploitation among those who are outside the narrow corridors of power. In addition, this tendency has made most of the institutions at the local levels ineffective. The gradual erosion of responsibility, the upward assumption of power, and the centralized controls have muffled local initiative and made it difficult to arrive at quick solutions. The sufferer in this process is, of course, the public at large, who cannot receive prompt service or quick redress of their problems.

There is no reason why local institutions cannot be assigned the responsibility and resources for managing their affairs.

Schools, clinics, roads, water supply, sewerage, electricity, marketing of agricultural produce, distribution of inputs, etc., could be managed more efficiently by local private and public institutions. As the span of control is not too large, the supervision of action and redressal of problems can be more timely and have more intense community involvement. The argument is often advanced that these institutions are not properly equipped to carry out these tasks. They are not and never would be prepared to take over these responsibilities if they perpetually remained dependent on the discretion and goodwill of the higher level of government for their resources and survival. The whole process of fiscal resource generation and allocation has stimulated a disincentive for mobilizing additional resources in aggregate. The total development budget of the provincial governments comes from the Federal Government. The higher the deficit shown by a province, the higher the allocation is likely to be. The situation of the local councils *vis à vis* the provincial government is similar. Every tier of government is thus forced to indulge in greater fiscal irresponsibility, with no incentive either to utilize the resources more efficiently, or to bring about cost saving, or to generate additional resources locally.

The experience of other developing countries suggests that local communities are willing to contribute to and pay taxes and charges for services and projects whose benefits they can see as being available to them rather than some distant places about which they know nothing. This explains the reluctance to pay appropriate prices for public goods and services. The quality and availability of services to the public can improve significantly, the implementation of development projects can be expedited, waste and inefficiency can be minimized, and the higher levels of government can be freed to undertake more substantive policymaking and problem-solving tasks if the local institutions are gradually strengthened and given more powers, resources, and autonomy. The local communities, if they have the power of electing these institutions at regular intervals, will ensure that they perform effectively and efficiently. Organizations and institutions at the local level evolving organically and learning through trial and error are not only the best guarantee for sustained economic development, but also an excellent avenue for reducing ethnic and linguistic tensions and mistrust.

Finally, the role of government intervention in the economies of developing countries is perhaps the most misunderstood and misinterpreted issue. Nobody in his right mind would ask for a completely hands-off approach by government. At the same time, nobody would like to see a completely centralized and fully state-controlled economy. The truth of the matter is that government has an extremely important role to play. It must ensure a stable macroeconomic environment by adopting sustainable monetary, fiscal, and exchange rate policies, a system of incentives that encourages resources to be allocated efficiently and used optimally, and a pattern of growth whereby benefits are widely shared. But reorientation will be necessary; for the bureaucracy, from administering regulations toward managing development, for the planning ministries, from drafting comprehensive blueprints of five-year plans toward more selective interventions backed by better policy analysis, and for accountants and auditors, from a preoccupation with innocuous financial rules to obtaining value for money. Improving the quality of public-sector institutions responsible for the execution of policies and for the provision of public services is the most important task facing the country. The growth in government bureaucracies to create employment opportunities for party supporters and other unemployed youth may appear an easy way out in the short run, but would haunt any sensible government that wishes to restrain fiscal deficits, avoid inflationary pressures, and pursue prudent economic policies. Such a move is, in the ultimate analysis, likely to be counterproductive. Instead, countries in similar situations to Pakistan have discovered that opening up the economy through liberalization of trade regulations and other controls and providing incentives to attract foreign and domestic investors is the only viable option for generating stable employment which contributes to accelerated economic growth and welfare. Creating 'improvised employment' through the public sector is a short-term palliative whose costs are enormous in terms of fiscal imbalances and inflation. India has started a vigorous and successful programme of setting up joint ventures with major computer multinationals for software export. The employment created in this way ensures skill formation, technology transfer, and foreign exchange earnings for the country.

The excessive dependence of the people of Pakistan on the government is a legacy of the colonial heritage that has not been reversed despite over fifty years of independence. And where has this led to? Private and local initiative has been shifted, and unrealistic expectations have been raised of the political leaders which cannot be realized. The example of the Sattar Edhi Trust illustrates the enormous potential of private initiative in social and other services that exists in this country but which has not been properly tapped.

The encouragement and promotion of non-governmental organizations active in social service not only relieves the government of the financial burden of maintaining and operating them, but also makes these services accessible to all and sundry without discrimination. That the philanthropic spirit among the good-hearted Pakistanis has not yet been fully tapped is evident from the enormous offers of help and contributions received by the Edhi Trust.

The future course for Pakistan to achieve a structural transformation of the economy therefore lies in a strengthening of the partnership between public, private, and community sectors. There are some functions, such as defence, law and order, the judiciary, and macroeconomic management, that can only be performed by the government and the public sector, while others, such as production, distribution, and trade of goods and services, can best be performed by the private sector. There are still others, such as education, health, water supply, and basic infrastructure at the local level, that can be managed by the communities. This division of labour has worked well in other developing countries and there is no reason why it should not do so in the multi-ethnic, multicultural environment of Pakistan. It would strengthen the institutions, generate social capital, and create feelings of trust that would help to overcome the ethnic, sectarian, and linguistic tensions.

EPILOGUE

Pakistan's Economy in the Post-Nuclear Era

28 May 1998 heralded a new era for Pakistan—strategically, politically and economically. The testing of nuclear bombs in response to the earlier tests conducted by India established unequivocally that Pakistan possessed nuclear capability. These tests have advanced our national security interests, reestablished the strategic balance in the subcontinent, stirred the developed countries of the world out of their slumber and indifference and attracted renewed attention to the problem of Kashmir—the fundamental source of tension between India and Pakistan. On the domestic front, these tests were welcomed by all strata of society, and people from all regions of the country. This decision to go ahead with the tests, despite strong pleadings form the Western powers and particularly the US to do otherwise has, however, resulted in imposition of economic sanctions by the G-7 countries.

A weak and fragile economy heavily dependent on a whole variety of external capital flows (See Table 1) was severely hit by the disruption of these flows. The freezing of foreign currency deposits of about $11 billion was inevitable under the circumstances (as the reserves in the system were only $1.2 billion when the freeze was announced) but the impact on investor and depositor confidence was disastrous. The growing divergence in the movement of official and market exchange rates discouraged the inflows of workers' remittances and virtually suspended other private capital flows. As the expected disbursements from the IMF, the World Bank, the ADB and Japan for balance of payments supports were withheld in the light of the economic sanctions the possibilities of default on external payments became imminent.

SOURCES OF EXTERNAL CAPITAL FLOWS
TO PAKISTAN

Official	Private
Multilateral Institution	• Foreign Direct Investment
IMF purchases	• Portfolio capacity investment
IDA concessional loans	• GDR Flotations
IBRD/ADB	• Asset-backed securities
• non-concessional loans	• Private Placements
• Balance of payment support	• Commercial bank medium-term
• Project aid	loans
IsDB borrowings	• Short-term swap loans
Grants from the UN system - EU	• Foreign currency deposits
	• International bond issues
Bilateral Donors	(Eurobonds)
Grants	• Short-term commercial loans
• Technical Assistance	• Trade financing
• Project	• Workers' remittance
Concessional Loans	• Deposits of foreign banks in the
Export Credits	Central Bank
Commodity and Food Aid	

The magnitude of the problem can be illustrated with the help of external financing requirements for the fiscal year ending June 1998 (based on the projections for 1997-98). The combined effects of current account deficit (excluding private and official transfers), amortization, and repurchases of existing obligations, and build up of international reserves required external financing flows of $11.5 billion. It was expected that private transfers ($2.8 billion), project and food aid (1.4 billion), commodity aid ($1.7 billion), balance-of-payments support loans (1.5 billion), foreign direct investment, portfolio investment and other private flows ($1.8 billion) and short-term credit including foreign currency deposits and swap loans, etc. ($2 billion) would have financed these requirements. The sanctions and the freezing of accounts, will together, create shortfall of $4.5 billion according to the official estimates. Debt servicing alone requires more than $5.2 billion. It is therefore obvious that unless this shortfall is met through revival of the lending from the IMF, multilateral institutions, Japan and resumption of workers' remittances and other private capital, Pakistan would not have adequate resources to fully service its external debt and other obligations.

While the short term management of the economy has become highly difficult some policy lapses could have been avoided. The unfortunate controversy over the Independent Power Producers (IPPs), who would have together brought in approximately $5 billion of new foreign direct investment into the country and met the shortages in electricity generation, has damaged the image of Pakistan in foreign financial markets. At a time when Pakistan badly needs every single dollar the opening of this new front with foreign investors has scared away other potential investors. In contrast to this, India took a decision in the aftermath of the economic sanctions to approve most of the applications from foreign investors which had been pending for a very long time. This has had two favorable effects. First, the country signalled that it is open for business to the foreign private investors and would facilitate and encourage them to bring in new resources for infrastructure development and manufacturing. Second, the Indians indirectly created a powerful lobby of multinational corporations—which argued strongly within the US for the easing of economic sanctions against India. Even in the case of Pakistan, the exemption granted by the US Congress for exporting wheat was largely motivated by the US farm interest lobby. The prolonged and unending saga of the IPPs as a blanket proposition rather than picking out those companies which have indulged in corruption or malpractice should have been avoided. It can only be speculated at this stage that a more positive attitude towards IPP investment would have encouraged second generation investment in the form of transmission, disbursement, equipment manufacturing and ancillary service industries.

Another area where opportunities have been lost is the privatization of state-owned enterprises and financial institutions. There was a widespread expectation that the Nawaz Sharif Government, so deeply committed to private enterprise and initiative, would accelerate this process. This would have helped generate some exceptional financing—both in foreign currency as well as domestic currency—to ease the debt situation and also avoided subsidies or passing on high utility costs to the consumers. But the record eighteen months later is that of indecision and lack of any perceptible action. Financial institutions such as Habib Bank, United Bank and other DFIs under new private management would have introduced some element of dynamism in the economy and contributed towards relaxation of the credit crunch that is currently being felt by the business sector. The change in the top management of these banks is indeed welcome but without coming to grips with the problems of portfolio contamination, branch network and personnel practices and the uncertainty ensuing from the announced intentions to privatize these banks any significant progress will remain elusive.

Non-interference from the political leadership, the recovery of outstanding loans amounting to Rs 130 billion owed to the exchequer by a few thousand borrowers and improvement in the performance of the financial sector under the new management would have helped the competitiveness of the production enterprises particularly those exporting their goods. Consistent and indefatigable efforts to recover these loans (at a discount) would have had several beneficial effects. First, the defaulters would have been forced to liquidate their foreign currency deposits kept at home (thus reducing the country's foreign liabilities to that extent) or would have brought their money kept overseas (thus adding to the foreign exchange reserves of the country). This injection of liquidity would have allowed the banking system to make credit available to private businesses at affordable interest rates.

Non-performing assets have so far only increased intermediation costs and consequently resulted in larger spreads between deposit and lending rates. The recovery of these assets would therefore reduce these spreads and lower the interest rate structure. Not only would private businesses save on their financial costs of servicing the existing debt they would be able to invest in new enterprises as the lowering of the cost of capital would make many of these enterprises attractive. The lowering of interest rate structure would also help the government and the public sector enterprises. For example, if a three percentage point reduction in interest rates is achieved through recovery of non-performing assets and lower administrative costs it would reduce the domestic debt servicing obligations of the Government by about Rs 24 billion annually. This saving can either be utilized to reduce the budget deficit to 4 per cent of GDP or partly utilized to increase the allocations for development expenditure. The multiple effect of increased development spending would raise the level of economic activity.

The above line of analysis is applicable to tax recovery and recovery of public utility charges. The implementation of the principle of equal burden of taxation from all sources of income, the broadening of the tax base by applying the General Sales Tax on all traders, manufacturers and importers (above a given threshold level of income) and detecting and penalizing tax evaders would go a long way towards placing the country's public finances in good shape. It is not at the level of the Federal Government alone that there is enormous potential for tax collection but this exists at the provincial and municipal levels as well. The rate of growth in capital appreciation in urban immovable property has been phenomenal. None of the provincial governments or the large municipal corporations have derived any benefits from these capital gains. Should the tax base for assessing property tax on land and real estate be adjusted to the prevailing market values the additional revenues accruing to all the four Provincial Governments and the cities of Karachi, Lahore, Islamabad, Peshawar, Faisalabad, etc. would not be, according to my estimates, less than one per cent of GDP. The current tax collection from the provincial and local levels of government is insignificant. As education, health, water supply and sanitation are the services provided mainly by these two levels of Government the benefits from increased tax revenues, if allocated for these basic services, would accrue to the poorer segments of the population. The recovery of charges from the consumers of electricity, gas and water and plugging off leakages in theft and better manpower utilization would also help lower the tariff charges for consumers.

The combined impact of reduced interest rate, lower utility charges and complementary development expenditure in infrastructure and social services would improve the competitiveness of the export sector.

Higher export earnings, in turn, should be able to lower the external financing requirements for the same level of economic activity. But there are a large number of non-price barriers that also act as a disincentive for new exports. The Export Promotion Bureau should live up to its name and mandate by helping new exporters overcome these barriers.

Even after implementing all the above measures our economic problems may get worse. This will be due to the exogenous forces of globalization, financial market integration, currency convertibility and liberalization of capital flows. The lessons from the recent financial crisis in East Asia, Russia and emerging markets in general are sobering. The judgements and actions of credit rating agencies, analysts, fund managers, investment bankers and speculators can create such a constellation of negative forces that the national authorities can feel helpless and are unable to exercise any meaningful control. Contagion effects of shocks originating elsewhere can hurt the Pakistani economy severely. This risk of financial turmoil can be magnified if the domestic economic management is weak and policy implementation lacks credibility. The way out of this dilemma is not to shut out foreign capital but to strengthen the domestic financial and corporate sectors, enhancing the powers and capacity of the regulatory agencies and to ensure that economic fundamentals such as exchange rate, fiscal deficit, inflation, external debt service and interest rates remain strong and on track. Short term capital inflows including foreign currency deposits of residents and non-residents have disrupted the functioning of emerging markets through abrupt massive withdrawals. The recent financial crisis in the emerging markets has underlined the limitations of our understanding of the appropriate pace and sequencing between policies aimed at microeconomic stablization, removal of microeconomic distortions, liberalization of capital flows and institutional restructuring. There is hardly any consensus as to how to deal with these flows but countries such as China which have attracted long-term foreign investment flows for the expansion of their manufacturing and export capacity have weathered these storms better but there is no guarantee that this conclusion will continue to remain valid in the future. The policy instruments for managing capital inflows are blunt and the experience with them is only rudimentary.

The only valid lesson from Pakistan's own experience is that it is unwise to rely on sustained large flows of external savings to finance consumption in excess of domestic savings on a consistent basis. Domestic savings—both public and private— have remained consistently low over time and in relation to other countries with similar income levels. The addiction we have developed in the past with foreign sources of capital—aid, borrowing, remittances, foreign currency deposits may have mitigated the immediate pain but has also numbed our nervous system. It would be foolish to argue that a country with a per capita income of $450 should insulate or abandon external capital inflows. The main proposition is that domestic savings should be maximized and the sources, types, terms and volume of foreign inflows should be closely aligned with productive investment requirements to derive high returns in the form of growth and poverty reduction.

Pakistan at a glance

POVERTY and SOCIAL	Pakistan	South Asia	Low-income
Population mid-1996 *(millions)*	133.5	1,266	3,236
GNP per capita 1996 *(US$)*	480	380	490
GNP 1996 *(US$ billions)*	63.6	478	1,597
Average annual growth, 1990-96			
Population (%)	2.9	1.9	1.8
Labour force (%)	3.3	2.2	1.7
Most recent estimate *(latest year available since 1930)*			
Poverty: national headcount index (% of population)	34	..	..
Urban population (% of total population)	35	27	29
Life expectancy at birth (years)	63	62	63
Infant mortality (per 1,000 live births)	88	73	68
Child malnutrition (% of children under 5)	40	63	43
Access to safe water (% of population)	60	78	76
Illiteracy (% of population age 15+)	62	51	34
Gross primary enrollment (% of school-age population)	74	99	107
Male	101	109	112
Female	45	89	102

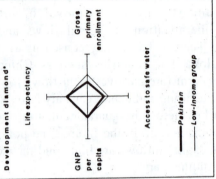

Development diamond*

Life expectancy

GNP per capita — Access to safe water

Gross primary enrollment

—— Pakistan
—— Low-income group

KEY ECONOMIC RATIOS and LONG-TERM TRENDS

	1975	1985	1995	1996
GDP (US$ billions)	11.3	31.1	60.6	64.8
Gross domestic investment/GDP	16.2	18.3	18.7	18.6
Exports of goods and services/GDP	10.9	11.2	16.4	16.5
Gross domestic savings/GDP	4.9	6.7	15.7	14.2
Gross national savings/GDP	7.0	25.2	21.1	18.2
Current account balance/GDP	-9.4	-4.1	-3.5	-6.5
Interest payments/GDP	0.9	1.0	1.6	1.4
Total debt/GDP	50.7	43.2	49.9	46.1
Total debt service/exports	20.6	24.9	26.6	27.4
Present value of debt/GNP	:	:	:	39.9
Present value of debt/exports	:	:	:	206.0

	1975-85	1986-96	1995	1996
(average annual growth)				
GDP	6.7	5.1	5.1	4.6
GNP per capita	4.5	1.2	2.7	0.3
Exports of goods and services	8.4	8.3	-3.1	2.0

Economic ratios*

Trade

Investment

Savings

Indebtedness

—— Pakistan

—— Low-income group

STRUCTURE of the ECONOMY

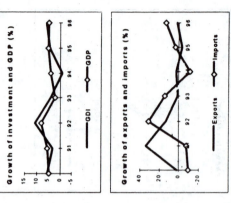

Growth of investment and GDP (%)

GDI ⟶ GDP

Growth of exports and imports (%)

Exports ⟶ Imports

(% of GDP)	1975	1985	1995	1996
Agriculture	32.0	28.5	26.0	25.8
Industry	23.4	22.5	24.4	24.5
Manufacturing	16.7	15.9	17.2	16.9
Services	44.5	49.0	49.6	49.7
Private consumption	84.4	81.2	72.5	73.4
General government consumption	10.6	12.1	11.7	12.3
Imports of goods and services	22.2	22.8	19.4	20.9

(average annual growth)	1975-85	1986-96	1995	1996
Agriculture	4.5	4.1	6.6	5.3
Industry	7.1	6.3	4.6	3.6
Manufacturing	8.0	6.0	3.7	4.4
Services	7.1	5.1	5.0	4.7
Private consumption	5.7	4.7	7.0	6.6
General government consumption	7.3	3.0	5.4	6.8
Gross domestic investment	7.3	4.3	4.2	5.6
Imports of goods and services	4.9	3.6	3.9	13.6
Gross national product	7.8	4.3	5.6	3.1

World Development Indicators 1998 CD-ROM, World Bank

Note: The diamonds show four key indicators in the country (in bold) compared with its income-group average. If data are missing, the diamond will be incomplete.

BIBLIOGRAPHY

Adams, Richard H. and Harold Alderman (1992), 'Sources of Income Inequality in Pakistan: A Decomposition Analysis,' *Oxford Bulletin of Economics and Statistics.*

Ahmad, Viqar and Rashid Amjad (1984), *The Management of Pakistan's Economy* 1947-82, UGC Monograph Series in Economics, Oxford University Press, Karachi.

Ahmed, Ehtisham (1989), 'The Distributional Consequences of a Tax Reform on a VAT for Pakistan', World Bank Research Working Paper.

——, (1992), 'Taxation Structure and Policies in Pakistan,' paper presented at the LUMS Conference on Financing Pakistan's Development in the 1990s, LUMS, Lahore.

Ahmed, Ehtisham and Nicholas Stern (1985), 'Employment and Wages in Pakistan,' World Bank Discussion Paper, Washington DC.

Ahmed, E and S. Ludlow (1989), 'Poverty, Inequality and Growth in Pakistan', Background paper for 1990 World Development Report, World Bank, Washington DC.

Ahmed, Sadiq (1994), 'Explaining Pakistan's High Growth Performance over the Past Two Decades: Can It Be Sustained?' Policy and Research Working Paper No. 1341, World Bank, Washington DC.

Ahmed, Viqar and Rashid Amjad (1984), *The Management of Pakistan's Economy: 1947-82*, Oxford University Press, Oxford.

Alderman, Harold, Jere Behrman, David Ross, and Richard Sabot (1996), 'The Returns to Endogenous Human Capital in Pakistan's Rural Wage Market', *Oxford Bulletin of Economics and Statistics.*

Alderman, Harold (1993), ' Poverty, Household Food Security, and Nutrition in Rural Pakistan', International Food Policy Research Institute.

Alesina, A. (1994), 'Political Models for Macroeconomic Policy and Fiscal Reforms' in S. Haggard and S. Webb, *Voting for Reform*, Oxford University Press, New York.

Amjad, Rashid (1992), 'Employment Implications of Development Policies for the 1990s', Paper presented at the LUMS Conference on Financing Pakistan's Development in the 1990s, LUMS, Lahore.

Aslam, N. (1987), 'The Impact of Foreign Capital Inflow on Saving and Investment', *Pakistan Development Review*, No. 26, Islamabad.

Augenblick, Mark and Scott Custer (1990), 'The Build, Operate, and Transfer Approach to Infrastructure Projects in Developing Countries', World Bank Policy Series.

Azhar, B.A. and S. Sharif (1974), 'The Effects of Tax Holiday on Investment Decisions: An Empirical Analysis', *Pakistan Development Review*.

Azhar, B.A. (1991), 'Taxation of Agricultural Income', *Pakistan Development Review*.

Azhar, T. (1991), *The Quest for Power: Pakistan's Policy Options for the Nineties*, Ferozsons, Lahore.

Balassa, Bela (1971), *The Structure of Protection in Developing Countries*, Johns Hopkins Press, Baltimore.

_____; (1986), *Export Incentives and Export Growth in Developing Countries*, World Bank, Washington DC.

Banerjee, Abhijit and Andrew Newman (1994), 'Poverty, Incentives, and Development', *American Economic Review*.

Bardhan, Pranab (1995), 'Research on Poverty and Development: Twenty Years After Redistribution with Growth', World Bank Annual Conference.

Barro, Robert J. and Jong-Wha Lee (1994), 'Losers and Winners in Economic Growth', *Proceedings of the World Bank Annual Conference on Development Economics*, Washington DC.

Behrman, Jere (1994), 'International Perspective on Schooling Investment in the Last Quarter Century in Some Fast-Growing East and Southeast Asian Countries', *Asian Development Review*.

———, (1995), 'Pakistan: Human Resource Development and Economic Growth into the Next Century', Background Paper for Pakistan 2010, World Bank, Washington DC.

Bencivenga, Valerie and Bruce Smith (1991), 'Financial Intermediation and Endogenous Growth', *Review of Economic Studies 1991*.

Bergsten, Fred and Marcus Noland (1994), 'Pacific Dynamism and the International Economic System', Institute for International Economics, Washington DC.

Bhagwati, Jagdish (1993), *Protectionism*, MIT Press, Cambridge, Massachusetts.

Bhagwati, Jagdish and T.N. Srinivasan (1993), 'India's Economic Reforms', Ministry of Finance, Government of India, New Delhi.

Bilquees, Faiz (1988), 'Inflation in Pakistan', *Pakistan Development Review*.

Bird, Richard (1991), 'Tax Administration and Tax Reform: Reflections on Experience', World Bank Study, Washington, DC.

Birdsall, Nancy, David Ross, and Richard Sabot (1993), 'Underinvestment in Education: How Much Growth Has Pakistan Foregone', *Pakistan Development Review, Islamabad*.

Birdsall, Nancy (1994), 'Inequality, Savings, and Growth', Williams College Research Center, Connecticut.

Birdsall, Nancy and Richard Sabot (1994), 'Human Capital Accumulation in Post-Green Revolution Pakistan', Williams College Research Center, Connecticut.

Birdsall, Nancy, David Ross, and Richard Sabot (1995), 'Inequality and Growth Considered: Lessons from East Asia', *World Bank Economic Review*.

Bourguignon, Francois and C. Morrisson (1995), 'Inequality and Development: the Role of Dualism', OECD, Paris.

Burki, Shahid J. (1981), 'Pakistan's Development: An Overview', World Development, London.

Burki, Shahid J. and Robert Laporte, Jr. (1984), *Pakistan's Development Priorities: Choices for the Future*, Oxford University Press, Oxford.

Burney, Nadeem (1986), 'Sources of Pakistan's Economic Growth', *Pakistan Development Review*, No. 24 (4), Islamabad.

Burney, Nadeem (1987), 'Workers' Remittances from Middle East and their Effects on Pakistan's Economy', *Pakistan Development Review*, No. 25 (4), Islamabad.

Byerlee, Derek (1994), 'Agricultural Productivity in Pakistan: Problems and Potentials', *World Bank Agricultural Sector Review*, Washington DC.

Caprio, Gerard et al. (1990), 'Monetary Policy Instruments for Developing Countries', World Bank Policy Series 528.

Casterline, J. (1984), 'The Proximate Determinants of Fertility', *World Fertility Survey*, London.

Central Statistical Office (1971), 'Twenty Five Years of Pakistan Statistics', Karachi.

Chenery, Hollis (1974) , 'Redistribution with Growth', Institute of Development Studies, Sussex.

Cline, W. (1995), *International Debt Re-examined*, Institute of International Economics, Washington.

Cnossen, Sijbren (1991), 'Design of the Value-Added Tax: Lessons from Experience', World Bank Study, Washington DC.

Deininger, Klaus and Lyn Squire (1997), 'Economic Growth and Income Inequality: Re-examining the Links', *Finance and Development*, World Bank.

Department of Income Tax (1995), *Facts and Figures on Income Tax*, Karachi.

Diaz, Hugo (1995), 'Pakistan—Poverty Assessment', South Asia Department, World Bank.

Easterly W. and Levine R. (1996), *Africa's Growth Tragedy* (mimeo), World Bank, Washington DC.

Ebinger, Charles (1981), *Energy Planning in a Strategic Vortex*, Indiana University Press, Bloomington.

Ercelawn, A.A. (1990), 'Absolute Poverty in Pakistan: Poverty Lines, Incidence, Intensity', Draft Mimeo, Karachi, Applied Economics Research Center, University of Karachi.

FAO, *Year Book of Agriculture Statistics*, Rome, (various issues).

Faiz, Asif (1992), 'Financing Infrastructure Development', Paper presented at LUMS Conference on Financing Pakistan's Development in the 1990s, LUMS, Lahore.

Faruqee, Rashid (1995), 'Pakistan's Agriculture Sector: Is 3 to 4 Percent Annual Growth Sustainable?', South Asia Country Department, The World Bank, Washington DC.

————, (1994), 'Structural and Policy Reforms for Agricultural Growth: the Case of Pakistan', South Asia Department, The World Bank, Washington DC.

GATT (1995), *Trade Policy Review*, Vol. I and Vol. 2, Geneva.

Gilani et al. (1981), 'Labour Migration from Pakistan to Middle East and its Impact on the Domestic Economy', Vol. 1, 2, and 3, PIDE Research Report Series No. 126-8, Islamabad.

Goldstein, M. et al. (1992), *Policy Issues in Evolving an International Monetary System,* IMF, Washington DC.

Government of Pakistan *(1975-1996), Economic Surveys*, Finance Division, Islamabad.

Government of Pakistan (1993), *Report of the Prime Minister's Task Force on Agriculture*, Islamabad.

Griffin, Keith (1989),'Alternative Strategies for Economic Development', OECD Development Center, London.

Guisinger, Stephen (1981), 'Trade Policies and Employment: the Case of Pakistan' in A. Krueger et al. (eds.), *Trade and Employment in Developing Countries*, University of Chicago Press, Chicago.

Guisinger, Stephen and Gerald Scully (1991), 'Pakistan: Liberalizing Foreign Trade', mimeo World Bank.

Hamid, Naved (1992), 'Industrial Incentive Structure: A Need for Reform,' paper presented at the LUMS Conference on Financing Pakistan's Development in the 1990s, LUMS, Lahore.

Hamid, Naved and A.R. Kemal (1991), 'Pakistan Industrial Sector Review Study', prepared for the Asian Development Bank.

Hamid, Naved, Ijaz Nabi, and Anjum Nasim (1990), 'Trade, Exchange Rate, and Agricultural Pricing Policies in Pakistan'. World Bank, Washington DC.

Haq, Mahbubul (1963), *The Strategy of Economic Planning: A Case Study of Pakistan*, Oxford University Press, Oxford.

Haque, Nadeemul and Peter S. Montiel (1991), 'Exchange Rate Policy in Pakistan: Recent Experience and Prospects', paper presented at the LUMS Conference on Financing Pakistan's Development in the 1990s, LUMS, Lahore.

Haque, Nadeemul and Peter S. Montiel (1991), 'Fiscal Policy Choices and Macroeconomic Performance in the Nineties', Paper presented at the LUMS Conference on Financing Pakistan's Development in the 1990s, LUMS, Lahore.

Haque, Nadeemul and Peter S. Montiel (1991), 'The Macroeconomics of Public Sector Deficits: The Case of Pakistan', Policy and Research Working Paper No. 673, Washington DC.

Haque, Nadeemul and Peter S. Montiel (1993), 'Agricultural Pricing Policy in Pakistan', International Food Policy Research Institute Working Paper, Washington DC.

Haque, Nadeemul and S. Kardar (1993), *The Development of Financial Markets in Pakistan* (mimeo).

Hossain, Akhtar (1994), 'The Search for a Stable Money Demand Function for Pakistan', *Pakistan Development Review*.

Hossain, Akhtar (1990) 'Monetarist vs. neo-Keynesian Views on Acceleration of Inflation', *Pakistan Development Review*.

Hussain, Akmal (1988), *Strategic Issues in Pakistan's Economic Policy*, Progressive Publishers Limited, Lahore.

Husain, Ishrat (1984) 'Raising Resources for Development', Chapter 5 in Burki and Laporte (ed.), *Pakistan's Development Priorities. Choices for the Future,* Oxford University Press, Oxford.

———, (1991), 'How Did the Asian Countries Avoid the Debt Crisis', World Bank PRE Working Paper No. 785, Washington DC.

———, (1992), 'External Debt and Foreign Aid to Pakistan', Paper presented at the LUMS Conference on Financing Pakistan's Development in the 1990s, LUMS, Lahore.

Husain, Ishrat and Kwang Jun (1991), 'Capital Flows to South Asian and ASEAN Countries: Trends, Determinants, and Policy Implications', World Bank PRE Working Papers, Washington DC.

Husain, S.M. (1970), *Empirical Studies on Pakistan Agriculture*, Pakistan Institute of Development Economics, Karachi.

International Finance Corporation (1996), Annual Report, Washington DC.

International Monetary Fund (YR) (1947-1997), *International Financial Statistics*, Washington DC.

International Monetary Fund (1996), 'Pakistan Recent Economic Developments', IMF Staff Country Report No. 96/8, Washington DC.

Irfan, Mohammed (1982), 'Wages, Employment, and Trade Unions', *Pakistan Development Review*, No. 21 (1), Islamabad.

Irfan, Mohammed and Zeba Sathar (1984), 'Reproductive Behavior in Pakistan: Insights from Population, Labor Force, and Migration Survey,' PIDE, Islamabad.

Irfan, Mohammed and Rashid Amjad (1984), *Poverty in Rural Pakistan*, ILO/ARTEP, Bangkok.

Irfan, Mohammad and Meekal Ahmed (1985), 'Real Wages in Pakistan: Structure and Trends 1970-84', *Pakistan Development Review*, No. 24 (3-4), Islamabad.

Irfan, Mohammed (1986), *Mortality and Health Issues*, UN ESCAP, Bangkok.

Isfahani, H. (1994), 'Financing Pakistan's Infrastructure', Background Paper for Pakistan 2020, World Bank.

Islam, Nurul (1970), 'Factor Intensities in Manufacturing Industries in Pakistan', *Pakistan Development Review* No. 10 (2), Islamabad.

_____, (1981), *Foreign Trade and Economic Controls in Development: The Case of United Pakistan*, Yale University Press, New Haven.

Joshi, V. and I.M.D. Little (1996), *India's Economic Reforms 1991-2001*, Oxford University Press, Oxford.

Karamat, Ali (1982), *Pakistan: The Political Economy of Rural Development*, Vanguard Publications, Lahore.

Kemal, A.R. (1994), 'Structural Adjustment, Employment, Income Distribution, and Poverty', *Pakistan Development Review*, No. 33, Islamabad.

_____, (1992), 'Self-Reliance and the Implications for Growth and Resource Mobilization', *Pakistan Development Review*, No. 31 (4), Islamabad.

Kemal, A. R. and Syed Nawab Haider (1991), 'The Privatization of Public Industrial Enterprises in Pakistan', *Pakistan Development Review*, No. 30 (2), Islamabad.

Kemal, A.R. and Mete Durdag (1990), 'Budgetary Deficit and Performance of Pakistan's Economy', Pakistan Institute of Development Economics, Islamabad.

Khalilzadeh-Shirazi, Javed and Anwar Shah (eds.) (1991), *Tax Policy in Developing Countries*, World Bank, Washington, DC.

Khan, Ahmad (1992), 'Determinants of Income Tax Base in Pakistan: A Policy Review', *Pakistan Development Review*, No. 31 (4), Islamabad.

Khan, Ashfaque, Lubna Hasan, and Alia Malik (1992), 'Dependency Ratio, Foreign Capital Inflows, and the Rate of Savings in Pakistan', *Pakistan Development Review*, No. 31 (4), Islamabad.

Khan, Mahmood Hassan (1975), *The Economics of the Green Revolution in Pakistan*, Praeger Publishers, New York.

_____, (1979), 'Farm Size and Land Productivity Relationships in Pakistan', *Pakistan Development Review*, No. 18 (1), Islamabad.

_____, (1981), *Underdevelopment and Agrarian Structure in Pakistan*, Westview Press, Boulder, Colorado.

_____, (1991) 'The Structural Adjustment Process and Agricultural Change in Pakistan in the 1980s and 1990s', *Pakistan Development Review*, Islamabad.

Khan, Mahmood Hassan, Syed Nawab Haider Naqvi, and Ghaffar Chaudhry (1989), 'Structural Change in Pakistan's Agriculture', Pakistan Institute of Development Economics, Islamabad.

Khan, Mohsin (1986), 'Exchange Rate Policies of Developing Countries', *Pakistan Development Review*, No. 25 (3).

_____, (1990), 'The Macroeconomic Effects of Fund-supported Programs', IMF Staff Papers No. 37.

_____, (1990), 'Macroeconomic Policies and the Balance of Payments in Pakistan: 1972-1986', IMF Working Paper/90/78, Washington DC.

_____, (1994), *The Behavior of Non-oil Commodity Prices*, IMF, Washington DC.

_____, (1997), 'Public and Private Investment and the Growth Process in Developing Countries', *Oxford Bulletin of Economics and Statistics,* Oxford.

King, Robert and Ross Levine (1992), 'Financial Indicators and Growth in a Cross Section of Countries', World Bank Policy Series 819.

Krueger, Anne (1978), *Foreign Trade Regimes and Economic Development: Liberalization Attempts and Consequences*, Ballinger, Cambridge, Massachusetts.

Krueger, Anne, Maurice Schiff, and Alberto Valdes (eds.) (1992), *The Political Economy of Agricultural Pricing Policy*, Johns Hopkins Press, Baltimore.

Krujik, Hans de and Myrna Van Leeuwen (1985), 'Changes in Poverty and Income Inequality in Pakistan During the 1970's', *Pakistan Development Review* No. 24 (3-4).

Krujik, H. de (1987), 'Sources of Income Inequality in Pakistan', *Pakistan Development Review,* Vol. 26, Summer.

Lee, Rama and Iwasaki (1986), 'Effects of Foreign Capital Flows on the Developing Countries of Asia', ADB Economic Staff Papers, No. 30, Manila.

Lewis, John (ed.) (1988), *Strengthening the Poor—What Have We Learned?*, Overseas Development Council, Washington DC.

Lewis, S.R. (1970), *Pakistan Industrialization and Trade Policies*, Oxford University Press, Oxford.

Lipton, Michael (1988), 'The Poor and the Poorest: Some Interim Findings', World Bank Discussion Paper, No. 25, Washington DC.

Lipton, Michael and Martin Ravallion (1995), 'Poverty and Policy', World Bank Policy Series, WPS 1130.

Little, Ian, Tibor Scitovsky, and Maurice Scott (1970), *Industry and Trade in Some Developing Countries*, Oxford University Press, London.

Low, Patrick (1995), 'Pakistan: The Uruguay Round and Trade Policy Reform into the Next Century', Background Paper for Pakistan 2010, World Bank, Washington DC.

Mahmood, Naushin and G.M. Zahid (1992), 'Measuring the Education Gap in Primary and Secondary Schooling in Pakistan', *Pakistan Development Review,* No. 31 (4), Islamabad.

Mahmood, Zafar and Mohammad Ali Qasim (1992), 'Foreign Trade Regime and Savings in Pakistan', *Pakistan Development Review,* No. 31 (4), Islamabad.

Maier, Gerald (1984,1990), *Leading Issues in Economic Development*, Oxford University Press, Oxford.

Malik, M. (1988), 'Some New Evidences on the Incidence of Poverty in Pakistan', *Pakistan Development Review,* No. 27 (4), Islamabad.

Malik, Sohail, Safiya Arab, and Nargis Sultana (1994), *Pakistan's Economic Performance 1947 to 1993: A Descriptive Analysis'*, Sure Publishers, Lahore.

Malik, Sohail (1991), 'Poverty in Pakistan: 1984-85 to 1987-88', International Food Policy Research Institute Working Paper, Washington DC.

———, (1992), 'Rural Poverty in Pakistan: Some Recent Evidence', *Pakistan Development Review*, No. 31(4), Islamabad.

McKinnon, R. (1973), *Money and Capital in Economic Development*, Brookings Institution, Washington DC.

Mehdi, Istaqbal (1984), 'Experiment in Social Income Accounting in Pakistan', *Pakistan Development Review,* Islamabad.

Mellor, John (1991), 'Agricultural Link to Nonagricultural Growth: Urbanization, Employment, and Poverty', *Pakistan Development Review,* No. 30 (4), Islamabad.

Mohammed, Azizali (1992), 'Monetary Management in Pakistan', paper presented at the LUMS Conference on Financing Pakistan's Development in the 1990s, LUMS, Lahore.

Morris, P. (1985), *India's Financial System*, World Bank, Washington DC.

Nabi, Ijaz (1992), 'Foreign Direct Investment: Lessons from the Asian Experience', paper presented at the LUMS Conference on Financing Pakistan's Development in the 1990s, LUMS, Lahore.

Nabi, Ijaz, Navid Hamid and S. Zahid (1986), *The Agrarian Economy of Pakistan*, Oxford University Press, Karachi.

Naqvi, Syed Nawab Haider (1964), 'Import Licensing in Pakistan', *Pakistan Development Review*, Vol. IV, No. 1, Spring, Islamabad.

_____, (1966), 'The Allocative Biases of Pakistan's Commercial Policy', *Pakistan Development Review*, Vol. VI, No. 4, Winter, Islamabad.

Naqvi, Syed Nawab Haider and A.R. Kemal (1991), *Protection and Efficiency in Manufacturing: Case Study of Pakistan*, International Center for Economic Growth.

Naqvi, Syed Nawab Haider and Khwaja Sarmad (1984), *Pakistan's Economy through the Seventies*, PIDE, Islamabad.

Naseem, S.M. (1977), 'Rural Poverty and Landlessness in Pakistan', in *ILO Report on Poverty and Landlessness in Asia*, Geneva.

Nasim, Anjum and Asya Akhlaque (1992), 'Agricultural Taxation and Subsidies', paper presented at the LUMS Conference on Financing Pakistan's Development in the 1990s, LUMS, Lahore.

Nasim, Anjum, Naved Hamid, and Ijaz Nabi (1990), 'Trade, Exchange Rate, and Agricultural Pricing Policies in Pakistan', World Bank Comparative Series.

Nehru, Vikram and Ashok Dhareshwar (1994), 'New Estimates of Total Factor Productivity Growth for Developing and Industrial Countries', Policy and Research Working Paper No. 1313, World Bank, Washington DC.

Noman, Akbar (1992), 'Liberalization of Foreign Trade and International Competitiveness', paper presented at the LUMS Conference on Financing Pakistan's Development in the 1990s, LUMS, Lahore.

———, (1994), 'Economic Growth and Public Policy: the Case of Pakistan—A South Asian Miracle', Unpublished.

Noman, Omar (1988), *Pakistan Political and Economic History since 1947*, Kegan Paul International, London.

Pakistan and Gulf Economist, Karachi, 1987-1998.

Papanek, Gustav (1967), *Pakistan's Development—Social Goals and Private Incentives*, Cambridge University Press, Harvard.

———, (1992), 'Alternative Development Strategies', paper presented at the LUMS Conference on Financing Pakistan's Development in the 1990s, LUMS, Lahore.

Pasha, Hafiz (1995), 'Political Economy of Tax Reforms: The Pakistan Experience', *Pakistan Journal of Applied Economics,* No. 11 (3-4), AERC, Karachi.

Pasha, Hafiz and Aisha Ghaus (1992), 'Provincial and Local Government Taxation', paper presented at the LUMS Conference on Financing Pakistan's Development in the 1990s, LUMS, Lahore.

Pasha, Hafiz and T. Hasan (1982), 'Development Ranking of Districts of Pakistan', *Pakistan Journal of Applied Economics*, AERC, Karachi.

Peree, E. and A. Steinher (1989), 'Exchange Rate Uncertainty and Foreign Trade', *European Economic Review,* No. 33, July 1989.

Population Welfare Department (1984), 'Population Program of Pakistan', Islamabad.

Porter, Michael (1990), *The Competitive Advantage of Nations,* Free Press, New York.

Psacharopoulos, George (1994), 'Returns to Investment in Education: A Global Update', World Development, United Kingdom.

Qureshi, Sarfraz and Akhtar Shah (1992), 'A Critical Review of Rural Credit Policy in Pakistan', *Pakistan Development Review,* No. 31 (4), Islamabad.

Ravallion, Martin and Gaurav Datt (1995), 'Growth and Poverty in Rural India', *World Bank Policy Research Paper,* 1405.

Riaz, Tariq (1984), *Pakistan: The Energy Sector,* Ferozsons Ltd., Lahore.

Riordan, E. Mick and T.G. Srinivasan (1996),'Pakistan's International Linkages: Evolution and Prospects', World Bank, Washington DC.

Romer, Paul (1986—a), 'Increasing Returns and Long-Run Growth', *Journal of Political Economy.*

_____, (1986—b), 'Human Capital and Growth', Carnegie Conference Series on Public Policy.

_____, (1994), 'The Origins of Endogenous Growth', *Journal of Economic Perspectives.*

Ruttan, Vernon (1987), *Lectures on Technical and Institutional Change in Agricultural Development,* Pakistan Institute of Development Economics, Islamabad.

Sakr, Khaled (1993), 'Determinants of Private Investment in Pakistan', *IMF Working Paper/93/30,* Washington DC.

Sarmad K. and Z. Mahmood, 'Disaggregated Import Demand Functions for Pakistan', *Pakistan Development Review,* No. 26 (1), Islamabad.

Sathar, Zeba (1979), 'Rural-Urban Fertility Differentiatals in Pakistan', *Pakistan Development Review,* No. 27 (4), Islamabad.

_____, (1984), 'Does Female Education Affect Fertility Behavior in Pakistan', *Pakistan Development Review,* No. 23 (4), Islamabad.

————, (1985), 'Differences in Household Characteristics by Income Distribution in Pakistan', *Pakistan Development Review*, No. 24 (3-4), Islamabad.

————, (1987), 'Seeking Explanations for High Levels of Infant Mortality in Pakistan', *Pakistan Development Review*.

————, (1991), 'Population Policy and Demographic Change in Pakistan', Seminar on Eighth Five Year Plan (1993-98), Islamabad.

Sathar, Zeba and Cynthia Lloyd (1994), 'Who Gets Primary Schooling in Pakistan: Inequalities Among and Within Families', *Pakistan Development Review*, No. 33 (2), Islamabad.

Shabsigh, G. (1995), 'The Underground Economy: Estimation and Economic and Policy Implications—the Case of Pakistan', IMF Working Paper 95/101, Washington DC.

Shabbir, Tayyeb (1994), 'Mincerian Earnings Function for Pakistan', *Pakistan Development Review*, No. 33 (1), Islamabad.

Shaikh, Abdul Hafeez (1992), 'Financing Development through Improved Public Sector Management', Paper presented at the LUMS Conference on Financing Pakistan's Development in the 1990s, LUMS, Lahore.

Shaw, E. (1973), *Financial Deepening in Economic Development*, Oxford University Press, New York.

Sodersten, Bo and Goeffrey Reed (1994), *International Economics*, St. Martin's Press, New York.

State Bank of Pakistan (various issues), Annual Report, Karachi.

Stewart, Peter and Jenny Sturgis (1995), *Pakistan: Meeting the Challenge*, Euromoney, London.

Sundrum, R.M. (1990), *Income Distribution in Less Developed Countries*, Routledge, London.

Thirsk, Wayne (1991), 'Lessons from Tax Reform: An Overview', World Bank Study, Washington DC.

Thomas, Philip, (1966) 'Import Licensing and Import Liberalization in Pakistan', *Pakistan Development Review*, Vol. VI, No. 4, Winter, Islamabad.

Wellenius, Bjorn (ed.) (1989), 'Restructuring and Managing the Telecommunications Sector', A World Bank Symposium, Washington DC.

White, L. (1974), *Industrial Concentration and Economic Power in Pakistan*, Princeton University Press, Princeton.

Winters, Alan and Merlinda Ingco (1995), 'Pakistan and the Uruguay Round: Impact and Opportunities—A Quantitative Assessment', World Bank, Washington DC.

Winters, Alan and W. Martin (1996), *The Uruguay Round and the Developing Countries*, Cambridge University Press, Cambridge.

World Bank, World Development Report 1996, Washington DC.

World Bank (1996), *Financial Flows and the Developing Countries*, A World Bank Quarterly, Washington DC.

World Bank, *World Development Report 1995*, Washington, DC.

World Bank (1995a), *Global Economic Prospects and the Developing Countries*, International Economics Department, Washington DC.

World Bank, *World Development Report 1994*, Washington DC.

World Bank (1993), *The East Asian Miracle: Economic Growth and Public Policy, Policy Research Report*, Oxford University Press, New York.

World Bank (1995b), *Pakistan: Poverty Assessment*, World Bank, Washington DC.

World Bank, *World Development Report 1990*, Washington DC.

World Bank (1988), 'Pakistan Education Sector Strategy Review', Washington DC.

World Bank (1969), *Water and Power Resources of West Pakistan: A Study in Social Sector Planning* (Vol. I and 2), World Bank, Washington DC.

World Bank (various issues), *World Development Report*, Oxford University Press, New York.

Yeats, Alexander and Francis Ng (1996), 'Open Economies Work Better!' International Economics Department, World Bank, Washington DC.

Zafar, Ali (1991), 'Privatization and Liberalization in Pakistan: An Assessment of the Reforms', Pakistan Institute of Development Economics, unpublished, Islamabad.

Yeats, Alexander and Francis Ng (1996), 'Open Economies Work Better!' International Economics Department, World Bank, Washington DC.

Zafar, Ali (1991), 'Privatization and Liberalization in Pakistan: An Assessment of the Reforms', Pakistan Institute of Development Economics, unpublished.

INDEX